Stolen Life

consent not to be a single being

Stolen Life

FRED MOTEN

DUKE UNIVERSITY PRESS DURHAM AND LONDON 2018

Designed by Amy Ruth Buchanan
Typeset in Miller by Westchester Publishing
Services

Library of Congress Cataloging-in-Publication
Data
Names: Moten, Fred, author.
Title: Stolen life / Fred Moten.
Description: Durham : Duke University
Press, 2018. | Series: Consent not to be a
single being ; [v. 2] | Includes bibliographical
references and index.
Identifiers: LCCN 2017036322 (print) |
LCCN 2017044096 (ebook)
ISBN 9780822372028 (ebook)
ISBN 9780822370437 (hardcover : alk. paper)
ISBN 9780822370581 (pbk. : alk. paper)
Subjects: LCSH: Black race—Philosophy. |
Blacks—Race identity—Philosophy. |
Philosophy, Black.
Classification: LCC HT1581 (ebook) |
LCC HT1581 .M684 2018 (print) | DDC
305.896—dc23
LC record available at https://lccn.loc.
gov/2017036322

Cover art: Lauren Halsey, *kingdom splurge
(3.7.15.15)*, 2015, The Studio Museum in
Harlem, installation view. Photo: Texas
Isaiah. Courtesy of Lauren Halsey.

CONTENTS

ACKNOWLEDGMENTS

Earlier versions of some of the essays collected here appeared in the journals *CR: The New Centennial Review*, *Floor*, *Palimpsest*, PMLA, and *Social Text*. Earlier versions of others appeared in the following books: Alys Eve Weinbaum and Susan Gillman, eds., *Next to the Color Line: Gender, Sexuality and W. E. B. Du Bois* (University of Minnesota Press); Brenna Bhandar and Jonathan Goldberg-Hiller, eds., *Plastic Materialities: Politics, Legality, and Metamorphosis in the Work of Catherine Malabou* (Duke University Press); and Ulla Haselstein and Klaus Benesch, eds., *The Power and Politics of the Aesthetic in American Culture* (Publications of the Bavarian American Academy, Volume 7, Universitätsverlag). Thanks to all the editors involved.

PREFACE

What it is to be given (as) something to hold, always in common, has really got a hold on me. It's not mine but it's all I have. I who have nothing, I who am no one, I who am not one. I can't say it and I can't get over it. I can't fathom it and I can't grasp it. It opens everything and, in that exhaustion of what it is to acquire, a choir is set to work. More and less than tired, more and less than one, we just want to sing that name, which is not the only name, though it's not just any name. Movement in the history of that name and naming is insistence in the history of study. Theory of blackness is theory of the surreal presence—not in between some things and nothing is the held fleshliness of the collective head. There, we study how blackness and imagination are compact, in reconstructive flight from imposition, its sovereign operations, which keep on taking their incalculable toll. Beyond that, in the im/possibility of anything beyond that, those operations are resisted and refuted, often by way of simulations of that sovereignty. Wherever sovereignty is thwarted, whenever it's unsettled, everywhere, all the time, the radical events and things of our surround are shadowed by control, by its biopolitically antibiotic effects, which destroy, they say, in order to preserve, and then take an even more incalculable toll. To invoke the more (or less) incalculable is to recognize how life-in-danger takes certain conceptual apparatuses over the limit, in unnatural defiance of their rule, placing *them* in danger, such that the difference between internal and external imposition, or that between major and minor struggle, fails properly to signify. Dispersed, broken sovereignty and its various shadows are what apposition always turns away, what animated ground refuses to uphold. The double burden of our atmosphere has a double edge whose interstice we inhabit, with which we are preoccupied, as anti-occupation.

On the ground, under it, in the break between deferred advent and premature closure, natality's differentiated persistence and afterlife's profligate singularities, social vision, blurred with the enthusiasm of surreal presence in unreal time, anticipates and discomposes the harsh glare of clear-eyed, (supposedly, impossibly) originary correction, where enlightenment and darkness, blindness and insight, invisibility and hypervisibility, converge in the open obscurity of a field of study and a line of flight. Consider what it is to be concerned with the fluorescence and efflorescence of generation's self-defensive care, its prefatory counterpleasures, which reveal the public, intramural resources of our undercommon senses, where flavorful touch is all bound up with falling into the general antagonistic embrace of inhabited decoration, autonomous choreography, amplified music, of which what happens in the yard or at the club or on record are only instances unless the yard is everybody's and the club is everywhere and everything is a recording.

All that intellectual descent neither opposes nor follows from dissent but, rather, gives it a chance. Consent to that submergence is terrible and beautiful. Moreover, the apparent (racial) exclusivity of the (under)privilege of claiming this (dis)ability serially impairs—though it can never foreclose—the discovery that the priority of the imposition, of sovereign regulation, of constitutive correction, is false. In order to get the plain sense of this you have to use your imagination. Certain critico-redemptive projects, which are always accompanied by the disavowal of what they valorize as becoming, encompass one way to understand such usage, such being put to use, such means; but in the meantime, in the improvisation of beginnings and ends, way on the outskirts of town, in the blur over the edge, critique and redemption submit to a poetics of condensation and displacement when blackness, which already was and was always moving and being moved, stakes its claim as normativity's condition.

Generation puts normativity in play, past the supersensible's interdiction of the representations it demands, through the ones who (refuse to) represent. They wear the material they work like a bad habit, out of uniform(ity), between thread and protocol, seen and heard and danced as a kind of skin, a vehicle for passage, in and through the merely epidermal. What if we could speak of generation's elementary structures, certain submarine, supercutaneous areas of unfamiliar resemblance, without losing sight of the best place to look for them, where they can change, where the antenormative persists in being numerous, in the immensity of its constant aeration and free alteration? Why is this uncountable finitude—its mass immeasurable as the masses, the weight of their hard, studious pleasure in and as the things they live among—so vulnerable to the noumenal prophylaxis of the very idea of a single source who doesn't dance, who has no skin, who can't be seen or heard?

Too often life is taken by, and accepts, the invasive, expansive aggression of the settler, venturing into the outside that he fears, in search of the very idea as it recedes from its own enabling condition, as its forms are reclaimed by the informality that precedes them. Genesis and the habit (the ways, the dress, the skin, the trip, the jones) of transcendental subjectivity don't go together; can generation and origin—the thin, delusional line between settlement and invasion—be broken up, as well? The generative breaks into the normative discourses that it found(ed). They weren't there until it got there, as some changes made to previous insistence, which means first things aren't first; Zo just wants to travel, to cities. Do you want some? Can I have some? (Octavia Butler might have called it the oncological difference; she sounds dispossession as our xenogenetic gift; migrating out from the outside, always leaving without origin.)

Generation, in its irreducible sociality, in the infinitely inspiriting dispersion of its finitude, is identified as pathology; the informal is understood as formlessness, the structured, structuring force that settlers, running diabolical errands, take for wilderness; juvenile court judges passing phobic judgments, prior to any experience, on the socioecological space they invade, where everyone dies before they get old. The self-appointed judge makes settlements in his favor, against whatever is already preoccupied in and with the scene, which he kills without finding, erecting unsustainable homes and prejudicial legalities in order to protect himself, which is to say his expansion. The most effective mode of such protection places prejudice under the cover of an appeal to its eradication, which now becomes a hidden, metaphysical foundation of judicial ownership, legislative priesthood, or whatever other vulgarly temporal authority of the ones who find relative nothingness everywhere. Effective protection is their insubstantial, antisubstantial ruse, even in its viciousness, as the thinking and wracking and locking up of bodies. But the suspension of such sentencing, the abolition of its degenerative grammar, is already on. Its reconstitutive enjoyment and distribution is a project, a hermitage, a multipurpose room. That admission to the study and the making of law is open shows up most clearly against the backdrop of denials of jurisdiction that variously enable and are enabled by the supposedly elect(ed). Before and against the grain of that negation habits are sewn in cotton, sown like cotton, on the hard, veered, spread-out row of volunteers, their (de)livery of touch, their handing and tilling, their disruptively autonomous agriculture, in the shadow of scientific management, under its ground, making rhizomatic criminal law.

This comes into relief as black forms of life that anticipate and appose epidermalization, criminalization, and genocidal regulation. In the inexclusive mobile situation and idiom, to which we people who are darker than blue have been inexclusively given, our runaway history gives us this: that affirmation in and through negation, situated mobility, and differentiated presence is blackness; that blackness is generation's more-than-arbitrary name; that she is our more-and-less-than single being; that critical celebration of tumultuous derangement, of the constitutive force of dehiscence, of the improvisations of imagining things, is written in the name of blackness, on and under its skin, in its paraontological difference from, which is its paraontological differentiation in and as, the people who are called black. What it is to be—to be with and against—that name has something to do with what Luce Irigaray calls "the fecundity of the caress." The caress makes social space like a garment, social fabric biopoetically brushing up against a wall that opens out into a room or rises up as a resting place—slave ship, favela, space ship, project. It's like the preparation of a table, or a piano. It can't be sung alone.

Stolen Life is a set of social essays, to use Amiri Baraka's term.[1] In play is not only the reversal of an all-but-canonical valorization of the political over the social, but also a commitment to the sociality and sociability of the essays themselves. Their tendency to rub up against one another in a mutual overstepping of bounds is also meant to indicate common effort as well as differential approach. The essays are, more pointedly, concerned with how it is that a kind of impossible publicness emerges in and from the radical exclusion from the political, as the refusal of that which has been refused. Life which has been stolen steals away in this refusal in a range of insurgencies that, insofar as they call regulation into question, can be said to anticipate its beginning and its end. The essays collected here are concerned with, among other things, pedagogy, criminality, and the social force of neura*typicality* given at the intersection of the artistic and the autistic. There's a lot of stuff in here about how we go to school, and how we play, and how we see. Because of this pointedness, which is more emphatic here than in the rest of its companion volumes, the contents of *Stolen Life* resist collection. Or, perhaps more precisely, there is resistance to the power of the executive even as another mode of desegregation is intimated. If a certain devotional and club-like buzz is alive and well here—because rubbing, worrying, brushing, and handing bear certain irreducible phonic effects—it is in echo of everything I've been taught on various dusty roads.

chapter 1

Knowledge of Freedom

I

At the beginning of *In Praise of Nonsense: Kant and Bluebeard*, Winfried Menninghaus calls our attention to an exemplary expression of sovereignty's ambivalence toward its own non-fullness. "'All the richness of the imagination,' [Immanuel] Kant cautions in the *Critique of Judgment*, 'in its lawless freedom produces nothing but nonsense.' Nonsense, then, does not befall the imagination like a foreign pathogen; rather, it is the very law of imagination's own 'lawlessness.' Kant therefore prescribes a rigid antidote: even in the field of the aesthetic, understanding must "severely clip the wings" of imagination and 'sacrifice . . . some' of it."[1]

The paralegal disturbs Kant, is anoriginal disturbance in Kant. Whatever violent overturning it enacts (however softly), whatever ante-invasive evasion it performs (however smoothly), was already online, as something there, then gone, exercising options that even the bloodiest constraint can neither liquidate nor reduce. Nonsense is fugitive presence. You could think its animated flesh, with and against Hannah Arendt's hard grain, as "the dark background of mere givenness," *and* as "the dark background of difference." Feel it get down right there, though it keeps on moving, right there, where difference and givenness are inseparable in never being one.[2] Its diplopic print is not marked "before and after" but shows up as smudge, bend, ecstatic shift, common and impure. This recidivist fringe just won't act right no matter how much the power of judgment tries to make it "well behaved."[3] Law enforcement, in whatever exclusionary attempt to ensure equilibrium, belatedly responds to what shows up as (de)generative dehiscence requiring suture and irregular wholeness in need of incision.

Note that the very image of imagination is more and less than one. *Phantasie*, in its anarchic productivity, ludic, labored, hanging at the corner of the ordinary and the merely (given, phonetic, culinary, gestural, cultural, sensual), is shadowed by *Einbildungskraft*, the jurisprudential faculty's tasteful, emphatically regulatory straight edge and end. Menninghaus argues that for Kant, *Phantasie*, "imagination in its pure form—which is by the same token its *vitium*—produces 'tumultuous derangements' that shatter the 'coherence which is necessary for the very possibility of experience.'"[4] Judgments of taste, in their unifying and developmental power, defy tumult in the interest of that possibility. But if Kant prescribes what Menninghaus calls a "politics of curtailment" of the imagination which, in its pure productivity, sunders every enclosure and maddens every work, infusing them with the anoriginal, dispossessive, recollective impurity that is its dispossessive own, he does so by acknowledging the prior resistance (unruly sociality, anarchic syntax, extrasensical poetics) to that politics that calls it into being.[5]

Menninghaus's work is structured by the revelation of this ambivalence in Kant that can be said to disrupt and appose origin in general.[6] I want to consider this necessarily irregular opening of the regulative and to think it in relation to Kant's deployment of race as the exemplary regulative and/or teleological principle. As Robert Bernasconi's work in particular shows, Kant uses race and the raced figure to ground the distinction between natural history—the production and discovery of purposive and singular, if internally hierarchized creation—and natural description's cataloging of a diverse set of observed natural facts potentially attributable to different origins. The regulative discourse on the aesthetic that animates Kant's critical philosophy is inseparable from the question of race as a mode of conceptualizing and regulating human diversity, grounding and justifying inequality and exploitation, as well as marking the limits of human knowledge through the codification of quasi-transcendental philosophical method, which is Kant's acknowledged aim in the critical philosophy. Similarly, the racial and racist conceptualization and, therefore, regulation of blackness is inseparable from its naming, so that the precritical impulse to categorize and catalog supposedly natural facts, above which critical philosophy would rise, or over which it would conceptually leap in its use of teleological principle, casts a sleepy and dogmatic shadow over that which newly awakened criticality is supposed to illuminate. What if the ones who are so ugly that their utterances must be stupid are never far from Kant's mature and critical thoughts? What if they, or something they are said and made to bear alone, are the fantastical generation of those thoughts? It is as if the exclusive property they are and have is the generative facticity that constitutes and solicits fact and grasp, having and being. It is as if that darkness, which gives and takes away the given in and as differentiation without beginning or end, could only be contained if it were yoked to a set of phenotypical particularities whose arbitrary collection and categorization were shamefully deployed by the one whose theorization of how to know better should have allowed and required him to know better. Wholly without standing, the ones who are said and made to bear alone that which is so essential as to be unbearable alone stand in for a general improvisation, a practice of dispossession, that critical philosophy must now put in its proper place. This is how the radically and essentially improper—a giving of givenness, a handing over of being-handed—is brutally emplotted and enclosed, constantly submitted to a torturously accountable category and its imperatives; this is how, along with that local habitation, the unnameable comes to bear the imposition of a name. This nominative, genetic, historico-geographic enforcement, whose constitution is the enforcement of naming, genesis, and geographical history as the foundations of normative politics and subjectivity, is given in a set of brutally regulatory discursive maneuvers (the conception and deployment/erection and collapse of what Denise Ferreira da Silva calls the "global idea of race") in which blackness's repression has generally been taken for its history.[7] This is so even as what is continually revealed, if not confessed, is that what is now, in the wake of those maneuvers, called blackness makes those very maneuvers possible and—for and as eternally thwarted and dispersed sovereignty—necessary.

In Kant, these erstwhile foundations form a rich field of material figures (where the ones who work the ground *are* the ground) that animate and destabilize. This cultivation is like a floating bridge that moves and facilitates movement between eighteenth-century exclusionary fantasies of Africa and America and the cultivated nature and organized fantasia of the English garden; between the domesticated and anthropomorphized beast (of burden) and the irreducible wildness of the cultured flower. I am concerned with the extent to which it could be said that the black radical tradition, on the one hand, reproduces the political and philosophical paradoxes of Kantian regulation and, on the other hand, constitutes a resistance that anticipates and makes possible Kantian regulation by way of the instrumentalization to which such resistance is submitted and which it refuses. A further elaboration of those material figures is demanded such that we understand the strife that ensues in the space between two fantasies—the black (woman) as regulative instrument and the black (woman) as natural agent of deregulation—as a turmoil foundational to the modern aesthetic, political, and philosophical fields. Thus my interest in the resistance to "this politics of curtailment" that

Kant prescribes. Such resistance, which might be called a radical sociality of the imagination, moves in preparation for the question concerning the law of lawless freedom; but it must be said immediately that this question, which is nothing other than the question of the free irruption of thought, is here and now inseparable from the racialization and sexualization—at once phantasmatic and experiential—of the imagination.

Menninghaus characterizes that politics as a cultural reorientation toward "sense" as a power of meaning that permeates and orders all details of a discursive event into a totality. The distinction between the material surface of a discursive event and the depth of its meaning, accompanied by the preference for the intelligible pole of this opposition, became the characteristic framework for numerous social practices. These entailed a transformation in pedagogy and practices of promoting literacy as well as a reform in reading and study, in universities and in the bureaucracy. In academic teaching, the institutionalization of hermeneutics as the new vanguard science responded to this comprehensive revolution in the discursive network of writing and reading. This network's new practices and its underlying assumptions surpassed the academic science of hermeneutics in its breadth, while at the same time undercutting its subtle problematizations. The poetics of nonsense arises within the horizon of this discursive system, in the border area between late Enlightenment and early romanticism. In Michel Foucault's sense, this poetics can be read as one of the diverse "points of resistance" that are "present everywhere in the power network," as countermovements that do not simply exist outside the new sense-paradigm, and yet are not merely its parasitic "underside."[8]

This is to say that Kant's conceptualization of race, of blackness-as-race or racial difference, is not just one instance among others of him stretching his own wings, of his evasion of their regulative, if partial, amputation or even that weighting of them with lead that, before Kant, Francis Bacon prescribed. Rather, Kant's conceptualization of race—as a way of ordering the dispersive facticity that composes the open set of human differences; as an instantiation of the bridge from natural description to natural history—inaugurates the culmination of the critical philosophy where culmination is best understood as invagination, as a folding that opens the whole that it would also enclose. Kant's imaginative deployment of blackness is also his enactment of those simultaneously constitutive and disruptive properties, those irreducible improprieties, that will have accrued to blackness in the interinanimative development of the knowledge of race, the justification of racialized power and the sciences of man. The author of the critical philosophy and the founder of the aesthetico-scientific concept of race that guarantees and endangers that philosophy's systematicity, is Black Kant. This is, in turn, to say that we must note, along with Menninghaus, the precariousness of that "'ideal' liaison between beauty and imagination" that the strict regulation of "genius's excessiveness and unreason" can never fully protect, that genius's paradoxical policing of the understanding that is supposed to police it can never fully unleash. That liaison is subject to the dangerous internal difference, the irreducible materiality, that structures the beautiful, the pure. The irreducible materiality of the beautiful and the irreducible irregularity of the imagination define an enclosure that will have always been disruptively invaded, as it were, from the inside. This troubled interiority is either domesticated by way of a cycle of projection and importation; exoticized and eroticized as an object of irreducible difference, attraction, incorporation, and exilic hope; or theorized as an interdicted and invisible view, derived from the (ad)vantage from which it can neither see nor be seen, neither impeded nor enhanced by whatever strange preoccupation. While, as Menninghaus points out with regard to what he calls the escape of nonsense "for a brief moment in the history of Romantic Literature," refuge is found, what he describes as that which "acquires the character of a hyperbolically artistic form rather than of a natural power prior to all culture" is what I prefer to think of as the immanence of a radical informality that precedes the distinction between nature and culture.[9]

Kant's second sight is of the divisive excess at the heart of his own work. This visionary versioning of the critical philosophy persists despite the institutional retrofitting to which it is almost immediately submitted.[10] Having blurred the distinction between invention and discovery in every sensual improvisation of its own priority, because "diverse 'points of resistance'" are "present [*always*] and everywhere,'" im/pure imagination disrupts and apposes beginnings and ends in general. At stake is another topography altogether. It requires us to speak of and from the underside or underground as refuge; it demands that we fathom (un)sounded depths of surface, outside's complex interiority. At an incalculable cost that he helps to impose (something that is in but not of), Kant helps to make such canted thinking possible. This impurity in Kant, the phantomic reality of his philosophy, emerges through an irregular opening of the regulative that comes fully into relief in relation to Kant's deployment of race—and, more pointedly, of blackness—as teleological principle's radical exemplar.[11] Kant's blackness is given in his fantastical generation of the concept of blackness, whose relation to generativity as such is not just one such relationship among others. Kant knows that the only way to regulate (fantastical) generation is to deploy it as inoculation, so that the philosophical body is resurrected or, perhaps more precisely, transubstantiated by means of the dehiscent and constitutive force of a more than critical power that critical philosophy will have soon learned to neglect. Critical neglect is how generation comes to seem the same—little literalist objects who, having chosen not to object, sign on as privileged beholders, working new galleries and reclaimed city streets like security guards, in melancholic fashion, isolate instances of thwarted *Einbildung* regulating the monolithic uniformity they project with robotic efficiency and speed almost everywhere they look.

Of course, regulation (negation; uncut critique) encloses blackness, as its very name—one just wants to resist regulation's hegemony, to recognize its surroundings, to put it in its place as an effect of the irregular. Blackness, or, to be more precise, what Laura Harris calls "the aesthetic sociality of blackness,"[12] is the collective head, as that head's incessant division and (re)collection, moving in and against and as the situation of its nominative enclosure. Enclosure, engendering, and epidermalization of the irregular, of the alternative, mark the conceptual boundaries of regulatory technique. But to begin in the vicinity of Kant's theory of race, in order to consider how the deployment of difference in the regulation of difference and the deployment of imagination in the regulation of imagination go together, is to consider that something other and more than that, which can only be approached through that, is at stake.

To be sure, an increasing number of initiatives are taken up by aspiring individuals who follow the impulse to prove that genealogical isolation is initiatory. They seem committed to not knowing what they're not missing. On the other hand, in "Nomos and Narrative," Robert M. Cover notes that it is "remarkable that in myth and history the origin of and justification for a court is rarely understood to be the need for law. Rather, it is understood to be the need to suppress law, to choose between two or more laws, to impose upon laws a hierarchy. It is the multiplicity of laws, the fecundity of the jurisgenerative principle, that creates the problem to which the court and the state are the solution."[13] Though Cover is ambivalent regarding the abolition of this solution, which he understands to be violent, of necessity, his advocacy of a certain resistance to the very apparatuses whose necessity he denaturalizes makes it possible for us to ask some questions that the state and the understanding find not only inappropriate but also inappropriable. What if the imagination is not lawless but lawful? What if it is, in fact, so full of laws that, moreover, are in such fugitive excess of themselves that the imagination, of necessity, is constantly, fugitively in excess of itself as well? Will law have then been manifest paralegally, criminally, fugitively, as a kind of ongoing antisystemic break or breaking; as sociality's disruptive avoidance of mere civility that takes form in and as a contemporaneity of different times and the inhabitation of multiple, possible worlds and personalities? In response to this anoriginal priority of the differential set, the courts and the state (as well as critics of every stripe) will have insisted upon the necessity of policing such collaboration. Meanwhile, relations between worlds will have been given in and as a principle of nonexclusion. The line of questioning that, in Kant's wake, Cover requires and enables brings the jurisgenerative principle to bear on a burden that it must bear: the narrative that begins with the criminalization (and engendering racialization) of that principle. In studying the criminalization of anoriginal criminality, one recognizes that the jurisgenerative principle is a runaway. Gone underground, it remains, nevertheless, our own anarchic ground.

While Kant assumes the necessity of the understanding as an office of law, regulating the imagination in its fecundity, Cover reveals the constituted indispensability of the legal system as an institutional analog of the understanding designed to curtail the lawless freedom with which laws are generated, and subsequently argues for a duty to resist the legal system, even if from within it, in its materialization in and as the state. In the concluding paragraph of his unfinished final article "The Bonds of Constitutional Interpretation: Of the Word, the Deed, and the Role," he argues that "In law to be an interpreter is to be a force, an actor who creates effects even through or in the face of violence. To stop short of suffering or imposing violence is to give law up to those who are willing to so act. The state is organized to overcome scruple and fear. Its officials *will* so act. All others are merely petitioners if they will not fight back."[14] But insofar as some of us cling to Samuel Beckett's notion that "the thing to avoid . . . is the spirit of system," we are left to wonder how else and where else—in what marooned exhaustion, what communal isolation—the resistance of the jurisgenerative multitude is constituted.[15] Moreover, we are required to consider an interarticulate relationship between flight and fight that American jurisprudence can hardly fathom.

That man was not meant to run away is, for Oliver Wendell Holmes, sufficient argument for a combat whose true outcome will have become, finally, eugenic rather than abolitionist. To assert a duty to resist, enacted in and by way of the vast range of principled fugitivity as opposed to the absence of a duty to retreat, is a reading against the grain of Holmes's interpretive insistence on honor, on a certain manhood severely husbanding generativity, a patrimonial heritage manifest as good breeding and as legal violence against bad breeding, given in the prolific but inferior productivity of the unintelligent, whether black or (merely optically) white.[16] Reading Cover (un)covering Kant, always against the backdrop of a certain multiply lined, multi-matrilinear music, requires regeneralizing fighting back, recalibrating it as inaugurative, improvisational, radical interpretation—a fundamental and anticipatory disruption of the standard whose cut origin and extended destination are way outside. This implies a kind of open access to interpretation that in turn implies the failure of state-sanctioned institutions of interpretation insofar as they could never survive such openness. One must still consider interpretation's relation to force, as Cover understands it, but also by way of a massive discourse of force in which, on the one hand, the state monolith is pitted against the so much more than single speaker and, on the other hand, in which the state, as a kind of degraded representation of commonness, is submitted to an illegitimate and disruptive univocality.

Meanwhile, criminality, militancy, improvisatory literacy, and flight collaborate in jurisgenerative assertion, ordinary transportation, corrosive, caressive (non)violence directed toward the force of state interpretation and its institutional and philosophical scaffolding. It's a refusal in interpretation of interpretation's reparative and representational imperatives, the mystical and metaphysical foundations of its logics of accountability and abstract equivalence, by the ones who are refused the right to interpret at the militarized junction of politics and taste, where things enter into an objecthood already compromised by the drama of subjection. In the end, state interpretation—or whatever we would call the exclusionary protocols of whatever interpretive community—tries to usurp the general, generative role of study, which is an open admissions kind of thing. What does it mean to refuse an exclusive and exclusionary ontic capacity or to move outside the systemic oscillation between the refusal and the imposition of such capacity? This question is the necessary preface to a theory of paraontic resistance that is essential matter for a general theory of the generative or, to be more precise, a theory of blackness.

As Bernasconi argues in his reading of Kant's theory of race and that theory's importance for the development of the critical philosophy:

> Kant's interest in the question of the color of Africans . . . seems to have kept him focused on the question of the adequacy of mechanistic explanations offered in isolation from teleology. In Kant's first essay on race the purposive nature of racial (which meant for him color) differences was assumed but not argued on the basis that because neither chance nor mechanical laws could have brought about the developments that enabled organic bodies to adapt to the climates into which they first moved, those developments must be construed as preformed. He was more direct in the 1785 essay when he wrote that the purposive nature of color was visible in the Negro race. . . . The blackness of blacks provided Kant with one of the most powerful illustrations of purposiveness within the biological sphere. But perhaps it worked as a powerful example among his White audience because it addressed their fascination with the fact of Blackness."[17]

In the concluding phrase of this passage, Bernasconi sounds an echo that prompts consideration of the mutually generative, derivative, and endangering interplay of Kant and Frantz Fanon. I hope to show that what that interplay requires us to understand as the epidermalization of the alternative can be more rigorously and precisely imagined as the animaterialization of the fantastic in chromatic saturation. Bernasconi views the structuring power of Kant's racial thinking through a Fanonian lens, in the interest of what Lindon Barrett refers to as seeing double, which the lens induces as an effect of certain complexities of crossing and encounter and as the divided enhancement that blackness—the dispersive gathering of crossing and encounter, poised but mobile in the break between fact and experience like a cantilevered bridge—performs on vision in any case. There's a transverse, experimental drama of body-made questioning that Fanon could be said both to produce and discover. But this counterpublic scene's most immediate necessity, carried out in (musicked) speech, as general endangerment in the interest of general safety, is to place the body itself in question. There's another sense of the blackness of blacks that passeth show as well as understanding; in/visible life is on the double edge. Bernasconi's having sought out Fanon's distorted cosignature calls attention to the fact that blackness indicates a phenomenality, a lived experience, that exceeds the visibility of the color and negates the visibility of the person who bears it even as it amplifies the dynamic hum of blackness's facticity, of what it is to have borne being thrown and how it is possible to have carried movement in depths of sound that are deeper than sound. Double seeing, as Barrett shows, is audiovision: it will have been undone were it to remain uncut, if seeing's straight, single line were undisturbed by the differential force of the resonator. The written, sight-read note is put in a kind of anoriginal trouble by surreptitious accompaniment and tangential proliferation. In his righteous harassment of those disciples of Kant who think the concept of race—and the fact/phenomenality of blackness/black people—has nothing to do with the emergence of the critical philosophy, Bernasconi helps prepare us to recognize the work of blackness (which shows up as an already-given Fanonian turbulence) in Kant. To engage Kant, our enemy and our friend, is to be held and liberated by the necessity of alternative frequencies, carrying signal and noise, that thinking blackness—which is what it is to be given to the reconstruction of imposition—imposes upon him as well. An already-given remix of the doctrinal enunciation of the end is amplified and he becomes our open instrument.

This is to say that doubleness at the convergence of (necessarily cut and augmented) seeing and (the irreducible materiality of) thinking, having been freed from its mundane determinations by delving ever more deeply into their airy ground, lets us know that a difference remains continually to be established not only from the tradition of philosophical racism (whose originary mythologic is a regulatory exertion that is always after the fact) but also from the antiracist philosophical reply (whose negative dialectical subordination to the tradition it would critique as a redoubled belatedness). Both are driven by a nocturnal logic in which it is understood that absence, darkness, and death corrode and that black bodies are such corrosion's agential sign, held tightly within the sensual register and regulation of in/visibility. This agonistic double session, the divided and divisive attempt discursively to mobilize and then fix the locale of absolute negation—as a fleshly object of fear and loathing, identification and desire—is, in Achille Mbembe's words, the convergence of "a demoniacal lie that the Enlightenment's greatest philosophers are guilty of: the assumed existence of a *hole* at the bottom of the African's being" and an Afro-diasporic response that "has allowed itself to be inhabited and 'voiced' by the demon of the Other" in the interest of "the repression of a fantasy of which one is not the author."[18]

While Fanon's questioning body means to give the double its due by blowing up division and collection with a new, explosive affirmation, there is a powerful tendency in Fanonian thought that would not repress but deploy this fantasy in the hope of unleashing what is supposed to be its destructive acidity. It is in this regard that Fanon could be said to reauthorize a massively productive misapprehension in which blackness bears the deviant's alluring, dangerous fertility. Both tendencies amplify only part of Fanon's polyphonic richness, thereby working to regulate the vast, common plain (of which the whole Fanonian mix is a part) from which it comes. The difference between that plain's general capacity for radical chant, radical song, radical (non-) sense, radical cant, radical form, and those forms of dis/located embodiment that are mistaken for things which are not remains to be thought. "The fact of blackness," that quintessential and quintessentially derivative Fanonian phrase, given in the original as "*l'expérience vécue du Noir*," is a beacon for such thought, though the critical obsession with its imprecise rendering into English loses sight of translation's more than foundational findings and capacities, which phonobinocular fantasia often induces a little past the days' and the years' deep midnight. It is usually around three o'clock in the morning when one comes to realize that fact(icity), reflection, and phenomenality are all bound up with one another; that the capacity to overturn is not given in nothingness but in animated thingliness, to which blackness corresponds; that what is at stake in that correspondence is a matter of (is the *material-ity of*) relation—between things and thingliness, blacks and blackness—and study, determined by the protocols of improvisation and review, invention and inventory. The anticipation of what one is tempted to call either or both Deleuzean and Derridean protocols, operating at the animative intersections of minority and exhaustion, deferral and distancing, is brilliantly illuminated in Nahum Dimitri Chandler's steady insistence:

> Let us also mark here that one, such as Du Bois . . . is led to [a] larger perspective because the African American problematic solicits such. It is, from its inception, a displacement from putatively primordial origin. Its development, that is of the situation specific to African Americans, and there is always such specificity, comes about only by way of social processes that are excessive to any locality, no matter how locality is defined. Thus, the very particularity of the African American situation is what sets in motion, or calls for, a form of suprainhabitation of thought or demands that a certain meta-perspective take shape right in the midst of experience, self-consciousness, or the particularities of existence. It solicits the development of a paraontological discourse.[19]

Chandler reopens the Du Boisian field of paraontological difference, where everything is predicated on the animating facticity of deadly, richly internally differentiated but radically nonindividuated lived experience in the relegation zone, which turned out to be resistance's refuge, where renaming is the unnameable's inadequate preface. One such as Du Bois serially lets us know that there is no such one though such more + less than singular refuge is easily mistaken either for source or void. What remains there to be discovered and inhabited, serially and in the insistence of its previousness as an anarchic fact underground, is blackness, which, rather than the hole that negatively bodies forth corrosive force, is continually reconceived as a binding and universal general disturbance—the differential (w)hole at the bottom of (not just the African's) being.[20] The generality of the disturbance, the ubiquity of the Earth's irruption into world, is not negated by, but set to work in, (dis)location. Here in the world, where we stay, for a while, on the move, the interplay of nationalism and humanism makes world citizenship and necropolitical upheaval in, against, and for the state equally impossible. Here on Earth—which serially redoubled and remixed vision brings to light in and against the questioning, nationally liberated human body in subjection—citizenship, spatiotemporal contemporaneity, and the general distribution/imposition of their abstract equivalence are not only im/possible but unnecessary.

Consider that when Fanon gestures toward the positive force that animates corrosive negation and remains in its wake, he not only echoes but retroactively authorizes a corresponding motion in Kant's work that orients the exemplarity that brings critical philosophy's drive and limit. In Kant, blackness is an emphatic visible difference that stands in for race and its powerful illustration of purposiveness, which he defines as "that the existence of which seems to presuppose a representation of that same thing." Purposiveness is exemplified in things "whose possibility must be grounded in an idea of them." It is theory—the general idea of the object-in-representation—that compensates for difference, an intelligible "lawfulness of the contingent as such," a teleological impetus that trumps both chance and mechanistic rule. As such it is "an extravagance for our theoretical faculty of cognition, but not thereby useless or dispensable, but which rather serves as regulative principles partly to restrain the worrisome pretensions of the understanding. Nevertheless, it is prescribed by the understanding '*a priori* as law.'"[21] In other words, the understanding, in its unexplained and unattainable completeness, having been invoked as that which polices the imagination in its lawlessness, is itself both constituted and restrained by imaginative excess. Regulative principle, given in the open and incalculable constraint of a supersensible and nonsensical surround, paradoxically, by way of the specific, unadorned sensuality of a visible difference, embodies purposiveness. It is, therefore, a foundational aesthetic experience of blackness, contained in the register of the merely sensual, held in the relay between the agreeable, which in any case blackness cannot attain, and the disagreeable, which blackness could be said almost to define, that Kant appeals to espouse the importance of teleo-logical principle. Blackness, which constitutes and exemplifies race or racial difference, is the sensible instantiation of the principle of the supersensible, which in turn grounds what Paul Guyer calls "the intersubjective validity" of judgments of taste.[22] But blackness, precisely insofar as it is "merely" sen-sual, is not subject to the intersubjective validity of judgments of taste that it could be said to (under)ground.

As mere sensuality, blackness occupies and quickens a series: the stupid, the irrational, the deformed and/or deformative, the unfinished and/or disruptive, the driven and/or transportive, the irregular and/or anti- and ante-regulative, the blurred and/or blurring, the curved, the canted, the arabesque, the parergon, the outwork and/or mad absence of the work, the outlaw, the would-have-been-outside, the thing of nature that defies or defers, rather than presupposes, representation, the social whose life in exhaustion of the given has often been mistaken for death. That series will have always been inseparable from a "natural" history of inequality that it animates and by which it is animated. Disagreeable blackness is sent, as it were, into what is characterized as a predispositional servitude, a captivity in which the embodiment of the need for constraint, whose own founda-tional and constitutive constraining force has been deployed and forgotten, precisely insofar as she is supposed to be incapable of self-regulation, is given over to the ultimate form of governance, namely that phantasmic and im/possible condition of being wholly for another. This is all bound up with what Fanon speaks of as the possibility of the impossible, the shudder/shadow of death held in the struggle where reciprocal recognition is staged, as it were, with and by an irreversible reluctance. This struggle, which is, of necessity, interminable is, precisely insofar as it is interminable, rec-ognition's condition of im/possibility, a formulation Fanon reproduces without discovering. This doesn't mean that struggle (and its accompany-ing modes of organization) is unnecessary; it just means that it is neither sufficient nor originary. The enclosed incompleteness of the subject in struggle, of the object in representation, is held in the open materiality of things.

Meanwhile, Fanon opposes reciprocal recognition to the reluctance to recognize when it is, in fact, this interplay, subjectivity's serially explained and enclosed incompleteness, that must be understood in its antagonistic relation to the instrumental sociality of things in common. What remains is the task of studying the richness of the relation between instrumentality and uselessness, where being-instrument is profoundly other than being-for-others and disrupts an ethical regime where benevolence is inseparable from accumulation, a duo best understood, in Stevie Wonder's terms, as "the end of an endless end."[23] The vast problematic of arranging the impossible ethics of interminable struggle, of the infinite end, is the field where either mournful or delighted justification and imposition of exploitation is interinanimate with the constant tension between material ground and imaginative leap, each of which must be disavowed by the modern subject that they constitute, each of which must be invoked not only in the interest of such constitution but also in the interest of the other's disavowal. Blackness is the in/audible, in/visible, subterranean, and submarine focal point of this matrix. Nothing has ever been so positivistically, absolutely, and brutally seen as the ground, the earth, the dirt, under the feet and the institutions of man; nothing has never been so bound to the buried, hidden, underground that undermines what it is supposed to uphold. This basic materiality's essential aeration is a constant threat—soil turned over bears the imminence, as irreducible immanence, of overturning, which is, finally, what we have in common.

Insofar as it is an aesthetic experience that initiates this work of disavowal, it is possible to see the justificatory roots of a range of anti-aestheticisms, most notably Adrian Piper's, that justify themselves by linking the aesthetic to the paradoxically xenophobic expansionism that drives modernity. But rejection of aesthetic acculturation in the name of that trace of the disagreeable that reemerges in and as conceptual assertion and catalytic ethical performance seems anomalous in its swerve away from the aesthetic realm that constitutes something like a retroprojective ground for (or the locale of the culmination of) the critical philosophy upon which Piper's own ethics and epistemology are based.[24] Can any avoidance of the national and/or racial market that aesthetic acculturation implies maintain proximity to the rational and ethical field whose foundation is, according to Kant, the teleological principle, the structural guarantor and embodiment of the purposive, that blackness-as-race exemplifies? If Kant's movement within an imperative to

maintain the unmaintainable distinction between thingliness and humanity is any indication, the answer is no. Race or the raced figure, particularly
the figure of the black, occupies and enacts a kind of force field—the not but
nothing other than human—that maintains that distinction while embody-
ing the necessary danger of its inevitable collapse. It is the very mark and
location of the noncategorical, of the outlaw that guarantees the law. This
is how the exemplary figure of abjection, exploitation, pity, and revulsion is
also always the exemplary figure of danger, threat, and irreducible, unavoidable attraction. Racial slavery constitutes the condition of concretization and
dissolution for these concepts and figures (though I will argue emphatically
that it is not their origin). In an age which locates humanity in the very drive
or impulse to be free of any externally imposed law and to push against
the limits of the law in general, the black slave's desire to be free must be
dehumanized, pathologized, naturalized as somatic and mental defect or
disease; or mythologized as its opposite, as antimotivic absence, docility,
preternatural cheerfulness, contentment, and/or imperviousness to pain.
More to the point, and to return to ground Menninghaus prepares, that desire
to be free, manifest as flight or escape, as a fugitivity that may well prove to veer
away even from freedom as its telos, is indexed to anoriginal lawlessness.
The question of breaking the law is immediately disrupted by an incapacity for
law, an inability both to intend the law and intend its transgression and the
one who is defined by this double inability is, in a double sense, an out$_2$law. At
the same time, one is now both able and obligated to speak of something
like the natural and lawless freedom of this natural servant. The imagination,
the black, and the thing (*das Ding*) all partake of the "lawless freedom" that
attends the anti- or ante-intentional; all are in need of some external, regulative force that they also crystallize as that force's effect.

In such a context, amputation/castration/"clipped wings" emerge as psycho/
somatic remedy in need of remedy. After "emancipation," so-called natural
tendencies to break and/or (a)void law, to violate, for instance, the limits
of a juridical rationality whose protective function was directed toward or
through rather than for the "freedman," were criminalized, attached to some
primordialized excess-as-category, some spiritual tendency for mayhem that
must, paradoxically, be thought as a certain criminality of imagination or
pathologization of form that, again, is deployed to mark both the human
and its excluded, inhuman essence. Race, then, is an always already troubled
concept, the consolidation or protection of which is the occasion for, among
other things, the massive exertion of theoretical energy. It is, finally, black

resistance to such foundational strife, or rather, the yoking of such resistance to blackness, that constitutes the ground whereby the figure of the black not only occupies the space wherein the difference between thing, criminal, and human would be maintained and always collapses but at given moments is the exemplary figure of the thing, the criminal, *and* the human. To be figured as the exemplary human—and as the very opening through which access to the human is given—is perhaps the greatest index of racism. But what is most important is that blackness itself, insofar as it stands in for the inadequacy of mechanistic explanation, operates for Kant within the realm of the transcendental—it is a physicality that is indexed to something more than the "merely" physical. Though not subject to the intersubjective validity that grounds judgments of taste it is, again, the field or the ground—that takes the form of an imaginative leap—within which the universalizing strain of subjective individuation is intelligible.[25] For us, as apposed to Kant—who bears but does not speak for, disavows but is constituted by, supposedly mute and decidedly mutative disagreeable blackness—there is a certain romanticism to be entered and exceeded insofar as it marks the occasion of a recovery or rehabilitation of the "merely" sensual even as it calls upon us to consider how the material instantiates the teleological, the transcendental. And all this requires a deeper consideration of the nature and fate of the material, the physical. But what is the materiality and physicality of blackness? I would tend to agree both with Kant and Du Bois that simple description doesn't come close to getting at that animaterial, metaphysical thing in itself that exceeds itself.

In the end, the question of ownership, of property and the proper, will always be the field upon which the specifics of these general structures are laid out. Finally, race is the locus of the conceptual and practical protection and the uncontainable endangerment of the proper. The black slave is, again, the key manifestation of this double icon but she is also always a strong reminder that both this danger and this saving power can neither be limited to nor contained within that iconic figure. The comingling of the constraints of and the resistance to the proper and the law turns out to be the very essence of the modern conception of personhood. There is an impurity at the very heart of the modern subject that the notion of general and abstract equivalence cannot regulate.[26] What is figured as external threat to that illusory structure of equivalence—a material ruse in the perpetuation of inequality— is the shadow of its already fatal internal differentiation. The figure of the outside that guarantees the equality of "all men" is the embodied shadow of a difference internal to all men (as an exterior comportment, a line of flight), an interior paramour (as Wallace Stevens would have it) or blackamoor (as Denis Diderot would have it), one that might have been conceptualized otherwise. The anxiety that structures racism as a capitalization of difference and the justification of the derivation of inequality from difference by way of abstract equivalence is this: that race, insofar as it guarantees the field of equivalence that it supplements and thereby ruptures, anoriginally endangers the inequality it is deployed—or, more precisely, nominated—to protect. It then becomes, as Foucault argues, the locus and method of a massive interplay of policing and exploitation, repression and desire, as in the current terror-driven war on terror that produces the objects of its prosecution and persecution in the violent enforcement of lethal state legality's response to the resistances and flights that prompt it. Implicit, here, is that race moves against its own regulatory derivative. This given activation—the prefigurative (under)ground of anti- and anteracism—is the universal, differential formation of form or the informal condition of possibility of forms of life. Against and before the brutal fixity of the name, it is called, among other things, blackness, which must be imagined in its paraontological difference from black people, who suffer the name as a kind of (under)privilege, whose animating, anominative structures they are given to imagine and enact in a massive calling to social study. Cedric Robinson famously recalls this as "the black radical tradition" to let us know that if the paraontological difference is an irreducible dehiscence it is also a sociopoetic activity, a dance, a passage, a step, by The Step Brothers, The Soul Brothers, Soul Brother Number One who is not one, her bridge, his line, their *pas du tout* in the name of the stepbrother, their generative antigenetics, the general, variable heritability of our dissent, the way we get down, when we doin' it to death, in death's earhole, all and nothing at all.[27]

THOSE OF US WHO are given to black study serially return to this fugitive preoccupation. None of us can, and some of us would never, get away from it. Instead, we try to get away with it, get down with it, but it always runs away. There's a logical fallacy concerning where it comes from and a wary negation of the wishful thought that, out of nowhere, it keeps on coming. These difficulties often take the form of an axiomatic enclosure where paraontological force is forgotten in the deployment of antiontological method, where the paralegal force of the supernaturally empirical is obscured in legal empiricism's vigilant attendance upon the unnatural. This problematic comes brilliantly into relief in the opening movement of Bryan Wagner's *Disturbing the Peace: Black Culture and the Police Power after Slavery*.

> Perhaps the most important thing we have to remember about the black tradition is that Africa and the diaspora are older than blackness. Blackness does not come from Africa. Rather, Africa and its diaspora become black during a particular stage in their history. It sounds a little strange to put it this way, but the truth of this description is widely acknowledged. Blackness is an adjunct to racial slavery. Certainly we will continue to discuss and disagree about the determinants that made blackness conceivable as well as about the pacing of their influence. That process is very complex, mixing legal doctrine from ancient slave systems with social customs from the long history of enslavement between Christians and Muslims to produce a new amalgam that would become foundational to the modern world. Blackness is an indelibly modern condition that cannot be conceptualized apart from the epochal changes in travel, trade, labor, consumption, industry, technology, taxation, warfare, finance, insurance, government, bureaucracy, communication, science, religion, and philosophy that were together made possible by the European system of colonial slavery. Due to this complexity, we will likely never be able to say with confidence whether blackness begins before or during the sugar revolution, or consequently whether slavery follows from racism or racism follows from slavery. We do know, however, what blackness indicates: existence without standing in the modern world system. To be black is to exist in exchange without being a party to exchange.[28]

Though its subtitle declares its concern with black culture (and certainly this is not in any way a false declaration), *Disturbing the Peace* is more fundamentally about blackness. The implication here is not just that blackness and black culture are not the same; what is further and more importantly implied is that blackness and black people are not the same, however much it is without doubt the case that black people have a privileged relation to blackness, that black cultures are (under)privileged fields for the transformational expression and enactment of blackness. For Wagner, blackness is "existence without standing"; it is "to exist in exchange without being a party to exchange." It is a peculiar condition of and within the modern world system. It is existence under the coercive surveillance of the state though the fundamental condition of this existence is that the very state that watches you can neither see you nor see from your perspective. To say this perspective is unseen and not seen from is not to say, according to Wagner, that it is unknowable. There is a tradition that emerges against this backdrop that is, according to Wagner, knowable by way of its relation to the law. There is an empirical legal history that allows Wagner to trace the contours of blackness. As he puts it, "It is the history of law that gives us what we need to track the tradition's continuing labor of self-predication."[29] This is to say that while blackness is not simply an effect of the coercive brutality of the state, its self-making is only visible against the backdrop of the state and its coercive legal apparatuses. This is how blackness comes into relief. For Wagner there is "a statement against which the black tradition has continually dramatized its own emergence."[30] Again, that statement is legal—the death sentence whose utterance serially reveals the determinate and degenerate grammar of slavery, settler colonialism, and their ongoing afterlife.

Consider Wagner's sense of blackness as counterstatement by way of Hortense Spillers, who takes pains to show that the counterstatement is indissolubly linked to a statement of its own and therefore to imply that black study is, and is concerned with, the improvisational encryption that counterstatement accompanies. This hidden indication—its continuing reconstitution of knowledge and knowability, intelligence and counter-intelligence—is a problematic whose irreducible sociality remains an irreducibly paraontological matter for which neither ontogeny nor sociogeny can fully account insofar as their interinanimation is put off by their competing claims to access to the originary. For Wagner, the origin of blackness in the laws that blackness speaks against but cannot silence decisively undermines any "insistence for a positive cultural property such as soulfulness."[31] Wagner is driven, in and by his own historiographic tendencies, to avoid the positive in favor of a constant illumination of that which blackness would negate in order more fully to understand blackness as that negation. Rather than begin to imagine something on the order of an anoriginary criminality with which blackness is inextricably linked—or to think blackness, perhaps more precisely, as the paradoxically anarchic principle and expression of a jurisgenerativity that demands a reconfiguration of the very idea of law—Wagner moves by way of an assessment of crime as part of a state language (itself part of a more complex state apparatus) to which blackness responds in ways that are labeled by the state as criminal. The idea of an anoriginal, jurisgenerative criminality requires us to ask after the possibility of the priority of counterstatement to statement in much the same way that Robinson—on frequencies beneath but parallel to Gilles Deleuze, Foucault, and, before them, Karl Marx—intimates the priority of resistance to power (when as the coercive, regulatory, and accumulative apparatuses of racial state capital respond to the already given insurgency of blackness at work). But more than that, it demands that we consider how improvisational para-statement—the extragrammatical run-on, that informal incompletion where the sentence lives against its own execution—continually and ubiquitously establishes itself otherwise, elsewhere and at another time, neither here nor there nor here and now, as a kind of anoriginal (declaration of) independence. What if the priority of resistance to power, or counterstatement to statement, were something on the order of a previousness without origin (or even a haunted, precedential re- or misunderstanding of origin as anoriginal disturbance)? If this were the case, we would move more fully into the realm of a sociohistorical paraontology in which blackness improvisationally passeth understanding as an antiquity constantly constituted and reconstituted in modernity, always in irreducible entanglement with the terms and powers of modernity, forever in anticipation of modernity and its exhaustion.

Wagner is concerned with something about the black tradition that we have to remember rather than discover. Even if an ongoing historical unfolding is understood to remain possible, it will have been determined by an absolute natal occasion rather than still be moving after the fact of a previousness whose insistence does not take the form of an originary enclosure. That the truth of this origination is widely acknowledged has nothing whatever to do with whether it has been thought. What if, as Robinson asserts, there remains that facticity of blackness which cannot be understood within the context of this genesis? Then the corresponding task entails not only a consideration of that remainder, not only a critique of that origin and of origin in general, but also a disruption of the regulative methodological hegemony of understanding. Indeed, what if regulative, regulated understanding is that indelibly modern institution that responds to a condition that not only precedes it but also calls it into existence? The specific invocation of law that follows Wagner's remembrance is, in this regard, necessary. What is at stake in the interdiction of a paraontological approach—and what such interdiction's relation is to the racialized policing of the imagination (a belatedness of which racial slavery is a belated example)—remains to be seen. The ongoing history of blackness is available only by way of some attendance to its paraontology, whose most prominent feature is what Chandler refers to as "originary displacement."[32] It is through the gift and givenness of displace-ment, in the displacement of origin that blackness enacts, and within which the supersensible nature of blackness becomes sensible and/or makes sense, that paraontology (for which what Ian Hacking calls historical ontology and what Fanon calls sociogeny are suggestively inadequate synonyms) comes into relief in its generality. This is to say that the most important thing we have to imagine about the black tradition—about the radical, paraontological totality that is its motive force—is that it is common. Blackness is (in) com-mon. Blackness is (in) universal exchange. Blackness is, therefore, older than Africa and its diaspora in the broadest and most ancient senses that this sentence can bear. What remains in us of Africa—as the very condition of possibility of the remainder—is its ordinary trace. Such imagining is (in) the (double) vision of a paraontological difference.

That difference is elided both by Wagner's initial temporal determination of blackness and the delimitation of blackness as indication that immediately follows. While he cannot know exactly when blackness began, he does know that it had a beginning, that it was derived, that it is, most fundamentally, derivation, or the derivative, as such. Wagner has behind his claim a catalog of institutional departments and comportments that combine to guarantee and to narrate the durative imposition of the nonposition or, at least, of posi-tion's vacancy; and his capacity to tell what blackness indicates follows from his capacity to assert that it has an origin. In Wagner's estimation, existence without standing is an after-effect of state-sponsored annihilative terror in which a mode of being is reduced to a structure of designation. The at-tempted imposition of bare existence is activated when ontology is supposed to have been left by the wayside. This nakedness is only in relation to the ones who confer it and its conferral is nothing other than a kind of withhold-ing. Blackness is, in this crucible of refusal, a null set offering neither resis-tance nor explanation. Here, it is the existence of the impossibility of existing but for the eternal, brutal imposition of the deadly gift of that impossibility. That the one who conveys that gift bears that gift, as that gift, is something we keep having to remember to forget. Being and nothingness converge, here, in this hellish river of thwarted interracial intersubjectivity we keep crossing, as dual, dueling singularity, in the fucked-up dance of the nothing that is not there and the nothing that is. Blackness names what is not (there); even its thingliness is nil in relation to something, some point, some pure, abstract and ascendant singularity the possibility of whose presence we continue to assume against the grain of natural social history's constantly lived assertion of and insistence upon its absence. In, or perhaps more precisely, underneath Wagner's account, which legalistically assumes the historical can be accounted for in a judiciously chosen and carefully analyzed set of historical facts, blackness names what is not there as the ghostly bearing of so being named and the radiation of that bearing as ghostly affectivity. In that bearing what is given is a kind of abjection machine, an industrially productive thought experiment always at work in the imaginal and algorithmic production of identity.

But what if we remember not to forget that the black man is not? Any more than the snowman? Then, in contradistinction to Wagner and the wide acknowledgment he invokes, we might move by way of the assumption that blackness is older than Africa, older than its diaspora, older than racial slavery, older than its beginning, older than its name or its submission to the operation of naming. It is the anarchic principle that calls originary nominalization into being and, therefore, into question; it is the subjunctive, substantive, anticipatory accompaniment of every eviscerative indication. Does racial slavery give blackness its name or does it serve to solidify and disseminate an ongoing naming? Who is the agent, and what is the context, of that naming? These are questions concerning the natural history of racial capitalism, as Robinson theorizes it, and of antinomian race war, as Foucault theorizes it. Both theorizations require us to consider the possibility that the history and historicity of blackness is underived from the generally acknowledged temporal, geographic, and psychoeconomic origin Wagner demarcates wherein (b)lackness begins with an exchange to which one is not a party, in a state of which one is not a citizen. This is to say that Wagner also carries out a Fanonian protocol—conflating (the blackness of) the black with a general and implacable anonymity in the eyes of the state and in the vision of whatever mode of etiolated personhood the state makes—against the grain of Fanon's most powerfully paraontological counterequation.

> Being black is belonging to a state organized according to its ignorance of your perspective—a state that does not, that cannot, know your mind. To borrow a formulation from the eve of decolonization, we might say that blackness suggests a situation in which you are anonymous to yourself. It is a kind of invisibility.

Taken seriously, these facts about blackness are enough to make problems for anyone who wants to talk about blackness as founding a tradition. Conceptualized not as a shared culture but as a condition of statelessness, blackness would appear to negate the perspective that would be necessary to found a tradition. To speak as black, to assert blackness as a perspective in the world, or to argue the existence of the black world is to deny the single feature by which blackness is known. Because blackness is supernumerary, it is impossible to speak as black without putting yourself into tension with the condition that you would claim. Speaking as black can mitigate your condition, or make you into an exception or a credit to your own condition, but it cannot allow you to represent your condition, as speaking is enough to make you unrepresentative. You can be clean and articulate and also black, but to be all these things at once is to admit to an existence defined by its division (or its doubleness).[33]

Note that as in Fanon, this protocol seems always to move in excess of itself, as a seeking out of something—even though it may have been battered into the airy thinness of a perspective—in the nothing that law makes, thereby not only breaking the law it explicates but also imagining that there is something on the order of an originary criminality that is before that law, that calls that law into existence by calling *its* name. Those who are driven to prove the impossibility of this dangerous supplement still desire it or, at least, its effects. While Wagner leaves unasked the question of why there is something (extra) not so much rather *than* but rather *in* nothing, he certainly does not leave its social desire unrequited; his book is, in fact, a richly devoted outlaw covering/recovery of its siren songs. Nevertheless, what remains is to consider that there is something called "blackness" that has been transformed by its name and by its deployment as a name that has, itself, in turn, been altered by that to which it refers. If the name and the referent acquire and dispossess, continually attempt to own and disown, one another, such an operation fails to undermine the referent's previousness. The referent is before its naming, just as the name is prior to, and therefore independent of, that to which it refers. What lies before the name is given in and structured by the name each in their mutual anticipation of the other. This off derivation, which anticipates that from which it is derived, is a general flight that keeps taking off somewhere between Saul Kripke and Jacques Derrida, on the one hand, and Gottlob Frege and Martin Heidegger, on the other. Perhaps these names denote mere positions placed around the capaciously indeterminate and open circle of a philosophical rhythm that blackness lays down, when name and referent don't so much acquire but *complement/*

ac*comp*any one another, in a kind of subcanonical Niels Bohr–McCoy Tyner operation in which experiment and theory are in mutually abrasive and enabling contact, against the backdrop of a global field of in/human acquisition and inquisition. What if such brutality turns out to have softened certain annihilative rigidities of designation and, in so doing, established the entanglement of two distinctions: that between being and beings, on the one hand, and that between sense and reference, on the other? Then, on the good foot as it were (the distinction between blacks and, and the distinction between race and), blackness will have been revealed as entanglement's gravitational feel.

I have been concerned with the implications of Wagner's momentary deferral of saying what blackness is so that he could reveal what "blackness" indicates because it is only after a prior historicization (i.e., a laying down of the facts of the case) and a subsequent nominalization that Wagner attends to the question of the (strange) meaning of being black's continual estrangement of meaning. The shift from indication to existence is precipitous; the one from blackness to being black is subtler; it is practically imperceptible except from a vantage point given in the more dramatic slide it prefaces— in which being black comes into relief against "being a party." Being black in Wagner's more self-contained Fanonian formulation is an anti- or nonsubjective condition. It is the condition, to be more precise, of *a* black, the one who is barred from being *a* party, with which Wagner is concerned. This condition of a black—this "lived experience of the black" (as illegitimately opposed to blackness's peculiar and common facticity)—is defined by a relative interdiction of subjectivity (that comes into relief as the forgetting of the general interdiction of subjectivity). The ontological question is thereby suspended. Or, as the Fanon whom Chandler illuminates might say, a black, in his condition, offers Wagner no paraontological resistance. I employ this black lit, echoplexed version of Fanon's phrasing because Wagner writes from a position that many contemporary critics now occupy, a position structured by this presumed incapacity for ontological resistance (and a corollary criminalization of paraontological imagination's already-given criminality) that sanctions a deferral of attention to the question of ontology in its relation to blackness or, more precisely, to the pressure that blackness puts on both ontology and relation. Because Wagner speaks of blackness in order first to get at its origin and then to get at what it indicates, the question of its (suspension of) ontology is suspended or displaced in an assumption of its conflation with black people (in their impossible representative manifestation as a black person), whose very personhood is supposed to have been suspended in the interdiction of their capacity to have standing in the world system, to be a subject, a citizen, a party to exchange. Wagner's privileging of juridical reflection over the paraontological, of historical fact over facticity in/as historicity, is not announced as such; ontology is not dismissed but bound over, held in a jusrisdictional vacuum. This methodological preference takes the form of a negligence that barely appears against the backdrop of such rigorous, caring, and careful thinking and scholarship. The effects of this choice, in all their quietness, are of great moment, however, to those of us who remain concerned with the possibility of resistance that blackness offers from below the history of being sent. I'll try to show how that resistance is better understood as paraontological insofar as it is directed toward the structure of dominance not only in society but in ontology as well. Paraontological resistance is an ontic affair, irruptive as a sociokinetic mode of everyday study. What remains to be thought is also another way of thinking being—something best understood as imaginative misunderstanding apposed to the regulative power of understanding and its racist enactments.

In the end, however, it is Wagner's devoted care that ought to animate any engagement with him. This care is evident when he assumes the capacity for a black to have a perspective, even though such a perspective would hardly be possible where the capacity to be a citizen or to be a party to exchange are not. Perhaps a black's perspective is something like what Frank B. Wilderson III considers under the rubric of black (or a black's) positionality[34]—a view that is from relatively nowhere and of relatively no one, which is to say not only that the no one in question does not see but also, as Wagner asserts, that she is not seen. Wilderson rightly demands that we consider—by way of the powerful analytic of antagonism as opposed to mere conflict as the structure of antiblackness, and of antiblackness as the structuring force of the modern world, that he provides—how not being seen and being seen in crosshairs are all bound up with one another, which could only occur after thinking the implications of the fact that no one's necessarily unoccupied vantage is a lived, preoccupied impossibility in which even Wilderson detects something organic. Wagner's object is that organicity and he sees it precisely as a kind of criminalized underexistence. Though it seems to bear, in his own impossible view, no chance either of admittance into the world system or of transcendence of that system it might very well constitute a certain disorderly tendency whose force has heretofore been theorized without the protection, so to speak, of the paraontological difference. Perhaps invisibility was never an accurate description of this other mode of being unseen, particularly when that mode is understood to have been a kind of self-regard in its proximity to a whole other form of self-nomination. Anonymity, in this regard, is better known as paranymity; in this regard, invisibility slanders the ones who are more accurately described, in Cecil Taylor's phrase, as "dark to themselves."[35]

When Wagner gestures toward a perspective whose impossibility is required by his own axiomatic primitive, it is as if he strains against being a representative—or perhaps merely a citizen—of the state that is organized, in his words, according to its ignorance of that perspective; and against his understanding that though there is no facticity of blackness, there are facts about blackness that serve to negate that perspective and to found, in this negation, a tradition. It is Wagner's intention, therefore, to understand the black tradition as found(ed), which is to say discovered, in statelessness, after the fact of an assumption that statelessness is the negation of the very possibility of common cultural property. Stateless is the name given to the ones who are subject to, but not subjects, of history. The stateless ones are anti-ontological. And, deeper still, they are defined by an absolute dispossession. They are nothing in having been thrown and, moreover, their being thrown is not theirs, is not something they can have, for they can have nothing. This is to say that they can have nothing in common. This is to say that they cannot even have their nothingness in common. This is, moreover, a matter of law. They are derivatives of the law that authorizes these conditions. And it is by way of an examination of their relation to the law that Wagner intends to describe the contours of their interdicted perspective, their outlaw tradition.

But what if there is an ontic facticity of statelessness that is greater than what the law lays down and irreducible to the external imposition of a set of facts? Wagner's insight that statelessness is not a condition but a perspective is of massive importance because it moves toward the necessity of imagining the actual existence of nonstatist, nonstatic, anti- and anteperspectival sociality. To sense such sociality is to enact it, in and as study of and in the (sur)-real, in the underground that accrues to no-thing's militant flight, which takes the form of a tilling, a cultivation, an overturning of ground, in and as but from thingliness. The paraontological questions, which are given in the recognition of the paraontological difference, remain: what is this refusal of perspective? What is statelessness? What is blackness? What I would like always to show is this: that statelessness is not relative nothingness; that insofar as blackness is and comes, rather, from absolutely nothing it is, indeed, something after all, namely, the commonness of the improper; that blackness is exchange, the dispersive gift of anoriginal dispossession; that dispossession is what we are and what we have in common; that it is the undercommons.[36] If such assertion is what Wagner would call "recourse to the consolation of transcendence," it is so only insofar as it assumes an immanence that is fundamental and irreducible.[37] Ultimately, I share Wagner's stated objectives, which are "to name the blackness in the black tradition without recourse to those myths that have made it possible up to this time to represent the tradition as cultural property"; to "track . . . the emergence of the black tradition from the condition of statelessness"; and "to describe its contours by tracking the tradition's engagement with law."[38] I simply differ from him regarding the origin of blackness and of law. Wagner disruptively exposes certain myths of origin in order to replace them with others, thereby begging the question of the anoriginal, which the paraontological thinking of blackness instantiates and of which those myths (and Wagner's) are an expression. Anoriginal expression bears a jurisgenerative grammar. It is before the law, as the law's ani*mater*ial foundation. The state brutality Wagner understands to be originary responds to the ante-interpellative call of an already given, anterelational exchange—the exhausted and exhaustive making of the living of the party. In his theoretical and historiographical merger of policing and production, Wagner contains blackness within the history of its juridical regulation even as he demonstrates that blackness—as precisely that perpetual disturbance that is, for Kant, endemic to and constitutive of perpetual peace—not only exceeds such placement but is its anticipatory and (juris)generative displacement. The history of blackness can be traced to no such putatively, and paradoxically, originary critical or legal activity. In the social exhaustion of racial state capitalism's sanctioning of politics as the systemic ordering of life in death, which is before that sanction and brings it online, there's a hymn to the name and the thought that are above and below every name and every thought—the name and the thought of blackness.

Before Menninghaus, Arendt took critical notice of Kant's thesis on the unregulated imagination's nonsensical productivity.[39] While she agrees with Kant that such production requires that the imagination's wings be clipped, Menninghaus directs his attention to that production and the aesthetic and political possibilities it bears. I want to move in Menninghaus's wake while considering that nonsense itself (in the richest sense of the term)—as much as its suppression or regulation—is essential to the unexplainable completion of the critical philosophy. The imagination, in its lawless freedom, is melodramatic; this is to say that Kant's imagination is just so, not only in the very idea, construction, and deployment of teleological principle, of the purposive, of the supersensible, but also in the more general idea of beauty as a symbol of morality, of beauty and morality as links in the chain of significa-tion, as operative within a system of legibility. What's important, here, is to recognize that the melodramatic imagination is indispensable to the critical philosophy, is the dark invaginative foundation—and the secret, antifounda-tional rupture—of its systematicity. Moreover, what the melodramatic imag-ination seeks (teleological principle, purposiveness, a path to the ethical that guarantees it, a bridge as internal and external limit) must be empirically determined—as in a gesture or in the frenzied stillness, tantamount to move-ment, to flight, of the Other's picture, the irreducible thingliness of the Other that grounds and, as it were, invades the picture with a kind of criminally ontic scandal—though what is sought still remains, as it were, in a realm other than that of the empirical, namely that fleshly realm, again to invoke Spillers, in which irreducible animateriality remains unenclosed by body and soul. The lawless freedom of the melodramatic imagination, its constant irruptive and disruptive escape from the system it engenders, is structurally correspondent to the gestures that conjure it and which it conjures. There-fore, I'm interested in the incalculable rhythm of the incalculable relation between the beauty of things and gestures that conventional aesthetic judgment finds unbeautiful and the morality of paralegal assertions and disruptions that conventional moral reason finds unreasonable.

When Kant discovers that what Paul Guyer later calls the "intersubjec-tive validity" of judgments of taste can transcend the merely empirical, it means that the problem of taste can be incorporated into the system of the critical philosophy so that what might be called the immanent aesthetic will have been linked to the transcendental aesthetic's intuitive frame and therefore will have been, as it were, transcendental all along.[40] But intersubjective validity also raises the question concerning the location of systematicity—is it in the natural world or in us? Representation intervenes, allows detachment from and disinterest in the natural world or thing. A moment of abstraction—from the thing's bare existence to a representation that will have seemed to make that existence possible by radically augment-ing it—is what allows this expansion of the Kantian system. It is a moment of expansion that operates as a kind of bridge between the sensual and the conceptual and between the representation of the thing and the presentation of subjectivity. That moment of abstraction is nothing if not an imaginative flight, bringing a kind of graceful absence into philosophical presentness like a paraontic shadow. Things—and the supposedly intentionless moves they make—are ennobled by this representational supplement, which is also an envaluing. At the same time, the representation constitutes an irreducible endangering of the thing's ontological status. It's not just that, as Derrida has shown, the logic of the supplement bears the trace of an irreducible lack, but also that the question of the thing's being is lost, hushed, as if that question partakes of the bad taste that generally accrues to things, as if it requires submission to "the rabble of the senses," to that rabble's attendance upon things. Representation bridges the gap between thing and object even as it seeks to guard against the danger such passage makes possible; at the same time, representation collapses the bridge between the ontic and the ontological. So that the completion of the critical philosophy is also a kind of contention with and in and as an antinomy; it is a being-possessed of the dispossessing force of the antinomian: the rabble of the senses must be placed in some contrapuntal relation to imaginative riot, rebellion, and uprising, all of which are often misunderstood as correspondent to a riotous inability to plan. Moreover, uprising's backlit echo in gest/ure, more properly understood as the trace of a constantly reirruptive soliloquy, a heretofore unthinkable social interiority, is understood as self-interested rejection of study and, more generally, as an expression of the irrational that is also, necessarily, in bad taste. I've been preparing myself to offer a corrective to this formulation that moves through Kant's subtle, serial admission of the debt critical philosophy owes to what cannot be simply dismissed as the irrational.

That debt is manifest in Kant's ability to see beauty as a symbol of morality. But Kant certainly did not think that black(ness) was beautiful. In his early observations on the beautiful and the sublime, blackness, in what he understood to be its irreducible nonbeauty, is detached from the very possibility of truth and rationality, a detachment that is given immediately in the supposed ugliness of the black visage. Strange, then, that in his elaboration of the critical philosophy, race, as embodied in the racial difference that blackness exemplifies, is itself the exemplary form of teleological principle which not only grounds the distinction between simple description and natural history but also, in so doing, helps to make possible that completion of the critical philosophy that is manifest in the very idea of the purposive, in its linking of beauty and morality. Perhaps part of the beauty of blackness lies in that it has been and continues to be the condition of possibility of the critique of judgment. If so, this beauty justifies an inquiry into the morality symbolized by a raised fist. Moreover, we can justifiably consider why that gesture seems pretty consistently to evoke the abandonment of moral legibility in a range of texts that directly and indirectly insist upon a logic of white supremacy they attempt to deny or disavow. The price for entering what one has never left is, on the one hand, the ultimate surrender of the optic and aim of moral legibility and, on the other hand, the forced self-refusal of access to (a certain) beauty and to the question of beauty.

These texts move within a history of the antifoundational refusal of beauty's gestural fugitivity even as Kant—both in spite and because of his foundational antiblackness—allows us to consider beauty as a kind of fugitive foundation. On the one hand, another beauty in the interest of another reality; on the other hand, this other beauty demands a fundamental reworking, a rewalking and reconstruction, of the bridge between beauty and morality. The scandal of the supersensible is that it manifests itself sensually; the scandal of the work is that its completeness falters in the presence of ineradicable complaint, a radical misunderstanding that no explanation can mute. The gesture in question is, finally, a refusal of a certain system of judgment, a testimony in and as a critique of the testimonial modes that system offers. It is, moreover, a kind of demand, a strenuous assertion of what Charles Mingus, in another context, calls the *terribly* beautiful whose intersubjective validity is bound up with what disturbs and disorders the faculties of mind, with what troubles and extends the harmony of those faculties, especially when that harmony, or its representation, is aligned with political normativities and their corresponding (il)logics.[41] The gestural emancipation of mind's dissonance inhabits a sexual cut of sexual difference, where the choreo-iconography of blackness in action, its irruptive and disturbing presence, the assertion—in its desire—of the play of nothingness and abundance, is both sacred and ordinarily occult. According to Mingus, it is the black woman, who bodies forth the terribly beautiful; the raising of her arms accompanies other modes of testimony in the frenzied gatherings of Wednesday night prayer meetings, marking the subterranean knowledge of the Earth, where she lives, and the surreptitious negation of the world, where she stays. Her flown, animate dwelling materializes the jurisgenerative principle whose fecundity Cover illuminates. There is a kind of ornamentation—a ruptural amendment; a serration; a work of undoing at the work's broken edge—where lawfulness and lawlessness meet. That something works this way might be surprising since precise, which is to say unnatural, description of it takes such a tortuous path. See how nonsense escapes precisely through the constant and demonstrative making of sense that poetry—which Kant argues is the carrying out of the imagination's free play as a business of the understanding, but which we seem continually to misunderstand as the informal, form-giving, nominative force of endlessly self-(dis)organizing blackness is supposed to enact. To take care of the understanding's business, Kant says, poetry must paradoxically restrain that "play of sensations" in a reduction of its (phonic) materiality, an ordinance that protects the exclusionary universality of a totality that cannot stand, in its orderedness, in the face of the rough nonsense or extrasense—the nonreduction of sense that is more than sense—of the aesthetic event and its ordinary serrations. It is no accident that irruptions on the surface of the event, that irruption as (the surface of) the event, will have constituted the severest challenge to that Kantian notion of freedom that depends upon smooth containment. The romanticism of the black radical tradition is at issue here; it's played out in the sensual, nonsensical depths of surface, on the plain of imagination in black performance, whose spectrum is so broad that it includes its own falling into shadow.[42]

Elsewhere, I have considered that plain as J. L. Austin's rebellious domain. His work was devoted to the proposition that the proper object and methodological apparatus for philosophy was ordinary language—the material of everyday discursive events or, in his parlance, speech acts. However, when Austin sets out on the path toward a general theory of language he moves along lines determined by the paradigmatic opposition of material surface and semantic depth. Austin's Kantian desire for universality in language and in the theory of language requires the reduction of phonic substance, the dismissal of the "phonetic act" as "merely the act of uttering certain noises."[43] Still, Austin's anticipation of deconstruction comes upon an effect that, perhaps efficaciously, is never fully crystallized as method. He submits his own work (his own logical direction, his own diegetic comportment) to that effect—a liberating cascade of breakdowns in which linguistic categories are cut by the everyday events of speech so that, within the plain of the ordinary, the distinctions between words and gestures and between words and sounds emerge and recede in order to let us know that the extraordinary is the always surprising path through the ordinary that is made by way of the montagic, transversal sequencing of events. That sequence is, in turn, structured by the logic of the surprising, multiple singularity of the event—that it is unprecedented, that it is infused with the plexed singularity of its fellows. The event in question is ill legality, the repeating head of a step aside or across; the object at hand is phonographic, paraliterary, and ungraspable. Such movement in sight and sound, such dispossessed and dispossessive fugitivity, in its very anticipation of the regulative and disciplinary powers to which it responds, reminds us, along with Foucault, that "it is not that life has been totally integrated into techniques that govern and administer it; it constantly escapes them."[44]

Ed Roberson, who is later beautifully echoed by Aldon Nielsen, speaks of this fugitivity as "the calligraphy of black chant."[45] I'd like to think of it as the chor(e)o-phonography of black Kant, pronounced cant, marking not only that version of Scottish pronunciation that my teacher, Julian Boyd, insistently claimed on Kant's behalf, but also channeling a certain cantilevered reach toward or projective structure for science and history whose attachment to the natural is more accurately understood as what Nathaniel Mackey would call a "broken claim to connection."[46] "Race" in Kant is incantatory gesture, the mark of an incapacity that drives philosophy (the black can't of philosophy, philosophy's unpayable debt to the unmeaning jargon and illegitimate rhetoric, the phono-material suasion, it keeps trying to leave behind). The proper valuation of that gesture is made available to us by inhabiting what Kant devalued and, at the very moment of his deployment of it, disavowed and by considering what even Kant couldn't imagine, namely the beautiful art of what is supposed to be unbeautiful.[47]

Black chant, is, among other things a transverse reenactment of black Kant, pronounced cant, of blackness in Kant insofar as it intones the foundational interplay of sense and non-sense, sense and reference, being and beings, blackness and blacks, at the racial crossroads where modern philosophy takes its own path, reinitializing itself as the inhabitation of the conflict between flight and constraint.[48] What I am imagining, in other words, is a kind of black genius in Kant that must be conserved—an incantatory, ante-Kantian frenzy, a tumultuous derangement, wherein a terrible reality is lent to song and word in their interinanimation. You will doubtless recognize the invocation of a Du Boisian analytic that emerges in an essay called "The Religion of the American Negro," first published in 1900 and later revised and republished in 1903 as "Of the Faith of the Fathers," Chapter X of *The Souls of Black Folk*, a text that has become unfamiliar due to the cavalier familiarity with which we often treat it. Indeed, my invocation of the text counts on that combination of proximity and estrangement as the very possibility of the work of reinitialization I am attempting. I suspect that the place to begin again is where Du Bois's most famous and influential text begins, precisely in order to show how that text, seminal though it may be, is, in fact, not the beginning.

> Herein lie buried many things which if read with patience may show the strange meaning of being black here in the dawning of the Twentieth Century. This meaning is not without interest to you, Gentle Reader; for the problem of the Twentieth Century is the problem of the color line.[49]

What does Du Bois mean by "the color line"? What forms and formulations are necessary to, and implied in, that phrase? It seems to me that there are two intellectual modes that emerge from Du Bois's thought, the body of which, in the richness of what Spillers might call its enfleshment, is endlessly troubled and irreducibly troubling: (1) a mode that takes the problem of the color line as its starting point without ever offering anything more than a cursory foray back into the ground of that formulation, "the meaning of being black," as it digs and veers into the underground of black being, which we'll come back around to under the rubric of the paraontological totality; (2) a mode that carefully and painstakingly prepares to work that ground and inhabit that underground in spite of whatever problematic determinations and rejections of (stain and) soil (and blood), where uncut vision doubles itself and is, therefore, undone.

This is all to say that while *The Souls of Black Folk* emphatically announces the thought of the color line, that thought is only insofar as it is interinanimate with the thinking of blackness, which lies anoriginally *before*, and is therefore irreducible to, the color line. Much of the most advanced work in contemporary black studies understands blackness as an effect of the color line, which is to say the white/nonwhite binary which orients it and by way of which it is plotted. That work often moves by way of a specific and, again, self-contained Fanonian elaboration of this racial geometry. That thesis, in its most extreme development, understands blackness not only as effect but, more decisively, as death-driven epiphenomenon, something on the order of an always already imposed and interdicted "right to death" that is, at the same time, uninflected by that salvific force that Hegel understands as a link between sovereignty and self-negating decision. This elaboration of blackness as death-bound emanation is also determined by incapacity or refusal to think blackness as if it were neither bound by nor originated in the white/nonwhite binary. Such thinking would require something on the order of an ontological distinction between blackness and blacks insofar as the color line is a dubious operation and delimitation of the ontic. Here, I am considering as ontic the field of racialized existence in which blacks, within a general structure of difference, have been made, against the grain of their own anoriginal, collectively unselfconscious self-making, to signify a certain deanimated otherness-in/as-blackness while having been devoided, in the same horrific and impossible figuration, of the idea of blackness as a form of life. The field I am characterizing as ontic or, more precisely, as a sclerotic and isolated substitute for the ontic, is, in short, the realm where blacks will have been reduced to an already reduced, already etiolated, notion of the thing. Critical and creative inhabitation of that field, which is to say that border, when it is figured or understood as genesis, could more properly be understood as a kind of forgetting (of the meaning, which is to say the question) of black being; on the other hand, precision demands—ante-genetically and, therefore, against the understanding's grain—that blackness practice a fundamental in/determination of being in nothingness. In establishing a protocol for remembering the essence of our existence, Du Bois's early work is driven by the distinction between blackness and blacks in ways to which we remain insufficiently attuned; in ways, this is to say, that are not simply in passing but which would constitute the axiomatic foundation of our work. Chandler's ongoing, careful, monumental elaboration of that distinction shows that it would, finally, be more proper to consider Du Bois's distinction as a paraontological one that moves in a kind of critical anticipation, finally, not only of the ontological distinction between being and beings that Martin Heidegger recovers but also of the critique of Heidegger's desire for a unique word for being, a critique that is at the heart of Jacques Derrida's intervention.

In particular, Chandler shows that *The Souls of Black Folk* is a cross-sectional assemblage of a decade-long elaboration of the question of blackness in which Du Bois was engaged at the turn of the last century.[50] As such *Souls* is indispensable but also incomplete, and indispensable because of its incompleteness, which has had a palpable effect on the development of black studies and postcolonial studies, both of which can be said to emerge, at least in part, from Du Boisian protocols. In its general disavowal of incompleteness, philosophy will have sought to secure itself from the disruptive force of Du Bois's thinking and, deeper still, from the troubling force of blackness in philosophy that Du Bois's work will have begun to illuminate. At stake, here, is the notion that blackness is a general force of fugitivity that racialization in general, and the more specific instantiation of the color line, exacerbate and focus without originating. Such focus could be said to create the condition wherein blacks are privileged insofar as they are given (to) an understand ing of blackness. Du Bois's historical philosophy—his constant attention to black social life, to its constant escape both from and within the anti-ontic state of racialization, to the irreducible constraint such constancy of escape implies, and to its continuing ante-ontic disruption of the very ontological foundation upon which the ontic is anarchically, disruptively grounded— causes us to recognize the paraontological as the ontological's (im)proper name. It does so by way of the rigorous elaboration of the strange, brutal career of that privilege as (emerging from and as) underprivilege—as the underground works and workings of a social energy worthy of the conserva- tion that in any case it performs as self-transformation. What critics who operate within a general movement that is characterized as against race fail to understand, say, in Du Bois's "The Conservation of Races," is that rather than a bridge between the most excessive articulations of German Romantic racialism and their vulgar and violent elaboration in the twentieth century, Du Bois's work attempts to constitute a thinking of blackness as a dehiscence both anticipatory of and internal to the normative discourses of race. This requires understanding blackness, in Robinson's terms, as that which can- not be understood within the context of its genesis, particularly when that genesis is (mis)understood to be the color line, the violent instantiation of the white/nonwhite binary.

Put simply, Du Bois's early work understands blackness as that which is before the binary that has been said to define our existence. His understand- ing of this "insistent previousness evading each and every natal occasion" (in Mackey's words) thinks blackness, in its essential fugitivity, in ways that anticipate Jacques Derrida's elaboration of *différance* as that "non-full, non- simple, structured and differentiating origin of differences" which, in its very structure, undermines the very idea of origin.[51] This is to say that in his early essays, Du Bois offers us the reinitialization of a thinking of blackness that is absolutely necessary to any understanding of black people even as they move us toward some sense of the irreducible importance of blackness (as fugitiv- ity in being, as *différance*) in the history of philosophy. Du Bois advances the black reconstruction of the previous by way of the black deconstruction of the natal. His public intellectual life is an extension of the subterranean tradition where the social life of the taken that has been taken for things has always taken form.

At the same time, Chandler's renewal of a general invitation to think "the problem of the negro as a problem for thought" moves through an examination of the exemplary figure of Du Bois that not only solicits the very logic of exemplarity but also shows that no thought, including that of Du Bois, is commensurate with the problematic we inhabit. In the wake of Du Bois's own knowledge of this interplay of limit and the illimitable, Chandler refreshes the question of how to proceed in the absence of a solution, an adequate theoretical orientation, a satisfactory standpoint, arguing that, "We must desediment the dissimulation of a war."[52] That we are at war, and have been, and that the denial of that war is the primary modality of its prosecution, is a crucial and inescapable truth from which, nevertheless, the world we inhabit remains in flight. Flight, in this instance, takes the form of fight and perhaps it is the very idea of world itself that requires such brutal dis/engagement, that constant interplay of proximity and distance that structures the settler's regime as scandalous romance with marronage. What if Kingston, or Jamestown, or Jonestown are maroon communities? Then the marooned's rigorous exposure of the pretense of disowning the maroon's strict commitment to ownership, *which he lives as settler and which the settler lives as war*, is fundamental to the black radical tradition. It instantiates critique as alternative, insovereign, anti-subjective earthly life and those of us who attempt to follow and extend that line must be thankful for its gifts and mindful of its costs. The toll of war is deathly, particularly when its limits, when the materiality of passage not only within but also from it, are placed in the erasure that ensues when the ongoing is taken for the endless; and when and where a certain anticipatorily (counter)violent commitment to the murderous, given in the militant recognition of its constantly denied hostility, is recognized by terrorists as the terror which they insist they have a right to suppress. How do we think and live this problematic, which is one of rhythm, and of historicity, if not musically, if not poetically, if not as a problem, precisely, of poetry and music, of improvisational, anarchically principled (dis)organization? Chandler's Du Boisian reiteration proclaims not only the fearsome drone of our violent regulation but also the fantastic abandon that we are. We are passage, limit, and their asymmetry. Our history—no, our historicity—is this: that our passage, in limit, is illimitable. For Chandler, this is not only Du Bois's lesson but also his practice, which remains the most complex of gifts: the gift of thoughtful contracceptance of our gift, and the terror that bore it, and that it bears.

Chandler shows that the justness of Foucault's claim that war is politics by other means, which reverses Carl von Clausewitz's famous dictum, is anticipated in Du Bois's discovery of the generative and ordinary anarrhythmia of black social life, in which war, ownership and politics are a/voided beneath the surface of their exclusionary constitution and their delusional constitutive force. He also shows that the irreducibly social, emphatically underpolitical opening Du Bois marks and helps to conjure is an address, an entrance, a studiously reinitializing activity of planning that can't be plotted. Here, two of Chandler's signature critical figures—originary displacement and paraontology—are of great help and importance because they serve to reveal the problematic facticity of blackness, in and against the grain of its disavowal *by* subjective authority, as the mystical foundation *of* subjective authority. When thought takes up the figuration—the necessarily failed embodiment—of blackness in and as the Negro, its own constitution (in purportedly successful embodiment), as well as its agential subject, is put in question. The very ground and moment of contemporary critical thought is disturbed by the irruptive movement of what is buried there. The anoriginal displacement of philosophical foundations carried out in the social life and thought of the more + less than ones whose exteriority helps to constitute philosophy's limits, and the paraontological disturbance that emerges from what is simultaneously accurately and imprecisely called non-being, require constant critical recursion, as in this this footnote, which takes up Derrida's "Introduction" to Edmund Husserl's *The Origin of Geometry*:

> "Thus, undecidability has a revolutionary and disconcerting sense, it is *itself* only if it remains essentially and intrinsically haunted in its sense of origin by the telos of undecidability—whose disruption it marks." Might this not help to outline in some philosophical form, for another history of science if you will, that which would recognize the irruptive generality of that anonymous practice of generations, of the regeneration of the generations, announced in the historial passage that has gone under the heading of African American since, perhaps, 1619, and which acquired a nodal rearticulation across the opening decades of the twentieth century in the movement of sound as something once called, respectively, the spirituals or the blues? I prefer to note such historial movement as general, not restricted to art in any simple sense, where living and what has been called death is, too, "making a way out of now way," to turn an old and idiomatic phrase.[53]

What follows from this meditative (re)turn of phrase, this lyrical challenge to philosophy's normative phase, is a project of reading that takes up the matter of a certain "reciprocity," in Chandler's words, between origin and end animating and intimating a radical untimeliness, a second timeliness common, in the unlikeliest sense, to the historiality of philosophy and the art(s) of black life. Why should what remains almost entirely unthought in philosophy turn out to be its impetus? And why should that impetus be understood, when it is thought, though such "thinking" seldom deserves the name, to have taken the form of what is figured as the unthinking thing? The second time around, like the incommensurate and almost impossible to imagine double session of the electron's return to origin, intimates that field of variance, that impossible waywardness, in and through which eccentricity preserves and is preserved in a radical dislocation where undecidability and uncertainty simultaneously trouble and instantiate the very idea of duality. In short, the trajectory Chandler establishes proposes to show that desedimentation is given in the arts of black life *as* thinking. The social, aesthetic, and intellectual implications of this showing are massive, not only for life in and as black study but also for black studies and for the study of philosophy, to the extent that anyone remains engaged in these thwarted, yet essential, yet neglected, fields. What is it to operate on the border of those fields whose anafoundational distillate, "[Du Bois's] persisting and ex-foliating formulation of the 'problem of the color-line,'" remains unread?[54] If, in beginning to read Du Bois, we begin also to sense the depth of a problematic that his contribution elaborates in and with a disruptive and disrupted fullness, which is given in and as authentic sociological methodology, that ought not be mistaken for representing an academic discipline but, rather, stands alongside psycho-analysis, the critique of political economy, genealogy (in the Nietzchean instantiation and Foucauldian elaboration), phenomenology (in its Husserlian/transcendental instantiation and its various heretical elaborations from Heidegger to Fanon), and grammatology as essential to modern thought's capacity to think itself in the most profound and rigorous, but decidedly anadisciplinary ways. But one says "alongside" only in order to establish a deeper and more disruptive understanding of Du Bois's radical displacement. He is neither exalted in his apposition to this line nor would he seek such exaltation. He aerates the very ground modern thought occupies and upon which it's subject claims standing. It is this aeration, this constant digging and tilling, that Chandler reads and extends. At stake is the force of blackness in the establishment of a sociological aesthetics and an aesthetic sociology whose mobile fundament is the problem of the *genus*, of the general, of generation's ongoing ungendering.

Therefore, fecund enjoyment of the beautiful sociality of Du Bois's text is not optional. The militant care of its warlike force—which is given not only in its arrangement but also in its unique capacity to rearrange, and be rearranged in, *our* reading—bears the loving care of thoughtful, abrasive caress. Ex-foliation is what Chandler calls that caress when he feels and studies it in Du Bois. For Chandler, removal of the skin's outermost layer, the dead cells, so that what survives can also thrive, comes closest to providing an image of that dislocative, unlocatable, extrametrical, anamatrical (e)motion wherein it is the same thing (which da Silva teaches us to understand as no-thing) to think and to live, to think and to love. Ex-foliation anticipates epidermalization, whose critical examination by Fanon can be seen, now, to have been anticipated in Du Bois, in an x-chromosomal anticipation of Du Bois that Du Bois always echoes and sometimes approaches as Chandler shows us by way of protocols Spillers establishes. This is an underchromosomal, anarrational, extrachronosocial field of feel at which we never quite arrive and from which we never really depart. Ex-foliation renews without disavowing. Quickeningly, affectionately ex-foliation is reading in the flesh. It bears an attunement—as anageneric index of and impure passage to whatever comes beyond the limit of every im/possibility of and in (the) world—to the diurnal irregularity of every interruption of the story of life and death. *That* caesura, *that* jam, *that* break, *that* social hesitation. We run to it because we're still in it.

With this in mind, Chandler's elaboration of Du Bois's elaboration of blackness as what Andrew Benjamin has called "anoriginal difference" ought not be mistaken for the erasure of a set of seemingly intractable differences.[55] Insofar as underprivilege is the gift of having to discover and claim some understand as an effect of imposition to be disavowed, regulated, or negated in the interest of an absolute negation, it is necessary to recognize the force of a certain privilege in Kant, one that makes it altogether likely that today he would have chosen to sound a bit more conventionally self-regulated than Roberson, a bit more normatively expository than Du Bois, a bit more philosophically controlled than Fanon—eschewing the way they've all been touched and handed, an underprivilege that guarantees access to a couple of realizations that are impossible for Kant: (1) that black is a gathering of chance in the submerged city, ready to erupt, at the city's unruly, disagreeably ornamental outskirts, where the *metoikos* is homelessly at home; and (2) that in this city there are no men, there is no Man. To inhabit this marginal, underground city, where the informal is the condition of possibility of form, has required a shift of emphasis—from the resistance of the object to the insistence of things; from the existence of the freedom drive to the persistence of escape—in the interest of voiding state-sponsored normativities and the statist antistate shade they project. Upon what is the resistance of the object grounded? Can that ground be said both to prepare and disqualify that object, displacing its resistance? These questions animate the unraveling black study that is gathered before you, in need of your remixing, though hopefully it's already starting to resound an annular, anoriginal distortion, between belated inauguration and its distended mirror image, illuminating and enacting the transition from the one to the other as stolen life.

II

In 1989, in the tradition of answering the question concerning Enlightenment, Derrida declared:

> Of course I am 'in favour' of the Enlightenment; I think we shouldn't simply leave it behind us, so I want to keep this tradition alive. But at the same time I know that there are certain historical forms of Enlightenment, certain things in this tradition that we need to criticize or deconstruct. So it is sometimes in the name of, let us say, a new Enlightenment that I deconstruct a given Enlightenment. And this requires some very complex strategies; requires that we should let many voices speak. . . . There is nothing monological, no monologue— that's why the responsibility for deconstruction is never individual or a matter of the single, self-privileged authorial voice. It is always a multiplicity of voices, of gestures. . . . And you can take this as a rule: that each time Deconstruction speaks through a single voice, it's wrong, it is not 'Deconstruction' anymore. So in ['Of an Apocalyptic Tone Recently Adopted in Philosophy'] . . . not only do I let many voices speak at the same time, but the problem is precisely that multiplicity of voices, that variety of tones, within the same utterance or indeed the same word or syllable, and so on. So that's the question. That's one of the questions.
>
> But of course today the political, ideological consequences of the Enlightenment are still very much with us—and very much in need of questioning. So a new Enlightenment, to be sure, which may mean

deconstruction in its most active or intensive form, and not what we inherited in the name of *Aufklärung*.[56]

The black radical tradition is in apposition to enlightenment. Thrown shade, off to the side of its derivative, apposition remixes, expands, distills, and keeps radically faith with the forces its encounters carry, break, and constitute. Stolen by it, it steals from it, steeling itself to it in preservative, self-defensive, disjunctively anachoreographic permeance. It's (the effect of) critique or rationalization unopposed to the deep revelation instantiated by a rupturing event of dis/appropriation or the rapturous advent of an implicit but unprecedented freedom. It's the performance of something not quite like a detour of Kant onto an Heideggerian path, a push toward a critical rhythm in which *Aufklärung* and *Lichtung* animate one another in the dark, as in a clearing always already after hours underneath what Fillmore had already lost to the west, warmed by arethic rays in a public their privation made. The improvisation through their opposition is enacted in (interruptions of) passage, tone, pulse, phrase, silence. No one cares if the history of philosophy's fatal attraction to the sun is borne or encompassed in this or that nocturnal gathering. What's at stake is (the) ensemble's open gift of its own obscure radiance, marked by the market insofar as it is touched by the mother. The dark *mater* that is and animates this tradition sounds black light beneath lit(erature), remaining unfelt and unsavored in philosophy's consumptive grasp.

Another way to put it would be this: there is an enduring politicoeconomic and philosophical moment with which the black radical tradition is engaged. That moment is called the Enlightenment. This tradition has been concerned with the opening of a new Enlightenment, one made possible by the ongoing improvisation of a given Enlightenment, improvisation being nothing other than the emergence of "deconstruction in its most active or intensive form." That emergence bears a generativity that shines and sounds through even that purely negational discourse which is prompted by the assumption that nothing good—experientially, culturally, aesthetically—can come through terror. The black radical tradition improvises terror, through the philosophy of terror, in ways that don't limit terror's discursive or cultural trace to an exclusively descriptive approach toward some either immediately present or heretofore concealed truth. There is also a prescriptive component in this tradition, which is to say in its narrative and in its narratives, that cuts the mythic and/or objectifying structures and effects of narrative while at the same time always holding on to the resources that flow from narration's partnership with description. Social presence is given there so powerfully that it inheres even in certain reactions that, in the very force and determination of reaction, replicate terror's preconditions. Such replication is done, for instance, in the vexed ethics of encounter of which Olaudah Equiano tells and which Fanon cites and theorizes. I'm after another recitation of that fugitive, improvisatory trace.

So this is on the way through some narratives or, more precisely, to some passages that might provide a passage through narrative. This is an essay for a kind of narrative and its recitation, the kind that would be adequate to slavery. The narrative that must be recited is of, among other things, deprivation; deprivation of, among other things, the apparatuses of narrative construction such that such recitation will seem only to have taken place by way of other apparatuses benevolently given—which is to say violently imposed—by the one who took you and your ability to tell, your ability to tell and your ability to know, your ability to tell and to know in the interest of that which you would know or would have known—namely, freedom—in a way that is other than simply negative. How to tell the story of a rupture that has broken the ability to tell and how to have that telling be free and be in the interest of freedom? As William Andrews might put it, this essay is for the telling of a free story.

What I want to get at is that that telling must be situated at a frontier, on the border that is the condition of possibility of "the law of genre."[57] Such a telling must simultaneously fulfill and exceed the generic responsibilities of narrative, must be both *récit* and recitation. It must move through and reorient the paradoxical space-time of "foreshadowing description," thereby exhibiting that which, because of its material access to presents that are no longer or that have not yet been, might have been called ecstatic temporality.[58] This telling must also occupy the space of a frontier between narrative and rationalization, between narrative and the theory of narrative, between narrative and the improvisation of its discourse and of its story and, above all, of its subjectivity and of what that subjectivity knows and of what that subjectivity is both constituted and capable. This telling must also be situated on the frontier at which "Man" is improvised. I'm interested in how the free story that forms the paradoxically anarchic ground of the black radical tradition will have rationalized that conception of "Man," improvising through its exclusionary force and toward theory and practice that reconstitutes both the methods and the objects of ethics, epistemology, and ontology. With regard to this last formulation one must see how this telling lies in the break between singularity and totality, between the unlocatable origin and as-yet unlocalized end of their mutual philosophical and politicoeconomic systematization.

If I suggest that we improvise notions of genre and of narrative; and that we descend into the rhythmic break between "foreshadowing" and "description" rather than treat their oxymoronic linkage as a fateful and convenient bridge that erases itself in its presencing of origination and destination; and that we honor and extend—by way of improvisation—the black radical tradition's ongoing improvisational abolition of "Man," knowing full well the danger of a kind of negative reification such a distancing romance holds; and that we venture a continued movement out-from-outside of a range of conventional philosophical and historical understandings embedded in the oppositional relation of singularity and totality; I'm thinking of, and hopefully through, a pivotal—but certainly not exclusive—moment in the tradition that marks the intersection of these tasks and their unfulfillment, the event of their dis/appropriation. In the epilogue to *Invisible Man*, Ralph Ellison writes: "Our fate is to become one and yet many—This is not prophecy, but description."[59] The impasse this impossible fate represents and the unresolvable caesura this passage is and contains (and implicit here is an argument for the profoundly generative and regenerative force of this phrasing—which is less and more than a sentence, less and more than a proposition—its ability to spawn negations and affirmations of itself that hold prominence in the contemporary extension of that strain of the tradition in which social development is foregrounded), marks a need to know some things again, as if for the first time, about knowledge and (language and their relation to) freedom. So what I'm interested in, here, is freedom and the relationship of certain narratives of slavery to the question of freedom not only in the historical context in which they were written but in the no-less-desperate context of our fiercely urgent now. We know something—narratives and understandings of narrative and understandings of the relation between narrative and freedom—that we need to know we know. Where does that knowledge comes from and what are the im/possibilities and theoretical and political problems regarding our access to its source?

Ellison's meditation on the one and the many is one of a seemingly infinite set of such formulations within and across a great range of traditions, all of which, as members of that set (and as participants in the logic of Set), operate in or take the form of a mis/chance or im/possibility. That set, and the very idea of Set, "exists"—if we are allowed to speak of the existence of mathematico-metaphysical objects—at a threshold where it is necessary, yet seems unfathomable, to imagine a phenomenology of totality and singularity that would reveal some opening of the possibility of political agency, of another mode of organization unopposed to freedom. That phenomenology would have to provide a sense—neither sensible nor intelligible, more than sensible, more than intelligible—of a whole not bound by the interminable oscillation of systemic relation and nonrelation. Such a phenomenology would move beyond the endless and always asymmetrical tension between individual and society or self and Other or subject and object; finally, it would move beyond any ontological formulation of and in difference that displaces the whole and leaves us at the site of a discursive contest of infinite curvature where our reality never escapes the forces power exerts over responsibility and determination exerts over improvisation.

That phenomenology and its object, whose interinanimation I call *ensemble*—the improvisation of and through the opposition of totality and singularity in and as a descent into the generative cut between description and prescription—must, therefore, faithfully reclaim the honor of the whole, an honor which is real only within the complex, radical, and realist attention and devotion we pay to the earth. It is, to sample a phrase often repeated by Derrida, both a scandal and a chance—a peculiarly vexed burden and responsibility, an enabling disability—that the performance of that devotion in the black radical tradition must slash through the Enlightenment tradition and, importantly, through that tradition's allegiance to the active misprision of singularity and totality—phenomena certain tendencies within poststructuralism both critique and extend in the analysis and affirmation of the always already multiple essence of singularity that is embedded in the ontological and epistemological questioning of totality. Indeed, the theory of ensemble is enabled by the tradition of singularist and differentiated thinking of the whole it extends and improvises, most particularly as that tradition—at its heretofore highest level of intensity and internal tension— begins to be articulated through calls either for its dissolution or continuance in the impossible language prompted by the incommensurable conjunction of community and difference. In short, the possibility of a nonexclusionary whole is opened by the most radical critiques—those of identitarian politicoaesthetic thought in addition to those of poststructuralism—of any prior holism.

The point, here, is that those critiques which pay descriptive and prescriptive attention to singularity and totality while responsibly confronting the horrific effects of singularist totalization must be acknowledged and as-similated. But the fact that they offer only choked and strained and silenced articulations of the whole—that which allows our aspirations for equality, justice, freedom—means they must be improvised. The various discourses that are informed by identity theories open the possibility for such impro-visation in their directions toward other philosophical or antiphilosophical or antephilosophical modes of thought and representation. But it is pre-cisely in the thought of the Other, the hope for another subjectivity and an other ontology, that the metaphysical foundations and antilibertarian im-plications of the politico-philosophical tradition to which identity theories attempt to respond are replicated and deepened. Improvisation—and thus the possibility of describing and activating an improvisational whole—is thereby foreclosed. I want to offer here another chorus of ensemble—by way of what/whom you'll come to know as *Uncle Toliver*—as something out-from-outside, other than the Other or the same, something unbound by their relation or nonrelation and situated at an opening onto the site of the intersection of the knowledge of language (as prayer, curse, narrative [*récit* or recitation]) and the knowledge of freedom (as both a negative function of the experience of oppression and the trace of what Noam Chomsky calls an "innate endowment that serves to bridge the gap between experience and knowledge").[60]

This is a passage from Leon Litwack's *Been in the Storm So Long*: "In Nansemond County, Virginia, a slave known as Uncle Toliver had been in-discreet enough to pray aloud for the Yankees. The master's two sons ordered him to kneel in the barnyard and pray for the Confederacy. But this stub-born old man prayed even louder for a Yankee triumph. With growing exas-peration, perhaps even bewilderment, the two sons took turns in whipping him until finally the slave, still murmuring something about the Yankees, collapsed and died."[61] This passage improvises tradition/s. In *Been in the Storm So Long*—which is at once more than text, more than literary and/or historical—and in the singular icon of that work I'll continue to offer to you, an icon that inhabits and exhibits all the senses of the word *passage* and whose content is precisely that of an improvisatory whole, there is that which the Enlightenment's differentiated, Euro-phallo-centric, ontologically determined and necessarily and narrowly literate rational subject and the critiques of that subject which work in the name of an other differentiation preface but never approach: the voicing and revoicing of ensemble. This text/passage/voicing is, if you will, an autobiography of ensemble,[62] one that moves from thought through what Levinas calls an "ethical saying" to the possibility of ethical action that *we* must activate. The essence of that ethics is mediation, the *ensemblic* mediation of improvisation which is not arrested in or by the passage, (dis)appropriative event or death of the individual body and which, as such, is not held within the determination of any (impossible) exclusively singularized agency.

Mediation is material to this passage and opens a number of possibilities. There is a reading that would argue that the passage is dependent upon a name whose honor oscillates between decidability and undecidability, whose referent is lost to us, a voice given but dangerously supplemented by voicings and revoicings. There is another reading that would see Litwack's mediational stance as an extension of the material oppression and suppression of Uncle Toliver's originarily oppositional voicing, one that can only hope to reintegrate it with a tradition which is the locus and effect of a historical decision *not* to hear Uncle Toliver's other subjectivity, to distort that subjectivity's self-expression and self-reflection. What I'd like to argue, however, is that one might also think of the problematic of our necessarily mediated access to the discourse of Uncle Toliver and begin to imagine the immense ethics of mediation and the move away from the illusory ideal of an immediate presentation of our history that that history demands. For it is within this ethics—which is, ultimately, the ethics of ensemble—that mediation is neither the silence of Uncle Toliver (the absence or differentiated iteration of a simple and originary singularist subjectivity or an iconically presented collective one) nor Uncle Toliver's silencing (the suppression of an other subjectivity, whether singular or collective): it is, rather, the improvisational voice of the ensemble that is *Uncle Toliver*.

Here we have a narrative that could be simply placed within a differentiated Afro-diasporic expressive cultural tradition that will have been predominantly marked as a tradition of the end, a "vicious modernism" always already at the limit, of the disaster, a remarking of the worst as a repetitive suspension or long continuance, the interminable discourse of the slave, the paradoxically open vernacular. It is a *literary* tradition in all the in/determinate sense of Derrida's sense of the word. That is to say it is, finally, something more than literary, more than philosophical, more even than its "least inadequate name"[63]—autobiographical. Most importantly it is a tradition of the something more that holds all the material force of Uncle Toliver's thinking. Hear where Derrida speaks and *Uncle Toliver* is written:

So there was a movement of nostalgic, mournful lyricism to reserve, perhaps encode, in short to render both accessible and inaccessible. And deep down this is still my most naïve desire. I don't dream of either a literary work or a philosophical work, but that everything that occurs, happens to me or fails to, should be as it were sealed (placed in reserve, hidden so as to be kept, and this in its very signature, really like a signature, in the very form of the seal, with all the paradoxes that traverse the structure of a seal). The discursive forms we have available to us, the resources in terms of objectivizing archivation, are so much poorer than what happens (or what fails to happen, whence the excesses of hypertotalization). This desire for everything + n—naturally I can analyze it, "deconstruct" it, criticize it, but it is an experience that I love, that I know and recognize.[64]

Literature seemed to me, in a confused way, to be the institution which allows one to say everything, in every way . . . . To say everything is no doubt to gather, by translating, all figures into one another, to totalize by formalizing, but to say everything is also to break out of [franchir] prohibitions. To affranchise oneself [s'affranchir]—in every field where law can lay down the law. The law of literature tends to deny or lift the law. It therefore allows one to think the essence of the law in the experience of this "everything to say." It is an institution which tends to overflow the institution.[65]

Everything can be said, though said otherwise, with a difference, and therefore nothing can be said, for everything must be said otherwise, with a difference: the vernacular, where literature and slavery—those institutions strange and peculiar—converge, is where everything and nothing can be said; the vernacular, where name is given to the worst and to the other and what is given is renounced; the vernacular, where everything + n(othing) is named, where everything + n(othing) is said. The tradition of Uncle Tolliver, the tradition of what is thought to be the most intense critical naïveté, is what Derrida desires. It is not the tradition of the vernacular, of an other name, an other subjectivity, a hypertotalization, nor is it to be figured in the convergence of singularities, the iterative set (though it's closer to what is instantiated by the law of genre, an invagination, the formation of what is larger than the whole[66]). Uncle Toliver's tradition, the black radical tradition, our tradition, is the tradition of ensemble, of black light, where everything + n(othing) is unconcealed in murmur, in mo'nin', in lyricism's recessive self-destruction. If one reads within a thinking that keeps faith with the whole one notes the rhythms of improvisation and the sound of ensemble—their revelation of the inadequacy of the in/determinate, the same, the Other. This is the attention *Uncle Toliver* demands.

Such attention is required in part because of the place of Litwack in *Uncle Toliver*. Litwack's decision to enter the discourse that is of and that transcends the vernacular expresses a commitment to nonexclusionary universality that is tantamount to a formulation of identity. That identity is given in its improvisational materiality by a more than deconstructive expansion of the understanding of universal humanity such that those who, like Uncle Toliver, have been excluded from prior understandings of humanity because of ontological and/or cultural and/or biological determinations that are also a part of the Enlightenment's legacy—and whose exclusions have been the iterative irruption of those determinations—participate in the formation of that understanding. Litwack's identity becomes—in the dissemination of *Uncle Toliver*—the identity of Uncle Toliver. That identity requires that thought of the whole that moves through differentiating notions of identity.

But this is a simple passage, one designed to provide some sense of the violent imposition of silence that marks slavery and will have marked every disaster, every violent assault on or ritual destruction of the whole. We might gather from this simple recounting, this simple "objectivizing archivation," that slavery is that institution—violent and ritual dehumanization is that event—wherein nothing can be said, whereof nothing can be said, which arrives for us, even now, enveloped in the silence that accompanies the absence of specificity, the lack of an immediate resonance. But to speak here of simplicity—of a text, a passage, that tells, simply, the barest story and unearths, simply, the smallest remnant of a life that gives us, simply, an indication of the nature of a mode of being—is a matter that is, of course, not so simple. The passage, which can only be called *Uncle Toliver*, is more than a subject and more than a text; and its transmission of the whole of *Uncle Toliver* to us is far from simple. It arrives through various arrangements of the story of Uncle Toliver, the story of a man who could not tell his story as a matter of law and as a matter of the materiality of his life and death. But the mediation that gives us that story does not obscure the position and situation spoken through his silence. It is spoken so profoundly that the entirety of the Enlightenment tradition and its critical other is invoked, reopened, revised, improvised. The mediated and reconstructed voicing of the slave speaks through the vernacular and for freedom. The mediated and reconstructed voice of a man held as property arrives to us as a critique of Property. As the passage arrives once more, hear again its simplicity in a repetition that serves to further obl/iterate (ob/literate) that simplicity: the subject, the text—that which is more than the person and more than the text—of *Uncle Toliver* haunts and infuses us: "In Nansemond County, Virginia, a slave known as Uncle Toliver had been indiscreet enough to pray aloud for the Yankees. The master's two sons ordered him to kneel in the barnyard and pray for the Confederacy. But this stubborn old man prayed even louder for a Yankee triumph. With growing exasperation, perhaps even bewilderment, the two sons took turns in whipping him until finally the slave, still murmuring something about the Yankees, collapsed and died."

How is this strange arrival possible? What is its significance for us today amid an attempt to provide a desperately needed critique of liberation within an argument for the necessity of something other than either a rejection of or an indifference to or a convergence with the (old or given) Enlightenment? Ensemble, figured in and improvised through the ethical mediation of another light's anacritical opening of the whole, is the improvisation of the singular identities of Litwack and Uncle Toliver and the totality generated by lingering in the music that airily fills the space between them. They speak in ensemble and are written there in a moment at which we are given, through the mediation of improvisation, the whole of the history of the whole and the whole of the history of singularist (and differentiated) totalizations of the whole. *Uncle Toliver* is, once more, the autobiography of ensemble and the history of an ensemble voicing and agency; it is not the recording of a differentiated, repressed, and oppressed ego by another ego in search of affirmation. *Uncle Toliver* is the reality which invocations of naive and idiomatic writing or calls for a voicing-toward-agency or overlordly assertions of the whole only imagine within the inevitable return to the best and worst of the Enlightenment that poststructuralism and identity politics must make. *Uncle Toliver* prepares the ground for the real formulation of a more than discursive ethics; we are propelled toward that view of the world that allows our knowledge of the passage, a view that demands a particular way of being in the world. In other words, our attention to ensemble, as it exists in and as *Uncle Toliver*, activates and improvises—keeps faith with— ensemble. It is an attention that will have always *moved through* the interminable attention to differentiating singularity or homogenizing totality that has always foreclosed the possibility of a general agency. Agency's dispersive disbursal is in the tradition of *Uncle Toliver*.

Uncle Toliver's narrative is part of a chain of recitation that moves from a never fully unveiled originary encounter to the specter of an impossible encounter to come, the encounter in the future that would mark the impossible justice of a strange, oppositional resolution. But the oppositional resolution that the bridge or passage would mark falls before its own form. Descent, not oscillation; descent, not the asymmetrical tensions and reemergent subjectivities of a gaze; descent, as in the future resonances of variations of an unknown tongue. We'll get to that, come back to that, recite that, by way of Olaudah Equiano, the one whose ambiguous relationship or durative encounter with European Man is embedded in the more refined naïveté of a narrative whose intensity must survive the transgressions of predatory mediation. In that ambiguity lies the shadow of the master that produces and obscures a certain paradox concerning the knowledge of freedom, knowledge that seems to be embedded in the interrelation of certain determinations of literacy and subjectivity that stem from—and are thus never fully to be activated against—the master. Equiano's literacy, and the subjectivity to which it is tied, is causally linked both to his freedom and his enslavement, connected as it is both to his resistance toward and the "benevolence" of some of those who owned him. How are these paradoxes or ambiguities to be written? Indeed, is the text not the manifestation and, as R. A. Judy argues, the captive of these ambiguities which are the function of a too-uncritical adherence to Enlightenment? To enter into this language is precisely to transgress a boundary that the language marks, on the border and at sea, where the ethics of mediation is played out at a different locus and in a different register. Every word, every sentence, every anecdote, the narrative itself, constitute a representation of the durative encounter that prompts, enforces, and allows that representation in the first place.

I don't mean, then, here to deny Judy's well-formed, form-breaking assertion of the existence of other than Western literacies, especially because it takes so brilliantly into account the intensity with which the production of literacies weighs against any notion of literate authenticity, containing possibilities that an oppositional or other literacy (or its subject) could never open, possibilities that far exceed some simple entry into already fully composed notions of literacy and its subject, possibilities that solicit Enlightenment, its subject and its oppressive psychic and politicoeconomic manifestations, by way and in the interest of a valorized unreadability, an errant and essentially unapproachable textuality that carries the trace of another being, another subjectivity, another literacy, another politics: the Afro-Arabic. Judy's analysis troubles the temporal and ontological constitution—namely the systemic relation and opposition of totality and singularity—which grounds the "old" Enlightenment and its phantomic subject by his projection of an other, pre-oppositional anoriginality.

Judy inhabits an improvisational tradition, one weighted toward the impossible generativity of an apocalyptic event/institution, and finds within it a certain self-deconstructive germ in the form of a fragmentary eighteenth century Afro-Arabic slave narrative called *Ben Ali's Diary*. Wary of the replication of certain deeply problematic metaphysical structures that can't help but animate canonical slave narrative, the most important being a unitary formulation of the subject which has its origins in an intensely racialized—as well as an intensely and gendered, sexed and sexualized—understanding of "Man," Judy discovers in *Ben Ali's Diary* a *récit* and recitation (which is to say rationalizations or theorizations) of an improvisatory suspension of subjectivity and of a certain desire for subjectivity and of any prior understanding of subjectivity's differentiated ground.

The Diary is, as Judy shows, improvisational and generative in the deepest ways; it is, and it instantiates, a poetics of recombination marked precisely by an ongoing anarchic seizure, excess and intensification of what it might be said to carry with it as deconstruction. The tradition does so precisely by its active embrace of improvisation in its relation to a material dissatisfaction with the opposition between singularity and totality and its political effects. That improvisation is present in European traditions as well but with this difference: their general repression of improvisation, an embarrassed refusal enacted by precisely that irrationalism against which it would guard. One could more judiciously call this irrationalism a wariness that manifests itself as a certain disabling decision neither to improvise nor to rationally encounter the revelatory *and* critical dis/appropriation that must ensue when one is confronted with the structures and effects of "other" traditions that generate and are generated by improvisatory practices. Not even Derrida is immune to this wariness (which, finally, we could call Eurocentrism), though what's cool in his work is the trace of improvisation (of which he is wary but to which, more often than not, he is attuned, especially in his writing, more complexly in his mediated and recorded speech) that emerges as if a certain elaborative moment in the generative history of philosophy-as-deconstruction always and all throughout the ensemble of tradition(s) carries along with it another level of intensity. What I'm after, after Judy, is a critique of the absence of that intensity in the heretofore almost always correspondent historico-philosophical phenomena of Enlightenment and Eurocentrism and in certain critiques of that absence and that correspondence which lose that intensity themselves. Judy seeks that intensity, that laughter out-from-outside of the house of being, by way of crucial questions regarding the development of that intensity in knowledge production and academic labor, allowing us to linger, for instance, at the intersection of the university and the plantation as places of work. What I'll do here is focus on some other important questions he raises and prompts. Is writing (a more or less conventional and complete autobiographical narrative) always writing-into-being as it is manifest in the totalizing virtuality of the racialized, gendered, nationalized, "universal" Kantian Subject? This question is a central one for it implies and opens a critique of being and its question as well as an improvisation of that subject, its exclusionary categorization and its conflation with being. It also raises another question: what are the effects of the personalized recounting of the horror of the African encounter with the European other, the middle passage and slavery? Finally, in a question prompted by Judy's work, what, asks Wahneema Lubiano in her introduction to Judy's text, are the effects—if any, either good or bad—of the depersonalization of that recounting, or at least, the valorization of a narrative which rather than establishing authorial subjectivity places the very idea of authorship/authority and the possibility of subjectivity on interminable hold? I employ the term *subjectivity* here, placed within the frame of possibility, in order to begin opening access to what lingers in the cut between the subject and its deconstruction, the virtualities of (European) Man and their others. While I was looking for some errant passages in narrative, Ben Ali and Judy had long since booked passage through narrative in poetical disruption and excess, in analytic torque away from what it is to be enslaved to freedom. In having done so, they make it possible to discern the generative incoherence Equiano stashes in narration's hold.

Here is an excerpt from the dedication of the first edition of Equiano's *Interesting Narrative*:

> Permit me, with the greatest deference and respect, to lay at your feet the following genuine narrative; the chief design of which is to excite in your august assemblies a sense of compassion for the miseries which the Slave-Trade has entailed on my unfortunate countrymen. By the horrors of that trade was I first torn away from all the tender

connections that were naturally dear to my heart; but these, through the mysterious ways of Providence, *I ought to regard as infinitely more than compensated by the introduction I have thence obtained to the knowledge of the Christian religion,* and of a nation which, by its liberal sentiments, its humanity, the glorious freedom of its government, and its proficiency in arts and sciences, has exalted the dignity of human nature.

I am sensible I ought to entreat your pardon for addressing to you a work so wholly devoid of literary merit; but, as the production of an unlettered African, who is actuated by the hope of becoming an instrument towards the relief of his suffering countrymen, I trust that such a man, pleading in such a cause, will be acquitted of boldness and presumption.[67]

This is a passage that acknowledges not only that Equiano's humanity is on trial but that his humanity places humanity on trial. The typography that links "such a man" with "such a cause" indicates a nonarbitrary relation between trial and humanity that is, in this very cause, not containable within this cause. What it is to be a man is to be such a man and what it is to be such a man is to be embedded in such a cause. Equiano italicizes these phrases; I have italicized two others, two instances, really, of the use of the word *ought.* He ought to regard his alienation as compensated by the knowledge of Christianity. He ought to apologize for daring this unlettered, African disruption of English literary merit. In both cases *ought* is shadowed by *nought*; obligation is cut by the force of an appositional negation that it behooves us to study. An articulate ensemble is held in this apposition; a theory of articulation is embedded in this apposition as well.

Thanks to Vincent Caretta, it's possible also to speculate that the dedication is an oblique and highly mediated assertion that is anticipatory of pointed challenges to his origins, authenticity, and authorship offered in the *Oracle* and the *Star,* two London newspapers, in late April of 1792. Caretta cites the *Oracle* as reporting the following: "It is a fact that the Public may depend on, that *Gustavas Vassa,* who has publicly asserted that he was kidnapped in Africa, never was upon that Continent, but was born and bred up in the Danish Island of Santa Cruz, in the West Indies. *Ex hoc uno disce omnes.* What, we will ask any man of plain understanding, must that cause be, which can lean for support on falsehoods as audaciously propagated as they are easily detected?"[68] That the dedication anticipates this challenge ought not obscure its appositional relation to a more direct response that appears in editions five through nine in the form of a note to the reader dated June 1792:

> AN invidious falsehood having appeared in the Oracle of the 25th, and the Star of the 27th of April 1792, with a view to hurt my character, and to discredit and prevent the sale of my Narrative, asserting, that I was born in the Danish island of Santa Cruz, in the West Indies, it is necessary that, in this edition, I should take notice thereof, and it is only needful of me to appeal to those numerous and respectable persons of character who knew me when I first arrived in England, and could speak no language but that of Africa.
>
> Under this appeal, I now offer this edition of my Narrative to the candid reader, and to the friends of humanity, hoping it may still be the means, in its measure, of showing the enormous cruelties practiced on my sable brethren, and strengthening the generous emulation now prevailing in this country, to put a speedy end to a traffic both cruel and unjust.[69]

That Equiano's claims regarding his birth and early childhood are falsehoods easily detected is, of course, far from easily established, as Caretta's meticulous research shows. It is, at the same time, equally difficult to establish their veracity despite the string of letters from gentlemen of good standing who vouch for Equiano both before and after the 1792 attacks on his character. What remains, however, is the possibility of a more thorough consideration and inhabitation of the distance between the "man of plain understanding" and the abolitionist "cause" that the *Oracle* is emboldened to dismiss. That Equiano is not such a man, that he is an other such man, or such that is other than man, and that his is a writing that emerges from something profoundly other than a plain understanding, must be interarticulate with his allegiance to such a cause and this gives us reason to investigate the necessity of the relationship between the imagination in its lawless freedom—more particularly, the imagination's fugitive comportment toward names and local habitations—and the drive or cause (for freedom) that animates Equiano's text even as that text makes its adamant and contradictory claims to divergent national appellations and the very abstract equivalence that he would deploy to bridge the gap between them. The regulatory bridge of commerce that Equiano invokes, crosses and recrosses, is, as David Kazanjian gets us to, only properly understood in the acknowledgement of its improper underside, something akin to what Fanon ambivalently calls "a zone of occult instability"—the dangerous market of the open sea that operates on the order of what Chinua Achebe, under the influence of Fanon and in echo of the riven, given name of the great Igboland market town of Onitsha, which is now famous for the production of a kind of literature for which the Igbo Equiano's famous narrative (and, in another and surprising way, the narrative production of Wole Soyinka, even in his bemusedly admiring Fanonian dismissal of market literature) is a kind of troubled and unlikely precursor (as Kent Thometz argues). Fanon's ambivalence—which will manifest itself in one way as a profound absence within the discourse on his own origins and childhood in the Antilles (as if akin to the erasure of which Equiano was, and still is, accused; as if in echo of a general West Indian claim to Africa of which C. L. R. James will come to speak, which he and George Padmore come to enact; what's at stake here is the entire history of what Nathaniel Mackey calls the broken claim to connection, the attenuated appeal to origin that will have always operated, in the name of something before, as origin's deferral)—echoes a conflict between regulation and its disruption which, in its racialized structuring, will come not only to constitute a fundament of black intellectual life and formation but to mark the opening of such life's structuring irruption into modern European thought as well. As Chandler teaches us in and against the grain of Du Bois's exemplary anexemplarity, this is the problematic of one, such as; of such a one; of the one, as such.

Often, such irruption of the one who is not the one bears a specifically, though not exclusively, phonic materiality, which asserts sense as surface *and* depth in challenge to a regulative paradigm whose hallmark is the reduction of the former in the interest of the latter. Interestingly, reaction to this paradigm structures the veiled, Adornoesque dismissal of Pops (and/or Miles) that Fanon offers on *Wretched of the Earth* (railing against the "jazz howl hiccupped by a poor misfortunate Negro"); it's bound up in Fanon's conflicted critique of the style of the native intellectual—a style of reflexive and muscular contradiction; "a harsh style full of images, for the image is the drawbridge which allows unconscious energies to be scattered in the surrounding meadows; a vigorous style, alive with rhythms, struck through and through with bursting life . . . full of color, too, bronzed, sunbaked and violent."[70] Fanon's is a Kantian critical discourse on nonsense, on the tumultuous derangements of a certain politicoaesthetic imagination that might more improperly be understood as the essential resistance of the object that manifests itself as lawlessness, as a kind of being against the law, as the lawless freedom and the struggle for freedom in unfreedom, in quite specific modes of discipline and regulation that we call slavery and colonialism. Here resistance's priority to power is understood even by Fanon as a kind of projection of the native, the projective construction of an ontological totality or native (mass?) intellectuality or na(t)ive intellectual style that lies before national consciousness and its pitfalls, as its most essential pitfall but perhaps, also, as something like a potential vault or vaulting whose activation emerges as a function of loss. One simply wants to investigate, ultimately, the imperial conditions of the Romantic attachment to nonsense and one recognizes a certain prefiguring of modernism's attachment to "African art in motion." If we ever get anywhere this will be thought in relation to the tumultuous derangements that emerge in the socioimaginative constitution of reality. The ambiguity is shown in what elsewhere appears as a kind of valorization of actual events (as opposed to inner truth—surface over depth), as the call for intellectuals to linger in the necessarily rhythmic and muscular music of the "zone of occult instability" wherein "our lives are transfused with light."[71] Now he'll valorize the ways "the contact of the people with the new movement gives rise to a new rhythm of life and to the forgotten muscular tensions, and develops the imagination."[72] These contradictions or ambivalences must be read carefully in that they body forth something of what they refer to, the rhythmic contradictions of which they speak. Note that a certain change in the oral traditions, a change that is at the same time already there and activated as a function of encounter, is noted by Fanon as if in anticipation of Menninghaus.[73] Meanwhile, what will have been the relationship between non-sense and the sensual, (the irregular and irreducible materiality of imagination)? The point, of course, is that the regulative reduction/irregular irruption of sensual materiality is the condition of possibility of sense and its normative sciences. Again, is there anything other than this ambivalence?

What if the appearances that most clearly tell of Equiano are those he might be said to have anticipated, a paraliterature of the market that emerges a century and a half after his death from the heart of the Igboland that he claimed as his native soil, from a city called Onitsha, which means "one who despises another," a place rife and gifted with antagonisms? As Chinua Achebe says, Onitsha "is where the spirits meet the humans, the water meets the land, the child meets the adult—these are zones of power, and I think this really where stories are created."[74] It is in these "zones of power . . . where stories are created," where the figure of the artist has always already and eternally been left behind by the people that blur the distinction between art and life, that the contest between the regulation and irregular irruption of exchange takes place.[75] This is the market and it is structured such that what it is to commence merchant indicates a more general, more fundamental, anoriginary commencement. Moreover, this regulative market within the irregular marketability of origin conditions the question concerning what the market will be. This is to say that the ongoing creation both of history and of a story, *récit* and recitation, are at issue in any reading of Equiano and that which he leads us to and violates. We'll be concerned, especially, with the trace, as well as the suppression, of antagonism, its relation to the creation of stories, to the forging of free stories, of the possibility of communist stories, and black stories. (Autobiographical) writing and commencing merchant go together, as Caretta points out and Kazanjian illuminates, but there is a political erotics of market writing that remains to be examined, something we could link with Fela Kuti, Ogali Ogali, and Samuel Delany, on the one hand, and with Funmilayo Kuti, Harriet Jacobs, and Nancy Prince, on the other. Vexations of name change and exterior mediation are necessary conditions for such erotics and their aesthetic manifestation. We're after motley inscriptions of objectional insistence, the self-disruptive anautobiographical crew that moves in apposition to the unities of lawful, gentlemanly, regulative understanding; the crew that steels itself with stealing itself, stealing away from itself and from such regulation in the very motion of embrace. There is a flight from the mercantile to the mercantile, which Wole Soyinka, in specific reference to Onitsha's mid-twentieth-century blurring of the boundaries between the literary and the bazaar, seems to characterize as a delusional, "reflection of a sudden inundation of false values."[76] On the other hand, in linking Onitsha's subvisionary effusion of narrative instability to Equiano, Kurt Thometz, by way of Achebe, suggests a genealogy—at once prefatory and present—of fantastic, (mis)understandings of another market we enact and await. In considering what this post(trans)national market is, we also consider what it will be, against the grain of a certain politico-financial maturity, given in developmental, autobiographical portraiture (*Bildung*), where having arrived figures the regulatory restrictions of an already given market: the administrative market, the market of the same, and its logistical containment and distribution of differences and occult instabilities. Eventually, such suggestion will have required sounding the articulation of market women and mill women; of market literature in Onitsha, market literacy in Abeokuta, and the texts offered by the mill workers of Lowell, Massachusetts; or of the textiles manufactured by the jute mill workers of Calcutta whose resistance to regulation and discipline, aberrations woven into the gunny sack, register the falsity of value as such.[77] This will have demanded a more thorough understanding than one can venture of Kant's own latent mercantilism in its relation to what Barrett speaks of as the turns of imagination—reproductive effects of regulation and subjugation wherein the imagination turns on itself in a kind of perspectival, navigational Dutch mastery—that are both productive and destructive of modern subjectivity; and a more detailed examination of ambivalence toward the vulgarities of the market—where locality meets excess *as* difference from Adam Smith to Thomas Jefferson, from Fanon to Soyinka—than there is power to offer.[78] What might softly be asserted, and perhaps even obliquely demonstrated, is something touching on the dangerous criminality of the market, the animative force of the commodity, their indissociability from blackness and its definitional exclusion from, and reconfigurative suspension of, the human. The ambivalent, because managerial, enthusiasm for the market in Equiano (or, say, Alexander Hamilton) is of interest here as counterpoint to the libertarian restrictiveness of certain farmers (always on that road of Jeffersonian increase where the yeoman turns or tends toward the planter). The question concerning the revolutionary and self-destructive nature of the bourgeoisie, whose clearing is a criminal underground, is serially renewed in echo of an already rich chorus on the broken market, on the disruption of the federal and the federated, on the minor, injured cosmopolitanism of the injured. The present experiment in distorted articulation universality and particularity, totality and difference—which attempts, by way of a neurotic oscillation as a method of truth, critically to extend, to tend, to end, the relation between the black radical tradition and enlightenment is another echo.[79] The blackness of this radical tradition is irreducible in the enlightenment, as well. This complex irreducibility is given and obscured in the severally mediated performance of a slave whom you will come to know as Uncle Toliver and his inspirited, (dis)possessed medium—historian Leon Litwak. Each mediates the other's membership in this gathering where "each," "other," and "membership" are under a duress so severe that (the determination of that) set undergoes serial rupture and expansion. Such mediation does not suspend the question of essence. Rather, blackness, in its irreducible relation to the structuring force of radicalism and the graphic configurings of tradition (what I want to say is tradition-ing—an accumulative movement that is montagic, that is driven by the cut) and, perhaps most importantly, in its very manifestation as the inscriptional, "material events" of a set of performances, requires another, nondismissive thinking of essence.[80] And this thinking converges (you could think such convergence, such "discrepant engagement," by way of Mackey) with the reemergent question of the human that articulation and the critique of articulation demands and disturbs.[81] As we'll see, Equiano's is a blackness in constant motion, a blackness as law of motion—always mediated (even in the supposed absence of editorial mediation), without origin(ary local habitation) or (unique) name, functioning as the mobile repository for the fragile and indispensable knowledge of freedom and its limits.

Dispersion is the condition of possibility of knowledge of freedom. Equiano knows something (else) about freedom. What's the relation between Africa and this something else that Equiano knows? Perhaps this: that Africa is not the origin but the condition of possibility and impossibility of this knowledge, which is animated by the refusal of origin and the refusal of that refusal that anticipates it. Blackness is the exhaustion of this knowledge, which tends toward its own dispersal. This knowledge is diffused and disbursed in black performance, whose irregularities bring the generality and general disruption of performance online. This knowledge—which comes into its own in the giving of itself, of its givenness, away—is the essence of black radicalism. But blackness is only in the break of its convergence with Africa. This decalage, this sexual cut, this intimation of an insistent previousness, is never resolved or recovered or rediscovered or returned to as a fixed and determinable natal occasion. The rupture is asymptotic and unsuturable. (Exhaustion of the) knowledge of freedom is activated in this infinitesimal and unbridgeable distance.

For this, I guess, we ought to be thankful. But fuck anyone and everyone that says so. The fullest expression of such gratitude, in the end and despite whatever superficial gentleness, will have been vicious, a ruthless negation, a savage nought (another obligation, an ought + n intimated through Equiano), the out and rooted critical lyricism of lament and prayer and scream and curse, the radicalism of sacred, anarhythmic, sociomusical graph in a line you could trace, if you wanted to, as the insurgent, anticolonial market life and art. Imagine Fela and Equiano, each (in) the other's wake, en route in late anticipation to America, that African nightmare through which one is constrained to move so that Africa might be lost and found. If alienation and distance represent the critical possibility of knowledge and freedom, they move within a field of articulation where Africa remains indispensable as previousness, not beginning, as provision, not end. Previousness is irreducible precisely because it is irrecoverable just as provision remains insofar as it cannot be achieved. We know this and what this knowledge lets us know, by way of modes of inscription that are always the very mark of cut convergence. This is to say that the necessarily African articulation of the question of the human is the question of a kind of competence in blackness; that in and as the posing and discomposition of the human, blackness simultaneously opens and closes the question of the human. This field of occasion, messing up the very ways things show up for us historically and geographically, is dispersal's and disbursal's polygraphic convergence. And it's not just that the tide has failed to wash this writing from the shore; the sound of the sea, the sound from the sea, is writing, keeps writing, the ensemble of the social through relation.

Ensemble is given through the object, the thing, the artwork, as the rebellion of its laws of motion. To address Marx's formulation of the human essence as the ensemble of social relations will ultimately require an address of the thing. Moreover, Kant's prophylactic meditations on the law of imagination's own lawlessness must be thought with what Theodor Adorno calls art's law of motion, the *Bewegungsgesetz* that has rebellion at its heart.[82] These in turn must be thought in with the antelegislative gathering of (art) work, object, thing, slave, and person that is given in the ensemblic, transversal, internally differentiated act of self-narration, where the ensemble of the social will have decayed, by way of development, into the ensemble of social relations whose substance is supposed to have been rendered, by the abstraction of embodiment, as a general equivalence. Serially, ongoingly, anoriginally, however, Equiano is the beginning and end of the general equivalent—this is to say that not only does he occupy the place where the theory of value intersects with the theory of the subject and with the theory of the state; but that he also operates such that he can never be rendered as the privileged example of the emptiness of equality or universality in general. Equiano has no place in the place he is supposed to found. Equiano does not take place. Abstract, universal equality's instantiation and hideout is Equiano's placelessness. Objectional things, like Equiano, in their radical, materiality, constitutive irrupt, likes teleological principles, into the abstractions that are fundamental to liberalism, capitalism, mercantilism, national humanism, as their *destruktion*. That which congeals, that which (un)conceals, does not lie still; the abstraction is not empty and it is not dumb; its substance neither freezes nor evaporates. This substance and its law of movement—its fugitive and disruptive exhahitation of that law; the constancy and fidelity of its escape, its faithful faithlessness—requires some thought on the relation between imagination and reason, here configured as lawless freedom and appositional enlightenment. This means traversing the passages between tariffs, teleological principles, and the mysteries of blackness as aesthetic social life.

Remember that Equiano is vexed by failures of self-regulation that he must acknowledge as his own incapacity to own; they are insistent transgressions of the state (of) authority that he craves. What is it that he disavows in attempted restraint? What does the transgression of restraint reveal? Equiano works between law and motion, between constraint and a privileged loss of control that is, then, retrospectively narrated. There is a delight in that narration, which is also always staging and restaging the encounter between mercantilism (law) and the mercantile (motion). The law of motion is, in this regard, a fugitive whose movement is (un)held between law and motion. In light of this consideration, Equiano's writing is structured by the centripetal force of a kind of stylistics of national unit/y and the centrifugal power of abolitionist differences and is an early exemplar of black intellectuality's architectonic volatilities—its internal fissures and interior agons that stem from the powerful conflict between imagination—a certain erotic, aesthetic, and political lawlessness of and in exchange that one might call, after Avery Gordon, the "abolitionist imaginary"—and regulatory, juridical, increasingly instrumental reason or understanding. Other complications arise: how to deal with the conceptual problematics that attend the abolitionist appeal to law, the abolitionist irruption into reason? How to understand their differential articulation with the deathly decay of the abolitionist orbit, with the allure that antiabolitionist formations carry for certain positions within the abolitionist trajectory? This other interarticulation of the centrifugal and the centripetal, the out and the rooted, is at the heart of black radicalism, where the struggle for freedom, which is also a collision with freedom, is an object of devoted study rather than an object of devotion.

A set of passages, then, to and for encounter, beginning with the problematics of medium and vessel:

1.

The first object that saluted my eyes when I arrived on the coast was the sea, and a slave ship, which was then riding at anchor, and waiting for its cargo. These filled me with astonishment, that was soon converted into terror, which I am yet at a loss to describe, and much more the then feelings of my mind when I was carried on board. I was immediately handled and tossed up to see if I was sound, by some of the crew; and I was now persuaded that I had got into a world of bad spirits, and that they were going to kill me. Their complexion too, differing so much from ours, their long hair, and the language they spoke, which was very different from any I had ever heard, united to confirm me in this belief. Indeed such were the horrors of my views and fears at the moment, that if ten thousand worlds had been my own, I would freely have parted with them all to have exchanged my condition with the meanest slave in my own country. When I looked round the ship too, and saw a large furnace or copper boiling and a multitude of black people, of every description, chained together, every one of their countenances expressing dejection and sorrow, I no longer doubted of my fate; and, quite overpowered with horror and anguish, I fell motionless on the deck, and fainted. When I recovered a little, I found some black people about me, who I believed were some of those who brought me on board, and had been receiving their pay: they talked to me in order to cheer me, but all in vain. I asked them if we were not to be eaten by those white men with horrible looks, red faces, and long hair. They told me I was not: and one of the crew brought me a small portion of spiritous liquor in a wine glass; but, being afraid of him, I would not take it out of his hand. One of the blacks therefore took it from him and gave it to me, and I took a little down my palate, which, instead of reviving me, as they thought it would, threw me into the greatest consternation at the strange feeling it produced, having never tasted any such liquor before.[83]

I was soon put down under the decks, and there received such a salutation in my nostrils as I had never experienced in my life: so that, with the loathesomeness of the stench, and with my crying together, I became so sick and low that I was not able to eat, nor had I the least desire to taste anything. I now wished for the last friend, death, to relieve me; but soon, to my grief, two of the white men offered me eatables; and, on my refusing to eat, one of them held me fast by the hands, and laid me across, I think, the windlass, and tied my feet, while the other flogged me severely. I had never experienced anything of this kind before, and although, not being used to the water, I naturally feared that element the first time I saw it, yet nevertheless, could I have got over the nettings, I would have jumped over the side.[84]

The sea and the ship are emblematic of encounter, the originary site of abjection, of the production or evocation of a shuddering affect that is quickly conceptualized in and as the mark of the aural and visual differences encoded in language and complexion.[85] This initial encounter remains. It is durative, domesticated, or inhabited in representation. It remains in every passage of the text, in the text's representation of the act of passage. Part of what the encounter generates in Equiano is a fear of being eaten, a terror that is shaped by prior experience in the culture of his claimed origin, in which food is given a double status—sustenance and (possibly) poison—and is thus to be regarded warily.[86] The young Equiano is scared of being consumed and rightly so as the ship is the white man's digestive system. He is consumed in the ship, situated within its bowels, swallowed by and radically drawn into the economy the ship symbolizes and instantiates, and incorporated as instrument into the dialectic of recognition initiated by the encounter and its originary abjectification. But this description of abjection as a kind of antibiotic processing foreshadows an emergent resistance. In that emergence Equiano embodies a reversal of the *pharmakon*, opening and marking the possibility of a contamination of what consumes him—a re-sounding and re-vision of the aural-visual assumptions and structure of European Man and his self-image. The abject, force-fed child takes poison for medicine while being taken, as poison, for sustenance.

2.

It was now between two and three years since I first came to England, a great part of which I had spent at sea; so that I became mured to that service, and began to consider myself as happily situated; for my master treated me always extremely well; and my attachment and gratitude to him were great. From the various scenes I had beheld on ship-board, I soon grew a stranger to terror of every kind, and was, in that respect at least, almost an Englishman. I have often reflected with surprise that I never felt half the alarm, at any of the numerous dangers in which I have been, that I was filled with at the first sight of the Europeans, and at every act of theirs, even the most trifling, when I first came among them, and for sometimes afterwards. That fear, however, the effect of my ignorance, wore away as I began to know them.

I could now speak English tolerably well, and perfectly understood every thing that was said. I not only felt myself quite easy with these new countrymen, but relished their society and manners. I no longer looked upon them as spirits, but as men superior to us; and therefore I had the stronger desire to resemble them, to imbibe their spirit, and imitate their manners. I therefore embraced every occasion of improvement; and every new thing that I observed I treasured up in my memory. I had long wished to be able to read and write; and for this purpose I took every opportunity to gain instruction, but had made as but very little progress. However, when I went to London with my master, I had soon an opportunity of improving myself, which I gladly embraced. Shortly after my arrival, he sent me to wait upon the Miss Guerins, who had treated me with so much kindness when I was there before, and they sent me to school.[87]

There was also one Daniel Queen, about forty years of age, a man very well educated, who messed with me on board this ship, and he likewise dressed and attended the captain. Fortunately this man soon became very much attached to me, and took great pains to instruct me in many things. He taught me to shave, and dress hair a little, and also to read in the Bible, explaining many passages to me, which I did not comprehend. I was wonderfully surprised to see the laws and rules of my own country written almost exactly here; a circumstance which, I believe, tended to impress our manners and customs more deeply on my memory. I used to tell him of this resemblance; and many a time we have set up the whole night together at this employment. In short, he was like a father to me; and some used even to call me after his name; they also styled me "the black Christian." Indeed I almost loved him with the affection of a son. Many things I have denied myself, that he might have them; and when I used to play at marbles or any other game, and won a few halfpence, or got some money for shaving any one, I used to buy him a little sugar or tobacco, as far as my stock of money would go. He used to say that he and I never should part, and that when ship was paid off, as I was as free as himself or any other man on board, he would instruct me in his business, by which I might gain a livelihood. This gave me new life and spirits; and my heart burned within me, while I thought the time long till I obtained my freedom. For though my master had not promised it to me, yet, besides the assurances I had often received that he had no right to detain me, he always treated me with the greatest kindness, and reposed in me an unbounded confidence. He even paid attention to my morals; and would never suffer me to deceive him, or tell lies, of which he used to tell me the consequences; and that if I did do, God would not love me. So that from all this tenderness I had never once supposed, in all my dreams of freedom, that he would think of detaining me any longer than I wished.[88]

The encounter remains in the memory of abjection and terror, an ineradicable and inconsumable trace even and especially in the context of the desire to resemble the one who'd once been feared. The paradox of freedom resurfaces in the fact of the abjectifying desire for and impossibility of resemblance. There is the illusion of resemblance—between the laws and rules of Equiano's assumed place of origin and those written in the Bible (a paradoxically divergent coalescence about which more later)—but that illusion is disappeared by the split between the theory and practice of Christianity; and in the absence of either an aural resemblance (a sound that is an absolute sounding-like; the absence of accent) or a visual resemblance (effect of some magical phenotypical transfiguration), resemblance must be reformulated and relocated by and in Equiano's relation to language—to tone, grammar, and the *written* mark. Resemblance is to be made manifest in literacy, as that which would become the mark of the same, the "universal," the "human."

Equiano's overcoming of terror corresponds, then, with a desire for resemblance that is enacted in his virtual acquisition of English(ness). The ability to speak, read, and write English "tolerably well" is connected to an ability no longer to look on white men as spirits; instead he looks on them as superior men and wishes to resemble them, to "imbibe their spirits and imitate their manners." (This opens, of course, the possibility of a kind of intoxication and reintroduces the motif of consumption and the notion of pharmakon that goes along with it; this notion of intoxication is bound up with the possibility of transportation or ecstasy and this imbibing of the spirit returns, along with the motif of consumption, during Equiano's conversion [again, about which more later], prompted by his attendance at a "soul-feast" at which nothing material was eaten or drunk and at which the entire complex of metaphors regarding consumption approaches resolution.[89]) Equiano "therefore embraced every occasion of improvement," many of which were afforded him by the Misses Guerin who taught him to read and also were responsible for his baptism, thereby foreshadowing the resolution of a dialectical motion from the white's inhabitation of the interstitial identity between God and Man to the white as superior man to the Lord. Nevertheless, there is a certain reconstruction of language, a certain refusal to understand, that is embedded in the desire, manifest in the re-citation, to move from the abject to the same. It is a desire for "self-improvement" through the knowledge of language that is, again, wholly within the frame of the encounter. Equiano must be "given" this opportunity—the imposition, in fact, of a brutal usufruction—by the one by whom he is taken and to whose will he remains open and subject. The gift, too, bears pharmakonic complications, as if independence depends upon the terror of random kindnesses: enter the Misses Guerin who offer Equiano the gift of (their) language; his profit, of course, is the ability to curse. Again, one might reconfigure this ability: as a mode of resistance, disabling the language, making it halt or limp or move unreliably for—which is to say against—its framers; as an infiltration or improvisation of the language, a contamination or a disprovement, if you will, of that with which one would have been improved. The problem, though, is that even this reversal of improvement is doubled by another kind of fall: one learns to curse when before, in Africa, one had had neither the need nor the tools "to pollute the name of the object of our adoration."[90]

Nevertheless, this reversal, the improvisation of improvement, is what must occur in the absence of any absolute mimesis. The accent remains—like the trace of the encounter—as the sound-alike is re-sounded. The written shifts uncontrollably; the letter moves. That movement is not the authentic difference of the African and his experience, a difference constitutive of the maintenance of the dialectic of recognition in the discourse of abolition. Its manufacture is manifest in prefaces that, in an attempt to figuratively confirm an imagined, already written and canonized otherness, speak of "round, unvarnished tale[s]," thereby betraying the inability, which the author himself nurtures, to read Equiano except through the image of Othello, the phantasmatically stylized other whose self-deprecation conceals an intoxicating, sexually transgressive, predatory linguistic power; or in reviews that would vouchsafe the narratives' authenticity in spite of the artful mediation of some European editor which, finally, *must* have been there.[91] Remember, too, that legal codes and biologically determined boundaries would always have served to mark the absoluteness of the color line—which turns out to have been a problem of the centuries, as Chandler might say—even as the consumptive sexual and juridical appetites of the European (man) takes to itself that impurity against which it so zealously guards.[92] Note, then, the echoes of Shakespeare's construction of the colonized, enslaved, or racialized Other with which Equiano is determined and that he is determined to resemble: paradigmatic oppositional attitudes toward and within the white man and his language and his daughter.

3.

In pursuance of our orders we sailed from Portsmouth for the Thames, and arrived at Deptford the 10th of December, where we cast our anchor just as it was high water. The ship was up about half an hour, when my master ordered the barge to be manned; and, all in an instant, without having before given me the least reason to suspect any thing of the matter, he forced me into the barge, saying, I was going to leave him, but he would take care that I did not. I was so struck with the unexpectedness of this proceeding, that for some time I did not make a reply; only I made an offer to go for my books and clothes, but he swore I should not move out of his sight; and if I did, he would cut my throat, at the same time taking out his hanger. I began, however, to collect myself; and, plucking up courage, I told him that I was free, and he could not by law serve me so. But this only enraged him the more; and he continued to swear, and said he would soon let me know whether he would or not and at that instant sprung himself into the barge, from the ship, to the astonishment and sorrow of all on board.[93]

But, just as we had got a little below Gravesend, we came alongside of a ship going away the next tide for the West-Indies; her name was the Charming Sally, Captain James Doran. My master went on board and agreed with him for me; and in little time I was sent for into the cabin. When I came there Captain Doran asked me if I knew him; I answered I did not; "Then," said he, "you are now my slave." I told him my master could not sell me to him nor to anyone else. "Why," said he, "did not your master buy you?" I confessed he did. "But I have served him," said I, "many years, and he has taken all my wages and prize-money, for I only got one sixpence during the war. Besides this I have been baptized; and, by the laws of the land, no man has a right to sell me." And I added, that I had heard a lawyer, and others, at different times tell my master so. They both then said, that those people who told me so, were not my friends; but I replied—it was very extraordinary that other people did not know the law as well as they. Upon this, Captain Doran said I talked too much English, and if I did not behave myself well and be quiet, he had a method on board to make me. I was too well convinced of his power over me to doubt what he said; and my former sufferings in the slave-ship presenting themselves to my mind, the recollection of them made me shudder. However, before I retired I told them, that as I could not get any right among men here, I hoped I should hereafter in Heaven, and I immediately left the cabin, filled with resentment and sorrow.[94]

Thus, at the moment I expected all my toils to end, was I plunged into, as I supposed, a new slavery; in comparison of which all my service hitherto had been perfect freedom; and whose horrors, always present to my mind, now rushed on it with tenfold aggravation. I wept bitterly for some time; and began to think that I must have done something to displease the Lord, that he punished me so severely. This filled me with painful reflections on my past conduct. I recollected that, on the morning of our arrival at Deptford, I had very rashly sworn that as soon as we reached London, I would spend the day in rambling and sport. My conscience smote me for this unguarded expression: I felt that the Lord was able to disappoint me in all things, and immediately considered my present situation as a judgment of Heaven, on account of my presumption in swearing.[95]

Equiano tells of a lessening of the original terror of the encounter and that telling can be construed as the mark of the submergence of any possible resistance and a capitulation to an oppressive Eurocentric model of self-measure and self-fashioning. The absence of terror is connected to Equiano's relation to the ship that is the locus of his sense of himself as (virtual) Englishman, the site of a delicate shift from the phantasm of consumption to the fantasy of assimilation. But as we see, his status on board the ship must have a double implication, and a resistant, improvisatory, asyntagmatic use of language occurs at the very moment that the virtuality of his Englishness is again unconcealed, namely in the reemergent encounter with the other—the redoubled image of another consuming, digestive ship—that corresponds to his sale; it is now clear that the absence of terror was a finite deferral and not an erasure. The other side of that implication is also indexed to his virtuality as an Englishman, which leads to the first of his many ineffectual appeals to English law. These appeals signify not only the juridical difference between himself and the English but the impotence of the law with respect to the achievement of freedom, on the one hand, and salvation on the other. Finally, the law pales in comparison to a certain kind of knowledge (more precisely, faith, though we'll see that neither faith nor law work in opposition to the other) that is bound up with the improvisation of a future state, one indexed both to freedom and salvation. Equiano's text demands that we confront questions concerning the relation between knowledge of freedom and knowledge of salvation and of what these have to do with the knowledge of language and the knowledge of the Lord.

So the double of Equiano's narrative of his original encounter with his other is the story of his next being sold. This sale comes just as Equiano has begun to believe he will finally obtain his freedom. Equiano views his sale as the result of an unguarded expression of emotion. Still, though unguarded expression, namely cursing, produces negative effects, those effects can be warded off by another form of unguarded expression—a pouring out of the soul, with unfeigned repentance and contrition of heart. Earnest prayer relieves Equiano: "In a little time my grief, spent with its own violence, began to subside; and after the first confusion of my thoughts was over, I reflected with more calmness on my present condition."[96] It's as if the opposing profuse strains of unpremeditated expression cancel one another out and are replaced by reasoned reflection and the accompanying possibility of a kind of redemption.[97]

Mediating between curse and prayer is the moment of an improvisatory contamination of the oppressor's language, the encounter in which Equiano "talked too much English." That impasse between imitative and resistant uses of the language is itself marked by an interruptive logical displacement such that at the very moment when it would seem we have a resistant encounter to valorize we must also see that encounter as the emergence of an interruption of the encounter as such, an interruption made possible by Equiano's knowledge of freedom and its constraints. When Captain Doran asks Equiano if he knew him he seems to imply that Equiano ought to have some prior knowledge, a certain antemetaphysical bondsman's understanding or competence, that would allow him to recognize Doran. The self-recognition that would emerge in Doran by way of Equiano's affirmative answer is interrupted, however, and in that deferral Doran must bestow upon Equiano, in the form of a violent requisition, a moment of self-recognition, a moment that would make Equiano know what he is so that Doran's identity can be confirmed. "You are now my slave," says Doran, but here recognition is missed again. Though Doran's utterance would be performative, as if in the face of Equiano's failure (or refusal) to recognize his new master, Doran hopes to instantiate, by speaking, their relative statuses: you are now, despite the deferring, non-deferential absence of your immediate recognition of this fact and of what it implies about our identities, my slave *because I say so*. Still, in the break that postpones immediate knowledge of his condition and of his identity vis á vis Captain Doran, another knowledge is implied, precisely that knowledge which animates Equiano's resistant speech. The "too much English" that Equiano talks when profanely calling out the name of the Lord is a function of the too little English he talks when his response is supposed to establish the identities of lord and bondsman. When Equiano responds, answering that he did not know Captain Doran, that he did not recognize the master or his mastery, that he did not know himself to be this master's slave, he lays claim to that knowledge in his expression of it. In not knowing what Captain Doran would have him know, Equiano knows, and has, plenty of nothing.

Of course this moment of misrecognition—at which the condition of possibility of a renaissance of resistance is revealed—is shadowed by another recognition. One lord is denied but another Lord is affirmed as the author of Equiano's misfortunes. Here, swearing and resistant response, a stated intention to carouse and an oppositional legal assertion of independence are connected precisely in the fact that that legalistic assertion of independence is, more precisely, a declaration of in/dependence contingent upon the mediating effects of an already extant ownership. Lordship and lordship return in and as one another's figures at moments of resistant or unguarded expression that constitute a devolution of their originary animus, like the "I answered I didn't know" that marks the negative assertion of the trace of knowledge of freedom. The question, of course, of the origin of that trace is vexed and impossible. Embedded in that question, however, is a possible improvisation of the very idea of the lord in its relation/opposition to the bondsman. That improvisation, emerging at the site of another question concerning the language of improvisatory resistance's origin, in which knowledge of freedom is expressed, is one to which we'll return by way of another consciousness, moving out-from-the-outside, that the oppositions of lord and bondsman, Lord and bondsman, curse and prayer, allow us only to imagine.

One thinks again and often, in an inevitable return, of the image/figure of the ship in the narrative: the proliferation of the gaze to and from the ship in Equiano, all determined to a certain extent by his first encounter with it. The ship is never not both engine and figure of consumption and containment and is never to be thought outside of its structuring determination as both abstraction and embodiment of the white man. Note, then, Freeman Equiano, impatient with the ship he was on for taking on too much water, again expressing himself unguardedly: "Damn the vessel's bottom out!" Of course, his "conscience instantly smote [him] for the expression,"[98] but we are led to believe repentance was ineffectual, for the ship—described as transfixed, fascinated, abject, and productive of abjection—soon founders on the rocks. The fear and horror that transfixion or encounter produces reconstitutes and reconfigures the terror Equiano felt as a child and to which he claims to have grown a stranger; the terror that the ship once held, and which had shifted to a terror of being transferred from one ship (and its correspondent comfort and identification with one's "original" captor) to another, becomes a terror of being torn away from the ship as such. "All my sins stared me in the face [another abject encounter or transfixion]; and especially I thought that God had hurled his direful vengeance on my guilty head, for cursing the vessel on which my life depended."[99] We must think what it means to curse the ship, to curse what is figured and embodied by the ship, to curse that upon which one's life depends. Here, again, lie the problematics of the curse and the ship and all amid a development toward reflection, reason, "good English." The vessel or ship must somehow be maintained, and yet that ship's maintenance is to be figured within the thinking of a kind of contained sabotage that reworks, contaminates, poisons. The ship is that in which one must be contained and yet what the ship contains must always itself contain some dangerous supplement that enacts not so much the reversal of encounter, or the return of the gaze, but their prior refusal. Freeman Equiano returns to England and confronts his "benevolent master," Capt. Pascal: "He appeared a good deal surprised, and asked me how I came back. I answered, 'In a ship.'"[100] Mad, smart-assed, atypical in affect, unsubjective in an abjection that is more and less than itself, still acting out in the refusal to act as if he knows his master, knowledge of freedom given in knowing all but nothing, Equiano establishes the transportation of enlightenment on a ship of tools.

III

What is to be done with financial instruments that won't mature? With regard to this, and other questions, Kazanjian is indispensable. In his extraordinary encounter with Equiano, and the powerful examination of racial capitalism that encounter requires and allows, Kazanjian excavates the historic coincidence of the publication of Equiano's *Narrative* and the debate in the U.S. Congress on the tariff of 1789.

> On August 1, 1789, less than one month after the passage of the Tariff of 1789, Olaudah Equiano published *The Interesting Narrative of the Life of Olaudah Equiano, or Gustavus Vassa, the African* in London. An account of his life from his birth in West Africa in 1745 to his experiences of capture, middle passage, slave labor, manumission, "free" labor, and antislavery agitation, the *Narrative* traces Equiano's attempts to tie fragments of his African past to the Euro-U.S. present forced upon him, and thereby to constitute a new identity. Yet each of those attempts prove fleeting, for each persistently threatens to collapse, to recoil on him and recode him as slave, as raced property. Persistently transgressing fixed institutional identities, Equiano just as persistently finds the space of transgression an unfixed and unstable one, a space occupiable for only a brief moment, if at all. Of these attempts, one of the most important, given the tenacity with which Equiano pursues it, is his engagement in the transatlantic merchant marine trade. As he puts it . . . , "I at length endeavoured to try my luck and commence merchant."[101]

Kazanjian continues:

> However, like many other black men who entered or were forced to enter the merchant marine trade in the late eighteenth and early nineteenth centuries, Equiano encountered an increasingly hostile terrain, signified by the "many instances of ill-usage" and "injuries done to other Negroes in our dealings with whites" . . .
>
> In the increasingly frequent "instances of ill usage" and "injuries" of black mariners on the North Atlantic we can locate quotidian traces of the constitutive relationship between racial, national and gender codification and formal, abstract equality glimpsed in the 1789 tariff debate . . . . Neither an aberration from, nor a contradiction of, the

formal and abstract equality that animates modern citizenship under capitalism, hierarchically codified identities actually sustained that very equality. Consequently, we need to understand mercantilism not simply as an economic policy, but rather as a set of discursive practices that articulated formal and abstract equality with the codification of race, nation and gender in the North Atlantic during the eighteenth and nineteenth centuries. Certainly . . . black mariners do sometimes deploy the practices of mercantile capitalism sufficiently to buy or to maintain their freedom from slavery and to become relatively socially and financially secure. Yet we will also see that black mariners are increasingly, systematically, and ritually barred from the formal and abstract equality of mercantile capitalism by mercantilist discursive practices.[102]

Kazanjian is concerned with the relation between Equiano's commencing merchant—his entrance into a transnational mercantile economy as a trader that is also a reentrance into that economy in which he already was ensconced as the traded—and the commencement of the United States, whose movement from a condition of immaturity to one marked by the ability truthfully to act and reason is bound up, according to Madison, with its own entrance into the mercantile economy as an entity capable of raising revenue without oppressing its constituents. For Kazanjian, the ability successfully to obtain both these objects can be thought along lines Marx establishes while helping to make possible a critique of the idea of the state as the field in which the general interest and the particular interests of each of its citizens are reconciled. But what and who constitutes "the general interest"? The vicious contest of its ongoing formation, wherein interest is only properly understood as antagonism and wherein the generality of antagonism is structured and obscured by the genocidal particularity of the settler's antiecological antiblackness, remains the bloody open secret of American development While Marx offers us theoretical frameworks within which to understand those phenomena of political figuration and national self-imaging that allow the interests of an elite to stand for the interests of the people, the critique of "the people" as mathematical object + mode of enclosure whose rigid exclusions are given as voracious grasp is a field (nigger) equation or, as in the case of Equiano, the live—because serially appositional—reckoning of those who remain at and under sea.

In Madison's view, and in the view of the other Federalists, the general interest required the levying of a tariff and, more generally, the inception of a monetary policy that would remedy the moral and financial retardation of the prior confederation of newly independent American states. Kazanjian is finely attuned to how Madison's discourse on the formation of the state echoes discourse on the formation of the subject. So that we might say that the subjectivity of the state—its authentic agency, independence, authority, maturity, majority, sovereignty—is bound up with its relation to the potentially divergent objects of raising revenue and nurturing its constituents. The state, like the subject, is where the general and the particular converge—in this case around the erection of a set of variously permeable barriers placed before articles that are incorporated by (constituents of) the state through trade. In this regard, the weakness of the Articles of Confederation, which only arrested the state's development, is shaken off when the politicoeconomic aspirations that are inscribed with whips and chains upon the articles of trade are transcribed on the state's (re)founding document. If the state is a kind of subject whose constitution tends toward the further development of an essentially mercantile agency that depends upon the subordination of the traded, then what are the conditions within which Equiano, the traded become trader, moves in the interest of developing his? Held within a transatlantic and transnational compact in which the refusal of his constituency is fundamental to the general reformation of the state that the United States embodies, Equiano's shadow graduation is a volatile experiment.

Kazanjian begins in this way:

> On July 4, 1789, four months into its first session, the U.S. Congress celebrated thirteen years of formal independence by passing its first tariff bill. The bill placed duties of 5–15 percent on approximately thirty different goods, ranging from nails to carriages, with the highest rates reserved for "articles of luxury." When James Madison proposed this "endeavour" with the first nonprocedural words ever uttered in the new Congress, quoted above, he called the representatives "first attention" and "united exertions" to a national economic policy, offering the tariff as a way "to remedy the evil" of a nearly bankrupt treasury.[103]

Kazanjian rightly argues that the tariff debate, from its outset, indicates a complication held in and against the desire for a kind of solvency given in the convergence of financial maturity and national unity. Madison is all about the formation of a potent and rational agency—which is not reducible to unity however much unity would foster it, however much the illusion of unity might cover it—to fabricate and enforce that specific and exclusionary understanding of the general interest given ideological expression in *The Federalist Papers*. Madison desires a state potency enabled by monetary policy's enforcement of an idea of the general interest that is the privatized and privative attenuation of the very national unity it constructs. And yet the potency of the state is the condition of possibility of the unity of the nation, which is theorized as a serially lost-and-found priority to the state. This simultaneously amputative and prosthetic construction of a simultaneously remembered and anticipated unity is the very mechanics of the privatization of the general interest. Kazanjian shows that when monetary policy extends and materializes ideological inscription it is a masterpiece of regulated, regulative imagination—enlightenment's greatest, most fragile, and most enduring work of art—which is not given in the object as such but in the performance of its continual decline and restoration, as the union fades in its increasingly lying self-assertion and blooms in the calculated, calculative, thorny governance of its constituents.

If we continue to follow along with Kazanjian, we see that for Madison, bankruptcy threatens the nascent union with disintegration into the implicitly plural and antagonistic realm of the representatives' "constituents." It is in response to this that he calls the legislators' "first attention" and "united exertions" to a national economic policy. Therefore, Madison suggests that this tariff will do more than fill the treasury; it is a national policy precisely because it promises to transform these potentially plural and antagonistic "constituents" into united subjects abstracted from their particularities and antagonisms and represented as formally equivalent units of a national population—units he elsewhere calls "citizens" who will engage in lively economic exchange.[104]

In his analysis of the forging of national unity, Kazanjian alerts us to a framework that will have continually generated radical misunderstandings of such unity and the subjective units that are supposed to comprise it. The subject as national unit is abstracted from particularities and rendered into something like a formalized stand-in for the fiction of a general interest made of "formally equivalent units of a population," individual state-sanctioned para-sites, as it were, of the convergence of a rationally manufactured generality and a rigorously evacuated particularity.[105] If the national unit—the constituent, the citizen—is merely an empty, formal equivalence emerging at the intersection of abstraction and embodiment, then this is all bound up with the fact that the general interest of the nation is nothing more than the metonymic imposition of an oligarchical desire that operates politically much like the "intersubjective validity" of judgments of taste operates aesthetically. Such deformation of generality necessarily accompanies the liquidation of difference when the citizen's qualities are ceded, as it were, to the state that is his condition of possibility as a unit simultaneously forged and submerged in national unity. The agency that is given to the state is then deployed in the interest of enforcing precisely that national unity that produces and is embodied by the formal, empty national unit. Kazanjian makes it possible for us to understand how the "freedom" of the citizen or national unit comes to stand in for gendered and racialized oligarchical power.

Kazanjian requires and allows us to be concerned, then, with the movement between the entrance into rational economic exchange and the formation—or, at least, the capitulation to the idea and ideality—of the national unit, and if Equiano is the exemplary figure of such movement it is because his capture by and exclusion from it makes it possible. As Kazanjian shows, the newly born potency of the state is instantiated in the imperial masculinity of its constituents, "whose unity depends upon racial slavery."[106] The development of the nation and its units is emergence into the antisociality of racial capitalism, which is predicated upon a metaphysics of static and state-sanctioned completeness that Robinson describes as "the terms of order."[107] Equiano's commencing merchant is his initiation into subjection's scene, its staging, whose temporal paradox Judith Butler delineates and recognizes as an ontological paradox, and whose ethical paradox Saidiya Hartman delineates and recognizes as a moral paradox. Butler asks, by way of Athusser, what receives, even as only an unformed vulnerability, the state's invitation to subjection, while Hartman frames—or brings into some unretrievable relief—an impossibly uncaptive priority to the "incompatible predications of the freed."[108] What emerges when we consider what comes before the denial and imposition of subjection? Does Equiano know something about freedom, universality, and their interinanimation that must be considered in any analysis of his commencing merchant and of the desire such advent implies?

Kazanjian's focus is marked by an absolutely necessary disbelief in freedom, universality, and their interinanimation. This will become apparent in his reading and I want to understand the effects of such disbelief, especially since Equiano's narrative is structured so much by a faith we are constrained to join Kazanjian in being unable to share. This is because "[r]ather than simply being excluded from [the] capitalist calculation of 'freedom,' black merchant mariners came to be ritually invoked as the limit of that logic" so that the making of the national unit is dependent not on the elimination of antagonism but on the formation of a unity that is nothing but antagonism—a unity without solidarity given in the abstraction from and eradication of racialized and gendered differences.[109] Immersion in this crucible of highly controlled form, as the fuel that drives it, is the enactment of antagonism. This is to say that what is constructed in the formal equivalence of national units/citizens is an attenuation of the universality of difference in the name of a unity that simultaneously assumes, enforces, and disguises separation. More precisely, if universality is given in the materiality of what Denise Ferreira da Silva calls "difference without separability," the state is the mechanism that generalizes the brutal abstraction of a nation of separate but simultaneously equivalent and unequal units.[110] In the embodiment that seeks to literalize, and therefore liquidate, difference in separation, what is rendered, instead, is separation's figural abstraction of fleshly difference. Carceral freedom, unequal equivalence, and antiuniversal unity are racial capitalism's deadly and uncontainable yield. Kazanjian recognizes that in this regime difference is under assault and that if this is so it is not because antagonism is detached from, but rather focused on and amplified in what the Federalists call "fellowship," which turns out to be an alias for leadership figured as an absolute need. The assault on difference works in tandem with an assault on, rather than an imposition of, universality. To commence merchant and engage the impossible naturalization of and into the transatlantic theater of emergent national unity, is to enter into forms of antagonism that accompany a figural resolution of the strife between difference and solidarity that is always an assault on both. They are submitted to the deformative force of a quite specific mode of antagonism that is precisely aligned with the interinanimation of commencing merchant and initiating subjection. We move, then, in the waning particularity of the individual citizen to a certain national particularity that will become the only quality available to the otherwise radically indifferent national unit who is, now, the figure of national unity. We'll come to see how, in the precise interplay between abstract and formal equivalence and inequality, the national particularity that differentiates the United States from its others will become a racial particularity that explains and ameliorates the interior inequality, the internal difference, within the United States. This difference is never not gendered, never not sexual, and it shows how the story of the nation is always also a story of kinship, how wounded kinship tends to merge with wounded nationality. In this regard, as M. NourbeSe Philip constantly shows, the transatlantic, in its irreducible blackness, is score and scar of a flesh forcibly mobilized and impossibly united as a state of exception.

When Kazanjian proceeds to his reading of Equiano he does so purposefully and emphatically by way of Marx. His formulation of the notion of the formal and abstract equivalent, the citizen or national unit, takes up the terms in and with which Marx thinks money early on in the first volume of *Capital*. Marx and Kazanjian show that the state is in the business of producing formal and abstract general equivalents in two forms—in the form of the citizen as national unit and in the form of money. (Monetary) policy produces them both. It is in this light that we look to Equiano again and again. He is neither money nor a citizen but, in occupying the undefined space between these poles, he lets us know how deeply the traded + trader falls not in between the two. What's Equiano's relation to the state? He is produced by it, as are its citizens and its revenue, even as he is figured as other to the national particularity that makes such production possible. What happens when he commences merchant where commencing merchant founds not only national and individual particularity but, more fundamentally, national and individual subjectivity? This is a question concerning the objectional force in mercantilism of the thing who is not one, particularly when he is a merchant, particularly when commencing merchant is essential to the production of national unity and national units, particularly when the delineations separating subject/citizen from object/commodity from money begin to blur. Moreover, in oscillating between lament at having been produced but not claimed by the state, and lament at having been forced to be productive of and for the state, narration takes the form of a blurred refusal of the conditions it narrates, as Kazanjian effectively demonstrates, wherein Equiano's "instances" and "injuries" repeatedly bring him to—or, more precisely, just short of—himself as the racial-national limit of mercantile capitalism and its promise of formal, abstract equality. Equiano is, in this regard, a kind of vanishing point that brings the transnational mercantilist perspective online. Barrett might say that a broken picture of the world of western modernity is given in the discontinuities of Equiano's (non)performances. Held between gesture and event, Equiano provides the frame for the portrait of (trans)national unit/y while also serially revealing that frame's necessary necessary emptiness. Kazanjian's analysis of Equiano's exposure of mercantilism's limits and race's prenatal entanglement with the value form, along with Barrett's revelations concerning the right angular rigidity of those turns of imagination through which racial capitalism is supposed to forge national and intrasubjective completeness, demands that we prepare ourselves for something like an analytic of the invaluable and the appositional.

To be a citizen you have to own yourself, buy yourself (everyday), sell yourself, equate yourself with money, figure yourself as/in relation to the commodity. Equiano invests in this, commences (ownership of) himself in commencing merchant. All this is in the nature of subjection but it isn't just answering the inaugurative, interpellative call of the state and its apparatuses; it's literally trying to be like the state when the state is constituted like an exemplary subject when, in the levying of taxes or the setting of monetary policy, it buys itself, owns itself, comes into its own as itself as force or power. Is there something in or of Equiano that lies before this self-controlled and self-emancipated majority? What will it have been to turn away from this investment? What's the choreography of this critical move, this sidestep in apposition, away from the constant relay between the state subjectivity of the citizen and the noncitizen's subjection in and to the state?

There's a discourse of revelation that begins to move Equiano against the grain of the master discourses of state and subject. The Lord—which word might be said to signify a sovereign imposition upon phantasmagorical materiality, some generative and general swarm of frenzied feasting soul in loving flesh—cuts enlightenment and the law.[111] This revelatory discourse is immaterial (or abstract). All goes back to the work of dematerialization and rematerialization that Equiano acts out. This work is given in Marx, after the black radical tradition's anticipation of it. Aunt Hester's rematerialization of and through Frederick Douglass is already there in Equiano. If the Lord cuts the law in ways that bespeak what Kazanjian identifies as a certain unruly confluence of coagulation and fluidity, object, and practice, then perhaps some discourse of the flawed, some *mater* discourse of extrarational, counterspeculative reproduction might emerge in light of an irreducible dehiscence between generality and the general equivalent.

Kazanjian shows how the state forges tax policies that help to construct the notion of a general interest in the general equivalent and the idea of citizenship that is its corollary. But while there is a real connection between the discourses and practices of valuation and those of subjection or identification that link what we understand about the subject/citizen with what we understand about the commodity, these modes of generality are subject to divergent modalities of restriction. The appositional and the invaluable work that dislocation. As Kazanjian argues,

> When capitalism first emerged as an economic and political force, Marx argues in the first volume of *Capital*, it worked to break down current ways of making sense of and giving value to social relations, while simultaneously instituting a new way of making sense of or giving value to social relations. Marx describes the process of breaking down in part 8 of *Capital* (vol. 1) in economic terms as "a process which divorces the worker from the ownership of the conditions of his own labour" through expropriation, so-called "bloody legislation," against the expropriated, the agricultural and industrial revolutions, and colonization. In turn, in the first chapter of *Capital* Marx calls the new, capitalist way of making sense of social relations, or the form in which social relations are valued under capitalism, the "value form."[112]

For Kazanjian, this mode of making sense is problematic in precisely the way that the formation of state subjectivity is problematic; it occurs by way of a denial or suppression of difference, particularity, and antagonism. He shows how Marx "explains that two materially different objects, such as a coat and linen, are equated with each other on the basis of a third commodity shared by the coat and the linen. That third commodity is abstract labor, or labor which has been abstracted from its particular qualities."[113] But what if there is an entanglement of coat and linen that resists the suppression of differences that remain obscure if they are thought to belong either to the coat or the linen? If the construction of a general equivalent, abstract labor, elides differences it is because generality has been yoked to equivalence. Obviously there is a massive question concerning the uses and abuses of generality. The point, here, is that a certain antipathy toward it presupposes the answer to that question rather than calling it. Kazanjian argues, by way of Marx, that "the value form transforms the particularistic aspects of social into the universal and abstract form of 'human labor in general.'"[114] Kazanjian goes on, though, to show how Marx argues for a certain reparticularization or rematerialization that is produced by the value form that he himself reformulates. Kazanjian quotes, then reads, Marx:

> However, it is not enough to express the specific character of the labour which goes to make up the value of the linen. Human labour-power in its fluid state, or human labour, creates value, but is not itself value. It

becomes value in its coagulated state, in objective form. The value of the linen as a congealed mass of human labour [*Gallerte*] can be expressed only as an "objectivity" [*Gegenstandlichkeit*], a thing which is materially different from the linen itself and yet common to the linen and all other commodities.

The exchange of the coat and the linen gives a formal, abstract, and universal meaning to what were the "fluid," particular human actions of weaving or tailoring. Yet this formal, abstract and universal meaning has a substantiality "coagulated," "congealed" and "objective." The value form produces a universal abstraction with a form that has jelled or solidified anew. In other words, the value form effectively departicularizes the particularisms of precapitalist social relations and then reparticularizes those social relations.[115]

For Kazanjian, embodiment is the modality through which the maintenance of particularity shows up as the reparticularization of social relations. He understands embodiment is both part of the value form as well as a kind of disruption of that form's movement in and toward abstraction. But what if embodiment enforces abstraction? What if the individuative limits of the body make the movements and relations of equivalence and the form of value possible? At stake here is not genealogical isolation, but the carnal and animative ruptures of genealogical imposition. Perhaps the work of black radicalism is most clearly characterized by the kind of aggressive, violent reticence we might associate with nonperformances of a substantive universal abstraction borne in performances of a fleshly universal machine. It would be in this regard that we might speak, just off of Marx and Kazanjian, of "the 'double existence'" of the commodity [who sounds]: as the invaluable, she is general; in difference, she makes differences.[116] This assertion, of course, goes somewhat against the grain of the tradition's most dominant self-construction as being constantly in transition or in development against the forces of coagulation that Kazanjian associates with the value form and which history teaches us constitute intractable barriers to black individuation. If to be valued is to suffer the brutal and final imposition of form, then perhaps the invaluable emerges not in formlessness but, rather, in a giving and receiving of form that is both substantive and indeterminate, where thingliness fades into the presence of nothingness. Such irregular, violent *mater*iality, transcendent only in its immanence, divine only in its ordinariness, sacred only in its constant profanation, is what is sought after in and before Equiano's commencement. We seek an open secret mercantilism cannot admit, some life, stolen from, and stolen away in and by, the stolen.

This animation is a condition and an object of racial state capitalism; it is, and it lies, before it in ways that Dipesh Chakrabarty attends to in *Provincializing Europe*.[117] He does so in a way that requires some fine-tuning of our understanding of the work or movement or resistance of the object of racial state capitalism, which is to say some attunement to that confluence of commodity and laborer that we might now begin to think of in terms of a certain animation of absolute nothingness.

There is, in the early Marx, something of an upheaval in the theory of the object; but this upheaval never crystallizes into a full understanding of the peculiar confluence of commodity/worker that, in a sense, constitutes the strange and revolutionary historicity of slavery in its relation to (the end of) racial state capitalism. Such an understanding is precisely what Kazanjian, within the context of a brilliantly experimental band with which I have here been trying to jam, advances. That understanding is given to us in the life and afterlife of the enslaved, providing an ani*mater*ialization of the Marxian categories as they remain not fully activated in their embeddedness in an inadequate idea of the thing (held, as it were, in objecthood). When Chakrabarty thinks Marx's relation to an Aristotelian economics that is hamstrung by its inability to think abstract human equality we see another path toward what must occur, namely some understanding of the way Marx is held up, as it were, by an inability fully to think the life of the object. The voice of labor-power (the abstract and general voice of a metaphysical presence in Marx) must be cut and augmented by a sounding that ruptures the commodity and everything her embodiment is supposed to guarantee. This is a sound that already moves outside of any illusory completeness in presence that speech supposedly gives—it is the material and differentializing force or accent that invaginates and revolutionizes the generality of labor outside the interplay of abstraction and embodiment. Where Chakrabarty rightly recognizes the inescapable need—registered in the method as well as the target of Marx's analysis—of generality (as in the degraded case of abstract labor), Kazanjian rightly exposes those abusive ruses of generality to which Marx was also attuned. What links them is a righteous antipathy toward the thing, figured as coagulation. For Chakrabarty, the generality of labor power is its life, its animation or fluidity; for

Kazanjian generality is precisely the condition of influidity and congealment. Kazanjian links fluidity (animation) and particularity, Chakrabarty links animation (fluidity) and generality; the thing neither fluid nor animate in their estimations—is neither particular (for Kazanjian) nor universal (for Chakrabarty). But perhaps some invaluable and in/organic apposition occurs, even if only for a minute, in the diffusive entanglement of thing and labor.

Kazanjian valorizes the confluence he sees between particularity and fluidity because he valorizes indeterminacy. Abstract equality/equivalence is, for him, a violation of indeterminacy precisely because it departicularizes social relations and represses antagonisms. Moreover, generality, for Kazanjian, is a violation of indeterminacy that is, if not the basis of freedom, the possibility of some violent and reticent approach to and departure from it. And this valorization of indeterminacy is linked with a kind of suspicion toward substance. But it seems that every reduction of substance in the modern episteme, from Marx's, Nietzsche's, and Freud's, through Ferdinand de Saussure's, J. L. Austin's, and Edmund Husserl's to Chomsky's and Derrida's, are themselves abstractions committed precisely in generality's name. The Saussurean reduction of phonic substance, foundational for structuralism and its aftermath, is traceable not only to the seventeenth- and eighteenth-century rationalists (as outlined by Derrida in *Of Grammatology*), but also to the dematerializing move that Marx initiates by making the crucial distinction between labor and labor power, whose echo emerges when Saussure submits the sign to the critique of value. When Kazanjian redoubles the reduction of substance, thereby liquifying the coagulate, in order to align Marx with those who would valorize the interplay of particularity and indeterminacy, he replicates a move that, in Marx, is precisely designed to foster detente between generality and a certain historical determinism. What if Marx is not entirely wrong in this desire? Or what if Kazanjian is entirely right in attempting to establish for indeterminacy a certain epistemological security? Can what appear as the impossible relations that somehow must obtain between the particular and the universal, determinacy and indeterminacy, be made available by a kind of exhaustion of the very problem in certain false starts and broken ends? This is a question of mediation, as Adorno understands it:

> Subjectivity changes its quality in a context which it is unable to evolve into its own. Due to the inequality inherent in the concept of media-

tion, the subject enters into the object altogether differently from the way the object enters into the subject. An object can be conceived only by a subject but always remains something other than the subject, whereas a subject by its very nature is from the outset an object as well. Not even as an idea can we conceive a subject that is not an object; but we can conceive an object that is not a subject. To be an object also is part of the meaning of subjectivity; but it is not equally part of the meaning of objectivity to be a subject. What is the content of the object's excess of its premature other?[118]

But what we might be able to challenge is not so much the notion of the inherent inequality of mediation but, rather, the directionality of that inequality. More specifically and precisely, we might think by way of, and perhaps through, the thing that exceeds or is before the conception of the subject as well as the specific prematurity of the subject in its entanglement with the thing, with the thing's thought, that thought's expression and habitation in the quotidian, in otherwise systematic rhythms, in the suffering of the suffering that is seemingly without voice, in the industrial, in and as the commodified, in the mute, mutant, mutated language of the mute, mutated, mutant instrument as it moves, finally, in the irrepressibly nonidentical. Philosophy provides a punctuated trajectory of refuge for the ones who refuse it by enacting a nonidentical and prior exteriority. This movement of things against owning lies, along with the advent of the subject, before us unto the diffusion of the thing itself.

On the one hand, the outset of the subject has yet to come. On the other hand, that which passes for the subject now is an object in a quite different way. The premature subject is an object otherwise, which is just as Adorno would predict in diagnosing subject's and object's abortive synthesis. That prematurity is equivalent, in this regard, to the subject's premature birth. If the subject is premature, then so is its inherent status as object. Does this mean that the prematurity of the subject is, more specifically, a prematurity of objecthood in the subject? What would it mean to think and to inhabit the object? Is this what's at stake in the notion of the becoming-object of the object? If so, it is a question for which Adorno has no patience. His exile and his damagedness did not sufficiently prepare him. He would effect a return while claiming the ability to conceive an object that is not a subject (as opposed to the inability to conceive a subject that is not an object). Is a critique of that conception, that moves by way of its asymmetry, possible? The object that is not a subject has resources that Adorno fails to think. What is the meaning of the object that exceeds any birth as or merger with the subject? Everything toward which black study tends is, for Adorno, impossible. But it's not the possibilities of black subjecthood nearly as much as the historical exhaustion of the possibilities of black objecthood—of blackness as an ongoing appositional underground of the premature—which are now in the gravest danger.

Abstract labor is abstracted in and as the object/commodity. As such, the abstraction is coagulated, congealed, objectified, inanimate, without interiority—which is to say, internal difference. It is, in this respect, a kind of Friedian object, without what he would call "syntax." In other words, as Kazanjian understands it, "The value form, [Marx] repeatedly intimates, produces a universal abstraction that paradoxically has particularized substantiality."[119] The indeterminacy of fluid activity has been solidified into a determinate and inanimate object. Kazanjian would agree with Amiri Baraka that "hunting is not those heads on the wall." Yet Chakrabarty, in a move that, for the moment, more fully aligns him with Marx, recognizes what is made possible by such abstraction, recognizes the necessity of generality or of some general equivalent not only for capitalism but for the analytical theory—and, thus, for the abolition—of capitalism. Chakrabarty's commitment to the general, even to a certain enlightenment notion of universality, leads to a different kind of reading of Marx in which there is some interplay between particularity and universality rather than an eclipse of the former by the latter (which is not to suggest that Kazanjian's work is devoid of such interplay or of interest in such interplay). For Chakrabarty, this means thinking abstract labor as living labor. But if Chakrabarty thinks abstract labor as living labor, this does not mean that he thinks the fullness of the relationship between abstract labor and the object/commodity, which is to say thinking the life or animation of abstract labor even in its figuration or representation as commodity or object. Kazanjian's thinking of this relation is both sharper and less sharp than Chakrabarty's. The congealed, inanimate nature of the object is a fatal representation of abstract labor, according to Kazanjian, operating here at his most inadvertently Heideggerian. For Chakrabarty, the animation of abstract labor is unaffected by its interaction with the object/commodity precisely because the object/commodity remains almost entirely unthought. That which is fatal, in Kazanjian's view, is, in Chakrabarty's formulation, repressed. Chakrabarty rightly diagnoses the need for the idea of generality that is constituted and deformed in the notion of abstract labor. Kazanjian accurately describes how abstract labor is inextricably tied to the object/commodity.

But what about the commodity/object's "double existence"? The object is animate and its animation is (in or of) its substance. One might be particularly interested in its phonic substance, in that substance's irreduciblity and in the implications of that irreducibility for a certain theory of meaning that has come to serve as the foundation for, among other things, precisely the kinds of critical reading of Marx that Kazanjian and Chakrabarty provide. But eventually one tends toward an unlikely tendency, a kind of impossible tangent or convergence, in and as the irreducible nearness and distance of the slave, where abstract labor, labor, body and flesh, or, if you prefer, generality, difference, determinacy, and indeterminacy, or, if you're really out there, earth, sky, gods, and mortals meet. At the fourfolds' triple crossing what is gathered in the notion of the thing as substance is nonconformity to the limits of understanding. Its dislocation is where something and nothing therefore converge, when thinking and its disruption dance at the marriage of meta/physical substance and bare materiality, as nonautonomous passivity resists regulation naturally, historically. What can we make of passage, of the improper event that cuts the subject's staging and his scene? Perhaps this: that appropriation as nearing, dispossession as distancing, are interinanimate; that the universalizing force of appropriation is animated by the very dispossessive power that troubles it; that generality conceals itself—and is at the same time nearest in its concealment—in difference.

The point is that maybe what I have been referring to as object must also pass through some terminal romance with what might be called the (improper and inappropriable) "event of the thing," which is to say, its disappearance.[120] At this point—this atopic gathering, this preservation of strained nonlocality, this inappropriative event or dispossessive force, this simultaneous establishment and dissolution of the proper, of the worker's relation to the proper at its most fundamental, of her own animation, this flight at the heart of the presencing of the present—there's a general statelessness of emergency. One name for the general difference—the ungendered inequivalent; not the national unit but its cut augmentation—is Equiano. What is so named is independent of the vexed question of who it was that bore that name. But either way there were many names, just so you'll know that our general interest is in the unnameable and just so you'll know that, just the same, there is and must be a hymn to the name that is above and below every name.

This is all to say, as has been said many times before, that slavery is more than just the constitutive outside of bourgeois capitalism and bourgeois subjection. The general difference is an anarchically performative principle of dis/possession. The animation of the object, which is inseparable in slavery from the animation of labor, is a dis/possessive force. Here's where the genuine greatness of all the generative differences that we call Marx begins to emerge even if as a kind of sensual deficit. This is to say that Marx offers us a profound analysis of the force and role of dis/possession in the provenance—indeed, as the very historicity—of capitalism. This is what Chakrabarty and Kazanjian both read in "The Chapter on Capital" in the *Grundrisse*. Marx discusses this dis/possessive force in terms of its effect on the worker, on the history of a set of relations of ownership, mediated by the community, between the individual worker and nature (most often figured as the land, the earth, "the natural condition of production," which is, in turn, related to by the worker as "his own inorganic being; the workshop of his forces, the domain of his will"), the individual worker and the instruments of labor, the individual worker and the necessaries of life.[121] The dissolution of these relations is a necessary precondition of capitalism. But to what is Marx blind? The relationship between the dis/possession of the worker (which is to say the emergence of the capitalist as the one who appropriates the labor power of the laborer) and the dis/possessive force of the worker. But this is, of course, false. Rather, one should say that Marx produces this relation without discovering it; that a certain presence of dis/possessive force is unleashed when ownership is figured as a relation to nature and to instruments. The proprietor is only in his (relation to his) "inorganic being" (his being's extension, the exterior manifestation of that being that will come to constitute, among other things, an instrument of reflection whether it be nature, wife, or bondsman); the proprietor is only in his (relation to his) instruments, which are, again, always instruments of reflection. This bespeaks the obvious intensity of the relation between the proprietor's workshop of forces or domain of will and the instruments through which those forces or that will are exercised. Nature and instrument converge in the figure of the slave. This is all to say that capitalism depends on the eclipse, or liquefaction, of proprietorship even as it demands the reemergence or, better yet, the transfer of the very forms that proprietorship takes. Moreover, slavery is all bound up with the construction of abstract labor, thus the construction of general equivalence, thus the construction of the liberal citizen-subject or national unit. Kazanjian understands this declension and rigorously explains it, always in light of something else that defies explanation. Slavery is also all bound up with the diffusion of these elements, which Marx can't hear but which he foresees. The diffusion of the proper, the uncongealed particularity of slavery, is (phonic) substance's generality. This uncongealment is what we study—the forceful flesh, as Spillers and Alexander Weheliye show, of her invention.[122] That which is understood as merely congealed must be rightly misunderstood as animated, not so much self-performed or self-represented, but by some richly internally differentiated and externally transverse black and social operation performed, out of self and representation).

If slavery is freedom's in/organic being, then how does this impact a Marxian politics dependent upon simultaneously substantial and animate abstraction to theorize capitalism and its demise? Here's how: Slavery is capitalism's in/organic being, too (its anarchic and anarchronic teleological principle, its law of motion, its dimensionality); it is the diffusion of labor and proprietorship, on the one hand, and the diffusion of labor and proprietorship, on the other. Submission of the ownership of labor and labor power to a radically—which is to say immanently and inorganically—dispossessing force is a terrible enjoyment of loss that no politics can survive. Moreover, when freedom is figured as that "workshop of forces" or "domain of will" or zone of equivalence wherein proprietorship is variously exerted over living labor capacity and cut by that capacity-as-animated-substance in acts of objection—wherein labor power is exchanged—then the submission of proprietorship to the force of dispossession is, in fact, the condition of possibility, the improvised manifestation, not only of the freedom that accompanies capitalism but also of the freedom from (the struggle for) freedom. This is something about which Equiano comes to know—a dispossessive force that stands over against standing, like some animated releasement of *gegenstandlichkeit*; not an arrival so much as a secret opening or openness, a surround off to the underside of enlightenment, which Marx and, more generally, philosophy and political economy, can only ever sometimes almost, and almost always only ever murderously and acquisitively, want to discover.

There's an antelegislative gathering of (art)work/object/thing/slave/name/person that is given in the ensemblic, transversal, internally differentiated, autonarrational act. The social ensemble's molten, eruptive fluidity constantly unsettles the calcified imbalances of equivalence and relation. the irruptive (audiovisual) substance of the general equivalent. The naming of the general equivalent intimates a preoccupational dislocation of the place where the theory of value intersects with the theory of the subject and with the theory of the state and its operation such that it can never be reduced to the privileged example of the emptiness of equality or generality. The ensemble of its difference does not negate equality or generality; it is, rather, their fleshly refuge. Uncongealment unconceals with terrible, all but unbearable beauty. Natal occasion, and the inevitable alienation that accompanies it, are not quite what's at stake. Neither birth, nor merger, but explosion. What happens when dark matter and ante-*mater* meet. Revelatory, nonparticulate particularity; magnanimous, magmatic illumination; animated, daimonic ground.[123] We're after a kind of knowledge that moves from the other side of either reason or experience, intelligibility or sensibility; it is irreducible to any originary state of nature but for that predisposition to ensemble that resists the conflictual organization of "our" faculties. Ensemble can here be thought of as an irrationalization of the social that is also an irrationalization of rationalization itself. It is the general and generative misunderstanding that imagination enacts as lawful fugitivity. If Equiano's focus on the incidents and injuries that mar black mercantile subjectivity sometimes obscures the other side of the black commodity's double existence it is also the the vehicle through which the general blur, the generative swarm, comes to into view. In addition to joining Equiano in a kind of displaced and displacing resistance at the intersection of knowledge, language (curse and prayer), and freedom, Uncle Toliver, Mary Prince, and Ellen Butler irrationalize, improvise—we might even say, decolonize—that resistance, precisely in how they propose a slide away from the proposition of encounter, a movement out of the normal exigencies of emergent and contained subjectivity, discovering what Equiano produces. If he is an effect, then they are the theory and practice, of ensemble.

Recall that Equiano's encounter with Captain Doran is structured around a moment of misrecognition that forces the captain to remind Equiano of who he is so that Equiano can play his part in a dialogic moment whose object is the establishment of Doran's own identity. Equiano refuses the terms of that confrontation in the complex moment of what I termed a *declaration of in/dependence*. The dependence at that declaration's heart is, in a sense, deferred. What I'd like briefly to examine is its return. I'd like to think that return in terms of a certain transcendence, one in which Equiano moves from the refusal of an encounter with the lord to the acceptance of an encounter with the Lord. That return takes place during the time of Equiano's religious despair: a time at which he has come to know a certain separation of liberation from salvation; a time at which, it might be said, the strictures of a certain kind of subjectivity born in abjection and objection reemerge, overwhelming the anti- and antesubjectivity of existent apposition that constitutes Equiano's ongoing departure. The moment at which Equiano both prompts and refuses the lord's determination of who he was is overtaken—amid a desperate search for the certain knowledge of salvation that is somehow tied to the loss of intensity that generates and regenerates the knowledge of freedom— by the active search for the Lord's determination of who he was. (This search was urged upon him by a certain Mr. L—d—a clerk of the chapel wherein Equiano attends his first "soul-feast," the site which replaces the ship as the locus of consumption and assimilation—in the following manner: "He then entreated me to beg of God *to shew me what I was and the true state of my soul*."[124] This development carries with it the echo of that illusory absence of terror we came across earlier, one bound up with the slippage, in the traumatized mind of a child, from freedom to heaven ("While I was attending those ladies [the Miss Guerins], their servants told me I could not go to heaven, unless I was baptized. This made me very uneasy; for I had now some faint idea of a future state"), a slippage enabled by a disabling and rupturous instruction ("[The Miss Guerins] often used to teach me to read and took great pains to instruct me in the principles of religion and the knowledge of God") and by the illusion of a virtual assimilation that leads to an inordinate faith in the law which, when proven to be unfounded, turns to a rigid differentiation of faith from law.[125] Yet, at precisely the moment at which one would seem to be sliding inexorably toward the need for a rigorous critique and repudiation of the colonizing force of Western religion's formulation of the subject's provenance-in-abjection, one deferred by the refusal of the lord but fulfilled in the acceptance of the Lord, the paradoxically anarchic principle of improvisational apposition returns—in the voices of Mary Prince and Ellen Butler—to raise again a fundamental question: What's the relation between the knowledge of God (so deeply bound to heaven, the faint idea of a future state) and the knowledge of freedom (another, and one would hope more material, future state)? This question is also prompted by a certain intuition that the teaching of the Misses Guerin joined but did not erase or supersede the knowledge Equiano already had and which Ellen Butler theorizes. That knowledge was always with him and activated, again, an improvisation of that with which he would have been improved.

For Equiano the determination of the Lord and the securing of his future state are equivalent. They are bound to a kind of fundamentalism that returns again and again in abolitionist writing as an appeal to Christians to live up to the principles of their religion as those principles are written. There is, then, a profound textualism embedded in Equiano's search that is manifest in his obsessive reading of the Bible; but this textualism is never disconnected from an impulse to confirm the knowledge that comes from a certain innate endowment—before the ethical, the epistemological, and the ontological—tempered and sharpened by the experience of profound deprivation. At this point we might say that Equiano is given a revelation of a certain already extant knowledge—of freedom or of salvation, one given as the human, the other given by the Lord; one given in birth, the other given in rebirth—though for him liberation and salvation remain problematically differentiated. Therefore, for Equiano, "The word of God was sweet to my taste, yea sweeter than honey and the honey-comb."[126] It is as if the fall of sovereignty from Lord to lord, whose engine is the consumption of black flesh, would be reversed here by way of transubstantiation and the future it allows in sovereignty's recovery. We are still left in need of an off, insovereign thought of sweetness and of the ensemble that generates and is generated by it.

Two passages—the first, Prince, the second, Butler:

After this, I fell ill again with the rheumatism, and was sick a long time; but whether sick or well, I had my work to do. About this time I asked my master and mistress to let me buy my own freedom. With the help of Mr. Burchell, I could have found the means to pay Mr. Wood; for it was agreed that I should afterwards serve Mr. Burchell a while, for the cash he was to advance for me. I was earnest in the request to my owners; but their hearts were hard—too hard to consent. Mrs. Wood was very angry—she grew quite outrageous—she called me a black devil, and asked me who had put freedom into my head. *"To be free is very sweet," I said* [my emphasis]: but she took good care to keep me a slave. I saw her change colour, and I left the room.[127]

Marster neber 'low he slaves to go to chu'ch. Dey hab big holes out in de fiel's dey git down in and pray. Dey done dat way 'cause de white folks didn' want 'em to pray. Dey uster pray for freedom. I dunno how dey larn to pray, 'cause dey warn't no preachers come roun' to teach 'em. I reckon de Lawd jis' mek 'em know how to pray.[128]

"To be free is very sweet." Mary Prince says it twice, it is written for her twice, once in response to the question of how she—illiterate black devil—might possibly have known of freedom and in interruption of her mistress's reverse echo of the logic of the encounter between lord and bondsman that Captain Doran illustrates and Hegel theorizes; the other time as a part of the rhetorical—hear the echo of a certain per*suasion*/sweetness—climax she reaches in telling us that slaves were not happy.[129] Telling *us*, yes, because though we might be with her we also wish to know, and cannot understand, how she could have known freedom in the absence of what we would recognize as the experience of freedom (if we suspend a kind of thinking that moves through what is imagined as a radical questioning of the very idea of experience). And our curiosity is, of course, anomalous given the knowledge we have of freedom that transcends any experience we will have had of it so far: any experience of "personal liberty," any illusion of opportunity, any phantasm of accumulative self-possession, any etiolation of some either liberal or communitarian ethos. She knows she knows something we don't know we know.

The question is of the place of experience, of the projection or improvisation of experience: is knowledge of freedom always knowledge of the experience of freedom even when that knowledge precedes experience? Does double existence, and its double vision of freedom (as freedom from the struggle for freedom), leave lived experience by the wayside? If so, something other than a phenomenology is required in order to know it, something other than a science of immediate experience since this knowledge is highly mediated by deprivation and by mediation itself and by a vast range of other actions directed toward the eradication of deprivation. Perhaps that knowledge is embedded in action toward that which is at once (and never fully) withdrawn and experienced. What this knowledge of freedom requires is an improvisation through the sensible and the intelligible, a working through the idiomatic differences between the modes of analysis which would valorize either over the other.

Indeed, Prince requires something other than a reading and the trace she bears is precisely that nonunitary trait that improvises through race and origin as the condition of the possibility of experience and knowledge, performance and competence, of freedom. This is just as the knowledge she has is something apposed but not opposed to the textual and to the kind of improvisation the textual allows without determining. This something other than reading, this something other than the application of an unirrationalized understanding of reason, this alienative labor, is precisely what is exercised through Equiano in his quest for the knowledge of freedom and of God. And whence comes Uncle Toliver's prayer? Ellen Butler tells us but her telling, her more + less than rational theorizing, her improvisational re-citation, is only in that it is mediated. Indeed, the irrationalization of the resistance is in the disseminative effects of mediation. If so, Equiano's prayers and curses cannot be merely the products of the medicine/poison, bestowal/imposition of the narrative apparatuses of a violent other. And who or what is "de Lawd" to which Butler refers and what, if anything, does "de Lawd" have to do with the Lord? Mary Prince addresses this question by way of the transcendental clue embedded in the displacing effects of her own non-reply which, in being set alongside other iterations of refusal, seems to indicate something general and generative. The point is that in their *work*, Ellen Butler, Uncle Toliver, and Mary Prince evade the opposition we might figure around the imaginary poles of the readable Equiano and the unintelligible and illegible Ben Ali: they valorize neither literate, rational identity nor its destruction; neither curse nor simplistic prayer; neither material experience nor imaginative intellection: rather, they valorize ensemble, transmitted in the trace of whatever it is that one carries through the human: a generative grammar and affect, a knowledge of language and freedom given by and as de Law'd, by and as justice's improvisational presence.

For Chomsky, the fundamental questions concerning knowledge of language assume and require an innate endowment activated in the break (between speech and writing, between inner and outer speech, between silence and sound, between competence and performance, in the interstice that is and engenders rhythm, generated anew and improvised throughout from the strange combination of experience and n[othing]). Knowledge of freedom is also in that break, that hiatus: it's where Prince is—as if given by the mediating and improvisational force of de Law'd when that force is enacted in the improvised, nonexclusionary solicitation of the human. Butler's insight into our knowledge of prayer as a particular linguistic mode is also insight into our knowledge of freedom.

And Uncle Toliver's prayer—uttered in an unknown tongue, given aloud and transmitted through narrative mediation and through a citation and re-citation in the rhythmic interstice where ensemble fell—is a citation (one given under the collective name of the Workers of the Writers' Program of the Works Project Administration in the State of Virginia) that Litwack names, therefore paradoxically showing the mark of an unnameable flowing in his *récit*, his re-citation. But, again, Litwack's is not some predatory erasure but the echo of that already extant loss inherent in intelligibility, translation, and transcription whose presence is and allows the mediational "ethics" of ensemble. (Think of what is lost in the translation from Butler's "dialect" to "standard English": the constitutive cut that separates the Lord and de Law'd and is transformed but retained in the chain of re-citation that marks the writing of oral history.) *Uncle Toliver* is the gain and loss in this recording at the end of the chain of recitations that is history and that here is extended at the end of a chain of narratives, of the kind of narrative wherein knowledge of freedom is given to us and for us. The constellation of these recitations and narratives is where George Orwell's problem (how we know so little given so much evidence) and Plato's problem (how we know so much given so little evidence) intersect.[130] It's where the questions concerning the law of genre, the strange institution called literature (where the law is lifted, where everything can be said) and the peculiar institution called slavery (where nothing could be said as a matter of a law broken and reconstituted in the breaking and reconstitution of the law of genre, and the law of the law of genre, and their intersection) converge.

"One story told in Nansemond County concerns Uncle Toliver, who had the indiscretion to pray aloud. When rumor reached the great house that he had been praying for the Yankees, Tom and Henry, sons of the master, told the aged slave to kneel in the barnyard and pray for the Confederates. Uncle Toliver prayed as loud as he could for a Yankee victory. All day long they kept him there, taking turns in lashing him, but he would not give in. At last he collapsed, still praying, his voice a mumbled jargon. The only word that could be distinguished was *Yankee*. Sometime that night, while they were still lashing him, Uncle Toliver died."[131] It is as if a jurisgenerative prayer meeting awaits our attendance. It's on the other side of the tracks, and of subjective tracking. There is no global positioning and so call and response resist normative staging. The Law'd is called and the message is off. The lord, alerted but unaddressed, goes there either to murder or to disappear. But they are praying to us. When we act like we can hear difference in common we are the Law'd: mantic, monastic, jurisgenerative study of the generally earthy underside of our double existence.

So we pause at the recitation of lost names and mumbled jargon where the rest of Uncle Toliver's utterance remains unheard. In the space that jargon opens (a space off to the side or out-from-the-outside; an appositional spacing or displacement of the encounter in the interest of a complex presence that remains to be activated; a space not determined by the zero encounter that ruptures the subject or the nostalgic return to another subject before the encounter; a space where Uncle Toliver speaks through Tom and Henry— the sons of the master—and through the Workers of the Writers' Project of the Works Project Administration of the State of Virginia and through Leon Litwak to us: piercing and dispossessing disabling and enabling mediation and meditation), the rest is what is left for us to say, the rest is what is left for us to do, in the broad and various echoes of that utterance, our attunement to which assures us that we know all we need to know about freedom.

chapter 2

Gestural Critique of Judgment

Both Stephen Jay Gould and Louis Menand have discussed eminent biologist Louis Agassiz's revulsion at the bodies, especially the hands, of the black men who served him at a Philadelphia hotel during his first visit to the United States.[1] Agassiz's response to the waiters was, among other things, an aesthetic one and, if it is not too much to consider the impact of this experience on certain aspects of Agassiz's scientific achievements, that response might lead one to understand blackness as the disorder to which the ordering concept of race—with all its correspondences—(cor)responds in Agassiz's thought. Agassiz's work is crucial to the development of a "logic of white supremacy" that film critic Linda Williams feels compelled to enter for the sake of the analysis of that logic she offers in *Playing the Race Card*, her recent book on the politics and aesthetics of American racial melodrama in the age of the (theatrical as well as cinematic) moving picture.[2] Entrance into white supremacist logic is entrance into its aesthetics as well, and it's not surprising that Williams's work is instantiated by a primal scene not structurally unlike Agassiz's inaugural encounter with black men. Both Agassiz and Williams are disturbed and spurred to thinking and writing by black hands moving in gestures of service or defiance that, either way, body forth the disorderly intentionality of a person that white supremacist logic and aesthetics apprehends and comprehends as a thing, which is to say, as devoid of intentionality. More specifically, part of what compels Williams to examine the history of racial melodrama is that a black male juror in the O. J. Simpson criminal trial raised his fist—in relief and/or triumph and/or thanks—when the jury was dismissed upon the reading of the verdict. As if the gesture were evident of something that is, in turn, so self-evident as not to require either mention or elucidation, as if its presumed bad taste were directly linked to a failure, or even absence, of moral reasoning, Williams recites but does not comment on it. I am preparing myself to think that gesture, its improvisation through the opposition of action and event, by way of a refusal of the logic and aesthetics of white supremacy. I want to consider that gesture—and, for that matter, would like to open the path toward a consideration of the seemingly servile gestures of the men waiting on Agassiz—as one that embodies such a refusal and will, moreover, argue that such moments of disorder constitute a general, gestural critique of judgment that animates black art, black politics, and their relation to the law as well as to what Kant calls the "lawless freedom" of the imagination. I hope, finally, to offer an extension of this gestural critique of judgment as alternative to the illogic of white supremacy and, more particularly, to the neopragmatist political anti-aesthetics that bears that illogic's trace—that could be said never to have left the illogic that it claims to enter—even as it seeks to analyze, if not quite disavow, it.

The alpha and omega of *Playing the Race Card* is the verdict handed down in the Simpson trial, a verdict whose shadow is the fist that is raised after the verdict is read. The following passages could be called the structural poles of Williams's work:

> Like many people who watched the October 3, 1995, verdict in the trial of O. J. Simpson, I felt deeply implicated in its drama. The verdict in what some would call "the trial of the century," viewed by more Americans than any other event in the history of television, resonated profoundly with the earlier verdict in the trial of the police accused in the beating of Rodney King. And that verdict, in turn, resonated with a long history of racial villains and victims. This book is my attempt to understand how that long history came to inform these trials. Sometime between the verdict in the police beating of Rodney King on April 29, 1992—a verdict that sparked a major race riot—and the 1995 verdict in the Simpson trial—a verdict that sparked unprecedented white resentment—I realized that a book I had been writing on the American melodramatic imagination as played out in "moving pictures" would have to become a book about black and white racial melodrama. . . . It would be necessary to study a set of racially resonant music and pictures that have moved the American public to feel sympathy for racially beset victims and hate for racially motivated villains across a wide range of mass media.

> Working backward from my confused and outraged response to the verdict in the O. J. Simpson trial, I have sought to understand

the reasons for my own raced and gendered resentment—not to vindi-
cate it, but to better understand the deep-seated racial and sexual fantasies that fuel it . . . I began to see that the emotionally charged "moral
legibility" that we shall see to be so crucial to the mode of melodrama
is intrinsically linked to a "racial legibility" that habitually sees a Manichean good or evil in the visual "fact" of race itself—whether it is the
dark male victim of white abuse or the dark villain with designs upon
the innocent white woman. This genealogy has enabled me to take a
longer and deeper look at the psychic investments in these archaic, yet
ever-modernizing forms of racial victimization and vilification.[3]

It is a peculiarity of the form of a melodramatic trial that the exciting
action of a chase or rescue can never be, as in conventional melodrama, the
climax of the story. In place of the ritual suspense of chase, escape, or rescue, a trial provides an entirely different ritual of suspense: the waiting for,
and the reading of, the verdict. Verdict readings take place in courtrooms
where verbal displays of approval or disapproval are taboo. All the more
reason, then, for the melodramatic text of muteness to take over as defendants, defendants' families, defense attorneys, and prosecutors register
mutely eloquent postures of relief and vindication or sorrow and outrage.
These exaggerated gestures are almost pure moments of theatrical melodrama, functioning much like the tableaux of the nineteenth-century stage.
Because the verdict in the Rodney King case took the public by surprise, its
reading did not itself register as a memorable iconic moment, though its
aftermath of rage certainly did. The not-guilty verdict in the Simpson case,
however, partly because it was viewed as caught up in the melodrama of the
previous "King" verdict, was the most viewed moment of television in all the
medium's history. Every detail of the response to the defendant and his defense team was remembered and analyzed, since, true to form, the camera
remained trained on Simpson. Viewers could thus observe the way Simpson
exhaled and half smiled, the way Johnny Cochran, standing behind him,
first slapped his shoulder and then rested the side of his head against it; the
way, in another view, Kim Goldman, sister of Ron Goldman, let out a howl
of pain, and finally, in a gesture of "raced demeanor" that was not seen by
the television camera but was much commented on by the media, the way
one black juror, upon exiting the courtroom, raised his fist in what some
interpreted as a black power salute and others saw simply as the pleasure of
being set free.[4]

Williams's work is animated by the notion, implicit in these passages but made explicit at the outset, that blacks have now "taken on the full mantle of citizenship."[5] But the specter of an already existing, generally equivalent citizenship and subjecthood into which blacks have been grandfathered is itself haunted by the realization, which appears periodically in Williams's text, that this prior formation has yet to have been achieved and is persistently deferred by structures of mind and experience that continually place such abstractions on trial. If one can now be said retroactively to have always been included in the abstraction from which one's actual ordinary life excludes one and of which the transgenerational history of one's ordinary life constitutes a vicious critique even as one's exclusion from it also constitutes it, then a bind ensues, wherein the quickening power of Williams's text is subject to a periodic halting; it moves in fits and starts, overlooking and overrunning the barriers that punctuate its path. The rhythm of Williams's project is further troubled by its commitment to the disqualification of appeals to the critical-historical structure of blackness—to blackness as a critical-historical project—that might ground some questioning of her ascriptions of citizenship. According to Williams, any such appeal amounts to a kind of wallowing in injury that is antithetical to (the possibility of) critique as the foundation for new political dispositions. The success of Williams's arguments depends on her ability to traverse an untraversable temporal gap. The neurotic oscillation between an abstract citizenship that will have always existed and the fact that it has never and does not now actually exist constitutes a bridge whose very structure is inevitable collapse. The necessary and anticipatory compensation for this planned structural failure is the assumption that this absence of citizenship doesn't really matter anyway, or ought not. This step, this time warp, is the work's choreographic heart and beat, its placement and spacing within the conceptual and historiographical rhythm that drives and marks the official American intellectual idiom. This is borne out by history and by a kind of critical-affective knowledge that cannot be dismissed as the irrational, paranoid effect of remembered trauma however fleshly, gestural, guttural, or (extra-)musically paradiscursive it might be. To think (and to think *from*) this affect as the critical improvisation of a certain aesthetico-juridical reason that sometimes gets called melodrama and which is nowadays in ill repute would be to perform the constitutive outside of Williams's project. In moving from the fact that Williams's book just doesn't feel right to me, while operating within an intellectual tradition (a fugitive, black and sentimental [anti- and ante-]Kantian education that is attuned, against the grain of some of its own foundations, to life's constant escape) that dictates that I honor such a feeling as an occasion for—as not but nothing other than a mode of—thinking, I hope to offer some insight into the nature of blackness as a radical, abolitionist, critical-historical project that must have seemed unavailable to Williams even as it is that to which she could be said semiconsciously to respond.

I realize that my comments only make sense within the theorization of the transgenerational transmission of transgenerational injury and its relation to the convergence of identity, critique, and the possibilities and practically always already existent realities of abolition and communism. This is about way more than the imagined memory of somebody else's pain. It concerns, rather, what it is to be embedded in a structure/stricture for which such pain is constitutive but which is also productive of new instances, new recordings. *Playing the Race Card* has an affect disorder that could be called (neo-) pragmatism insofar as it is attributable to the white supremacist logic that its author claims to have been necessary for its composition. It's not just the book's continual betrayal of its own origins in an identity whose disingenuous self-declaration takes the form of a denial of its irreducible and constitutive mark, the injury done by a black man's gestural irruption; it is, rather, a kind of affect difference that produces deleterious pseudotheoretical and anticritical effects. Is this affect difference a racial difference? Williams's work is prompted by a profound feeling that sanctions her writing about certain stuff that she doesn't feel, and the presumption is that this secondary lack of feeling is, in fact, a critical advantage that, by the way, compensates for her project's embarrassing emotional impetus. The presumption might also be that she has a kind of fundamental inability to feel black and white melodrama like I do, for instance, and that this is, again, an advantage. I would object not only to the notion that this is an advantage but also to any implication that she couldn't have felt it (like I do). And yet this affect-difference *is* a racial difference (which is to say it emerges as the condition of possibility of some insight into the actual nature of racial difference). What if, instead of (or even in addition to) entering into the logic of white supremacy, Williams had entered into the logic of black radicalism, of what Cedric Robinson complicatedly and complicatingly calls "black Marxism," of what I am attempting to understand under the rubric of blackness-as-abolitionism?[6] This entry would mean presuming that there is such a logic, but it would also mean the continual renewal of the task of rethinking the very idea of logic in its relation to feeling, affect, injury; it would mean, in short, the critical extension of the project of critical philosophy and the critique of judgment that simultaneously completes and reopens that project. This means, in turn, arguing with a cunning self-consumption of reason that should in no way be accepted as standard. And if that argument is tied to or made possible by pain, so what? It's not reducible to pain, requires no unbreakable allegiance to pain and shows, finally, how wrong it is to relegate black stuff to the iconic bad example of such debilitating (co-)dependence. On the other hand, Williams's work clearly emerges from a certain feeling, a certain discomfort, a certain injury. What causes this injury? An event; an object; a gesture that must be made intelligible; the unruliness of blackness-as-abolitionism to which she has access but which she disavows in the name of an instrumental rationality which, when it runs amok, blatantly assumes and aggressively declines to think its own grounds. These remarks (against neopragmatism and for Neo) are meant to contribute to the preface to a discussion in which we actually think and talk about the consequences of pragmatism.

The initial premise that attends Williams's conceptual apparatus is this: no reasonable person committed to a mode of citizenship or personhood based on the abstract universality of reason could have found Simpson not guilty. That he was found so by some black people who constituted the majority of the jury, that some black people celebrated the fact that he was found so, indicates something like the *general* descent of black people into the irrationalism of racial melodrama—itself an expression of the illogic of white supremacy—and the internal, structural, *ahistorical* strife that, according to Williams, obtains there between competing identities forged in injury. Therefore, Williams's goal in *Playing the Race Card* was

> neither . . . to rehabilitate the mode of melodrama nor to weigh in on one side or the other of the "black and white" resentments about race. Rather I consider it sufficient to recognize melodrama's almost incalculable influence on American attitudes toward race and to trace the genealogies of an influence that, because it is too obvious or because it is too embarrassing, has been relatively ignored. The study of melodrama has the potential to explain why it is that in a democracy ruled by rights, we do not gain the moral upper hand by saying simply that rights have been infringed. We say, instead, much more powerfully: "I have been victimized; I have suffered, therefore give me my rights." To understand racial melodrama is to see why repeated calls for more accurate, or more "realistic," representations of racially marked characters

are powerless to overturn deeply embedded racial stereotypes that seem hopelessly outmoded yet live on in the culture. Until we understand the melodramatic imagination that these stereotypes serve, and the historical dynamic of its popular cycles, we will never grasp why we are compelled to feel for the raced and gendered sufferings of some and to hate the raced and gendered villainy of others.[7]

Her idea of what is sufficient is, to my mind, insufficient because I recognize that I cannot choose not to weigh in on one side or the other. However, despite the fact that I perceive that I have no choice, I make a preferential option for blackness-as-abolitionism. Williams has a choice and, in failing to make it, in refusing to see that she has no choice but to make a choice, she chooses whiteness-as-anti-abolitionism, which is to say, white supremacy and its (il)logic. The structure of equivalence and normative asymmetry are the interinanimate flipsides of white supremacist logic that Williams doesn't have to enter but which she definitely ought to try to leave. By normative asymmetry I mean an ultimately anti-aesthetic refusal of the disorderly; a general distaste for the ruptural and resistant incidence of sound and movement that is manifest all throughout the book at the level of its practical readings. This is to say that the book is disrupted by the very gestures whose occasion prompts the modes of reading—the melodramatic imagination—that she wishes to transcend but which she can address only by involuntarily emulating. *Playing the Race Card* is driven by a kind of normative commitment to normative surface, to the radical absence or absenting of irruptive, ruptural depth and darkness in the interest of an already existing political and aesthetic reality that comes immediately to light. Whatever emerges, de profundis, is a thing of darkness to be disavowed rather than acknowledged. Williams's work is meant to regulate the morally occult and the desire for the morally occult that animates melodrama. This regulative function places victimization and vilification as poles in a discursive game. This means that a pseudohistorical fiction of equivalence is offered and given over to the service of the normative asymmetry that governs U.S. race relations in the form of political, legal, and aesthetic judgments against irruptive resistances of things which have been, given over to and by a range of subjects in the process of self-making. Therefore, villainy and suffering are equivalent within the more general illusion of a field of black-and-white equivalency that turns out to structure and allow the logic of white supremacy in its contemporary guise. And, since the villainy of white supremacy is by definition countered only by the victimhood of black suffering, there really can be no logic or aesthetic of black resistance in Williams's formulation. Indeed, this presumed absence structures *Playing the Race Card*.

Of course, the supposedly methodologically warranted entrance into white supremacy presumes that Williams had not been embedded in that logic all along. I would argue, however, that her reaction to the Simpson verdict and, in particular, to the arm-raising gesture of the juror, is a function of an enduring and more than merely methodological inhabitation of that logic. She moves toward something on the order of a general pardon, an autoconferred absolution, which moves, in turn, by way of the erasure of whatever historical detail that troubles the delicate structure of equivalence. Every disorderly gesture takes on the status of the morally occult even though it is precisely such a structure that Williams would eschew in the name of a certain authentically modernized democratic reason, a kind of Rortyesque "postmodernist bourgeois liberalism" that moves through and against the "merely cultural" (even as it grounds itself in the supposed idiomatic specificity, the state-sanctioned ethnocentrism of a given national cultural logic) in the interest of making something that will misleadingly be called "new law."[8] Williams advocates the bare assertion of rights against principle and, moreover, against that complex interplay of the beautiful and the moral (the unbeautiful and the immoral) of whose contours Kant believed he had achieved an understanding that might serve a regulatory function. Williams also aspires to a regulatory function to be achieved by way of the understanding, an eclipse of melodrama in its connection to the very idea of a moral upper hand, in the interest of pragmatist technique. For Williams, the melodramatic imagination, in its lawless freedom, in its resistant disorderliness, in the disruptive and irruptive gesturality that is exemplified and, embodied by a raised black fist, produces nothing but nonsense. Like Kant, she calls for its wings to be clipped; like Kant she understands its flights to be performances of a difference that is always at least racial; but unlike Kant, as I hope to begin to show below, she has no sense of the simultaneously constitutive and deconstitutive force of the melodramatic imagination for the very regulative faculty she hopes to initialize.

It is my contention, then, that Williams moves within a prominent mode of misreading, one whose initial target is blackness and which moves aggressively against everything that blackness has come to represent, particularly the ongoing possibility of a general, often gestural refusal that I have been trying to think under the rubric of abolitionism. That misreading reduces identities forged in resistance to, in refusal of, injury to identities forged *in* injury; that misreading denies the necessity of a critical encounter with the injury done to peoples and to principles and fails to recognize that the formation of resistant identities moves by way of a critical resistance to normative and univocal modes and understandings of identity. Here she invokes some theoretical precursors:

> To be a visible victim in black and white racial melodrama is, as we have seen, to be worthy of citizenship. As feminist theorists Lauren Berlant, Wendy Brown, and Robyn Wiegman have all shown, the minoritized body is caught up in a rhetoric of injury in which the quest for liberation often translates to an opportunity to show one's wounds. In the case of *The People v. Orenthal James Simpson*, however, the wounds of the white woman were decisively trumped by the wounds of Rodney King and the long, shameful history of injustice toward black men. If, as Shoshana Felman puts it, the history of the failure of justice in the beating of Rodney King haunted the O. J. Simpson trial and made it impossible for the jury to see with any degree of empathy the injury of the white woman, then we need to understand what it means that it was African-American women jurors who rendered this verdict. For this was a group whose own wounds have been increasingly erased from the melodrama of black and white. It is regrettable, therefore, but not too surprising, that the verdict in the Simpson trial represented the revenge of black women on what they perceived to be white women's privileged occupation of the role of victim. Indeed, the failure of this jury to find Simpson guilty may have had much more to do with resentment toward Nicole Brown than with paranoia about racist police planting evidence.[9]

The black woman jurors show their wounds in this verdict, thereby declaring themselves worthy, within the protocols of white supremacy, of a citizenship that still remains to be conferred, but thereby proving themselves unworthy, according to Williams's critique of racial melodrama, of that very citizenship. Their participation on the jury is another moment in the history of an interminable and unpassable test; Williams is the professor. Williams thinks she knows what black women think, what the black women on the jury were thinking, in the unlikely event of their having entered the courtroom which is, her classroom, though this is an inaccurate formulation since she doesn't actually think that they were thinking. Rather, the black women on the jury, according to Williams, are simply and reflexively moving, in the bare, discursive ground figured in the black male juror's gesture. They move in a reflex outside of intentionality, a reflex prompted by black folks' irrational embeddedness in "the rigid binary of victimization by race and gender."[10] Attempts to defend the verdict as reasonable—to consider, for instance, the massive amount of official and underground evidence that the Los Angeles Police Department does, in fact, plant evidence in ways that are determined by racial difference—are fruitless, according to Williams. The verdict is an effect, rather, of blackness-*as*-irrationality, an irrationality not genetically determined but the effect, rather, of ill-formed identities and their subsequent historically determined politics. The vote to acquit was a reflex, not a reflective decision; it was, moreover, a venal attempt at revenge. (Deeper still the revenge will have been for white women's occupation of the privileged status of victim rather than for white women's culpability in a history of victimization. Still deeper, even if revenge could somehow be ruled out as the primary motivation behind the verdict, any taking into account of not only the specific police malfeasance, incompetence, and deviance from procedure in the Simpson case, but also of the regime of quotidian brutality—racially motivated and otherwise—that animates Los Angeles Police Department history as well as the entire history of criminal law's application to black life in the United States, is dismissed as paranoia). Again, history is invoked by Williams only to dismiss, erase, or reduce it to its irreducible discursivity. According to Williams, there can be no excuse for "a verdict grounded in emotion and racial storytelling," which is that to which the history of antiblack racism and the resistance to that racism has been reduced. Instead, that verdict— the product of identities forged in injury, the product of an identity politics trapped in history, where history is now mere "racial storytelling" and its attendant, irrational emotion—and its logic must now be understood within and as "the rhetoric of black and white melodrama."[11] Williams thereby enacts the forgetting of the history of injury that she calls for; such forgetting is a major analytic tool for her. Even more problematically, she enacts a mischaracterization of black resistance that is equivalent to forgetting or historical erasure. While others find it possible to discern resistance not only in a range of black performances that will have never shown up for Williams but also in the highly constrained and constraining selection of performances by blacks that she chooses to examine, Williams's critical vision is limited to what she sees as moralistic assimilation into the Manichean logic of racial melodrama. Meanwhile, we are left to consider that the verdict, and the gesture that could be said to represent it, might be best understood as a refusal of a citizenship and an accompanying subjectivity by those to whom these are perennially refused.

Another crucial precursor of Williams is Peter Brooks, whose book, *The Melodramatic Imagination*, upon its initial publication nearly thirty years ago, laid the foundations for the contemporary study of melodrama, foundations with which Williams, among a host of other white feminist critics, hopes critically to contend.[12] Brooks opens his text with a brief reading of the opening of Balzac's *La peau de chargrin*. It is a passage, according to Brooks, "where the description of a gesture and the interpretive efforts that it prompts indicates how we should read Balzac, how he locates and creates his drama, and, more generally, how the melodramatic imagination conceives its representations." That gesture occurs "when Raphaël de Valentin enters a gambling house to play roulette with his last franc, [and] a shadowy figure crouched behind a counter rises up to ask for the young man's hat." Brooks observes, "The gesture of surrendering one's hat forthwith elicits a series of questions from the narrator."[13] It is important, though I can't do much more than mention it here, that Brooks focuses on the surrender of the hat rather than the gesture or movement of a kind of ominous service that prompts that surrender, a choice that has implications for the tradition of veiled, vexed resistance-in-service that I mentioned earlier in relation to Agassiz. I would point out, instead, that the narrator's questions to which Brooks refers include one that indexes a racial discourse on criminality that moves from Samuel George Morton, whose fanciful comparative measurements of black and white cranial capacity were models for Agassiz's fantasmatic racial empiricism, to Cesare Lombroso's speculative taxonomies of the delinquent, and, ultimately, to James Q. Wilson and Richard Herrnstein's vulgar but influential decrees on the relation between "crime and human nature."[14] Brooks's opening invocation of Balzac's opening allows us to consider how melodrama is bound up not only with pseudoscientific racial theories of criminality but also with a certain underground, bohemian aesthetic lawlessness and its racial shadow. Brooks shows how Balzac might be said to have entered into that logic of lawlessness—determined and disturbed by the troubling, troubled the surface of things—whose workings sanction another kind of investigation into the interplay of criminality, human nature, and (a certain reduction of racial difference to) blackness-as-abolitionism. Brooks meta-melodramatically describes and analyzes Balzac's narration of and narrative slumming in the zone of the moral occult, of Fanonian occult instability, in order to recover or discover the sacred. But now that contemporary cultural theory is so committed to the severe and strident dismissal of the transcendental, particularly in the vexed, ugly beauty of its violent romance with blackness, it becomes necessary to chart, by way of Brooks and in sober awareness of the racial and sexual chauvinism that he fails critically to attend in his own work, the movement from Balzac's entrance into the logic of the underground to Williams's entrance into the logic of white supremacy. White supremacy, it turns out, is a kind of home that can be inhabited even by those who think they are calling the very idea of home, let alone that particular home, into question; on the other hand, the *metoikoi*, the outsiders, the eternal internal aliens, the impossible domestics, the wanderers, the hard laborers, the servants, the sick, the injured, the denizens, the noncitizens, the prisoners, the ones who move in shadow, under a death sentence, the necessarily fugitive slaves and their fugitive descendants, the commodities and the traces of the commodity, the things, stay—but do not live—there.

Brooks helps illuminate the opposing directions of melodrama's "radiation": between the materiality of acting out and motionless seeing; between regulative understanding and sentimentality; between non-sense and the ubiquity of sense; between fantasy and truth; between "magnificent lurid document and the baseless fabric of a vision"; between the thing and its ennobling representation.[15] This structure of complication is exacerbated by the fact that the loss of the sacred, of the wholly Other, must be thought in its historic relation to the discovery of the wholly Other—the anthropological war of which Derrida speaks, whose literary production is foundational to the discourse of racial difference. The black apparatus stands in for the newly lost, newly discovered, wholly Other of Euro-modernity. Williams says melodrama is an attempt to get back to what feels like the beginning. The black apparatus, as the very figure of the ontogenic and phylogenic primitive, can work for that, too, though like any figure (or more like any figure than any other figure), it cuts what it makes possible. This invention of and as loss is an all-purpose fantasy given in the empirical register. The fantasy might have been of a child being beaten and is linked, in Freud, to what Williams understands to have been a prototypical melodramatic text—*Uncle Tom's Cabin*—that, according to Brooks, is anticipated in Denis Diderot's critical encounter with Samuel Richardson, the writer "who spirits away the mighty phantom which guards the entrance to the cavern [so that] the hideous blackamoor which it masks stands revealed."[16] That hideous blackamoor is, according to Brooks, "hidden in our motives and desires."[17] The I, in this case, is wholly Other, determined by the unavoidably irruptive and repetitive occasion of a gothic-pastoral entrance into a scene that facilitates the encounter with, and discovery/recovery of, the degraded figure, the thing of darkness, the black apparatus that Euro-modernity (from Diderot to Williams) will now claim as its own in preparation for the necessary disavowal. You could call this disavowal, as it is anticipated in Diderot's preparation for it, a preview of antiabolitionism which will have made pragmatism a transatlantic phenomenon, one whose Europeanness is always showing, much to the chagrin of the American Ideologists.

In the wake of Henry James, Brooks speaks of melodrama as a movement of or within "general arrest and interruption" that could be said both to indicate and to become a "passageway."[18] He speaks of melodrama in relation to what James, in his description of his own representation of Isabel Archer's "meditative vigil" on or, next to Gilbert Osmond, indexes as a moment of internal theater that is at once interpretive and inventive. That vigil is described as a scene of "motionlessly seeing," and such seeing is offered to us as both an attitude toward the meaning embedded in gesture and as a gesture itself.[19] This interinanimation of rupture and flow, of stillness and motion, could be understood as both montagic and atonal, a force that animates the sounding, moving picture in nineteenth-century popular culture that is Williams's object of study. It's the violence of the encounter between arrest and passage that is of interest here. Such violence seems to admit of no basis for a connection borne of disconnection, in the absence of a bridge, in the exclusion of the middle. Brooks says that the logic of melodrama is the logic of the excluded middle.[20] What if we consider blackness, or, if you will, the black apparatus, as that logic's essential structure and interior negation? Blackness is the nonexcluded middle with a right to (refuse) philosophy. This unruly, performing, gestural, postinaugural apparatus of the logic of modernity moves in the form of a kind of hope and a kind of reassurance. This means that Americans ought not be concerned that, according to Williams, "melodrama might be the aesthetic form to which they most deeply respond."[21] Moreover, it means that it is necessary to consider what's at stake in the moment when Williams exhibits the "good taste" to decline reading a gesture. The answer lies partly in what is presented as an ineluctable drive toward a general debunking of the aesthetic, particularly with regard to the link between morality and beauty. Beauty is not matter for thinking in *Playing the Race Card*, while morality is so only insofar as thought is manifest as its disavowal. Despite the fact that in the latter stages of her argument

Williams acknowledges the impossibility of getting past or getting out of melodrama, her work always seems to move in the spirit of such transcendence and in the interest, more specifically, of avoiding what appears to be melodrama's preferential option for the powerless. I'm interested in the character of a preferential option for not making a preferential option as well as in such an option's implications. Is it too much to say that Williams seeks to extend the cool analytics of antiabolitionism that Louis Menand considers in *The Metaphysical Club*, in just such an impossibly nonpreferential manner, as the Holmesian turn into pragmatism? Is there a relation between "the logic of white supremacy" and pragmatism as the movement toward a neutral submission to the status quo that attends the disavowal of a kind of fervor that is aligned with (feminized, sentimental) blackness and the critiques (of property, of the proper, of judgment) that it embodies as cause and as a cause? The cultural critical implications of this question are bound up with the necessary assertion of a difference between melodrama as an anti- and meta-melodramatic analytic of always already racialized disorder and melodrama as a mimetic preference for such disorder—for such escape—in its racialization. Williams's work is animated by a kind of rage for order that is, in the end, an anti-aesthetic commitment to the fundamental categories of normative aesthetics. Her work leads to this question: What is the relation between beauty, morality, and the disorder that attends the escape of, or into, new political and aesthetic autonomies? The path to that question goes through another: What is antiabolitionism?

Antiabolitionism is a certain demurral with regard to the effects of and struggle for freedom (as the lawless freedom of the imagination and every materiality that makes such freedom possible and every materiality that such freedom makes possible). Slavery and mass incarceration, in their historical continuity with one another, are the material fields within which this problematic emerges, but the problematic is irreducible to those fields, is not but nothing other than determined by them. To be antiabolitionist is not to be proslavery. It is, however, to exhibit a kind of preservative concern for the disruption of the structures, effects, and affects that accrue to the system of slavery; it is to be nervous about—and moreover to attempt to discipline and contain—the forces that fugitivity unleashes. White supremacist intellectual culture in America is committed to the regulation of disorder, the capture of the fugitive. Its methodological character is the ongoing and aggressive deployment of an instrumentalist disposition (i.e., a tendency to reduce everything to the status of mere instrument while failing adequately, ruthlessly, critically to consider the very idea of the mere instrument and, thereafter, to think [the thinking] instrument). Neopragmatism—the formation that white supremacist intellectualism either openly avows or surreptitiously apposes—is, in its most elemental forms and aims, regulatory intellectual aggression turned toward the black *dispositif* in its irreducible fugitivity. In the particular manifestation that Williams exemplifies, neopragmatism reduces blackness-as-abolitionism to the status of the bad example. Whether as constantly perceived threat to the internal order of liberal democracy or as naive betrayal of the critique of liberal democracy, the aesthetic, political, and philosophical differences that blackness marks must endure this pathologizing impulse and are often constrained to contest it. I'm interested in the tradition of such contest even as I attempt to break the containment that it confirms. This is to say that I'm interested in isolating and enacting a kind of anti-instrumentalism at the heart of the black radical tradition: one that continually, and at first glance paradoxically, manifests itself through enactments of blackness as instrument and apparatus in melodramatic irruption.

In his analysis of the life and work of Oliver Wendell Holmes in *The Metaphysical Club*, Menand powerfully gestures toward the notion that pragmatism's foundational idea, "the belief that ideas should never become ideologies," is most properly understood as antiabolitionism (or as grounded in the occasion of the abolitionist problematic and abolitionist commitment).[22] On an earlier, but parallel, track, Daniel Bell's *The End of Ideology* leaves one with the conclusion that the end of which he speaks is most properly understood as anticommunism or, at least, the emerging triumph of anticommunist, capitalist, liberal democracy—a structure of power whose resistant occasion is the long trajectory of communist insurgence and possibility of which the various Marxist traditions are a part.[23] It is tempting to make the claim that the convergence of antiabolitionism and anticommunism is the end of the trajectory that stretches from pragmatism to neopragmatism (to neoconservatism and its interinanimation with neoliberalism) but perhaps this is too simple. It is probably better to consider, instead, the necessary commerce between antiabolitionism and anticommunism—and its accompaniment by an ongoing reactive insurgency against the common underground and outskirts of the city, the *polis*, the radical, spatiopopular constitution of politics—that is embedded in the emergence and development of the American Ideology and that is enacted by the ones who, again, stay, but do not live, there.

Holmes, like many of those figures in the North who tended toward antiabolitionism, came over the course of his career to associate abolitionism's ardency with a kind of aural and oratorical derangement, wherein normative, rational speech moves in supposed opposition to that speech which is so excited or excitable that it crosses a boundary and enters the realms of animality, criminality, and the inhuman as preface to its final devolution to the status of the theatrical, the melodramatic, the merely gestural. Such degraded speech is a kind of paraverbal analog to stealing oneself, to stealing away, something Holmes felt that a man was not born to do.[24] This is to say that the inhumanity of abolitionism's interinanimation of gesture and speech moves not only in the name and in the interest of those who are supposed to be inhuman (or not quite human or not but nothing other than human) but also in and as inhuman form (or the inhuman or prehuman absence of form), as if speaking for the slave places, or inscribes one in the "inhuman" condition of the slave who moves in the degradation of speech, a condition which American law and custom had long since constructed as coterminous with blackness by the time of the Civil War, which, Menand argues, is pragmatism's crucible. Therefore, one way to think of blackness-as-abolitionism is as the site where madness and melos converge. It's the site of a kind of unruly music that moves in disruptive, improvisational excess—as opposed to a kind of absenting negation—of the very idea of the (art)work, and it is also the site of a certain lawless, fugitive theatricality, something on the order of that drama that Zora Neale Hurston argues is essential to black life.[25] This melodramatics of black life that animates the abolitionist excess of speech in speech is the continual enactment of abolitionism as blackness, blackness-as-abolitionism. And if communism can legitimately be understood, at least in part, as the critique of private property, on the one hand, and the discursive/ organizational field in which the abolition of private property is initiated in the performance of a kind of somatic *theoria*, on the other, then perhaps it is not too much to ask that we consider black life/black performance as containing, in at least one of its major strains, the durative convergence/ emergence of abolition and/as communism. You could think about this convergence as song's disruption of speech, the cry's disruption of song, gesture's disruption of the cry, the criminal animation or animalistic derangement of the human, the movement of law into the interstitial space of theater or drama's irruption into the subject's pure locale and cause, and so on. Please forgive the speed of these connections. I make them in order to submit for discussion an understanding of the field delimited by blackness, black performance, black radicalism, communism and abolitionism as ground for another examination of pragmatism, its newness and its end/s; and, more importantly, as ground for a recalibration of the aesthetic.

Critiques of black political identity, which fall within more general critiques of the interplay of politics and identity, fail properly to consider two things: 1) that black aspirations for freedom that are tied to claims of injury and to intergenerational links—both of which constitute the opening onto a certain improvisation of identity—are interinanimate with the commitment to the investigation of a set of practices that could be called, to borrow a phrase, "the experimental exercise of freedom" or, more succinctly, escape; 2) that black radicalism has been, precisely in its relation to such experimentalism and the practical and, in every sense, laborious ruptures which prompt it, a profound anti-instrument (an object offering thingly resistance to its disposition and representation, an antiapparatus) in the service of a profoundly anti-instrumentalist critique of the instrumentalist flaw—the foundational pragmatist or pragmatic germ—at the heart of liberalism and its rationality.[26] This is to say that there is a strain of black radicalism that has, as one of its most elemental features, a tendency toward the deinstrumentalization of freedom. This strain could be said to constitute the deinstrumentalizing irruption at the originary heart of the Enlightenment and its impacted instrumentalism. This irruption is sometimes manifest in the appeal to and call for rights; at other times (and sometimes those other times occur, at the same time as these appeals) it is manifest as a refusal of rights, of a certain discourse and a certain set of procedures of right.

Joan Dayan asks, by way of Earl Warren, what it means to have lost the right to have rights.[27] Her crucial question augments another, offered by Gayatri Spivak, that anticipates it: What about the right to refuse right/s?[28] These questions prompt a few others: What does it mean to be against or outside of the law of the home and the state, the home and the state that you constitute and that refuses you? What does it mean to refuse that which has been refused you? What new infusion is made possible by such refusal? In the end, the assertion of a right to difference that critics like Richard Ford denounce—especially when it appears that that right is tied to a certain fetishization of a history of injury and that the ones who assert that right are calling for the state to protect it—is misunderstood.[29] What's actually at stake is the right to differ that difference bodies forth; the right to refuse right/s, the right to refuse, more precisely, the etiolated citizenship and subjectivity that have been refused you, the right to refusal which is the first right. Ford is probably correct to suggest that the right to differ ought not be protected. If he's correct, however, he is so accidentally, against the grain of his own analysis. It's not so much that the right to differ ought not be protected; rather, it's that it can't be protected, that it moves always against the obligations and constraints of protection. But differing, as the fugitive being that is the animating and *destruktiv* essence of being-enslaved, is not only movement outside the law's protection. It is also movement that must negotiate the fact that the slave is submitted to the structures that protect the master from dispossession. Escape is insecure, unprotected existence; it is an existence, an experience even, of dispossession that we have to embrace. The dispossession of the master is inseparable from a kind of autodispossession of the always escaping slave and her descendants. Escape requires a willingness to give one's all. This is uncomfortably close to having one's all taken. Leaving, differing, stealing away, is always under the threat of interdiction, of protected theft, of mastery's protected "right" to steal, of the roguish force that is always most powerfully wielded by proper subjects and proper states. At the same time, one's differing, one's all, is protected only when it is stolen. The right to differ is the right to go, the right to life, the right to refuse, the right to refuse right/s, the first right (of refusal), the right before rights. This is, before the law, and it manifests itself, melodramatically, as a political aesthetic of gestural refusal.

Blackness, as the aspiration for a kind of anti-instrumental freedom, is a disturbance of the surface of reality that is, a kind of transcendental clue, given in an irreducibly material immanence, of that which lies below. The irony is that this moves against an old and multifarious incapacity to think black things, to think that black things think, to exceed that mode of fetishization that assumes a kind of black instrumentalism and then either denounces or lionizes it. More precisely, the inability to see the anti-instrumental impulse in black thought leads to the erroneous linkage of black aspiration to a liberalism whose fundamental instrumentalism is misunderstood such that the denunciation of it becomes its recapitulation. So we have the effect of an assumption of black instrumentalism that leads to a dismissal of black thought when it fails to live up to this instrumental imperative that it was thought to speak for and embody. This charge comes from folks who think their instrumentalism protects them from liberalism while being unaware that their instrumentalism recapitulates the instrumental kernel at the heart of liberal transcendentalism's mystical shell. Meanwhile, the unfinished project of enlightenment is not but nothing other than the unfinished project of abolition. This is a project, and projection, of the (radical politics embedded in the) black aesthetic that has been held under the loving protection of blackness-as-abolition—of black radicalism, of blackness as the melodramatic imagination—in its necessarily unprotected state.

The raising of a fist, meanwhile and according to Williams, corresponds not only to the Simpson verdict but also to the riot that occurred in response to the verdict handed down in the case of the officers who beat Rodney King. Williams is careful to explain why she uses the word *riot* to describe that response, arguing that it was other than an uprising (which implies, according to her, knowing that against which one rises [the clear implication being that the folks in South-Central Los Angeles didn't know]) and arguing also that it was other than a rebellion (which implies organization [something which, again, Williams clearly implies to have been beyond the black folks in question at the time in question]). I'm not as fastidious as Williams about maintaining the distinction between these terms and the modes of movement to which they correspond. Instead, I want to try to make as much as I can of uprising's echo in the raising of a fist, a gesture more properly understood as the trace of the constantly reirruptive soliloquy, the heretofore unthinkable interiority, of the interior paramour that disowns Wallace Stevens and the underground blackamoor that dispos(sess)es Denis Diderot. For Williams, the gesture that corresponds to what she can only understand as the irrational is in bad taste. It remains for us to consider just how sweet such gestures are.

chapter 3

Uplift
and Criminality

This is an excursion into the stolen life of black things, the roughness of its phonographic edge. Considering stolen life requires that we move, in the words of W. E. B. Du Bois and in their transformative amplification by Nahum Chandler, in the sphere—the open set—of "the Negro Question." The plain of the ordinary, of common ground or of a common underground, of the common underground or outskirts of the city, before the distinction between urban and rural and the formation of modernity and its opposite that distinction engenders, is where this structuring incommensurability resides. What is given in Du Bois's composed and scholarly production of the question of the Negro is the possibility of an improvisational discovery: of a politics of the black ordinary and of everything that is both enabled and endangered by such a politics, which is to say by the anthropological and/or sociological attitude that the discovery of the concept of the object of the black ordinary demands. Focus on the danger is part of what I'll focus on here in the interest of saving the saving power. This means working by way of the paralinguistic and its chances, of mechanically reproduced aesthesis and its foreshortening effects on the distance the ethnographer seems to require. The political opening Du Bois's work marks and helps to conjure is the function of a double step: the first element of this choreography is the step away or outside, the movement of analytic detachment with regard to black sociality that is characterized, as Chandler has established, by a fundamental ontological question: *Who are they?*[1] The second step, which is only properly understood as that which lies before the first, as that which is productive of a second and, as it were, improvisational (fore)sight, is a voluntary, identificatory address of and entrance into the politicotheatrical scene of black sociality. It is characterized by an appositional answer to the first of the questions it anticipates: *They bear me.* This is no simple moment of identification but a slight, all-but-disidentificatory moment of avowal.

In Du Bois's case, he associates this address and entrance with his matriculation at Fisk University at the beginning of the 1880s. Such entrance has all the indeterminate force of an always already cut and augmented act of will whose effect stays with Du Bois, drives him every day and in a way that is always manifest as what might be called the constitutive and disruptive supplement to everything in Du Bois that would operate under the sign of regulation.

It seems necessary and just to speak of this paradoxically foundational ornament as surface, as materiality, as ordinary, but one must reserve the right, so to speak, to ask that it also be considered under the rubrics of the archi-trace, the maternal, the one who is fully and problematically before the law. The discernment of this scar that is deep in the heart and at the start of Du Bois's work demands gentle, militant reading, a reading that is governed by a particular poetics and by the commitment to the rich content of a lyricism of the surplus, of the dangerous, salvific, (im)pure sonority of unaccounted for things or of the unaccounted in things, of the ruptural accompaniment, of murmur and mummery, of the folding or invaginative residue moving at the excessive interchange (the moving bridge-like object) of a set, which is to say a history, of loss(es). It demands a reading that is possessed and, above all, dispossessive, one that moves in a cut romance with the criminal burn of the very idea. The extraordinary is in the ordinary like freedom is in unfreedom as the trace of the resistance that constitutes constraint. John Coltrane spoke of a set of harmonic devices that he knew would take him out of the ordinary path. This transport out of the ordinary path within the ordinary; this extraordinary path within the ordinary; this wandering in search of the extraordinary in the ordinary (where what Du Bois calls the "evident rhythm of human action" and the "evident incalculability in human action" are interarticulate) is the distressed rationality that drives the romantic poetics reading Du Bois requires and whose discovery is made possible by reading Du Bois and by reading in Du Bois what he calls, in a great 1905 essay called "Sociology Hesitant" (made available again by Chandler's and Ronald A. T. Judy's work), the "sudden rise at a given tune" that puts the given in play.[2]

So let's begin again by indexing the discourse on a set of given tunes—a strain or string of the black radical tradition that moves in (mis)translation, (mis)transliteration, and (mis)transcription, and in the phrasing that emerges from the difficulty of these. Here is a passage from C. L. R. James's *The Black Jacobins* that recovers and elucidates a "Haitian Fight Song" irrupting from the gap between enlightenment and romanticism, enlightenment and darkness, among other constructs and continents:

> But one does not need education or encouragement to cherish a dream of freedom. At their midnight celebrations of Voodoo, their African cult, they danced and sang, usually this favourite song:

> Eh ! Eh ! Bomba! Heu! Heu!
>   Canga, bafio té!
>   Canga, mouné de lé!
>   Canga, do ki la!
>   Canga, li!

> "We swear to destroy the whites and all that they possess; let us die rather than fail to keep this vow."

> The colonists knew this song and tried to stamp it out, and the Voodoo cult with which it was linked. In vain. For over two hundred years the slaves sang it at their meetings, as the Jews in Babylon sang of Zion, and the Bantu to-day sing in secret the national anthem of Africa.[3]

And here is Amiri Baraka in *Blues People*:

> It is impossible to find out exactly how long the slaves were in America before the African work song actually did begin to have extra-African references. First, of course, there were mere additions of the foreign words—French, Spanish, or English, for the most part, after the British colonists gained power in the United States. Krehbel lists a Creole song transcribed by Lafcadio Hearn, which contains both the French (or Patois) and African words (the italicized words are African):

> *Ouendé, ouendé, macaya!*
> Mo pas barrasse, *macaya!*
> *Ouendé, ouendé, macaya!*
> Mo bois bon divin, *macaya!*
> *Ouendé, ouendé, macaya!*
> Mo mange bon poulet, *macaya!*
> *Ouendé, ouendé, macaya!*
> Mo pas barrasse, *macaya!*
> *Ouendé, ouendé, macaya!*
> *Macaya!*

Hearns's translation was:

Go on! Go on! eat enormously!
I ain't one bit ashamed—*eat outrageously!*
Go on! Go on! eat prodigously!
I drink good wine!—*eat ferociously!*
Go on! go on! eat unceasingly!
I eat good chicken—*gorging myself!*
Go on! go on! etc.[4]

In his explication of this "extra-African" song and its translation, Baraka writes,

> It is interesting to note, and perhaps more than coincidence, that the portions of the song emphasizing excess are in African, which most of the white men could not understand, and the portions of the song elaborating some kind of genteel, if fanciful, existence are in the tongue of the masters. . . . What is called now a "Southern accent" or "Negro speech" was once simply the accent of a foreigner trying to speak a new and unfamiliar language, although it was characteristic of the white masters to attribute the slave's "inability" to speak perfect English to the same kind of "childishness" that was used to explain the African's belief in the supernatural. The owners, when they bothered to listen, were impressed that even the songs of their native American slaves were "incomprehensible" or "unintelligible."[5]

In placing such importance on the resistant force of African-inflected new world song—and on the forging of a politics and aesthetics of excess and ornament from conditions of constraint by way of the simultaneous and ongoing loss and transfer of Africa—Baraka, and James before him, follow in the footsteps of Du Bois whose long life came to an end in 1963, the year *Blues People* was published, which was also the year after James added his famous postscript to *The Black Jacobins* on the line that stretches from Toussaint to Castro. They echo, in particular, the following oft-noted passage from the final chapter of *The Souls of Black Folk*:

> The songs are indeed siftings of centuries; the music is far more ancient than the words, and in it we can trace here and there signs of development. My grandfather's grandmother was seized by an evil Dutch trader two centuries ago; and coming to the valleys of the Hudson

and Housatonic, black, little, and lithe, she shivered and shrank in the harsh north winds, looking longingly at the hills, and often crooned a heathen melody to the child between her knees, thus:

Do bana coba, gene me, gene me!
Do bana coba, gene me, gene me!
Ben d'nuli, ben d'le.

"This was primitive African music," Du Bois asserts—"the voice of exile."[6] In the first volume of his massive biography of Du Bois, David Levering Lewis provides some context and background for Du Bois's musical excursion:

As with much else to do with early Burghardt history, Du Bois has left several confusing and contradictory accounts of the "little black Bantu" ancestor who sang a sad West African tune, still heard at the fireside of his childhood. . . . Willie never learned the meaning of her song, the exact origin and translation of which have continued to defy linguists. . . . But it was the influence of the song, rather than the singer, that finally mattered to Willie. It was his one truly palpable tie to that African homeland he would spend an academic and political lifetime trying to interpret and shape. "Africa is, of course, my fatherland," he would write sixteen years after spending a few months during 1923 in Monrovia, Liberia. "What is it between us that constitutes a tie which I can feel better than I can explain? [The] song had been the earliest prompting of a very New England and supremely intellectual great-grandson to try to discern a few notes of a remote, vestigial and mysterious heritage.[7]

In a footnote Lewis takes advantage of the independent research into the song's provenance and meaning conducted by Mrs. Denise Williams, a collateral descendant of Du Bois, quoting Sulayman S. Nyang, who writes that

If the song is a creolized version of a Wolof song, it should go like this: Duga na chi pah, gene ma, gene ma / Duga na chipah, gene ma, gene ma / bena njuli, njuli. Translation: I have fallen into a pit, get me out. Get me out! / I have fallen into a pit, get me out. Get me out! / One circumcised boy, one circumcised boy, one circumcised boy, one circumcised boy.[8]

Lewis adds that this is "A strange song, it would seem, for a female ancestor to sing. I have not been able to solve this mystery."[9]

The discourse on such songs is rich with such addenda (marked by confusion in the face of an impudence to which we shall return). James's appeal to song is anticipatory, prophetic, reaching back to a not-fully-approachable Africa in the name of a postcolonial African future we still await. Meanwhile, Baraka, highlighting the fruitful impossibility of a direct appeal to African origin that James constantly discloses and retrospectively admits, lingers in an unintelligibility that works at the site of a rebellious excess whose condition of possibility is, paradoxically, an African origin and which manifests itself most fully in the unbridgeable distance that separates it from that origin. That sound which both never arrives at and goes past home is directed toward a future politics that exists as a function of such nonarrival. Finally, Lewis marks the chain of references to that origin that links Du Bois's texts over half a century and links himself to that chain. It's a chain of impossible interpretation correspondent to a broken matrilinearity that Du Bois and Lewis after him reveal and repress (whether by an assertion that the song can be detached from, or matter more than, its maternal singer or by folding that remote maternal claim on Du Bois into the long trajectory of the claim he makes on the "fatherland"). The song of the mother is given in a resistant, forceful materiality that emerges most clearly after the fact of a deprivation, the ongoing—which is to say substitutive—loss of the mother and of meaning, sense, depth. Such songs—which is to say the performative, overdubbed circulation of these songs, embedded in a kind of literary recording that Hortense Spillers characterizes as "put[ting] down tracks for some future investigation" and understands as the instructive, repressive, reiterative engagement of a radical black male tradition with the fantastic and *mater*ial black female archi-trace that lies before it[10]—are why it seems necessary to speak of black radicalism as a new thing, as something James might specifically think of as a new world thing (or that James Brown might think of as a new breed thing), even as we recognize the absolute necessity of thinking it as the old-new thing, the "sexual cut," the ruptural and regenerative ungendering or regendering that Lewis finds so mysterious. In the end, this is just a way of repeating with a difference Cedric Robinson's formulation—whose depth and beauty is inevitably cut even by what hopes to be a genuine augmentation—regarding the impossibility of understanding black radicalism within the particular context of its genesis.[11]

The period in Du Bois's career between 1896 and 1903, when he was researching and writing both *The Philadelphia Negro* and some of the essays that would be collected in *The Souls of Black Folk*, is a crucial moment in the history of black radicalism in part because it shows the massive tension between what Kevin Gaines, in his important book *Uplifting the Race*, describes as "two general connotations of uplift. On the one hand, a broader vision of uplift signifying collective social aspiration, advancement and struggle [which] had been the legacy of the emancipation era. On the other hand, black elites made uplift the basis for a racialized elite identity claiming Negro improvement through class stratification as race progress, which entailed an attenuated conception of bourgeois qualifications for rights and citizenship."[12]

One of the objectives of Gaines's research is the historicization of the concept of race that arises as a result of the "tension between elite racial and popular social images of uplift within black leadership and culture" (xv). He is interested in exposing and challenging "the limitations of black elites' defensive appropriation of dominant racial theories for the purpose of erecting a supposedly positive black identity." These limitations resulted, he argues, finally more from "[white] power, black vulnerability, and the centrality of race in the nation's political and cultural institutions" than from the "complicity of black elites."[13] I want to follow Gaines in his attempts to explicate the tension between these modes of uplift while veering off from his enabling path in order to show how that tension operates at a deep and fundamental level in the work of Du Bois at the turn of the last century. This is to say that there is at work in Du Bois, even when his discourse is most colored by the elitism Gaines astutely critiques, another voice that Nathaniel Mackey, after Robert Duncan, might call a meta-voice, whose features carry some important information regarding the history of blackness as politicoaesthetic assertion. One might even say that this meta-voice marks, in its most essential office, not the tension between two modes of uplift but that between a certain lingering with the ordinary and what Chandler might call the construction of a horizon.

This tension is bound to Du Bois's contribution to the discourse of black urban pathology. Gaines explicates that contribution, arguing that Du Bois thinks of urban fallenness in contradistinction to a kind of organic ruralism that has, as its most important feature, a connection to soil and earth that fosters the maintenance of the patriarchal family model or, at least, militates against the most thorough post–Civil War degradation of female sexuality— the descent into prostitution that is figured by Du Bois as an almost inevitable corollary of women working outside the home. But if you look at the chapters in *Souls* detailing black peasant life in the South, you see something that operates in a less agonistic manner with regard to the Du Boisian critique of urbanization, something that prefigures Gaines's own assertions regarding the structuring force of white power and black vulnerability. First, urbanization is seen as the effect of a kind of enclosure. In this case enclosure doesn't refer to (though it ought not be understood to operate in some simple contrast to) the peasant's forced removal from expropriated common land. Rather, this enclosure is *of* the peasant, a literal entrapment and attachment to the land by way of the disciplinary—indeed, carceral—managerial techniques imposed on debt-ridden tenant farmers by landholders and enforced by the state. Urbanization is, in this regard, a kind of fugitivity, an incapacitated mobilization that works not in contradistinction to idyllic Southern life but in chorographic articulation with Southern oppression, which itself responds to the irregular rhythms of ordinary movements already in place, under the feet, as it were, of whoever enacts, every day, the revaluation of their own irreducibly political being. If Du Bois understands the flight to town as available only to "the better classes of Negroes," such understanding ought itself be understood as an attempt to misunderstand the low-class, country conspiracy that constitutes our smuggled, runaway modernity.[14]

As Gaines knows, the reconstruction of the pastoral in *Souls*—the black reconstruction of the pastoral that it begins to narrate—contains no simple scenes of the gallant or even organic South. This to say not only that Du Bois is unsparing in his attention to the details of Southern oppression, but also, as Gaines argues, that even in what might be read as a certain rural nostalgia in *Souls* there is room for "innovative social analysis."[15] The question is how such analysis comes to occupy Du Bois's text, and this question is inseparable from other modes of disruptive inhabitation. This is to say that the other factor that strains (against) the pastoral in Du Bois—that he sees the Black Belt as a kind of breeding ground for the very pathology that Gaines understands Du Bois to locate more originarily in the urban North—is so closely related, along a maternal and material line, as to be practically inseparable from the condition of possibility of innovative social analysis. That this is so is inextricably bound to the fact that the extension of regimes of forced and stolen labor beyond "emancipation" is also fertile ground for a certain mode of critique of their life-situation by Southern blacks. That *this* is so could be said, in turn, to both emerge from and body forth the social life Du Bois pathologizes—a social life that is not reducible to the structures of oppression to which it responds and which respond to it. Du Bois addresses the brutal plight of the black tenant farmer whose indefinitely deferred emancipation is putatively justified by the "opinion among the merchants and employers of the Black Belt that only by the slavery of debt can the Negro be kept at work."[16] We should join Gaines in his attunement to Du Bois's barely veiled confirmation of that opinion, which he describes as an "honest and widespread" response to the supposed listlessness, laziness, and ignorance of black workers. But Du Bois's normative elitism comes most sharply into relief when he seeks to explain and extenuate the social life of black laborers by referring to

> the obvious fact that a slave ancestry and a system of unrequited toil has not improved the efficiency or temper of the mass of black laborers. Nor is this peculiar to Sambo; it has in history been just as true of John and Hans, of Jacques and Pat, of all ground-down peasantries. Such is the situation of the mass of the Negroes in the Black Belt to-day; and they are thinking about it. Crime, and a cheap and dangerous socialism, are the inevitable results of this pondering. I see now that ragged black man sitting on a log, aimlessly whittling a stick. He muttered to me with the murmur of many ages when he said: White man sit down whole year; Nigger work day and night and make crop; Nigger hardly gits bread and meat; white man sittin' down gits all. *It's wrong.*"[17]

Some of what is problematic in this passage is so glaring that Gaines doesn't have to attend to it—the offhand invocation of "Sambo" that carries with it so much of the contempt that it is meant to combat; the facile confirmation of the idea that peonage might have been a legitimate response to the shiftlessness of the newly emancipated. What Gaines does note, however, is the way Du Bois so easily conflates crime and socialism, thereby marking, at this moment in his career, a particular commitment to bourgeois norms. Gaines goes on to express surprise at Du Bois's interpolation of "the ragged black man's" analysis, thinking it, along lines Lewis establishes, a mysterious song for Du Bois to sing.

If Du Bois's song is strange, marking the irreducible, material presence of a stranger in Du Bois, one who leaves the mark or gift of a certain estrangement for Du Bois that will await his claim, it is so because the thinking, the moral reasoning, of the ignorant worker disrupts and constitutes its own regulation. The class stratification that is signaled by land ownership and the internal differentiation that attends self-possessive discursive composure enact a kind of redoubled distancing. This is how Du Bois domesticates flight in the dramatization of a question and answer: "And what do the better classes of Negroes do to improve their situation? One of two things: if any way possible they buy land; if not they migrate to town." It is, at the same time, how Du Bois comes to ventriloquize the pathologization of fugitivity, as Gaines shows in his reading of Du Bois's analysis of the transfer of certain plantation irregularities from rural South to urban North. In the end, I want primarily to investigate "the murmur of many ages" that works as a vexed, multiplied coding of the voice, recorded in Du Bois's literary phonography but recorded also in the phonographic recording of his voice, disrupting a condescension at once regulative, elitist, and detached even as it troubles the very affective attachment that the writing fitfully implies. This murmur sets and keeps the time of that originary encounter of Du Boisian (ontosociological) questioning and answering with which I began. Later we'll hear (of) a kind of whistle, a pathogen in Du Bois's speech, that I have come to think of as this murmur of many ages, a transported maternal trace intensified by a technological feedback like a scar in and on the body of the voice. This whistle is a disruptive augmentation of the voice that I wish to place under the rubric of the criminal. This criminal essence of the black voice is mediated, technological, accidental, contingent, historically sedimented, performed, constructed, and no less essential for being all of these. I say this in critique of labeling or constructionist theories of criminality, blackness, and what might be called, by way of a movement that can be traced back to Louis Althusser, their articulated but incommensurable and unbridgeable combination.[18] Those criminologists who are known as labeling theorists argue along lines established in Karl Marx's critical ontology of the commodity. Just as the commodity's (exchange) value is understood by Marx to have been conferred from outside, so is deviance or criminality understood by labeling theorists as a function of nomination—"a consequence of the application by others of rules and sanctions"—and not a quality of the act or the person that is called deviant or criminal. But the hope for and history of resistance demands that we consider the question concerning the specific interiority of the deviant (act or person or act-as-person). Again, this is not to challenge claims of the constructedness of the category but to initiate an investigation into the essence of the constructed in this case and in general. In the end, black social life as innovative social analysis bears an outlaw sound.

What Gaines refers to as Du Bois's "telling juxtaposition" of crime and cheap/dangerous socialism moves as if in some appositional derivation from a more properly Marxian attachment to the revolutionary capacity of the proletariat that is, itself, dependent upon a discourse of uplift implied in the dismissal of the lumpen.[19] *Souls* and *The Philadelphia Negro* are bound by the valorization of hierarchical stratification and black leadership that Gaines so cogently diagnoses as fundamental to the ideology of normative uplift. This is to say that for Du Bois the cheapness and danger of the socialism that emerges in some articulated combination with crime in the South is all bound up with the fact that it is a socialism that will have emerged from the peasantry and/or urban (lumpen)proletariat without the guidance or the leadership of the better classes.

It's important here to note that this new enclosure that determines the character of the system of so-called free labor—an enclosure not of the common lands but of the peasant on private land—reifies the conflation of slave and prisoner that defines both these categories and therefore lies at the heart of the experience of blackness in a transition from slavery to freedom that is so fundamentally (de)formed and rendered so fundamentally delusional by convict-leasing (not to mention the no-less-intense nonextremities that attend what Saidiya Hartman teaches us more accurately to regard as the transition from subjection to subjection).[20] That system extends the criminalization of black social life that emerged as a central accomplishment of the power that black social life—as black resistance—brought into being. This is to say that the social death of slavery and imprisonment can only be understood as operating in some articulated combination with a necessarily political, necessarily aesthetic, necessarily erotic black social life. Each is the other's condition of possibility and this is to understand the criminality of black life in its relation not to laws codified and enforced by power but to power itself as the self-(re)generating mystical foundation of its own authority.[21] In this sense criminality is a drive originarily inscribed in constructed blackness or black radicalism but this criminality cannot be understood within the context of its genesis. It is constructed and exists as a function of construction, and yet it is before construction.

This makes it possible and necessary to understand Du Bois's adherence to the ideology of normative uplift as always disrupted by his deviance from it and from the morality of bourgeois production that attends it as means, end, and cause. A deviance is inscribed on the very discourse that puts that morality forward and this deviance must be attended. Movement between the critique of the interplay in elite black constructions of black social life—between class stratification and bourgeois respectability and the racist imposition of the minstrel stereotype—renders difficult such attention to this other writing, this other phonography, which works like a kind of dissonant echo, like some kind of accompaniment held a fraction after the initiative sound of its "original," and moves as if such harmonic thickness implied some perspectival time in the recording—the aspect or internal temporal constituency of the overdub. It's the overdub of or accompaniment to Du Bois's normative ideals—their doubleness, the repetition (with a difference) that is internal to them—in which I am interested and which I want to try to enter and unpack in order to extend (along with and against the normativity that in/voluntary, fugitive Du Boisians like Gaines and I share) the ongoing discovery of a particular concept of the criminal that animates black radicalism. It's recorded in Du Bois's writing and is evident in the recording of his speech as the form of a quite specific content toward which we are pointed (as the deviance from progress, rationalism, objectivity, scientific observation), and which we'll hear even in Du Bois's most severe adherence to these ideals.

Meanwhile, if, as Gaines points out, Du Bois helps to initiate the problematic discourse of black urban pathology that had its fullest flowering in the infamous report on the causes of urban unrest produced by the allegedly deceased Daniel Patrick Moynihan and others about thirty-five years ago and which still shapes much of the discourse on black urban life, then it is also worth noting that Du Bois's thoughts on the origin of black criminality had a more immediate scholarly impact, prefiguring the notoriously racist but inescapably valuable work of the historian of slavery Ulrich B. Phillips and his discourse on slave crime.[22] This convergence—unlikely given their mutual dismissal of each other's work—shows, in a way that Gaines's work predicts, how the assimilationist cultural politics of normative uplift can never be fully separated from the white supremacism it is supposed to combat. Here's Phillips at the opening of "Slave Crime," the penultimate chapter of his *American Negro Slavery*:

> The Negroes were in a strange land, coercively subjected to laws and customs far different from those of their ancestral country; and by being enslaved and set off into a separate lowly caste they were largely deprived of that incentive to conformity which under normal conditions the hope of individual advancement so strongly gives. It was quite to be expected that their conduct in general would be widely different from that of the whites who were citizens and proprietors. The natural amenability of the blacks, however, had been a decisive factor in their initial enslavement, and the reckoning which their captors and

rulers made of this was on the whole well founded. Their lawbreaking had few distinctive characteristics, and gave no special concern to the public except as regards rape and revolt."[23]

Phillips's belief in black biological inferiority and cultural backwardness—a belief that constitutes a major aspect of his retrospective defense of slavery; a belief that Du Bois will have characterized as both honest and dishonest; a belief to which Du Bois will have adhered in his understanding of the effects of slavery and from which he will have detached himself in his retrospective attack on slavery—does not restrict him from offering the kind of environmentalist account of the origins of black crime that Du Bois put forward a couple of decades earlier in Chapter XIII of *The Philadelphia Negro*, "The Negro Criminal." Moreover, black criminality, according to Phillips, has no "distinctive characteristics," and presents "no special concern" except for rape and revolt. The presumption here seems to be that special characteristics would arise as a function of some essential difference and that such a difference only manifests itself as a kind of propensity to rape and to rebel that magically lives in harmony with "natural amenability." Finally, note that these two distinctive characteristics give concern to a public that is understood, by definition and in a way so commonplace as to be almost unnoticeable, as excluding slaves and/or blacks. The slave is not a part of the public and yet this does not mean that the question of the slave's publicity or public—which is to say *political*—life is not a problem. As Phillips says a few pages later, "In general the slaveholding South learned of crimes by individual negroes with considerable equanimity. It was the news or suspicion of concerted action by them which alone caused widespread alarm and uneasiness."[24] Phillips slightly contradicts himself here, since now it seems that the special concerns regarding slave criminality are really a function of rebellion alone and not rape and, more specifically, are bound up with slave sociality and social organization, with the specter of an uncontrollable public life of slaves which was tantamount to revolt. Indeed, Phillips is valuable in part because of the rather lengthy catalog of slave revolts—in the North and South, as well as the Caribbean—that he produces. In some ways, Phillips picks up on the work of Thomas Wentworth Higginson and anticipates that of Herbert Aptheker, giving the lie to the old commonplace of slave historiography that happy and/or shiftless slaves never lifted a hand in the struggle for their liberation. Instead, the chapter on crime in Phillips is largely taken up with slave revolt and gives us some occasion for thinking the relation between rebellion and crime in such a way as to make possible a new understanding of the relation between criminality and blackness, taking care to think criminality as first and foremost black sociality, social life, social organization.[25]

If we jump back to Du Bois's formulations on the Negro criminal, we can hear what Phillips echoes: "Crime is a phenomenon of organized social life, and is the open rebellion of an individual against his social environment. Naturally then, if men are suddenly transported from one environment to another, the result is lack of harmony with the new conditions; lack of harmony with the new physical surroundings leading to disease and death or modification of physique; lack of harmony with social surroundings leading to crime. Thus very early in the history of the colony [of Pennsylvania] characteristic complaints of the disorder of the Negro slaves is heard."[26]

Du Bois goes on to enumerate complaints regarding the "tumultuous gathering" of blacks, folks swearing, cussing, and engaging in a supposed general kind of disorderliness. The environmentalist explanation that Du Bois offers constitutes a kind of justification of the colony's "anti-tumult" ordinances precisely by taking at face value the complaints against black gatherings. (Note in particular one such ordinance, passed in 1700 and recorded in Appendix B of *The Philadelphia Negro*, where blacks assembled in groups of more than four were subject to whipping if unable to certify that they were on their master's business.[27]) Moreover, as Gaines suggests, Du Bois is interested in promoting black assimilation to bourgeois norms of social organization precisely in the interest of racial uplift.

Black criminality as discord and disorder—or as the gathering of an ensemble that works outside of normative harmony; the atonality of another totality—is figured as a sign that black people need to develop social skills, as it were, to engage in already established normative modes of publicity that include not only high-minded social and political organization devoted to racial uplift but also wholesome forms of popular amusement that would form a vital supplement to respectable private domesticity.[28] This overlooks the fact, of course, that the supposed definitional impossibility of a black public, on the one hand, and the fear of this impossible or unreadable black publicity, on the other, is at the heart not only of notions of black criminality but founds or constructs blackness—black social life—as criminality. To be black, to engage in the ensemblic—necessarily social—performance of blackness, is to be criminal. This is essential to the construction of blackness and is to be indexed neither to environment nor genetics. It is of interest—

and will be taken up later—that crime is figured by Du Bois both as discord (between men and their conditions) and as a phenomenon of social organization. This ensemblic organization is something we'll come to think about under the rubrics of frenzy and fugitivity, where crime-as-revolt might be thought of as what Miles Davis came to understand as an ineluctably "social" music whose perceived disharmony and arrhythmia operates as an enactment of surreptitiousness and flight, a harmonic and rhythmic reorganization, if not disorganization, reconstruction if not destruction. It is, therefore, not amiss to think the musicality of black criminality–as–black rebellion and, moreover, it is important to consider what's at stake in the feat of black (musical) gathering. The first and most serious black crime is black sociality, something Robinson might understand as the preservation of an ontological totality, something I hope to understand as the continual and foundational cutting and expansion of this totality's masculinist circumference.[29]

This project means that the question of a certain criminalized sexuality is not to be put on the back burner. A fundamental issue, for Du Bois, is precisely the problematic of illicit and uncontrollable black sexuality. The locus of this sexuality is, however, not the predatory male but the insatiable female. This is a stereotype that Du Bois believes in and disbelieves at the same time, one that he must strive to address and overcome. Anna Julia Cooper's unprotected black female is at the heart of Du Bois's problem, as Gaines astutely points out. And the problem for Du Bois is not so much her supposed sexual insatiability but the fact of her being sexual at all. The black woman's transgression of domestic respectability—in working outside of the home, in seeking public and communal forms of sociality, amusement, and pleasure— is problematic for Du Bois in a way that recalls the ambivalences of normative uplift in Douglass when music and the discourse on music and rebellion in the second chapter of the *Narrative* emerge from a black woman's assertion of sexual autonomy and the resistance to sexual violation recorded in the first chapter. In that first chapter, the one who is constructed as property causes the very idea of the proper to tremble between the poles of appropriation and expropriation. Douglass—amid his moral denunciation of the master's cruelty—imagines some possible rehabilitative justification for his Aunt Hester's brutal and violative "punishment" by the master since, after all, she has attempted to determine the disposition of a sexuality she embraces and enacts. In so doing he prefigures the justifications of peonage or policing— in response to the black worker's attempt to determine the disposition of her labor—that are explicit and implicit in *The Philadelphia Negro* and *Souls*.

Aunt Hester's "resistant aurality," less than and in excess of the brilliant account/ing that Harryette Mullen offers by way of a term that sounds like that term, is a political phonography moving over the edge of speech, is part of that chain of song with which I began, a history of recording that Du Bois calls "the murmur of ages"; but his normative view of black women's publicity and sexuality—their engagement in forms of reappropriative challenge to the extraction of surplus from their bodies—leaves him unable fully to valorize a criminality by which he is, at the same time, possessed. It is a criminality attached, finally, to a black maternity that is at once constitutive and substitutive and that is construed, as Spillers first points out, as necessarily illegitimate and impossible. Du Bois intimately knows and obsessively indexes and represses this maternity. It is an inheritance that touches and unmans him, something handed to him that cannot be handled.[30]

The murmur is a sound, a rumble, given on the outskirts of normal, as opposed to the center of (speech) pathological, articulation. It's tied to acting and performance where mummery coincides with murmuring, where the dumb show would seem to indicate an otherness if not absence of articulacy, as in *A Midsummer Night's Dream* in which case murmuring and mummery, in the figure of Bottom, verge on animality (and I should just point out here that we're moving now in a constellation in which animality, sociality, criminality, blackness, and femininity circulate around a sound against or above speech, one that has, as Akira Lippit points out, the effect of making possible the construction, deconstruction, and reconstruction of the human, a project in which black radicalism is intimately engaged).[31] For Du Bois the murmur is laden with history, is the dubbed and overdubbed recording of a history of complaint, where the phonic *mater*iality of song operates, again, over the edge of speech, over the edge of meaning. If we take Mackey's work more fully into account, we see that complaint is better understood if seen and heard in its articulation with rebellion and escape at the place where expropriation and (re)appropriation combine idiomatically and accentually to disrupt the very idea of the proper—of property and proper speech. The murmur is an interminable doubling in and of what is supposed to be most properly one's own, namely one's speech. It's a phonography or deviant recording already inscribed upon or embedded in proper speech such that speech will have never been proper. Speech breaking from propriety, on the run from ownership. This is what Mackey thinks about, by way of Baraka on Federico García Lorca and then on saxophonist John Tchicai, under the rubric of fugitivity. Mackey begins by quoting Baraka's citation, in the epigraph to his poem "Lines to García Lorca," of lines from an African American spiritual: "Climbin' up the mountain, chillun / Didn't come here for to stay / If I'm ever gonna see you agin / It'll be on the judgement day."

Gypsies, though they do not appear explicitly in this poem, come in elsewhere in Baraka's early work to embody a mobile, mercurial non-investment in the status quo. One of the things going on in "Lines to García Lorca" is the implicit connection between that mercuriality, that nomadism, and the lines "Didn't come here for to stay," behind which lies a well-known, resonant history of African American fugitivity and its well-known, resonant relation to enslavement and persecution. Thus the resonant apposition of the poem's opening lines, "Send soldiers again to kill you, Garcia. / Send them to quell my escape." At the end of the poem Lorca's voice, "away off," invested with fugitive spirit, laughs

But away off, quite close to daylight,
I hear his voice, and he is laughing, laughing
Like a Spanish guitar.

The way fugitivity asserts itself on an aesthetic level, at the level of poetics, is important as well. The way in which Baraka's poems of this period move intimates a fugitive spirit as does much of the music that he was into. He writes of a solo by . . . Tchicai on an Archie Shepp album, "It slides away from the proposed." That gets into, again, the cultivation of another voice, a voice that is other than that proposed by one's intentions, tangential to one's intentions, angular, oblique—the obliquity of an unbound reference. That sliding away wants out.[32]

Mackey illustrates his analysis of fugitivity and the meta-voice with a fragment of multi-instrumentalist Rahsaan Roland Kirk's recording of his composition "The Business Ain't Nothing but the Blues," taking care to note how the voice and the instrument—in this case the flute—mutually cut and augment one another in a way that illuminates their already given internal difference and multiplicity.[33] Fugitivity, then, is a desire for and a spirit of escape and transgression of the proper and the proposed. It's a desire for the outside, for a playing or being outside, an outlaw edge proper to the now always already improper voice or instrument. This is to say that it moves outside the intentions of the one who speaks and writes, moving outside their own adherence to the law and to propriety. This fugitivity is at the heart of the murmur of many ages that Du Bois records. His recording of it is bound at once to his desire for it and for the outside that it desires and his proper fear of that fugitivity to the extent that it marks and carries that thinking or pondering that he associates with the combination of crime and, more generally, a certain lawlessness of imagination, with cheap, dangerous socialism, and with the improper as such.

There are a couple of things left to consider: How are we to understand the transition that occurs in Du Bois, the one that moves from the rejection to the embrace of socialism in every bit of what had been understood to be its cheapness, danger, and criminality? This question is all bound up with others: How are we to understand the constellation of (unsupervised, nonpatriarchal) maternity, sexuality, and promiscuity in its relation to the nexus of socialism and criminality? What's the relation between the phonics of fugitivity, the phonics of maternity, and socialism? This question is crucial precisely because it requires us to call into question the very idea of transition even as we explain its workings in the trajectory of Du Bois's thought. This is about the place of fugitivity in a maternal song that is inseparable from transgressions of proper bourgeois kinship. It's also about the trace of such song in Du Bois's speech and writing as not only his recording of the rural folk but his bearing of the maternal mark that bourgeois respectability demands be relinquished. In other words, we must be concerned with his operation within and ongoing reproduction (of the opening of discovery) of the political line formed by the tumultuous convergence of phonic materiality and maternity, criminality, and socialism, (what has often been dismissed as a kind of lumpen) peonage and (what has often been hoped for under the rubric of) proletariat.

At the end of his discussion of Du Bois, Gaines associates what might be called the revolutionary in Du Bois—the deviant, fugitive excess of normative uplift discourse and ideology—with Du Bois's affective critique of his own faith in the gathering and ordering of objective social facts as a necessary precursor to reform. This moment of reflection was prompted by the lynching of Sam Hose shortly after Du Bois moved from Philadelphia to Atlanta, and Gaines reads it as the beginning of Du Bois's never fully successful attempt to detach himself from the discourse of urban pathology he helped found and which continues to dominate discourse on the so-called black underclass to this day. Du Bois's recounting of this moment of self-analysis was recorded in 1961.[34] The truth of this recording lies precisely in a certain infidelity it bears that could be indexed to age, technology, and/or the oscillation between objective distancing and objectional identification. This interplay of truth and infidelity—which Adorno argues is art's *Bewegungsgesetz*, its law of motion—is pierced by the criminality that lies before it, one that, in the end, ought to give a certain pause right in between fidelity and its various modifiers and prefixes since it is perhaps more precise to say that the high fidelity of the recording accurately offers us a sound-image of Du Bois's scholarly and political intentions and commitments not only pierced but constituted by the low's high pitch.[35] I'm interested in the form as well as the content of a vocal performance that is almost everywhere cut and augmented by what might be perceived as a pathological disruption wherein every sibilant sound is subject to the rude extension of a whistle. It's as if Du Bois, prefiguring Kirk, is playing flute in accompaniment to speech that is already also his own improper, unowned disruption of the opposition between speaking and singing. Such broken form has something to tell us about that content and its condition of possibility, though perhaps I make too much of an involuntary impediment—or the surplus effect of the overcoming of this impediment— that you will not be able not to hear. I think, however, that this disruptive augmentation of Du Bois's *Sprechgesang* is emblematic of some things that certainly require attention. Is the whistle an effect of microphone distortion, of technological mediation and reproduction? Can it be attributed to, and dismissed as, an effect of old age as if the nonagenarian Du Bois is afflicted by the kind of microtonal, microfugal disorder that is sometimes said to characterize "late work," from Beethoven's to Holiday's, like some combination of natural disaster and supernatural depth? In a sense this doesn't matter since what I'm after, again, is some recognition of the accidental, contingent, and extraintentional nature of the voice's essential quality, some acknowledgment of the transgressive scar on the body of the instrument that is, nevertheless, inseparable from a pronounced politico-aesthetic agency of the ages (and the aged). Such scarring is important precisely because, in the end, it can't be detached from the vocal instrument it remakes, like the mutative force of the combination of muting and amplification that characterizes a fundamental aspect of Miles's exilic approach to the trumpet and to speech. In the end, it's as if he can't help but make this dirty sound, the black noise of overdubbing and overcoming, the disruptive addition to the instrument or the instrumental, the irruptive, resistant aurality of a runaway tongue in all its phonoerotic, pathographic materiality. Du Bois's whistle bespeaks (and exspeaks) the graphic wear and tear of long days on speaking, a kind of distress, the inscription of that against which a certain voice is raised,

the ordinary over(tonal)writing of everyday trouble, an irreducible immanence taking the way back into the strife between transcendental claims for
and on the moral law within and the vicious invocation of the transcendental as justification for an appeal to such law that is, at once, violation and
enforcement—as if starry heavens are made possible by the dust we can't
shake from our feet, the dust of daywork and journeywork, of lynching as
the disciplinary outrage of whiteness, which is to say, of dispersed, degraded,
defeated, and, nevertheless, dominant, modernized sovereignty. This is to
say that the troubled voice is not only where the trace of the spectacle is
laid down on top of the ordinary track, but also where the abstractions of a
discourse of (violated) rights and citizenship are animated by material that is
before the law and outside the house and its restricted economy. Audio cuts
and augments autobiography with another writing, the ordinary and inaugural inscription of and onto Du Bois. It's not just that Du Bois is, but that
he also depends on, a writing that overwrites his own attempts to erase it, a
dilemma that is both before and after, inside and out of, Du Bois's exemplary
position in the life and line of the thinking of black radicalism, the question
of the question of the Negro. Du Bois's speech is shadowed by walking pan-
thers and working women; haunted by citified Farmville promiscuity and
Lowndes County outlaw audiobiography. The whistle is also a clue regarding the necessary phonographic aspects of the enterprise of reading and one
needs to listen to (the racial-sexual force of [the sound of] phantasmatic
and material) criminality in Du Bois, especially in his denunciations of it.
The criminality to which we listen is of another order or is something at the
high or low and hitherto undetectable end of criminality's politico-aesthetic
spectrum. More than the denunciation of Du Bois's moralism and more than
the renewed—because demoralized—correction of stereotype is the audition
of the criminality that inhabits Du Bois's speech and writing.

In beginning with the question of an open set, one might have moved
this way: What is open to exploration in and by way of the phrases "criminal
ontology" and "ontological criminality"?[36] What is opened in the distinction
between crime and criminality? What is given in the range of movement
that ensues from this (at once Marxian and before or beyond Marxian) declension: being, wealth, city? Is criminality a thing realized in crimes? What
commerce is there between *metoikos* (the stranger, the foreign resident,
whom Robinson calls "the eternal internal alien"), *zoon politikon*, and the
criminal? What's the relation between what might appear to be the priority
of ontology over history and the priority within ontology of criminality over

law? These are members of the open set of The Negro Question, where color and democracy are situated relative to a gender line, where the historical and ontological relation between blackness and radicalism is set to work. Perhaps their effectivity can be maximized if in posing them one understands radicalism to be a kind of outrootedness, an irreducibly interior and transversal transformationality, and blackness to be an archive of performances, at once disrupted and expansive, moving by way and in excess of its points (Africa, the Antilles, Arkansas, Amsterdam [Avenue], the city, the City) and events (confinement, transport, exchange, confinement, employment, emancipation, confinement, the city, the City) of origin. The question of the City is an open set as well, operating before urbanization and its dialectic of modernization and regress that constantly brushes up against the engendering of the ordinary, of the everyday and its economies. The question of the city is inseparable from that concerning what it is to be, at once, of and outside of the house and the city, of an impossible domesticity's unattainable normativity, of the broken generation/s of the metoikos. It demands that the questioner consider the one outside the house, be concerned with what the outside does to the one, explore territories that have been thought to be outside the house of being, outside language. It requires an attempt to attune oneself to the outside language of the outside woman, the common-law outlaw, the shacked-up outside/r and, above all it, seeks to investigate and to inhabit that mode of interiority, that politico-aesthetic assertion, that inaugural, errant criminality that is the law of the outside, that the outside and everyday-laboring growl and hum of everyday people enforces and allows.

When Robinson speaks of the eternal internal alien, impossible domesticity is indexed. Deeper still, it is the impossible domestic who is indexed. She is one who does the labor of the house, who is constitutive of the economy and economics of home, and yet she remains irreducibly outside of the economy and the house, not just as stranger, but outside the law, outside of the law's protection even if open to the law's assault. This is what I mean by criminality—the status of the outlaw in all of its constitutive force in relation to the house, the family, the city, the law; the status of the outlaw in all of the deconstructive force and reconstructive danger to house, family, city, law of its ordinary imagination. This criminality is essential and historical. The outlaw, the impossible domestic, is before the law but not subject to it because not under its protection. She is, rather, the law's object or, more precisely, the thing or gathering or vessel of and before the law, up ahead and destructive of it. She can be prosecuted but she cannot and chooses not to prosecute. Citizenship is denied to the thing who denies citizenship. She enacts an ordinary apposition to, a denial-in-abolition of, citizenship precisely by way of imaginative, legislative sociopoesis. The impossible domestic apposes the citizen-subject. What a problem and what a chance she is for Du Bois (or for Marx, each in their own challenging adherence to certain Aristotelian and Kantian fundaments of political theory). She? A voice or meta-(metrical-madrigal-)voice disruptive of speech; the outside sound of the outside woman and her chorus, singing burial music, in the serial making and remaking of Antigone's antinomian claim, the lawless freedom of the imagination (improvising, not not looking in the very reconstitution of foresight as something Robin Kelley might call a "freedom dream," the surreal political "nonsense" of a utopian vision, the freedom we know outside of the opposition of sense and intellection by way of and *as* the transcendental and immanent aesthetic [clue] of the sound we make when we sing about it, such song's flavor, the movement that produces it and that it induces) that is constitutive of the political animal.[37] The infusion of maternal song in Du Bois, the murmur of ages, indexes her. So that this is about what the impossible domestic carries in her (pan-)toting, her handing and passing on of her little all, of everything, in her singing, her stealing and stealing away from being stolen, from being carried off, in her carrying and carrying off and carrying on, her production and dispersal of the wealth she is and carries where wealth is understood, in a new revision of the old Marxian way. Marx says wealth will not have been the aim of production. Rather,

> when the limited bourgeois form is stripped away, what is wealth other than the universality of individual needs, capacities, pleasures, productive forces, etc., created through universal exchange? The full development of human mastery over the forces of nature, those of so-called nature as well as of humanity's own nature? The absolute working-out of his creative potentialities, with no presupposition other than the previous historic development, which makes this totality of development, i.e. the development of all human powers as such the end in itself, not as measured on a *predetermined* yardstick? Where he does not reproduce himself in one specificity, but produces his totality? Strives not to remain something he has become, but is in the absolute movement of becoming?[38]

But our revision will have so cut mastery as to free up the forces of nature. This is about stealing and/in singing, out of which emerges another, voluntary, organization; another garden, another life outside, another city, another day/work and play, improvising through house and field. So this is also akin to Deleuze and Guattari's rhizomatic irruption into the arbor (and of the int-irrupted arbor into us) and hinges on the relationship between the volunteer (the plant or shoot or tendril that grows in spite of, and also in the absence of, and also as a residual function of, cultivation) and the meta-voice.[39] It demands concern with what the volunteer does to voluntarity, on the one hand, and, on the other hand, an aesthetics of criminality that is inseparable from, or is articulated through and as, art's *law* of movement. The occasion of the volunteer is, as it were, a movement between the force of (the out)law and the (out)law of movement. It is the anarchic, improvisatory quickening of jurisgenerative principle.

What kind of organization comes from this? She is outside the house she structures and makes possible by entering and she is outside her own impossible home within this "national" homelessness by leaving. She is embedded in and works a kind of leave-taking—at once palimpsestic and montagic—in the radical absence or absenting of home/origin. She leaves without origin, is not understandable within the context of her geneses and natal occasions, generally and ordinarily cuts and augments understanding with work-songs. This exteriority preserves the house that it dismantles so radically as not only to trouble or make impossible a certain tension between inside and outside but also fundamentally to disfigure, refigure, reconfigure owner-ship. This is a problematic, more specifically, of tools, of the ownership of tools. "The master's tools will never dismantle the master's house," ac-cording to Audre Lorde, who would know.[40] "Only the master's tools will ever dismantle the master's house," according to Henry Louis Gates Jr., who would know.[41] This impossible domestic, this female slave (a conflation Ar-istotle sees as barbaric), is the master's tool who will have never belonged to the master; the master's object who can make or break him. The one who will have never been the master's tool because she is the master's object anticipates the one who is assuredly the tool of mastery precisely by being subject to it. The point, however, is that what's happening here is beyond or before the problematic of dismantling or, perhaps more precisely, is of a dismantling that can only be spoken of within the context of something like an originary rebuilding. We have to move, rather, in what Chandler might call an originary displacement of building and dismantling, a displacement that emerges, paradoxically, from leaving (without) origin. We live in an im-possible originarity, the impossible domesticity, of reconstruction. We enact a deconstruction that only moves in its relation to reconstruction. You could call this improvisation, too. Impossible domesticity begins with irruptive reconstruction. It's marked and instantiated by a fugitive sound that is not just on the run from ownership but blowing a run that enacts a fundamental dispossession of ownership as such so that owning is, itself, disowned. This is black Marxism, black communism, where the originary reconstruction is understood as the preservation of the ontological totality, the reconstructive conservation, if you will, of wealth, of the wealth of who and what we are and will be. This is the condition of possibility of accumulation, primitive or otherwise; but it is also its disruption, deferral, originary displacement or anoriginal differing. Anoriginal stealing, anoriginal dispossession at the level of a disruption of regulative and lawful self-possession, the citizen-subject's necessary mode, his rational grammar and tone, the transformation, by way of protection, of voice into speech, a distinction that the impossible domestic operates before, as it were. There's much more to be said about teleological principle and certain outlaw actualities of black reconstruction through an analysis of some migratory outwork that Du Bois turns away from in *The Philadelphia Negro* before a long, tentative, and discomfiting embrace that *Black Reconstruction* signals; for now it must be sufficient to take note, in the interest of the city, of the imagination of the impossible domestic, the lawless freedom and/of the law of motion, her (every)day work, the work of the ordinary, the ordinary outwork, the madness, the flight, the criminality, in the presence of (the) work.

What more can be said about this criminality, this being against the law, to which the whistle brings us? Where else do we have to go in order to develop our understanding of it? The essence of blackness—as political, economic, sexual, aesthetic formation—is expropriative (or, both more and less precisely, ecstatic). Frenzied (in the way that Du Bois elucidates in his description of a certain highly eroticized black religiosity in *Souls*). Tumultuous. Plaintive. Trialed. Trailed. What happens when the law becomes the discourse to which we turn in order to get at the essence of what that very law is meant both to control and to slander? What does it mean to speak of the essence of a historical, constructed thing? This is not meant to romanticize crime; it is to say, however, that what we valorize as revolutionary or radical has to do with the criminal in a sense that is both very specific and extraordinarily broad, where the criminal can be understood as the resistant, cut augmentation of the proper. This means to think criminality not as a violation of the criminal law (however il/legitimate one thinks such law to be) but as a capacity or propensity to transgress the law as such, to challenge its mystical authority with a kind of improvisational rupture.

The anti-tumult law—which Du Bois ineffectively sought to apply to his own text (as the univocal voice of reason which, of course, bears itself as a kind of schizoid difference or transversal) and which is broken by the plexed multiplicity of his speech and writing—is a privileged place from which to begin an investigation of this criminality and its radical qualities. The whistle is, finally, a kind of clue at once immanent and transcendental, and the return of it or its like seems inevitable when and where righteous transgression and brutal repression meet. Deeper still, in cases such as this, what returns is a rich anticipation. But one shouldn't attach too much significance to such impediments of speech without having a sense of that surplus sound effect as something way more than an impediment. After the formation of such an apparatus what will remain, as always, is this: How will this event/music— the content it breaks and bears; the consent it holds and hands—continue visibly to mark the occasion of the volunteer?

chapter 4

The New International of Decent Feelings

In 1946, in the shadow of the previous century's most widely acknowledged versions of catastrophe, Louis Althusser described the formation of another International: "This 'International' of humane protest against destiny rests on a growing awareness that humanity is threatened, and has become, in the face of the threat, a kind of 'proletariat' of terror. Whereas the labouring proletariat is defined by sociological, economic, and historical conditions, this latter-day 'proletariat' would seem to be defined by a psychological state: intimidation and fear. And, just as there is proletarian equality in the poverty and alienation of the workers, so too this *implicit proletariat* is said to experience equality, but in death and suffering."[1] This new "equality" is perhaps more precisely understood as a new homogenization that now is manifest not only as the liquidation of dissent or of whatever marks the possibility of another way of being political, but even as the suppression of alternative tones or modes of phrasing.

In describing what he calls "the international of decent feelings," Althusser takes care both to imply and assert something outside of it, something on the other side of the limits within which this new equality operates. Recently, in response to the horrible events of September 11, 2001, and their aftermath, Geoffrey Galt Harpham—much like Albert Camus, André Malraux, and Arthur Koestler, the writers Althusser critically examined more than half a century ago—takes upon himself the task of resetting those limits and, just as in the work of Camus, Malraux, and Koestler (which embodies the angst-ridden and exclusionary leveling of a certain existentialism), the limit of the new international of decent feelings that emerges is terror. According to Harpham, terror now constitutes the fundamental "feature of the symbolic order, the vast mesh of representations and narratives both official and unofficial, public and private, in which a culture works out its sense of itself."[2] This is to say that terror now defines "our" collective identity. As it turns out, however, such a definition is nothing more than an intensified recalibration of the American exception. Intensified now because the U.S. response to terror is figured as the geopolitical reconstitution of the natural habitat—what Althusser might have referred to as the fatherland—of the human. The achievement of the human will now be understood as the adherence to "our" national interest. Humanity is equivalent to membership in "our" coalition though it is provisional, contingent upon a nation's or a people's willingness to do something to "help us." Harpham would seem to question this new configuration of the human but only reifies it by way of a thinly veiled romance with uncertainty, terror's primary manifestation, or with a supposed difficulty in "describ[ing] the most elemental of facts in a way that makes sense."[3] For Harpham, it is emblematic of such uncertainty that U.S. officials and their private policy adjuncts make charges of Iraqi complicity with the attacks of September 11 with no evidence save their feelings.[4] It is significant that Harpham's critique of such an appeal to feelings will ultimately align itself against evidence and analysis as if proper thought will have only taken place in the obsessive oscillation between false alternatives. We'll return to this later. For the time being, note that the abstract human equality that lies at the foundation of this new international has been revealed in all its exclusiveness with increasing intensity over the last few decades, and many of us who identify ourselves as Left intellectuals have perhaps grown too confident in its apparent eclipse. But here it comes again in Harpham's formulation and it has the same old features, features more insidious after the fact of their ongoing exposure and critique. The condition of possibility of the contemporary new international is the exclusionary nature of its concept of the human that is defined now by terror as limit-function. This is the essence of this old-new Left, this old-new International.

Significantly, the Third World simply fails to show up as a subject or collective subjectivity that is worthy of analysis for Althusser. The colonial question—which now seems to have been unavoidable in 1946 but was nevertheless avoided in the discourse of the international of decent feelings and its critique—is absent. And yet the military humanism that characterizes the international Althusser reads—and its contemporary recrudescence as manifest in Harpham's writing—is pinpointed by Althusser, thereby enabling the revelation of its cynical vulgarity in Harpham's text. It's the presentation of the Third World in Harpham's text that is the condition of his adherence to, rather than critique of, military humanism and its twisted sentiments. Meanwhile, in Althusser, it's as if Third World liberation is unforeseen, as if the colonized subject's very relation to the human is suspended by the irruption of the inhuman into what had been thought to be the human's exclusive domain. This is to say that the inhuman had become Europe's most pressing intramural matter, eclipsing momentarily the project wherein Europe had to discover, exploit, and, in exploiting, humanize the heretofore in- or prehuman.

Luckily for Harpham, operating within a practically Conradian recapitulation of the old paradigm, the inhuman is now returned to its natural locale, the Third World. This is the new exclusionary twist on the old international that must emerge when racialized imperial domination is an object of critique rather than a natural right. The justification of such domination can now be indexed to a delusion that Harpham takes to be self-evident—that the Third World is the place where the inhuman and terror converge and in a new and horrible, because ineffable, realignment. The new international of decent feelings, of humane protest against an uncertain destiny or against uncertainty as destiny, takes the daisy cutter as its most proper form. It's a First World affair, since the Third World continually finds itself unable to, or refuses to, achieve the humanity of counterterrorism that expresses itself in and as "our" dropped bombs, however temporary the satisfaction derived from such action might be. This is to say that for Harpham what's ultimately unsatisfactory about the bombings is not that they are inhuman or inhumane—they cannot be by definition because "we," the international of decent feelings, are perpetrating them—but that they are ineffective. Noam Chomsky—to whom we'll return precisely because the new internationalists obsessively return to him in order to renounce him—might say that this formulation is reminiscent of that liberal discourse that eventually emerged alongside American intervention in Southeast Asia whose fundamental point was that the war should have been stopped because of the impossibility of victory, because the satisfaction to be derived from the moral correctness of "our" intentions could not be achieved or sustained.

Althusser denounces the international of decent feelings because it attempts to erase antagonisms that are the necessary precursors of revolutionary theory and practice. Such cause for concern certainly has not disappeared. This erasure of antagonisms is bound up with the grotesque reduction and projection of terror that characterizes Harpham's discourse. The point is that when Harpham invokes what might be called "the Pentagonal we," it is merely the expression of the foreclosing power of a strange prematurity. This "we" makes we impossible. As Althusser argues, the terror that characterizes the proletariat is not some obsession with the horrible that might happen. "The worker is not a proletarian by virtue of what-will-happen-to-him-tomorrow, but by virtue of what happens to him every minute of the day. . . . Poverty, in the proletariat, is not the fear of poverty, it is an actual presence that never disappears."[5] This is to say that the most immediate refusal to be terrorized with which Harpham ought to have been concerned is his own. This speaks to the virtuality of a new international that is fragmented not by the Third World's inability to "help us" but by our ongoing inability viciously to critique the fatal simplicity of this implied self-construction. The decision to face the facts of suffering, to analyze the causes of suffering, is a necessary condition of empathy that would both follow from such critique and is its condition of possibility. Significantly, Chomsky serves as the axis around which revolves the simple opposition between feeling and analysis—which accompanies that between us and them—that Harpham reifies in the midst of something meant to pass for critique.

> It is bizarre to see the hard right promoting *feelings* and the hard left—if that is where Chomsky is; it has become difficult to place him anywhere—so coldly analytical. . . . And it is disturbing, too, to think that there are so many intelligent people for whom there is simply no event so ghastly, so outrageous, so monstrously murderous, so wanton and ignoble that the United States would not be held to be ultimately responsible for it simply on the grounds that *we* could have no share in *that*. It is Chomsky's refusal to be terrorized, his insistence that the terror really makes sense, that it has a germ of rational motivation, that this germ can and should . . . be incorporated into our national self-description, included among the narratives we tell about ourselves, that is the most terrifying, and terroristic, aspect of his thought.[6]

Chomsky's "cold" analysis is figured here as a kind of terror. It's aligned with the act that it's accused of rationalizing and, as such, is understood, along not only with the ones who perpetrate the act but with the kind of people who perpetrate and or rationalize such acts, as not just irrational but subrational, as geographically and historically foreign to the national-humanist zone of rationality. Of course whatever bombing we do in response to terrorist acts is not tainted by any sub- or prerational drive to rationalize precisely because its rationality is self-evident or is, in the absence of any evidence, something that "we" feel to be right. This is to say that it's self-evident that *we* could have no share in *that* (set of acts where the irrational or the unrationalizable and the monstrously violent converge), no matter how much like *that* whatever *we* do is, no matter how many times *we* did things like *that* before *that* was done to *us*. Such clotted logic leads to the formulation that equates the principled and persistent critique of American foreign policy's almost constant violation of the principles it espouses with mass murder or, just as problematically, with a kind of irrational fundamentalism whose fatherland is now not but nothing other than the Third World.

For some time a crisis concerning the specific features of Chomskyan political reason has been discernible in the arena of a certain Left critical theory. Now, in Harpham's view, the crisis is just as much about Chomskyan feeling or, more problematically, Chomsky's adherence to a discourse of reason and his supposed avoidance of a discourse of feeling. Why has Chomsky become such a problem? How do those who operate, as it were, under the protection of a kind of veil of the Left get so incensed by someone whose critique of capitalism, imperialism, and fascism has been so principled and uncompromising? Why is Chomsky's supposed absence of feeling so disturbing when so many other tragedies, ones he has taken pains and continues to take pains to bring to our attention, seem to have produced neither a discourse of feeling nor chagrin over the absence of such a discourse on the part of critics like Harpham? What it is that we decide to say we feel something about and what it is that seems to bear no relation to the question of feeling is of interest here.

Harpham's presumption is not only that one should feel something (which is to say something *more*) about September 11, but that the event is only properly approached by way of feeling rather than by way of an analysis that seeks reasons for, and reason in, the event, however monstrous such reason and such reasons might be. Note, however, that for Harpham the bombing of Afghanistan seems more able to bear such analysis, and that such analysis leads to the conclusion that American foreign policy since September 11 is just and justified. Whatever imperative there is to feel for the victims of "our" poignantly ineffective bombing is muted by its seemingly unassailable rationality, a rationality whose justification seems to be a kind of general confusion to which Harpham points but for which he has no remedy. Indeed, Harpham naturalizes this confusion that only serves, finally, to justify the ongoing execution of U.S. foreign and military policies that predate the event that is supposed to have prompted them. The point, again, for Harpham, seems to be that it's not that one should feel but that one should feel more about this than about other things, things that are either beyond or beneath feeling or things that are at least still subject to reasoned analysis, though the reasoned analysis that would place such things within the context of a general history of world terror is properly understood as tantamount to terror. I should feel more about this because I'm an American. I should feel more about this because I'm a New Yorker. I should feel more about this because of the ultimate sacrifice of our heroes. Such justifications are naturalized and unquestioned.

Meanwhile, the appeal to feeling that had earlier been critiqued is now repeated. Such inconsistency marks the spot where confusion represents itself as a kind of national-humanist rationality or as what Jacques Derrida has more precisely called "the onto-theology of national humanism."[7] What remains is the question of the compatibility of the assumption that one should in this case and with regard to this event feel, which is to say feel more, and certain fundamental principles of a Left politics that are now under the neopragmatist assault of self-appointed defenders of modernity and the fox-like guardians of the chicken coop of Enlightenment (as if the average rooster could have ever thought up something like that on his own). More specifically, this is to think about the question of this imperative to feel more here now given the history of American policy, a history that is ongoing, a history that never paused for a second, a trajectory that was never broken by the events of September 11 themselves, all claims regarding the fundamental disruption of world order to the contrary. American imperial policy took no time off to mourn. It does not stop to feel even if it incorporates and controls a powerful discourse of feeling. Perhaps we ought to defer the question concerning whether or how Chomsky was terrorized just long enough to note that U.S. imperial power and its ideological apparatuses and apparatchiks most certainly were not.

Terror, like fear, is, as Althusser says, "captivity without possibility of flight."[8] The "we" who bomb are embedded in such captivity though it is the captivity of the prison guard. In the end, Harpham's belated version of the pieties of the human condition fails to constitute, as Althusser might say, "a human fatherland. . . . The human fatherland is not the proletariat of the human condition," not the Pentagonal "we"; "it is the proletariat *tout court*, leading the whole of humanity towards its emancipation."[9] Already in 1946, by the way, even amid his "Catholic communism," we see Althusser beginning to deploy a strategic antihumanism in the service of another, nonexclusionary human ensemble. When Harpham renews exclusionary humanism, the task of its critique in the name of the human is also renewed, and this requires a renewal of the discourse of truth in order to combat exclusionary humanism's anguished and confused delight in the indeterminate. To wallow in so-called terror as uncertainty, indeterminacy, confusion, or the fear of these is wholly to deny the epistemological register within which operates terror's ongoing lived reality. Althusser appeals to a kind of Christian truth to which I cannot appeal; nevertheless, a discourse of truth is available to us—the simple, banal, inexhaustible record of what "we" do and of "our" motives for doing it. Harpham takes great pains to discredit this discourse, and the recourse to mystification it seems to require, as one of its elemental ritual forms, the renunciation of Chomsky as that discourse's primary purveyor.

In fact, it's not coincidental that one must turn to Chomsky and his critique of the workings of another old-new international in the mid-sixties in order to find some precedent for Harpham's discourse and some framework within which to critique it. In his 1967 "The Responsibility of Intellectuals," Chomsky writes of a "growing lack of concern for truth" manifest in statements animated by "a real or feigned naiveté with regard to American actions that reaches startling proportions."[10] Chomsky points to the example of Arthur Schlesinger, who "characterized our Vietnam policies of 1954 as 'part of our general program of international goodwill,'" noting that "unless intended as irony, this remark shows either a colossal cynicism or an inability, on a scale that defies comment, to comprehend elementary phenomena of contemporary history."[11] But Schlesinger's obtuseness seems no more extreme than that of Harpham who claims, in his conclusion, that "terror . . . is nothing other than the aggravated sense of the possibility that new forms of maleficence and horror are even now being harbored by our best intentions, lurking in the caves of our noblest ideals, ramifying in the dark, soft interior tissues of our most honorable attempts to secure peace and freedom in the world."[12]

As Chomsky points out, Schlesinger, in his capacity as a member of the Kennedy administration, was forthright about his own decision to lie in the national interest, a dishonesty he evidently thought justifiable. What's sad about Harpham is that he's not lying. Or, more precisely, his is a deception that seems inwardly rather than outwardly directed and therefore tells us something about the inner workings of the international of decent feelings in its present form. Self-deception, in discourse such as this, often manifests itself as an appeal to the self-evident. There are many, however, who would wonder what are the "honorable attempts to secure peace and freedom in the world" by the United States to which Harpham refers? Why renounce a mode of discourse that makes it possible to disabuse oneself of such evident delusions? These are matters of fact, of truth in its simplest and most uninteresting form, that finally allow the placement of the brutal and vicious attacks of September 11 within the context of an ongoing contemporary history of terror. Such contextualization is neither justification nor correlation. If it attributes reason to the bombers it does so within the context of a history of instrumental madness that goes past September 11 and right up to the contemporary manifestation of "our" participation in the imperial administration of Afghanistan, whose justification is, for Harpham, on the one hand unproblematically reasonable and, on the other hand, in its incomplete satisfaction, the occasion precisely for the present renewal of the grotesque discourse of sentimental militarism.

What's at stake in the denial of the truth—which is to say the facts—of this history of instrumental madness as instrumental reason? What's at stake in the refusal to acknowledge that "we" are by far its most consistent and powerful perpetrators? Again, Althusser points toward an answer. What's at stake is the very possibility of another collective political being, and the point of such refusal is not the origin of the current crisis but whether or not we stand for its closure or its perpetuation. The attempted foreclosure of such possibility reads almost like a hoax. Ultimately, Harpham raises the undecidable question of causality only in order to deflect the question concerning "our" ethical and political stance regarding its continuation. The question of what, if anything, caused the September 11 bombing is independent of the fact that U.S. foreign policy is foul, just as the question concerning what, if anything, the attacks caused or what, if anything, "our" bombing of Afghanistan will have caused is independent of the fact that it is foul. And yet we do know something about what such brutality has caused and will cause. To think these questions without implicating ourselves is monstrous. Quite simply, Harpham would exclude from "our" symbolic register the critique of "our" foreign policy, critique he equates with what he sees as a Chomskyan refusal to be terrorized. Rather, he places a premium on the ability to conjure uncertainty or indeterminacy from the brutal fact of the millions whom "we" have killed or who have been killed in "our" name and the ability to see U.S. sponsorship of and participation in murder as an effect of confusion and impotence.

However, Althusser provides the terms for a celebration of just such refusal as Chomsky's, though to do so is decidedly not to accept the perverse terms of Harpham's discourse, one which seems able to discern and judge the appropriateness of this or that person's feelings about an event which has come, for him, to define terror in and as an uncomfortably open futurity, even as his feelings concerning the ongoing everydayness of terror before and after this event remain unexamined. In the end, the question of whether or not the present crisis is old or new is not undecidable. It is both old and new. The real question is what you get out of trying to make it undecidable and of saying that a subservient comportment toward such undecidability constitutes "our" collective political identity. So that the facile appeal to the self-evident in Harpham that is neurotically poised between the false alternatives of feeling and analysis, particularly the appeal to the notion that the old world order has been shattered and that a new world order has been born, must be challenged. All that's new is the ground of the time-honored repeal American liberalism enacts on its principles, principles whose ongoing violation has been the rhythm track of the American Century; and that ground is nothing other than the brutal exploitation of a mode of victimization that the likes of Harpham seem to have found unacknowledgeable until September 11. What continually announces itself as the home or embodiment of Enlightenment, of modernity, of humanism, here reveals itself again as their ongoing negation; this is the true rhythm of the iron system, of instrumental rationality run amok; it's the backbeat and background of Harpham's essay.

Meanwhile, of Koestler, Malraux, and Camus, Althusser says: "We are entitled to *ask if these desperate people are not nurturing a secret hope, and are not serving a cause or master they do not invoke:* the cause of a 'Western' socialism without class struggle, that is, the cause of a Europe united in a verbal, moralizing socialism which conjures away social antagonisms, thus maintaining in actual fact, despite concessions of form, the essential positions of capitalism."[13] It seems too elevating to ask such questions of Harpham since even a moralizing socialism independent of social antagonisms has been struck from his horizons, however much he might avail himself of the ideological and pseudointellectual cover of certain putatively Left assumptions. His text speaks for a replicant ensemble that is, necessarily, farce, not tragedy, after all. Nevertheless, it seems important and just to point out how truly subservient to the mission of maintaining the status quo that ensemble's discourse on September 11 and its aftermath is. Its "we" is the collective subject for whom everything now is new and unprecedented, the one for and from whom declarations abound regarding the rupture and recalibration of military and political world order. This Pentagonal We, this pentagonal—as opposed to fundamentalist—Left sounds like this: "And yet, it seems that we must bomb. This is the most just of just wars, and if we were not bombing, we would be doing nothing at all except grieving and fearing."[14]

Note that in Harpham's text the question of an alternative—later used to bludgeon Chomsky who is understood as the one who produces no options—is closed. There is nothing to do but bomb, for this we, according to this we. There is no alternative but to engage precisely in that which is perversely given as unsatisfactory, as merely tactical. That the pentagonal we is left only with the option of bombing emerges as self-parodic yelps, in unselfconscious self-parodic sentences, as the sententious self-parodic drone—imbued with the rigorously precritical, noninquiring correctness of a Chris Matthews–model empty, though endlessly talking, head—that is the hallmark of a time-honored American discursive strain. It's the noisy parallel track to American military/corporate power—an elite discursive line on which a small minority talks to itself in public with the wack propriety of the so-called public sphere. It's sad that English professors now want, though I suppose many have always wanted, to join this community and speak its vulgate, mouthing the nerdy but homicidal schoolboy rhetoric (reminiscent of some kids playing *Battleship*) of "exit strategies" and "endgames."[15]

Thus a flock of so-called Left intellectuals whose membership degrades the set to which they claim to belong flock to add their voices to a choir that is peopled by the genuine victims of thought control in democratic societies, namely those like Thomas Friedman and Cokie Roberts who seem intent on convincing themselves that the lies regarding the purity of American motives mouthed in the Vietnam era by the likes of Arthur Schlesinger for elite public sphere consumption are actually true. These are people to be pitied more than hated but for the fact that they constantly play out their daily attempts at self-deception on media outlets that are interesting now only because so relatively few people actually pay attention to them, letting the rest of us know, if we didn't already, that this delusional public sphere is one vigilantly to be monitored from a safe distance, if not altogether avoided.

It might appear to be the case that Harpham's uncritical and naturalized identification with American power renews and reinitializes the subject of the new military humanism. But such an observation would be imprecise. What is performed, rather, in Harpham's discourse is not the military humanist subject but that subject's chronicler—the strange cross between public relations man and scholar who always seeks the crumbs of a kind of influence over policy but is always more likely merely to play the seamy role of the so-called public historian. This chronicler insists on his or her Leftism though the Left—particularly in its convergence with Third World subjectivity—seems to be its only object of critique. In this formation, a principled stand for nonviolence or the legitimate enactment by a citizen of a critique of his or her government's rapacious foreign policy is perversely described by Todd Gitlin as a "left-wing fundamentalist" alignment with an anti-Enlightenment, antimodernist formation whose primary twentieth-century manifestation as Nazism and communism is taken as much for granted as its supposed contemporary shift to Third World subjects in general and Islamic subjects in particular.[16] Meanwhile, one thinks of a certain connection between Harpham, Gitlin, and their ilk and Stephen Ambrose not because Harpham and Gitlin are plagiarists—neither of them have been accused of plagiarism nor is there any reason to think they should be—but because what both make clear, each in his own way, each in ways not formally unlike Ambrose's brand of allusiveness, is the infinite curvature of the military humanist sphere and its discourse. The words and phrases must be the same whether they're copied or arrived at by way of some almost wholly virtual, individual creativity.

What's particularly interesting is that entrance into this sphere is now securable by enacting a new manifestation of the old ritual exclusion of a broader public. Again, this new ceremonial form has, as one of its prime features, the renunciation of Chomsky that has now become a kind of inoculation, a kind of visa required for entry into this republic of letters. But what's at stake isn't Chomsky so much as the rest of the world that he has come to signify, the alternative public that he inhabits and helps to build, the ongoing enactment of (the drive for) another social life that, by the way, seems to me to constitute the clearest evidence of his feelings. More properly, Chomsky has become something like a sign of the myriad other modes of political being that do not fall under the umbrella of elite American exceptionalism and whose flourishing in the midst of the present crisis—as the construction and sustenance of new and active networks of information and organization, as renewed forms of cultural and political resistance—has occasioned the disciplinary efforts of Harpham and his crew. For them, the Left critique of U.S. foreign policy that maintains its principles after and especially in the wake of September 11 must be denounced and held off or away like some kind of viral embarrassment.

Meanwhile, the private public sphere is where the old-new Left can hope to be both rich and important while feigning an adversarial stance—in the very midst of their own self-absorbed self-deception where to be an adversary is uncritically to enact what Judith Butler calls a "passionate attachment"—to the power to which they have perhaps always been cathected.[17] Still, the rewards for entering this sphere are only the etiolated simulacra of money and fame. Like Sam Donaldson, Harpham thinks he's asking the tough questions. Now English professors, in the warmed-over imprecisions of the pragmatist degradation of European critical theory, stake their claim, thereby reducing September 11 merely to the occasion for this leftover political formation—both old and new in the most problematic senses of both these terms—shrilly to announce itself. This announcement, and its failure to silence the other speech that it denounces, is hereby noted.

chapter 5

Rilya Wilson. Precious Doe. Buried Angel.

I study art and am, in particular, interested in the aesthetics of what Cedric Robinson calls "the black radical tradition." It is by way of this tendency that I attempt to address Rich Blint's question of "how might a politically engaged aesthetics be useful in articulating alternative narratives of the occupation [of Palestine]" by way of or in a language inflected by a specific and necessary solidarity between the people of my tradition and the Palestinian people. But I'm at a loss. And really, I guess this is just to say that I resist the question while, on the one hand, knowing that it is a valid and important one and, on the other hand, not knowing at all how to address it. Let's say that in the face of the question's speed and clarity my impulse to resist wants to become deceleration (in the interest of directness) and blur (in the interest of precision).

But in the paper today (and in the paper today, *so* in the paper today) I saw the images—one a conventional photograph, the other the fantastic product of more complex digital technology—of two little black girls whose deaths and/or disappearances are the results, in multiple ways, of the brutal and callous state in which we live. The name of one of the little girls is unknown, but people in Kansas City—where her mutilated, decapitated body was found—have started calling her Precious Doe. There is no picture of Precious Doe save the computerized reconstruction of her face, copies of which now adorn the makeshift shrine that has been dedicated to her at Hibbs Park in Kansas City. We do, however, have a picture of five-year-old Rilya Wilson, a girl whose disappearance fifteen months ago from a Florida foster home was only recently noticed by that state's Department of Children and Families who took Rilya from her mother—twenty-eight-year-old former crack addict Gloria Wilson who said "the letters in Rilya's name mean 'remember

I love you always'"—so that she might be cared for and protected. There was a kind of ghastly hope this week in Kansas City that with the emergence of Rilya's story a face and a name finally had been found to match Precious Doe's body but it turns out that these little girls are not the same, that there will be no way to turn two tragedies into one. But to speak even of two tragedies is false. The images of Rilya and Precious resonate with those of all the children whose disappearance and death the United States oversees, enables, and perpetrates. These images resonate with that of the body of a young Palestinian girl buried in the rubble of Jenin. The caption attached to this last image reads, "buried angel" and that's the only name I've been able to find. She's lying on her side, her profile partially uncovered, like an Ana Mendieta performative photograph come to real, deadly life.

These images now, in their resonance, constitute a set, concretizing a bridge, which before might have seemed "merely" figural. That resonance bespeaks the ongoing ideological degradation of the human in what Sylvia Wynter calls the "overrepresentation of Man," the ongoing disappearance, in its reduction to matter, of what is supposed not to matter.[1] This disappearance, serially enacted by mainstream American journalism, keeps many of us from seeing things. Its iteration in the disappearances of three more little girls was decreed by racist, imperial power even before their deaths though they live now within the horribly beautiful irony with which their deaths defy such disappearance. They remain, even if unseen, in the ongoing disappearance that anticipates and redoubles their ongoing disappearance. This is the defiance of burial these images instantiate and record.

The images are accompanied by fugitive, improper names. Precious. Rilya. Buried Angel. These names move and work within a history of such naming, a history of radical imaging and imagination that troubles the aesthetic and the political like a scar, like a choke-cherry tree. Of course, Toni Morrison has mapped the terrain I'm briefly trying to cover here. Precious, Rilya, and Buried Angel all move in the resonance of *Beloved*, of *Dreaming Emmett*, and of the violated, exhausted motherhood these artworks invoke. Such exhausted motherhood is more than either possible or impossible because it comes most fully into its own at the death of a child (either by way of the brutal hand of the state or its vicious apparatchiks or by the tragic and horrible raising of the mother's own hand or by the desperate actions of the hand of the child or of another child). It comes most fully into its own as radical dreaming, radical imaging, as a radical imaginative sociality—grounded, unburied life. And one resists talking about this precisely because it seems improper, inappropriate, seems to be moving outside all legitimate and/or legitimating regulation, like the music that Nathaniel Mackey argues is the last resort, as well as the earliest product, of wounded kinship. But we need such music, such imaging, such naming to tell this story right and to start to tell another one. I guess all I can do here is affirm this truth and note its placement in the images and names I've mentioned here. This is finally about the terrible beauty of the radical image and if there is a call embedded in my words it's the call for an extension of the terrible and beautiful project of radical imagining, of radical imaging, of radical *poesis* and radical remembering. Let us pray to the buried angels and let the memorial content of our prayer be new struggle, new desire, and new will: "Remember I love you always."

chapter 6

Black Op

Black studies is a dehiscence at the heart of the institution and on its edge; its broken, coded documents sanction walking in another world while passing through this one, graphically disordering the administered scarcity from which black studies flows as wealth.[1] The cultivated nature of this situated volatility, this emergent poetics of the emergency in which the poor trouble the proper, is our open secret.

This open secret is the aim of black studies—a weight, a comportment, where what it is to carry converges with what it is to arrive, always more and less than completely. The critique of the structures and tendencies whose delimitation and denial of that aim appear integral to their own foundation has rightly been understood to be indispensable to black studies, which is "a critique of Western Civilization," according to Cedric Robinson.[2] This is to say that what is called Western civilization is the object of black studies. This black optics is an auditory affair: night vision given in and through voices that shadow legitimate discourse from below, breaking its ground up into broken air; scenes rendered otherwise by undertones that are overheard but barely. (Consider the rustle of a garment as the open, internally noncoterminous, interrogatory punctuation of a collective chop or clap; the worked, songlike irregularity animating Andrew Cyrille's brushed analytic of flavor; the breathy tortuousness of Jeanne Lee's brightening of taste; the seen, seared, heard, sheared relation between what is there and not there, on the outskirts of all belonging, that the music gives.) With its vast repertoire of high-frequency complaints, imperceptible frowns, withering turns, silent sidesteps, and ever-vigilant attempts not to see and hear, black studies, that vast, pleasurable series of immanent upheavals and bad, more than subjunctive moods, *is* the critique of Western civilization. Often this critique shows up in a range of unpaid, imposed pedagogical duties carried out at various faculty meetings and conferences; it is often manifest as a sublation of anger mistaken either for uncut ire or the absence of ire. Black students have to think about the give and take of such surplus being stripped from the thickness of their skin; then decide that it is best understood, best distilled, as the mood for love.

This is why Robinson is equally adamant that black studies' critical modalities are driven toward and directed by an aim—the ontological totality and its preservation—that, in all its secret openness, is called blackness. Black studies' aim has always been bound up with and endangered by its object. When the prosecutorial gaze that is trained on that object (Western civilization) passes over that aim (blackness, which is not but nothing other than Western civilization), the danger is brutally, ironically redoubled. Talk of the preservation of the ontological totality produces great consternation in certain circles, which is unsurprising given the scarred, grainy, phonic inscription that accompanies such utterance. When that sound is received as mere catastrophic effect, as an always already broken acoustic mirror, critique turns into litigation in the hope of silencing it. But catastrophe must be sounded for the terrible, beautiful resonance it bears of that anoriginal recording of constant incision and expansion whose irreducible priority persists only insofar as preservation is transformation. It is in the recognition of the interplay of rupture and irruption in and as the given that black studies aims and objects intermittently, inconsistently, but serially reconvenes, again and again momentarily escaping danger. Black studies break/s a rhythm whose tactile complexity must be maintained. It keeps moving, in and out of the institution, where smooth abrasion never seems to have a chance. Its inordinate feeling for divisions and collections requires every last bit of texture, as an opening gambit held in reserve—the "paraontological distinction" between blackness and the people (which is to say, more generally, the things) that are called black.

In abiding with this distinction, one might instantiate an adequate challenge to the voraciously instrumental antiessentialism, powered in an intense and terrible way by good intentions, that sanctions black studies' ongoing struggle with the misplacement of its aim and object. A kind of carelessness is revealed—as if the truth of old-new things is made available through their neglect—when invocations of home are subject to the continual misrecognition of their perpetual ideation of perpetual motion, while claims on homelessness are held to be everything other than the most radical mode of being-in-the-world. Similarly, when the strained desire the history of thinking imposes on those who have to think their way out of the exclusionary constrictions of that history succumbs to the antierotic power of summary judgment, the work that emerges is undone by what it misses. Behind such pseudocritical nonsolicitousness often lies a conflation of totality and the specter of a still univocality from which an etiolated idea of blackness is derived in order that it might be rescued by appeals to multiplicity that never fully regulate their own dismissive impulses. In fact, to be down with the dialectic of home and homelessness within which blackness persists, a dialectic that n(eg)ation language seems to bring into the sharpest audiovisual relief, one must have indexed (but more than this—grasped and inhabited in order to have thrown and departed) the ensemble of uptown operations that are migration's precedent, held, as they are, in captive movements that still take place and flight up the country. The mysteries of a certain kind of locomotive whine are always given and withheld by way of the underwater cables some alien folk lay down when they are barred from travel and forcibly removed. The submerged span remains as its own convention. So that out of the unjustified margin between the ascription of contagion as slur and the vicious infatuation surveillance imposes, blackness is a general, material aspiration, the condition of possibility of politics understood, along but also off Foucauldian tracks, as the irreducible unconventionality of race war— covert, gentle violence in the midst of conversion, an effect of conversion and imminently convertible in and as this essence of covering rolled back (flourished, ex-caped) and aggressively forgiving modesty. No government can take responsibility for it, however much it emerges in and out of governmental conditions; at the same time, it remains unresponsive to the governance that it calls and the governments that it rouses. The paraontological distinction brings the secrecy and openness of this gathering into relief as well.

All this—which was always so essentially and authentically clear in its wrought, inventive, righteous obscurity—now often suffers being revealed and reviled in critique that advances by way of what is supposed to be the closure of authenticity, essence, and experience, all of which continue to be made to share the most precise and predictably easy-to-dismiss name, local habitation, and communal form of life. That blackness is often profiled and found wanting in what it is and has, in work that involuntarily falls under the admittedly imprecise rubric of African American studies, is also unsurprising and is due not so much to chauvinistic reactions to real or perceived chauvinism but to the fact that blackness's distinction from a specific set of things that are called black remains largely unthought. Paraontological resistance to this particular brand of orthodoxy requires a paleonymic relation to blackness, which is not in need of a highlight it already has or an extrachromatic saturation it already is or a rampant internal differentiation it already bears. As such, it need not be uncoupled from the forms that came to stand (in) for blackness, to which they could not be reduced and which could not be reduced to them.

What is often overlooked in blackness is bound up with what has often been overseen. Certain experiences of being tracked, managed, cornered in seemingly open space are inextricably bound to an aesthetically and politically dangerous supplementarity, an internal exteriority waiting to get out, as if the prodigal's return were to leaving itself. Black studies' concern with what it is to own one's dispossession, to mine what is held in having been possessed, makes it more possible to embrace the underprivilege of being-sentenced to the gift of constant escape. The strain of black studies that strains against this interplay of itinerancy and identity—whether in the interest of putting down roots or disclaiming them—could be said, also, to constitute a departure, though it may well be into a stasis more severe than the one such work imagines (itself to be leaving). In contradistinction to such skepticism, one might plan, like Curtis Mayfield, to stay a believer and therefore to avow what might be called a kind of metacritical optimism. Such optimism, black optimism, is bound up with what it is to claim blackness and the appositional, runaway, phonoptic black operations—expressive of an autopoetic organization in which flight and inhabitation modify each other—that have been thrust upon it. The burden of this paradoxically aleatory goal is our historicity, animating the reality of escape in and the possibility of escape from.

What if the study of comparative racialization begins to extend and deepen its critical and imaginative relation to the terms *abolition* and *reconstruction* in a genuine, fundamental, fantastic, radical, collective rethinking of them that will take into account their historical ground while also propelling them with the greatest possible centrifugal force into other, outer, space? Then, even though these terms index a specific history in the United States, their continued relevance and resonance will be international as well as intranational insofar as the ongoing aggressive constitution of the modern nation-state as a carceral entity extends histories of forced migration and stolen labor and insofar as the imperial suppression of movements that would excavate new aesthetic, political, and economic dispositions—as well, of course, as those movements themselves—is a global phenomenon. Abolition and reconstruction might then be seen as ongoing projects animating the study of comparative racialization and black studies, two fields that will now be seen as each other's innermost ends, two fields that will have now been understood as constituted through the claim they make on, which is to say their thinking of and in, blackness.

Finally, one might plan to continue to believe that there is such a thing as blackness and that blackness has an essence given in striated, ensemblic, authentic experience (however much a certain natural bend is amplified by the force of every kind of event, however productive such constant inconstancy of shape and form must be of new understandings of essence and experience). It is so obvious (particularly after the recent lessons of Lindon Barrett, Herman Bennett, Daphne Brooks, Nahum Chandler, Denise Ferreira da Silva, Brent Edwards, Saidiya Hartman, and Sharon Holland, among others) that blackness has always emerged as nothing other than the richest possible combination of dispersion and permeability in and as the mass improvisation and protection of the very idea of the human. Thus, concern over the supposedly stultifying force of authenticity exerted by supposedly restrictive and narrow conceptions of blackness, worry over the supposed intranational dominance of blackness broadly and unrigorously conceived (in ways that presuppose its strict biological limitation within an unlimited minoritarian field), or anxiety over the putatively intradiasporic hegemony of a certain mode of blackness (which presumes national as well as biological determinations that are continually over- and underdetermined) indexes some other trouble that we would do well to investigate. Such investigation is best accompanied by vigilant remembrance of and commitment to the fact that blackness is present (as E. P. Thompson said of the English working class) at its own making and that all the people who are called black are given in and to that presence, which exceeds them (in an irrevocable, antenational combination of terror and enjoyment, longing and rejection, that Hartman in particular illuminates). Ultimately, the paraontological force that is transmitted in the long chain of life-and-death performances with which black studies is concerned is horribly misunderstood if it is understood as exclusive. Everyone whom blackness claims, which is to say everyone, can claim blackness. That claim is neither the first nor the last anticipatory reorientation but is, rather, an irreducible element of the differentially repeating plane that intersects and animates the comparativist sphere.

In this regard, black studies might best be described as a location habitually lost and found within a moving tendency. It's where you look back and forth and wonder how utopia came to be submerged in the interstices and on the outskirts of the fierce and urgent now. The temporal paradox of optimism—that it is, on the one hand, a necessarily futurial attitude while being, on the other hand, in its proper Leibnizian formulation, an assertion of the necessity, rightness, and essential timelessness of the already existing—resonates in the slim gap between analytic immersion and deictic reserve. This bitter Earth is the best of all possible worlds, a fact that necessitates the renewed, reconstructed realization of imaginative intensities that move through the opposition of voluntary secrecy and forced exposure in order to understand how the underground operates out in, and as, the open. What's the relation between the limit and the open? Between blackness and the limit? Between a specific and materially redoubled finitude called blackness and the open? The new critical discourse on the relation between blackness and death has begun to approach these questions. That discourse reveals that optimism doesn't require—indeed it cannot persist within—the repression of that relation; rather, it always lives, which is to say escapes, in the faithful, postfatal assertion of a right to refuse, in the prenatal instantiation of a collective negative tendency to differ, and in the resistance to the regulative powers that resistance, differing, and refusal call into being. The general insistence that we don't mind leaving here is inseparable from the fact that it's all right. Black optimism persists in thinking that we have what we need, that we can get there from here, that there's nothing wrong with us or even, in this regard, with here, even as it also bears an obsession with why it is that difference calls the same, that resistance calls regulative power, into existence, thereby securing the simultaneously vicious and vacant enmity that characterizes here and now, forming and deforming us. However much trouble stays in mind and, therefore, in light of a certain interest that the ones who are without interests have in making as much trouble as possible, there is cause for optimism as long as there is a need for optimism. Cause and need converge in the bent school or marginal church in which we flock together to be in the name of being otherwise.

chapter 7

The Touring Machine (Flesh Thought Inside Out)

In his review of evolutionary psychologist Robert Kurzban's book, *Why Everyone (Else) Is a Hypocrite: Evolution and the Modular Mind*, philosopher and linguist Jerry Fodor takes sharp exception to Kurzban's assertion that our brains, insofar as they are nothing more than a bundle of heuristics capable of performing discrete sets of computational operations, neither imply nor require the organizing principle/principal that we ordinarily call a self. Since Kurzban "says repeatedly that he knows of no reason why the science of psychology should acknowledge . . . selves," Fodor is happy to provide one: "Selves are the agents of inference and of behavior; you need executives to account for the rationality of our inferences; you need the rationality of our inferences to account for the coherence of our behavior; and you need the coherence of our behavior to explain the successes of our actions."[1] When Fodor asserts the necessity of the executive, a relation between the knowledge and the care of the self is implied, though what Michel Foucault claims to be the priority of care to knowledge is inverted. In the intensity of his normative philosophical self-regard, Fodor's executive is proximate to what Foucault, in a brief reading of Seneca's *De Ira*, calls the administrator. For Foucault, the administrative knowledge that Fodor sees as necessary prepares the way for renunciation, which, in the end, cannot abide with care. But insofar as Fodor's critique of Kurzban seems to leave renunciation by the wayside, to consider the representative generality that emerges when Fodor's self, which seeks to "explain the success of [his] actions," and Foucault's self, which prepares "for a certain complete achievement of life," are posed together seems nothing less than an imperative.[2] At stake in such a pose, in the assumption of the possibility of position, is not only how, but also that, one looks at oneself; how and that one gives, in Judith Butler's words, "an account of oneself" in the end, as an end, in a discourse of ends above means.[3] In the meantime, in a temporality of means that might not even be discernible as a moment's absence, the relay between abjuration and esteem that derives from philosophical self-absorption is endlessly refused in an ongoing flash of exhaustion and consent. "Our flesh of flames" burns bright in its submergence.[4] It's (neo-)plastic flash still folds beneath the water. *I want to study the poetic registration of this immeasurable apposition to the world.*

Michel Foucault, in sketching an outline of the "technologies of the self, which permit individuals to effect by their own means or with the help of others a certain number of operations on their own bodies and souls, thoughts, conduct, and way of being, so as to transform themselves in order to attain a certain state of happiness, purity, wisdom, perfection or immortality," presumes a clear difference between them and those "technologies of production, which permit us to produce, transform or manipulate things." This is to say that while these technologies "hardly ever function separately," they do operate against the backdrop of a sharp distinction between things and selves, which move within two different technological hemispheres—the technological manipulation of things and signs, which "are used in the study of science and linguistics" and the "technologies of domination and the self" that Foucault concerned himself with in the development of his "history of the organization of knowledge," his historiography of the present.[5]

Black studies, which does or should consider what Nahum Chandler calls "the problem of the negro as a problem for thought" within and by way of imperatives that are beyond category, is constrained to investigate the integration of these hemispheres and is particularly responsible for forging an understanding regarding the relationship between (the manipulation of) things and (the care of) selves.[6] This is to say that insofar as the ungovernability of things and signs within and outside or underneath the field that is delineated and enclosed by the manipulative efforts of selves caught up in the exertions of governmentality is, or should be, our constant study, we must be comported in and toward the juncture of technological breakthrough and technological breakdown. Black study moves at the horizon of an event where certain instruments, insofar as they can no longer either calculate or be calculated, are bent toward the incalculable. That juncture, that event, doesn't just imply and assume and consider movement; it is, itself, on the move, as a kind of fugitive coalescence of and against more than agential force, more than agential voluntarity; as a kind of choir, a kind of *commercium*, whose general refrain—like a buzz or hum underneath self-concern's melodic line—is that it's not your thing, you can't just do what you want to do. Such clamor might best be understood, in its constant improvisational assault on the understanding that was sent to regulate it, as anti-administrative, ante-executive action.

Fodor believes that evolutionary psychologists like Kurzban have taken the notion of the modularity of mind—an idea derived in part from the Chomskyan idea of innate and specific mental device, which states that such a device is evolutionarily developed to have a specific function—too far. Though Fodor is a major contributor to that notion, he believes that too much liberty is taken with and derived from cognitive impenetrability, the condition in which mental mechanisms are understood not only to be distinct but also independent, "encapsulated from beliefs and from one another."[7] And so he takes Kurzban severely to task for attempting to show that such encapsulation predicts the absence of the executive. For Kurzban, the fact that we can believe two contradictory beliefs is explained by the fact that the brain contains distinct, discrete modules—bundles of software, as it were—that are devoted to separate operations. It's not the mind or the self that believes contradictory things; it's just two different packages within the brain that do. Contradictory views correspond to different functions, different uses to which the brain is put that correspond, in turn, to different packages of mental processes. "An important consequence of this view," Kurzban adds, "is that it makes us think about the 'self' in a way that is very different from how people usually understand it. In particular, it makes the very notion of a 'self' something of a problem, and perhaps quite a bit less useful than one might think."[8] Fodor's concern and his critique are derived from his sense that Kurzban's psychological Darwinism—"the theory that . . . the traits that constitute our 'psychological phenotype' are adaptations to problems posed by the environments in which the mind evolved"—can explain negation (the relation or copresence of P and not-P) but not addition (the relation of P and Q).[9] He argues that Kurzban can explain how there can be impenetrability, but not how there can be interpenetrability, without an executive.

What I've been wondering, though—by way of the specificity of Fodor's critique of Kurzban but against the grain of what Fodor understands to constitute the ground of that critique; from the perspective of someone who is also interested in certain operations that have been done on bodies and souls, as well as on *Body and Soul*; in the light and sound, therefore, of a mode of social aesthesis whose predicate is that impenetrability and interpenetrability are one another's animation—is whether the self is better understood as something akin to what David Kazanjian calls a "flashpoint" marking a socially generated rebellion against the executive that is manifest in the form of the soloist who can now be thought as sociality's nonfull, non-simple, anarchic, anarchaic avatar.[10] The executive function is an exclusionary, hierarchical function that governs the space and adjudicates the relation between what negates and what carries and is derived from P. In this regard, Fodor writes that "it is not an accident that the belief P is a constituent of the belief P&Q; and it is not an accident that the sentence 'John prefers coffee' is a constituent of the sentence 'John prefers coffee in the morning.' If you have an executive, you can (maybe) make sense of all that. If not, then—so far as anyone knows—you can't. Intellectualism suggests the possibility of a unified treatment of logic, language and thought."[11] I want to suggest that it is something other than anti-intellectualism to think that what the executive excludes is a vast range of extrarational relations for which we cannot, strictly speaking, account; relations, which is to say things, that cannot be accounted for because they cut and augment inference; things like whatever occurs when believing P and believing Q is more or less and/or more and less than P and Q. All the things we are are more and less than selves. In general, the general is more and less, given in new sentences that some might see as unworthy constituents for which we cannot account, but which others might see more clearly as instantiations of the incalculable. Worked minds work wonders with 6.2 words, making do with less and more.[12]

Before a submarine poetics of plain, sous l'eau danse l'avenir dans le pre. We're something like, but both a little bit and a whole lot less and more than, the machine Alan Turing imagined and described: an infinite memory capacity, with an infinite amount of time, whose computational force allows us to chart the limits of what can be computed. This other thing—a something's else or extra—goes over the edge of that limit. It is as if it has been thrown over the side of the vessel, the state-sanctioned ship or self that navigates that limit. The self's or the subject's transcendence has usually been associated with what it is to stand on the edge of the abyss to which it is and has been committed. Transcendence matters to the one who stands there only if it is given in her immanence, her thingliness, her fallenness, her homelessness, her sounding, her submarine movement, her endless tour. Study of the socioaesthetic substance of black insurgency is inseparable from attending to the history of the interplay of calculation and displacement. This conjuncture manifests itself in frenzied, troubled, muffled speech over the edge of whatever is supposed to divide sacrament from profanation. Foucault, by way of Philo of Alexandria, recalls "an austere community, devoted to reading, to healing meditation, to individual and collective prayer and to meeting for a spiritual banquet (*agape*, 'feast')." These common practices, he argues, "stemmed from concern for oneself." Foucault then shows how the movement from self-care to self-knowledge is finally and fully instantiated in techniques of verbalization that are first deployed in the service of ascetic self-renunciation and then, with the advent of the human sciences, are given over to a mode of self-representation that is the necessary accompaniment to what Angela Mitropoulos calls "the proliferation and democratization of sovereignty."[13] The undercommon articulation I want to study, the symposium I want to join, marks the violent festivity of the knowledge and care of flesh—in the flesh and not in sovereignty's divided body—arrayed against the terror and privation that attend the long career of self-concern's attempt to regulate that for which it cannot account, either through renunciation or assertion. When drowned speech becomes fire music, embalming burned flesh with a runaway sermon's fragrant sound, an alternative is announced.

By way of the din of generative multiplicity, which sounds like an itinerant quartet's rhizomatic excess of itself, or like what kids' anarchic sounding does to speech, or like the evolutionary step of loved, invaluable flesh's instantiating interplay of artifice and intelligence, its blessedness inseparable from its woundedness, both new, interinanimate in beatitude, in poverty's radical theoretical attitude, M. NourbeSe Philip's Zong! *documents descent and dissent, experiments in ascension and consent, as an emergence in anticipation but after the fact of the ongoing imposition of a submarine state of emergency that the dispersed sovereign (the executive whose sentences are constrained to administer the brutalities of broken felicity, fractured enjoyment), having commenced merchant, is serially enjoined to declare.*

There's an unruly interplay of silence and chatter that Ian Baucom's assemblage and idiosyncretic archive, Spectres of the Atlantic, *replays. There, the Zong's exhausted, inspiriting cargo—132 or 143 or 150 persons (documentation of the number always changes as if marking an insistent incalculability) thrown into the sea whose trace was buried in the hold of the official language and documents of the governmental and financial entities that authored their disappearance—enacts its emergence and meta-emergence again. Thinking, but also living, between silence and chatter persists on other registers, in all languages: not only the silencing of things, the silence of an unheard case, of a muffled appeal consigned to lower frequencies, of disruptive wave and terminally colliding particle where no one can observe; and not only that other effect that constantly nascent and dying capitalism and colonialism produces, the ceaseless chatter of administration, regulation, and what Baucom calls "phenomenal busy-ness": but also the silence and chatter of song, which thinkers have been known to misrecognize as an unbearable lightness; but also the hard, sweet life of language on "the spectrum," where I am an initiate under the protection of my son. He moves between silence and chatter, where the set pieces that adults usually reserve for the forced participation of kids break down in the face of a constant contact improvisation that you have to be ready for, as Al Green or Danielle Goldman would say. The brilliant surprise of the silly abcs (ba, dc, fe, h . . . sung to the rhythm and melody of the old tune) or the belated christening of a dinosaur (the protocerealbox, his bones discovered in illicit breakfast reading) must be heard to be believed. But those impositions (How old are you? Are you ready for Santa Claus? Are you strong? Show me your muscles! Do you like school?) aren't the only scripts, all of which aren't so easily done without. Every returned I love you is treasure when every incalculable gift was occasioned by an unimaginable loss and when the gift is often harder to accept, or would be, if it weren't for what you had already been given by poems, which Charles Bernstein, thinking about Robin Blaser, calls "the flowers of associational thinking." Lorenzo gives me a fresh bouquet every day as I learn to stop mourning for something I never had.*

One of the hard parts of caring for a child with an "Autism Spectrum Disorder" is the problem of where he should go to school. And if you're picky about school to the point of not believing in it even though you love it so much you never want to leave it, if you're so committed to the conservation of the strange and beautiful that your mistrust of the normal is redoubled to a level of intensity that can actually keep up with your desire for your child to have a normal life, then the general necessity of the alternative (school), which may have been a principle you've been trying to live by, now becomes concrete and absolute. It requires you to go back to kindergarten, at least every Tuesday morning, in order to play and get dirty and paint and make birdbaths and talk about princesses. Lorenzo and I facilitate communication with the other kids for one another out in the woods, where all the flowers grow. On Tuesday afternoon I go to school with the big kids, whose interest in flowers often goes against the grain of their schooling, where critical and creative attendance upon both silence and chatter is frowned upon in the interest of a whole other kind of preparation. In the afternoon we try to read Zong! This means we get together to decide how to get together to decide how to read it. The implication of a collective enterprise is now explicit—I don't think anybody can do it by themselves. Philip's memorial bouquet—faded, fading, murmured, submerged, displaced, misspaced, overlaid, is an effect of a range of (a)voided superimposition exposed as beauty, the amplification of an associational field that evokes the mutual aid that it also requires, the terrible intimacy of the irreparable where everything is less and more than itself.

The logic of reparation is grounded on notions of originary wholeness, on the one hand, and abstract/general equivalence, on the other. Baucom thinks this in relation to credit and imagination but I wonder if it's not really bound up with a strange kind of empiricism. What's the relation between the logic of reparation and the logic of representation? And what does that relation have to do with telling the truth, or the story, or the whole truth, or the whole story, with truth telling as a way of making whole? The normative arc of becoming (a subject, a citizen) is part of this logic. What if there were a radical politics of innovation whose condition of possibility is memory, which remains untranslated, whose resistance, in turn, makes innovation possible? Not to resuscitate! No resurrection. Make it new, like they used to say, so that indexicality is an effect, a technique, so that the recording is part of an experimental impulse. The archive is an assemblage. The assemblage is an image of disaster. But I just want you to enjoy yourself and I want you to believe that. This is an enthusiasm. This is the new thing and a lot of what it's about is just trying to figure out how to say something. How to read. Not (or not only) how to offer a reading, or even an interpretation, but a performance of a text, in the face of its unintelligibility, as if one were forced/privileged to access some other other world where representation and unrepresentability were beside the point, so that the response to the terrors and chances of history were not about calculation, not bound to replicate, even in a blunted and ethically responsible way, the horrors of speculation, where new materialities of imagination were already on the other side of the logic of equivalence.

In a long set of unmade circles, the conditions and effects of miscommunication are brutal and glorious. They keep going till you stop—to revel in something that breaks you up; to rebel in dread of reverse and whatever brings it because if there were nothing it would be impossible and easier. I'm trying to talk about zones of miscommunication + areas of disaster + their affective ground and atmosphere and terrible beauty. They're the same but really close to one another but unbridgeably far from one another, connected *by some inside stories we keep running from, the way people flee a broken park when the island is a shipwreck. The crumbled refuge is a hold and a language lab. Half the school falls away from the other half that escapes. Help in the form of a madman's persistent gunship. The settler's exceptional and invasive mobile fortress. Aggressive, hovering neglect of the instructor. He says the constant variety of distraction makes collaborating impossible and the other story's been buried again, concrete taken for water. The serially disrupted plan should have been disrupted but the disruption is serial— the same, enlarged catastrophe whose sociomusical, sociopoetic anticipation will peek through every once in a while as suppressed reports of suppression. Somebody has to imagine that, and how we keep dying for the shit we live for. The slave trade's death toll takes another shock today and still we cannot quite engage, always a little turned away and elsewhere, a little alone. At 1:15 we have to see if we want to figure out a way to work through this, which is to say in this. To move in, which is to say through, the obscenity of poetry. This, too, is what* Zong! *is about, having claimed the catastrophe.*

Poetry is rhythm breaking something to say that broke rhythm, an afterlife installation where knowledge takes the form of pauses, a soundscape made of risen questions, a machine made out of what happened when we were together in the open in secret. It miscommunicates catastrophe with unseemly festivity, in an obscenity of objection; it knows not seems, it doesn't know like that, its Julianic showings go past meaning, in social encryption, presuming the form of life whose submergence it represents. But it doesn't represent. It more and less than represents. There's a rough, unsutured trans-action that moves against repair to make a scar. The new thing is a scar. It's hard to look at something when you can't look away. In Scenes of Subjection, *Saidiya Hartman says redress is "a re-membering of the social body that occurs through the recognition and articulation of devastation, captivity and enslavement." I don't know if redress is obscene; I just know that it's cognate with administration. The social life of poetry strains against a grammar that seeks to defy both decay and generativity in the name of a self-possessed equivalence that, in any case, you know you can't have because you know you can't have a case. Some folks strive for that impossibility, rather than claim the exhaustion they are and have, as if this were either the only world or the real one. Encrypted celebration of the ongoing encryption is an analytic of the surreal world in and out of this one. It's not about cultural identity and it's not about origin; it's the disruptive innovation of one and the voluntary evasion of the other.*

Catastrophe is the absence of the realistic account. Unflinching realism cannot account for such exhaustion. Attempts at such accounting are brazen in their hubris unless whatever such account moves up and down an incalculable scale. The assignment of a specific value to the incalculable is a kind of terror. At the same time, the incalculable is the very instantiation of value. The incalculable is what I think I mean by innovation. You could think about it in relation to Hannah Arendt's understanding of natality, but only by way of a suspension of her stringent exclusions. This is Hartman's encryption. The logic of reparation is vulgar. It's inseparable from representation understood as the thing—which is presumed to have a hole in it, whose fantasy in the hold is serially denied—made whole. To make whole, as if one could ever find completion, as if completion weren't an absolute brutality, as if the whole were static, as if it were the original, as if it were ever anything other than more and less than itself, as if the simple logic of the synechdoche could ever have been adequate to the mobile assemblage (the Benjaminian constellation where what has been comes together with the now), is an act of violence. The thing made whole is a heuristic device for attorneys and their postliterary critical clerks, who have no sense of time. Meanwhile, Jetztsein is the supplement like Selassie is the chapel.

The commitment to repair is how a refusal to represent terror redoubles the logic of representation. The refusal of our ongoing afterlife can only ever replicate a worn-out grammar. The event remains, in the depths. The event-remains are deep and we stand before them, to express them, as their expression. These bits are a mystery, a new machine for the incalculable, which is next, having defied its starting place. I almost remembered this in a dream, where we were just talking, and nothing happened, and then it was over, until just now, with your hands, and light on the breeze's edge. I just can't help feeling that this is what we're supposed to do—to conserve what we are and what we can do by expansion, whose prompt, more often than not, shows up as loss (which shows up, more often than not, as a prompt). More shows up more often than nought if you can stand it.

There's a mutual transformation that occurs when the thing is engaged, a mutual supplement that serrates fantasmatic scenes of repair, that is always manifest as getting through or past or behind it to its essence or its message. What if the message were displaced by the ongoing production of code, which is our social life and what our social life is meant to conserve? What if what we talked about under the rubric of silence were discussed under the rubric of space? Or, in a different register, air? Or water? What is it like to be in the world with some other thing? What does it mean to consider that the relation between the reader, the poem, and history is spatial, a special relation, a north Atlantic entreaty, a plea, an exhortation in the form of a world embrace in resistance to enclosure? To speak the space-time of articulation as futurity, as projection? There's a mutual transportation that occurs when the poem is engaged, a mutual indirection that turns the way back round, this beckoning descent onto the gallery floor or fire or flor or banquet or bouquet.

Fragmentation is also about more, an initiation of the work's interior social life, a rending of that interiority by the outside that materializes it. The logic of the supplement is instantiated with every blur, every gliss, every melismatic torque, every twist of the drone, every turn of held syllable. I want to attend to the necessary polyphony. I don't want to represent anything and I don't want to repair anything but I do want to be here more, in another way. I think, in the end, Zong! works this way but even if it doesn't work this way I want it to work this way. I want to work it this way, in coded memory, as the history of no repair, as the ongoing event of more and less than representing. Zong! is about what hasn't happened yet. It is a bridge, which is to say a witness, to the ecstatic and general before. It moves in the irreducible, multiply lined relation between document and speculation, where the laws of time and history, of physics and biochemistry, are suspended, remade, in transubstantiation. The ones who have been rendered speechless are given to and by a speaker, in code, whose message, finally, is that there is speech, that there will have been speech, that radical enunciation (announcement, prophecy, preface, introduction) is being offered in its irreducible animateriality. No mercantile citizenship, no transcendental subject, no neurotypical self matters as much as this: the refusal of administration by those who are destined for a life of being thrown, thrown out, thrown over, overlooked for their enthusiasms, which they keep having to learn to look for and honor in having been thrown, which keep coming to them, which they keep on coming upon, always up ahead, again and again from way back, as out recording, submerged encoding, faded script that can't be faded, joining the sound of the ones who have (been) sounded, under an absolute duress of water, flesh that keeps speaking to us here and now, in contratechnical, counterstrophic, macrophonic amplification of the incalculable.

At circle time on Thursday, Lorenzo declared that when he makes s'mores for Julian (which I wasn't aware that he'd ever done, because I think he's never done it) he makes them with bricks, sticks, and snow. He has become an anoriginal king of comedy. When everybody stopped laughing all the *other jokes started flying around. Have you ever seen a Bethany eat another Bethany? Have you ever seen a Christopher eat a dishtopher? The circle broke up into a whole bunch of fiery, delectable shapes driven further out by choco-late milk. Orchard Hill School became the river of rivers in North Carolina (centrifugal curriculum, vigor, local abstraction). Then it was time for me to go to real school and time for them to go to the sleds. I wish my class were at the surreal school. That's what I'm trying for. But I have been lecturing my ass off, driven by the Holy Ghost that Philip is giving away. The only way I'm gonna be able to shut up is to go to Chicago. But I hadn't gone yet last week so my poor students had to bear with me, sitting around the table, while I repeated myself again, hoping that it was in a different way and hoping that the difference mattered. Then I said, in desperation, that the thing about this class is that I just want to be in a band, preferably this band, pointing to the speakers, listen-ing to that first modification of the one/s that cause/s Baraka to use atom bomb and switchblade in the same phrase, Miles and them in '60, in Stockholm, with Wynton instead of Red, Jimmy instead of Philly Joe. There's a sped-up deep-ening of "All Blues" that was only gonna get faster and more lowdown over the next handful of years as the universal machines kept blowing things up. From there we went back to "The Buzzard Song," a Gil Evans installation, ar-ranged horns chasing measure into the room with the moving walls. Abram said, "Well, he's just so cool that he can play his way out of any situation."*

When we immerse ourselves in Zong!, throw ourselves into its terrible ana-lytic of flesh, its beautiful analyric of being-thrown, we are the touring ma-chine, dedicated to the thinking of the incalculable, suspended in the break of computation, held on the other side in always being sent, "consent not to be a single being," saturated in middle passion's insistent and ongoing worrying of inauguration, still in movement, in the quartet's sober enthusiasm, from which the soloist flashes, as striated glide, to introduce us, once again, to our multiplicity. Which reminds me of a little girl named Mykah, noted for her refusal of administration, her resistance to calculation, her tendency to get in over her head. She keeps caringly, carefully, not taking care of herself with others all the time, is so exorbitantly common that she keeps folks worried about her executive and her administrator, who seem too often to go on tour. One day, standing in front of a hollow place in a tree almost big enough for them to enter, Mykah said to my boy: "Come on, Lorenzo, let's take a walk into the future."

In "Will Sovereignty Ever Be Deconstructed," Catherine Malabou impa-tiently notes that political philosophy is still organized by the problem of sovereignty. This might appear to be a problem that political theory needs to overcome; on the other hand, perhaps the problem is with politics. In other words, what if the theory of politics understands and properly calculates its object? What if political philosophy is, and can be, nothing other than the theory of sovereignty? What if the biopolitical deconstruction of sovereignty (which Angela Mitropoulos describes as sovereignty's "democratization" and which we might think of as the condition in which every properly self-possessed, property-owning person is the king of his castle) marks the modern convergence of politics and its theory? What if that convergence is the very constitution of our contemporaneity precisely insofar as it keeps the strange untimeliness that demarcates what it is to be a contemporary (to be an other for another as Frantz Fanon once said, in a kind of militant despair)? What if our contemporaneity is the emergence of the citizen as general equivalent (the abstract and empty signifier that Malabou aligns with the symbolic life of those who are constrained to stand in for one another)? What if the citizen, serially remade, as it were, by his right to life, which is given in the regulation of her life, is nothing other than an executive function that turns out to be the form that sovereignty takes, the way that it shows up, the airy structure of its phenomenality? Such appearance, or manifestation, marks a movement that Malabou traces from natural history to biology—from the political subject to the living subject. And the living subject, the biologized subject, is not just vulnerable to but instantiated by a kind of instrumentalization of the one who bears and is the regulated right to regulated life that operates in and by way of something like a loss of enchantment, a purposive deficit that is given in the turn from natural history to biology, predicated on the absence of a teleological principle. When Immanuel Kant attempts to supply that principle, is he already engaged in something like the deconstruction of biopolitical deconstruction, allowing the biological and the political to touch? This is, I think, an interesting and nagging question, given the particular tools that he invents and deploys in the interest of that deconstruction. What's at stake is that resistance to instrumentalization is driven by a kind of panic in the face of generativity and destruction, of a certain unregulated interplay of fecundity and finitude that might be something like what Malabou has been elaborating under the rubric of "plasticity." The transcendental subject, the sovereign, dispersed in and as the new citizen with a right to life, returns in the interest of a certain security, in a way that recognizes what I think it is that animates Malabou's essay, the notion that there is nothing other than biological resistance to biopower. She allows and requires us to ask what if the *bios* is nothing other than mutual instrumentalization and, even, indebtedness within a massive field of means without end/s? Then, "biological determination" is what we would conceptualize, constantly and paradoxically, as a necessary and unavoidable indeterminacy within the general structure of the interplay of fecundity and finitude. This is what the reintroduction of plasticity allows us to approach.

More pointedly, Malabou's work requires consideration of the relationships between law and the sovereign, the sovereign and the state. If it's possible to detach law from the state, as Robert Cover suggests, then it might also be possible to detach law from the sovereign. Kant joins those philosophers who see the biological as an instrument of power. He fears the play of life and death in the state of nature whose politicization Hobbes famously describes as "the time men live without a common power to keep them all in awe, [when] they are in that condition which is called war; and such a war as is of every man against every man," delimiting life as "solitary, poor, nasty, brutish, and short."[14] What's just as crucial as the assumption of the need for a common power to keep men in awe is the simple fact that the anarchic in/determinations of the biological are submitted to statist terminology, a kind of transcendental clue that seduces us to consider its mirror image, that nature is nothing other than resistance to the state/sovereign. Unseduced, Kant lays down a certain pathway, which more recently Arendt follows and maps, that traces the interplay between teleological principle and the state (a universal history whose cosmopolitan intent is carried out by sovereignty-in-dispersion). Along that line we would speak of the administration of/in natural history, as opposed to biology, which has no executive. Insofar as Kant appeals to natural history he tries to deconstruct biopolitical deconstruction; insofar as he remains committed to sovereignty in the form of a kind of world citizenship, he remains committed to the biopolitical deconstruction. Natural (or universal) history reifies and recollects the dispersed sovereign. After all, even "the critique or deconstruction of sovereignty is structured as the very entity it tends to critique or deconstruct," says Malabou, such that "contemporary philosophers reaffirm the theory of sovereignty, that is, the split between the symbolic and the biological."[15]

By way of Foucault, and also by way of Eric Santner's updating of Ernst Kantorowicz, Malabou implies that the distinction between the symbolic and the biological (given first in the medieval notion of the king's two bodies and then dispersed throughout the citizenry) corresponds to the distinction between the body and (divested, devalued [insofar as they have been assigned and reduced to an exchange value], supposedly deanimated) flesh. She accesses Giorgio Agamben's assertion that the bare life of divested flesh is somehow incorporated into every body, as a kind of essence that dwells in the biological. Mere flesh is within, as well as outside, the symbolic economy, as the thing itself of incorporative exclusion. Necessarily degraded essence, flesh is within, at the core of, the body, as its reduction to the deathliness of merely living though the merely living, homeless, and adrift, are incapable, precisely in their unlocatability, of being or having a body. The merely living fall short of the basic spatiotemporal requirements of selfhood which is, in turn, the basic requirement of sovereignty. Flesh is unaccommodated, which further implies the impossibility of something like an analytic of flesh that might pierce the distinction between the biological and the symbolic by thinking the flesh as invaluable, as the continual disruption of the very idea of (symbolic) value, which moves by way of the reduction of substance. This is to say that the reduction to substance (body to flesh) is inseparable from the reduction of substance. Ferdinand de Saussure speaks, for instance, of the reduction of phonic substance as a fundamental maneuver for the formation of a universal science of language that is given in the terms of a theory of value; some thinkers (Jacques Derrida and Jacques Lacan) endorse this reduction in their different ways; others (such as Félix Guattari) assert that this materiality is irreducible; Malabou refines and extends that assertion, challenging the ascription of nonvalue to the one whose value is only in the arbitrariness of exchange or signification.

Malabou's challenge echoes without fully acknowledging a recent history of the theory of flesh that moves from detached analysis to immanent critique to ritual celebration. Before Malabou, before Agamben, Maurice Merleau-Ponty and Fanon move in a kind of mutual orbit.

And then we were given the occasion to confront the white gaze. An unusual weight descended on us. The real world robbed us of our share. In the white world, the man of color encounters difficulties in elaborating his body schema. The image of one's body is solely negating. It's an image in the third person. All around the body reigns an atmosphere of certain uncertainty. I know that if I want to smoke, I shall have to stretch out my right arm and grab the pack of cigarettes lying at the other end of the table. As for the matches, they are in the left drawer, and I shall have to move back a little. And I make all these moves, not out of habit, but by implicit knowledge. A slow construction of my self as a body in a spatial and temporal world—such seems to be the schema. It is not imposed on me; it is rather a definitive structuring of my self and the world—definitive because it creates a genuine dialectic between my body and the world.

For some years now, certain laboratories have been searching for a "denegrification" serum. In all seriousness they have been rinsing out their test tubes and adjusting their scales and have begun research on how the wretched black man could whiten himself and thus rid himself of the burden of this bodily curse. Beneath the bodily schema I had created a historical-racial schema. The data I used were provided not by "remnant of feelings and notions of the tactile, vestibular, kinesthetic, or visual nature" but by the Other, the white man, who had woven me out of a thousand details, anecdotes, and stories. I thought I was being asked to construct a psychological self, to balance space and localize sensations, when all the time they were clamoring for more.[16]

This means that my body is made of the same flesh as the world (it is perceived), and moreover that this flesh of my body is shared by the world, the world *reflects* it, encroaches upon it and it encroaches upon the world (the felt [*senti*] at the same time the culmination of subjectivity and the culmination of materiality), they are in a relation of transgression or of overlapping. . . .

The *touching itself, seeing itself* of the body is itself to be understood in terms of what we said of the seeing and the visible, the touching and the touchable. I.e., it is not an act, it is a being at (*être à*). To touch *oneself*, to see *oneself*, accordingly, is not to apprehend oneself as an ob-ject, it is to be open to oneself, destined to oneself (narcissism)— Nor, therefore, is it to reach *oneself*, it is on the contrary to escape *oneself*, to be ignorant of *oneself*, the self in question is by divergence (*d'écart*), is *Unverborgenheit of the Verborgen* as such, which consequently does not cease to be hidden or latent—

. . . It is by the flesh of the world that in the last analysis once can understand the lived body (*corps proper*)—the flesh of the world is of the Being-seen, i.e., is a Being that is *eminently percipi*, and it is by it that we can understand the *percipere:* this perceived that we call my body applying itself to the rest of the perceived, i.e., treating itself as a perceived by itself and hence as a perceiving.[17]

Merleau-Ponty discovers territory that Fanon had already begun to explore in Merleau-Ponty's wake, namely the difference and relation between flesh and body and the theory that emerges from bodily position and fleshly apposition (in and against and before imposition). In Fanon, the reduction to flesh that is implied in the loss of bodily schema is a reduction to the bare materiality of the thing whose very existence is ontologically and epistemologically dark to itself. Flesh, in its unlocatable immanence, because it is nowhere in being everywhere, nothing in being everything, is reduced to what it is made to signify. The immaterial is not given in flesh as the very animation of the invaluable but ascribed to or inscribed upon the flesh as mark/sign/value. Fanon is forced to inhabit the double edge of this experiment; a dehiscence is imposed upon him, his torn flesh opened to the experiment's irruptive possibilities. Who could fathom such enjoyment? Is it to his credit that Merleau-Ponty can want to approach it, that scandalous commitment to phenomenological exploration of which Edmund Husserl speaks, revealing the close proximity of coloniality to philosophy that Fanon had not only to interpret but also to negotiate? In their mutual orbit, where philosophical conquest is unsettled by a constant anticolonial insurgency, Merleau-Ponty and Fanon theorize the experimental inhabitation of flesh, in and as the naked declivity of being-perceived, pierces objecthood, making possible body and all the acts of consciousness that body, in turn, makes possible even unto the establishment of a real presence, a full inhabitation of and with rather than a kind of standing against or observing—given in and as an openness to things.

After Fanon and Merleau-Ponty, but in a way that is before them, in anticipation of them, Philip considers flesh that is mortified beyond the constraints of the symbolic (within which the keeping/writing of books instantiates the self as a financial instrument) in a violent hapticality while, for Toni Morrison, that hapticality brings us back to the revelation that Merleau-Ponty imagines, which is only materialized after the fact of a profound history of denial and deprivation that neither he nor Fanon fully take into account—the impossibilities that follow from not having easy access to the "lived body" due to the very possibility of body's already having been overwhelmed by a negative signification that takes the form of an imposition of race and a denial of gender. Together, this quartet of the flesh of the world, exploring a general and generative resistance to what ontology can think and narrative can tell, protect Malabou's approach to the investigation of what is it to achieve fleshliness and what is it to be relegated to it. Her investment in flesh would, in turn, result in a kind of analytic, "a complete lysis of this morbid body" that is the king's two bodies. What emerges in Philip and, here, in Morrison, on the other hand, is a ceremonial poetics:

> It started that way: laughing children, dancing men, crying women and then it got mixed up. Women stopped crying and danced; men sat down and cried; children danced, women laughed, children cried until, exhausted and riven, all and each lay about the Clearing damp and gasping for breath. In the silence that followed, Baby Suggs, holy, offered up to them her great big heart.
>
> She did not tell them to clean up their lives or to go and sin no more. She did not tell them they the blessed of the earth, its inheriting meek or its glorybound pure.
>
> She told them that the only grace they could have was the grace they could imagine. That if they could not see it, they would not have it.
>
> "Here," she said, "in this here place, we flesh: flesh that weeps, laughs; flesh that dances on bare feet in grass. Love it. Love it hard. Yonder they do not love your flesh. They despise it. They don't love your eyes; they'd just as soon pick em out. No more do they love the skin on your back. Yonder they flay it. And O my people they do not love your hands. Those they only use, tie, bind, chop off and leave empty. Love your hands! Love them. Raise them up and kiss them. Touch others with them, pat them together, stroke them on your face 'cause they don't love that either. *You* got to love it, *you!* And no, they ain't in love with your mouth. Yonder, out there, they will see it broken and break it again. What you say out of it they will not heed. What you scream from it they do not hear. What you put into it to nourish your body they will snatch away and give you leavins instead. No, they don't love your mouth. *You* got to love it. This is flesh I'm talking about here. Flesh that needs to be loved.[18]

Is Baby Suggs's fugitive sermon to the fugitives who embody the disruption of the distinction between things and persons, her injunction to them to love the flesh that they are, the flesh that has been unloved and devalued in an ongoing, violent valuation, an attempt at reinvestment, or does she preach the impossibility of flesh's divestment, therein further implying something like a radical displacement of the symbolic and its supposed force? This touches on a certain problematic of resurrection and transubstantiation that comes into quite specific analytic relief in experience of, which is always also to say over, the edge where being valued in exchange and having no value outside of exchange converge. In the age of the biopolitical deconstruction of sovereignty, such experience is racialized and gendered so that Malabou's resounding of Derrida's insight that "the dignity of life can only subsist beyond the present living being" comes fully into its own by way of the analytic of invaluable flesh that is given in that exhaustive "consent not to be a single being" that remains unheld in the hold's brutal emergency. This is something Hortense Spillers elaborates in her grammar, which must also be understood as a poetics, of (being-held in the terrible) interval.

> First of all, their New-World, diasporic plight marked a *theft of the body*—a willful and violent (and unimaginable from this distance) severing of the captive body from its motive will, its active desire. Under these conditions, we lose at least *gender* difference *in the outcome*, and the female body and the male body become a territory of cultural and political maneuver, not at all gender-related, gender-specific. But this body, at least from the point of view of the captive community, focuses a private and particular space, at which point of convergence biological, sexual, social, cultural, linguistic, ritualistic, and psychological features join. This profound intimacy of interlocking detail is disrupted, however, by externally imposed meanings and uses: 1) the captive body becomes the source of an irresistible, destructive sensuality; 2) at the same time—in stunning contradiction—the captive body reduces to a thing, becoming *being for the captor*; 3) in this absence *from* a subject position, the captured sexualities provide a physical and biological expression of "otherness"; 4) as a category of "otherness," the captive body translates into a potential for pornotroping and embodies sheer physical powerlessness that slides into a more general "powerlessness," resonating through various centers of human and social meaning.
>
> But I would make a distinction in this case between "body" and "flesh" and impose that distinction as the central one between captive and liberated subject-positions. In that sense, before the "body" there is the "flesh," that zero degree of social conceptualization that does not escape concealment under the brush of discourse, or the reflexes of iconography. Even though the European hegemonies stole bodies—some of them female—out of West African communities in concert with the African "middleman," we regard this human and social irreparability

as high crimes against the *flesh*, as the person of the African females and African males registered the wounding. If we think of the "flesh" as a primary narrative, then we mean its seared, divided, ripped-apartness, riveted to the ship's hole, fallen, or "escaped" overboard.[19]

Against and through every erasure, every legal record, every historiographic forgetting, every patrimonial repression, Spillers argues, "this materialized scene of unprotected female flesh—of female flesh 'ungendered'—offers a praxis and a theory, a text for living and for dying, and a method for reading both through their diverse mediations."[20] Bare life is supposed to be (degraded) essence, sacred and sacrificeable. But flesh and bare life are not the same. If, as Malabou once suggested, "the space which separates bare life from the biological body can only be the space of the symbolic," then flesh is the biological that, in its finitude and fecundity, is before the body.[21] The biological is the essence of the symbolic (its impetus, its initiation) just as flesh is the essence of the body. Essence is, here, as Malabou suggests, neither and both inside and outside. It has no place, it is insofar as it is displacement. Flesh might then also be thought as the irreducible materiality of Derridean *différance*, "the non-full, non-simple structured and differentiating origin of differences."[22]

Perhaps Malabou would say, by way of Levi-Strauss, that flesh, as Spillers theorizes it, as Morrison recites it, is a floating signifier, possessing a "value zero" that it is the very engine of the symbolic, the very instantiation of valuation. And they would agree except for the fact that it also constitutes the most radical endangerment of the system of value, of the symbolic, of the discursive. What happens, then, if the traditional placement of flesh within the outer depths of the king's two—symbolic and biological—bodies is refused by the Africanist presence's fleshly, thingly displacement of "American grammar"? What happens, then, if we follow Mama's Baby Suggs in claiming the monstrosity of "mere" flesh? This is another way of thinking about Malabou's assertion of the brain's plasticity, its explosive capacity to give and take form, which emerges for her most recently and most emphatically, in the impossible experience of the those with severe brain injury or impairment, the ones she calls the new wounded, *la nouvelle blessée*. It allows us to imagine Malabou's desire to put an end to the split between the two bodies, the symbolic and the biological, being performed in lingering for a while in/with the unclaimed experience of flesh—the merely biological, the mottled biothanatical, which is, itself, supposed to make no claims, which cannot itself be claimed though it can be bought and sold. Or to imagine, more broadly, that the discourse of cognitive science would take the deviant, nonneurotypical imagination of the Lorenzo Bird, the lover and the poet as its new, constantly self-disruptive standard. What they know of their blessing is given in what they know of their woundedness, by way of the analytic that flesh makes possible, as if there were something already there, in the persistence of its difference from, rather than in its reintegration with, the discursive body, in and as its very exhaustion and exhaustibility. This is what is given in and as Baby Suggs's festival of things.

There is something in the flesh, in its disintegration from and of the body, its personality, and its place. There is something to be thought from the flesh's givenness in displacement, the violence it does to positionality that instantiates positional violence. Sovereignty may very well be located or instantiated in the split between the king's two bodies, but this still requires us to consider that sovereignty, which can never be separated from the (symbolic) body, is detachable from the (biological) flesh, which would justify some interest in the fleshliness, the thingliness, of the ones whose sovereignty, subjectivity, citizenship, and selfhood are placed in question, in a question they consent to inhabit. It is this inalienable heritability of owned, disowned, unowned flesh and not "my body" that makes such questioning resound while rendering the difference and distance between the king's two bodies inoperative and inarticulate. The merger and dispersion of those bodies is biopolitics. In this sense, the merger of *bios* and *ta politika* is inseparable from and is manifest as the political rejection of the biological, which is given in the regulative conferral of the right to life. This is why, as Gayatri Chakravorty Spivak has suggested, the first right must be the right to refuse, and not to have, rights, even if it is exercised as the refusal of what has been refused which is, in the end, the monstrous emergence that occurs where right, power, life, and death converge.

In her desire for a rehabilitation of the biological that will have been accomplished by way of a liberation of "continental philosophy from the rigid separation it has always maintained between the biological, hence the material, and the symbolic, that is the non-material, or the transcendental," Malabou might be said to cause the brain to appear as reinvested, symbolical, transcendental, flesh.[23] But, in this regard, isn't the deconstruction of biopolitical deconstruction still a sovereign operation? Not only in Malabou's work but also in a great deal of philosophical reflection and cultural criticism, isn't the brain, in a way that flesh precisely exhausts, where the sovereign (the executive; the administrator) is said now to reside? Maybe the trouble we have with the king's head, its indefatigable resistance to all our would-be decapitative weaponry, is that it has a brain in it. Maybe we can appose the transcendental brain, and its scientistic underwriting of self-concern, to the flesh's dislocative immanence. Malabou says, "We are, for a great part, the authors of our own brains."[24] But who are "we"? How can "we" resist a tendency to isolate the brain from the rest of "our" (phenotypical/genotypical) flesh so that authorship doesn't reify an old administrative or executive function that is nothing other than a new version of sovereignty? How can we prevent the body's inspirited materiality (the brain) leaving the flesh behind? Or a plasticization of sovereignty, which is also a placement of sovereignty, a reconfiguration or opening of sovereignty's place, leaving behind what flesh-in-displacement allows us to think, a new analytic of sociality, a new analytic of thingliness-in-recessive festivity?

In the end, I'd like you to consider that the transition from a philosophy, or a natural history, to a biology of race accompanies and informs the pseudoscientific emergence of what we now recognize as the science of the brain; and that the Kantian revolution in moral, aesthetic, and political theory, and the theory of mind, are fatefully and fatally coupled with and enabled by the invention of the philosophical concept of race that submits difference to a sovereign power that will have been both refined (in the recovery of a single originary purpose, a monogenetic impetus) and dispersed (wherein that purpose is, as it were, replicated and reproduced as human mental endowment). Do so while keeping in mind that the revolution in theories and techniques of computation (especially the computation of risk and maritime positioning that helped significantly to fuel the transition from mercantilism to [the interplay of the dispersion of sovereignty and the refinement of private accumulation and the conceptualization and regulative exclusion of externalities that we call] capitalism) that began to emerge in the mid-nineteenth century with the work of Charles Babbage and which took more immediately practical and efficient shape in the mid-twentieth century by way of the contributions of Alan Turing, Norbert Wiener, and others coincided roughly with the inception and return of the Afro-diasporic revolutionary social movement and the new modes of consciousness (and their globalized dispersal) such movement reflected and helped to shape. The desire to study the black insurgency whose traces remain in and as the dissemination of phonic substance in literature and music is now inseparable from attending to the history of the interplay of calculation, displacement, and abolition. Baby Suggs's music—in the noise it brings to the opposition of score and performance, writing and reading; in its insistent worrying of the executive line—preserves what Foucault once called "the thought of the outside" so that the potential solipsism that autonomy and autopoiesis might be said to carry is given over to a desire for the informal, which will have been given, or will have been seen to have been instantiated, in every held, unheld, ruptured, ruptural social generativity that goes over the edge. Over the edge of the ship. Overboard. Thrown. Fallen. Inescaped. The touring machine is a diving bell, an instrument for sounding that becomes, at the end of exhaustion, ascent, accent, a certain songlike, sing-song quality, a sing sing sing kinda quality, a fugitive sing-sing kinda thing, an instrument whose forced movement in thinking the unregulated, the un-self-possessed, the un-self-concerned, its rubbed, performed, informal interiority, its flash, is flesh thought inside out.

chapter 8

Seeing Things

There's a more-than-critical criticism that's like seeing things—a gift of having been given to love things and how things look and how and what things see. It's not that you don't see crisis—cell blocks made out of the general meadow, all the luxurious destitution and ge(n)ocidal meanness, the theft of beauty and water, the policing of everyday people and their everyday chances that we call, in Cedric Robinson's brilliant shorthand, "racial capitalism."[1] It's just that all this always seems so small and contingent against the inescapable backdrop of constant escape—which is the other crisis, that is before the first crisis, calling it into being and question, that we might call, by way of Robinson and Nahum Chandler (and R. A. T. Judy and Hortense Spillers, who is the leader of that quartet), "the (para-)ontological totality." The ones who stay in that running away study and celebrate its violently ludic authenticity, the historicity that sends us into the old-new division and collection of words and sets, passing on and through, as incessant staging and preparation. This necessity and immensity of the alternative surrounds and aerates the contained, contingent fixity of the standard.

The alternative, and the ones who stand (in) for it, can only be defended in what Mário Pedrosa calls its "experimental exercise,"[2] which happens every day, and in the recognition of its exercise, which is what I think Karl Marx refers to when he speaks, in "Private Property and Communism," of the everyday engagement in criticism that is an essential part of a communist way of life,[3] and which sometimes he more than critically enacts when he engages in critique, in the elaboration of a general theory of crisis, and in the urgent address of specific instances of crisis. Questions concerning the theory and actuality of crisis are no less urgent now because crisis is always with us. Seeing things doesn't hide the crisis that critique discloses; rather, it locates it more precisely, within a general tendency for upheaval that it constitutes. Seeing things, the alternative seeing of things, the seen and seeing alternative, which a certain deployment of crisis is meant to police, is the crisis of genuine disclosure and generative disruption.

The crisis of deprivation on a global scale is a function of policing that responds to a global ecologic of generation that regulative power brutally (mis) understands as a crisis of law. This is to say that crisis is not only a function of policing but that it has a policing function; it is also to say that crisis is an ongoing, generative resistance to the regulation, the policing, that it generates. This poor description of the interplay of policing and crisis is trying reverently to disclose a reversal that already animates *Policing the Crisis*, the classic attendance of Stuart Hall, Chas Critcher, Tony Jefferson, John Clarke, and Brian Roberts to the range and force of the generative social and aesthetic upheaval of the alternative in England since World War II.[4] Hall and his fellows analyze the ideological manufacture of crisis as a mode of interpretive regulation. The racialization of already extant criminal activity allows its epidermalized "novelty" to be interpreted as crisis. But the criminalization of that activity, in its relation to the normalization of modes of propriation whose brutality and scale dwarf any and every instance of "mugging," is the real problem because, in the end, it was never about this or that instance or collection of instances of law breaking; it was, rather, about the social self-defense of jurisgenerative capacity of which mugging can be said to be a particular manifestation, noteworthy not because of its brutality or venality or degeneracy but only because of its enactment of self-defense through (re)propriative acts that are susceptible to a condition in which they reinforce the brutal axioms of ownership and exception.

Criticism, the capacity to see things in their branching and unfolding and generative differentiation, attends to generation while critique, as Marx deploys it, attends to the regulation and policing of generation; meanwhile, critique, which seems to be deployed almost everywhere in the normative human sciences to police generation, is so driven by its own implicit claims upon national identity or political subjectivity—which are themselves subject to a force, and have been understood by way of a logic, of dissipation implying a mystery of loss and of what was lost—has all but become degenerate. The neoliberal lament regarding "the crisis of democracy" (which was, according to Samuel Huntington and his fellows, a function of there being too much democracy) can be understood as the animating trace of certain folks, claiming to be on the left, whose lament of the current loss of "our democracy" is driven by nostalgic fantasies of a privilege supposedly held within the structure of, rather than given in resistance to, American exclusion. It's not coincidence that this convenient repression of American exclusion is usually accompanied by an assertion of American exception that either takes the form of an invocation of "our" best intentions or, more pragmatically, as the assertion of a right to do just about anything in the name of national defense, whose complete, completely delusional detachment from imperial aggression is sanctioned by the serial invocation of crisis.

When people respond to the suppression of the alternative—and Hall and his fellows brilliantly illuminate how state interpretation of the alternative as crisis is a fundamental element of that suppression—the word *riot* is deployed in order to augment that suppression; but when suppression of the alternative is more (im)properly understood as a response to the alternative, it also becomes possible to understand that with regard to the insistent previousness of the alternative it is more accurate to say, over Sly Stone's growl or Joe Strummer's sneer, that there is, and already has been, a riot going on. This is about the anoriginary force of tumultuous derangement, a generative sociopoesis given in and as everyday sensuality. To rise to the defense of this sacred, ordinary, generative violence—to protect it from the ongoing murder—is often to risk a kind of appropriation of the very propriative force one seeks to combat with an otherwise animating fugitivity. Such uprising can take the form of burnin' and lootin', but, even more easily, such appropriation can take the form of a critical account of the justificatory causes of burnin' and lootin'. Meanwhile, what always remains or, more precisely, what must be understood as the irreducible remainder that animates such physical acts as well as such critical accounts, are everyday and everynight things. It's not about the looting of loot or the assault of persons who take shape as shops and wares, or about the insurgents' loss of or exclusion from citizenship or belonging that supposedly makes the former inevitable; it is, rather, all about insurgence as the performative declaration of what we are and what we have and what we give. Put another way, the seemingly infinite production of crisis finds its limit in the infinite rehearsal of generative capacity, in the open field of a generative grammar, in the fecundity of a range of generative principles, all of which reveal the sclerotic constraints that are fostered by an empiricist attitude whose structuring force in the determination of Anglo-American intellectual identity can be traced back to a certain valorization of the grasp, and the philosophical nomination of the possessive individual to the office of manager of the enclosure, by way of the bloody fingerprints of a transcendental subject who is unable or unwilling to see things but who can neither let things go nor pass things on.

The riot that's goin' on is a party for self-defense. The question concerning its causes, its sources, shouldn't be left to liberal or neoliberal pundits and prime ministers, even when their more or less racist and ageist elitism leads them to say, with a kind of ignorant and imprecise accuracy, that the causes are cultural. What they don't mean is that *culture* is the imprecise word we give to regenerative resources of insurgent social life. There's another way of living that exhausts imposed arrangements. It's where and how people fight. When seemingly random and unorganized acts of self-defense erupt against the violence of the state and capital, the only important question is how to maintain their connection to the social field they are meant to defend. This is a question concerning the corrosive, reconstructive force of certain practices that Michael Herzfeld thinks of in terms of "cultural intimacy—the recognition of those aspects of a cultural identity that are considered a source of external embarrassment but that nevertheless provide insiders with their assurance of common sociality, the familiarity with the bases of power that may at one moment assure the disenfranchised a degree of creative irreverence and at the next moment reinforce the effectiveness of intimidation."[5] But what if we begin to consider, against the grain and over the edge of whatever combination of the critique of authenticity and the appeal to upright, paralytic sovereign recitations of the citizen consumer, that the social poetics Herzfeld is after is an undercommon intellectual project that begins to emerge precisely when the distinction between insiders and outsiders breaks down, when a certain kind of communal claim is made in a certain kind of walking down certain city streets, and when that claim is given in and as an active disruption of the nation-state, in and as a kind of masque in which the very habits of the damned are taken on and, thereby, altered in their free, constant, and already given alteration. Meanwhile, we confront the emergence of new black acts—of the kind E. P. Thompson describes in *Whigs and Hunters*—now outlawing autonomous cybersocial organization for self-defense under the self-regulating cover of the ones who internalize the embarrassment they refuse, which is the generativity noncitizens claim.

The notion that crisis lies in the ever-more-brutal interdiction of our capacity to represent or be represented by the normal is as seductive, in its way, as the notion that such interdiction is the necessary response to our incapacity for such representation. Their joint power is held in the fact that whether abnormality is a function of external imposition or of internal malady it can only be understood as pathological. Such power is put in its accidental place, however, by the ones who see, who imaginatively misunderstand, the crisis as our constant disruption of the normal, whose honor is given in and protected by its representations, with the anterepresentational generativity that it spurns and craves. This is the crisis that is always with us; this is the crisis that must be policed not just by the lethal physical brutality of the state and capital but also by the equally deadly production of a discourse that serially asserts that the crisis that has befallen us must overwhelm the crisis that we are; that crisis follows rather than prompts our incorporative exclusion.

There's a connection between poetry and violence that Amiri Baraka, among others, began to explore by way of these terms and which now needs to be re-explored in the full awareness that Baraka's movement extended, rather than disavowed, that antinomian opening of the field that can be traced back through Aimé Césaire, Charles Olson, and Sun Ra; Emily Dickinson, Harriet Jacobs, and Reyita; Nanny of the Maroons, Anne Hutchinson, and Tituba, and beyond. The poetics of the open field, especially when performed in the padlocked cell, was always tied to the social poetics of riot, of generative differentiation and expropriative disruption as the non-selves' self-defense, their seeing things as a performed social theory of mind. Baraka took it out, and sometimes tried to take it home, which drove it through him and even further out, in the name of an informant poetics, spreading the news and the new in the giving and taking of form, as lemons, and people, piled on steps, disarrayed inappropriately against every propriative and counterpropriative intention that claims to have put them there. We still enact, because we desire and cannot live without, the immense poetry of war, by which Wallace Stevens meant and didn't mean a poetics of social pregnancy, the international, antinational, incognate embarrassment of seeing things and making things. The poetics of the alternative is funereal and venereal, surviving in denotative self-defense and the righteous distortions it enacts in rough advent. There's a This is England poetics, a Luv N' Haight poetics, moving without moving in and against the brutal smallness of imposed needs and nationalized histories with the kind of out lyricism that only comes from being constrained to be somewhere else, that will have already come from the other side to keep on going, that had already come with those of us who are the other things we see till we might be eased with seeing nothing.

chapter 9

Air Shaft, Rent Party

I'm here to announce that the formation of a new political party is serially announced.[1]

Harlem Air-Shaft

This party is new because it's not political. This is the new political party to end all political parties. Like most genuinely new things, the new party is old. It's not the grand old party. It's not grand, just elegant, and nasty. It could be called the house party but don't let that mislead you into thinking that *house* implies ownership; this house party is of and for the dispossessed, the ones who disavow possession, the ones who, in having been possessed of the spirit of dispossession, disrupt themselves. They're preoccupied with disowning, with unowning, with homeless anti- and ante-ownership, and this is their party because they're always trying to give it away, like a bird in hand, hand in hand, hand to hand.

The party I'm announcing is serially announced. It serially announces itself, throwing off irruptions of itself that sound like somebody saying "Party over here," each instance of which sets off reverberations of itself all over the party. This party crusts and sugars over itself like that all the time. It keeps burning like that to be constantly driven by that burning, which results in this constant scarring. Party over here, party over here, party over here, this party is riotously other than itself. In constantly telling us that there's a party going on, the party is constantly showing us that there's a riot going on, which is how it gets itself smiling, like an antinuclear family affair. This riotous being-beside-itself of the party is kinda like this guy during the second great Los Angeles rebellion who was coming out of a Sears in South Central with a massive box of Huggies. The television news reporters, who were reporting on the riot as if it were a party, as if it were the violent birth or birth announcement of the last political party, put a mic in his face, because they couldn't put a mic in his hand because his hands were full, which meant that he couldn't try to take the mic, not because he was too small but because he was rocking the party he was in, which meant that he only had time to look into the camera, and say into the mic, "I'm not like this." He was rocking the party of the ones who are not like themselves, the ones who like one another, and who are like one another, because they are not like themselves. He was rocking the party of inseparable, unregulatable differences, the party that contracts the destruction and rebuilding of cities, and he rocked it so hard that the news reporter could no longer report. It was as if he'd slammed the mic when he was done to make sure it broke.

Now this whole slamming thing, indeed much of the activity that makes up the party, can rightly be taken as a sign of anger. The anger probably derives from the fact that even though the party is, and takes place in, and takes place as, a kind of refuge, refuge still indicates that those who take it are refugees and people tend not to want to have to live like that. It's all messed up though because tremendous amounts of love are circulated in refuge so you can't leave 'cause your heart is there. But insofar as you're always dreaming about leaving, which is to say that insofar as you're always leaving, you can't stay 'cause you been somewhere else. This is the party of the ones who are in more + less than one place at the same time all the time, the ones who are beside themselves, not like themselves, other than themselves, having inside-outed themselves in airy, fluid, black-and-blue solidarities. This is the party of the ones who are not self-possessed, the non-self-possessive anindividuals. This is the party of the ones in whom the trace of having been possessed keeps turning into this obsessive-compulsive drive for the total disorder that is continually given in continually giving themselves away. This is the party of the ones who continually say to one another, "I, who have nothing, I who have no one, adore you and want you so; I'm just a no one, with nothing, to give you, but o, I love you," so you see what I mean when I say that this new political party is not a political party, that it is the old-new, extrapolitical party of the ones who are none. This is that other thing, that other assembly, that other gathering, that other logos, that other set, that other party, the beforeandafterparty. The party I'm talking about is the rent party and I am here to announce it and also to call for the formation of a study group so we can study it. On the other hand, now that I think about it, there's no need for that since the rent party *is* a study group, where the theory of life is the theory of style, which emerges in a style of theory in which convolution, in the interest of revolution, is mobilized as the celebratory echo of the plain, the contrapuntal, the fugal, the fantastic. Actually, if you wanted to be academic about it you could say that the rent party is the Rent Party Department, Richard Iton, Chair Emeritus.

Of course, the Rent Party Department isn't really in the academy. I mean it's there, perhaps even insofar as we are here, but it's not really there. It's not really anywhere, which is cool because then it can *actually* be here, there, and everywhere as a kind of dislocation. Nowhere is usually a dissed location but not here. Professor Iton teaches us that musical announcements of this extrapolitical renunciation are often the most precise, bearing the way it belongs without belonging, that sharp, sped-up multiple weave of elongated essays and overpopulated pauses and hallways on what it is to always be longing. This animated urbanity in the cracks of the polis, this community sing whose improvised head reveals a tendency to get cracked in the head by the police, up here under the ground where falling feels like flying because it is and because we all fly when we fall like that, feeling each other in the space where we feel—because we bear—each other as differences, is where the fleshly thing you might have wanted to call a body, moving in and with and through each other in the open field we used to call everybody, populated by those abstract equivalences we call anybody, is given in its most essential form, which is nothing other than that ongoing giving of form that we call the informal, refuge for the no-ones, the not ones, the more + less than ones, the nones who are, in their constantly novitiate, base communitarian devotion, no-bodies. Even more than urban planning, this emergence of form in and from the informal, is the city we're always making, the city of plans, the city of terms, the city of terminals, the city of passage, the centrifugal refuge of the eternal middle, moved and moving, margined, monthly, weekly, daily, over here, over here, over here, the city of stateless practice.[2]

Rentals

Duke Ellington calls his design, encryption, and inhabitation of this city "Harlem Air-Shaft." Vijay Iyer and Mike Ladd update and reemphasize its antinational internationalism in "Rentals." For our fallen comrade Richard, who has ascended into the underground he prophetically described, this embrace of insurgent digging, and our ongoing and necessary embrace of that embrace, is the search for the black fantastic.

chapter 10

Notes on Passage

Refugees are the keenest dialecticians. They are refugees as a result of changes and their sole object of study is change.—**BERTOLT BRECHT**, "Denmark or, The Humor of the Hegelian Dialectic"

Refugees study change not only because they've been put through changes but also because changes are what they want and what they play and what they are. Refugees study a mode of study—the contrapuntal intersection of a set of interstitial fields, dislocation in a hole or a hold or a whole or a crawlspace. Such study is inhabitation that moves: by way of—but also in apposition to—injury, which is irreducible in the refugee though she is irreducible to it. There is, in turn, passage in acknowledging the theoretical practice of the one who emerges as if from nowhere, rooted in having been routed, digging, tilling, working, sounding, the memorial future of a grave, undercommon cell. She is the commodity, the impossible domestic, the interdicted/contradictive mother. Dangerously embedded in the home from which she is excluded, she is more and less than one. The question of where and when she enters—where entrance is reduced to some necessarily tepid mixture of naturalization and coronation, which is an already failed solution that is ever more emphatically diluted in its abstract and infinite replication—is always shaded by the option to refuse what has been refused, by the preferential option not for a place but rather for radical displacement, not for the same but for its change. Blackness is given in the refusal$_2$ of the refugee.

Cosmopolitanism has more often than not been thought to be an overview of the underground to which blackness is supposed to have been relegated. Overseeing and overlooking are crucial elements of this particular interplay of blindness and insight. The necessary detachment that links and animates

these elements becomes even more important as the various officially sanctioned modes of Euro-American cosmopolitanisms, and their Afro-diasporic
critical variants, emerge. Perhaps detachment within that diverse set
of cosmopolitanist theories is necessary to the illumination of the federated universality of a cosmopolitan drive. Detachment helps to enact a kind
of meta-cosmopolitanism to the extent that it redoubles a certain constitution of cosmopolitanism as the "womb in which all original predispositions of
the human species will be developed," a tendency whose subjunctivity persists as we await "the achievement of a civil society universally administering
right," whose own precondition is "a lawful external relation between states."[1]
Immanuel Kant tries to tell us why we have to wait for what he calls cosmopolitanism, noting that the safety and sanctity of this womb and its generative capacity is always threatened with deferral by states; and Gilles Deleuze,
reading himself into and out of Kant's conceptual framework, cautions us
against state thought such as the paradoxically static and statist conceptions
of cosmopolitanism that turn out to ground and sanction those antagonistic
external relations that Kant posits both as a natural order and as that which
nature drives peoples to transcend. Are lawful external relations between
states just as dangerous to the universal administration of right as their unlawful counterparts? What if cosmopolitanism, which is, of necessity, national is,
precisely because of this necessity, its own most absolute and eternal deferral?
What if cosmopolitanism is not just national, but also racial? Consider that
both lawful and unlawful relations between states operate, as it were, in the
medium of statelessness—which is also to say upon stateless flesh or, both
more generally and more precisely, earthly materiality that is posited as unem-
bodied and figured as unanimated. Racialized and sexualized, but also given
in the general distinction between man and dominion, statelessness is interdicted *materiality*. This is to say that statelessness ought not in any case be
seen simply as the field marked out by the difference between the citizen and
the noncitizen. On the one hand, statelessness is the field of their convergence
and coalescence and its modern determination and adjudication (even and
especially as what can rightly and all but generally be called the lived statelessness of the citizen) is enacted in and by ascriptions and impositions of
state-sanctioned or naturalized difference; on the other hand, and in the first
place, statelessness is the mobilization of a difference that cosmopolitanism
(as national, racial, sexual, and military humanism) is meant to regulate in
the name and in the service of the state and of the very idea of possessive and
individual interest that the state is meant to protect and to project.[2]

The kind of metacosmopolitan overview that proliferates in the various shades of official intellectual discourse does not simply exemplify this condition; rather, it might be said both to define and refine it precisely along an obscured but strangely faithful Kantian line. Such discourse usually briefly attends to the shadowed reemergence of this line, which seems inescapable in part because to step along it is to step into a kind of morass that is defined by the return of a couple of intractable, intersecting problems—the conflict between the empirical and the normative (or, you could say the constitutive and the regulative) and the conflict between the particular and the universal. But this line only *seems* inescapable—not because these conflicts are not real but rather because the set of terms that is marked and structured by them is neither limited to nor enclosed by the Kantian imagination whose freedom polices itself at the intersection of race, sex, and teleology. The racial/sexual mark in Kant, which regulates and is constitutive of cosmopolitan constitution and regulation, has been passed on down the Kantian line and does its business in the divergent formulations that compose the discursive field where philosophy and policy converge. The persistence of that mark (as the enclosure of the common ground of cosmopolitan thinking), its ineluctable place at the foundation of contemporary thought and society in the world that has often been called both first and free, and above all the simultaneously destructive and reconstructive force to which the philosophical concept of race, in its irreducible sexualization, responds, requiring that we access and mobilize it now under the name of a radical and universal differentiation, renders moralistic calls for a kind of voluntary and self-corrective deracialization and asexualization of culture downright silly and, for that matter, immoral.[3] At stake here is the necessary distinction between the delusional system, at once narcotic and regulatory, of possessive individual and national development, figured in what Ernst Kantorowicz calls "the king's two bodies," and the improvisational mechanics, at the convergence of fantasy and flight, of fugitive ensemble's dispossessed and dispossessive flesh.

Against the backdrop of the massive, and still massively discounted, history of (European) man's racial violence, which is part and parcel of the narcotic delusion sovereignty constructs for, as, and in itself, the burden of "voluntary" deracialization is generally placed on the backs of those whose access to the fantasy of man's full embodiment—the full, free, self-determining occupation of his position—is always refused and often refused$_2$. This strictly racialized responsibility for deracialization, an externality imposed upon those who desire, as well as those who disavow, the sovereign's impossibility, now often passes as a critique of blackness leveled from a vast range of colonial out-posts that have been and remain man's staging area and theater of opera-tions. Moreover, an expanding set of contemporary social theorists, who seem to believe in the achievement of this or that country, the discovery of the world, and the possibility of the new political dispositions these dreams imply, also seem to understand that these dreams require the repression of a range of assertive and insurgent social forms and performances that emerge in part from the experience and transgenerational transmission of transgen-erational racial injury. Constantly inducing pain in the interest of feeling none, the sovereign junkie is always high on his own supply and always in withdrawal, which takes the violently antisocial form of the expansion of his territory. He says he does this in order to protect his geopolitical corners. He says he needs his corners in order to protect an idea. This idea, the sover-eign's dream of his own unnatural highness, can't protect itself. This dream is maintained, in lieu of its fulfillment, as submission to the logistics and logic of racial capitalism and its ends. Its persistence-in-deferral is the very matter of neoliberal, neoimperial policy.

Against the grain of (the) man's brutal self-projections, which often result in the addictive tendency of his others to settle for the settler's delusional sovereignty, blackness still has the fugal, fugitive, radically imaginative so-ciopoetic work of refusal$_2$ to do. This work takes form in passage, as ill logics and logisticalities of sharing, as a general indebtedness that requires and allows a general corporate liquidation performed by means of what Édouard Glissant calls "consent not to be a single being."[4] Such work is inseparable from the hope for an undercosmopolitanism that might abolish the Kan-tian line and its recursions to and recrudescences of exclusionary state and national determinations—its conflicted, melancholic, imperial, and post-imperial patriotisms—even as it materializes antinational ways of being to-gether from the exhaust(ion) of internationalism. To speak of that hope is to sift and rub, delve and caress, in the interest of flight. One day, perhaps Walter Rodney will have called such common intellectuality underground-ings with his brothers and sisters; one day, perhaps Kamau Brathwaite will have called the striated unity of such thinking sub-marine.[5] This other ana-or extra- or subcosmopolitanism, which will not have been *from* but rather will have *remained* below, is proper—in its radical impropriety and expro-priative inappropriability—only to the dispossessed and to the trace of the dispossessed, a category whose membership is open, where dispossession is understood within the context of its historical racialization and engendering and ungendering and the ongoing challenge that resistance in and before these processes offers to possessive subjectivity. Thinking the undercosmopolitan requires being circulated. You have to be moved, in having declared that you shall not be, in this other place for *theoria*, impatiently racing for another vision in and of your patient habitation, the underground overview, the buried *übersicht*, of resurrected angels singing beneath and invisibly sensing, practicing, worrying, breaking the cosmopolitan line. Signs of the universality of this new condition for theory are ubiquitous and, in Nathaniel Mackey's words, both premature and postexpectant.[6] You have to give something up in desperate anticipation of the total loss at which we'll never arrive (those of us, I mean, whose imaginations resist being policed by and in the refusal to pay noninstrumental attention to the thinking of the instrument). There's still something (t)here—the commodity's general theory of elsewhere. It comes from nothing, from nowhere, which is the real presence of our displacement, which is everywhere, in everything. You have to seek it in places that some might think unlikely and beware, in yourself, the effects of the kind of thinking that produces certain traditional ideas of unlikeliness.

At that point, as a function of its movement, you might begin to ask: Is consciousness, of necessity, national? Is necessarily national consciousness a state phenomenon? Can you be a person, can you have a story, can you have rights, can you do right, without a state? These questions, instantiating a kind of relay between G. W. F. Hegel's *Elements of the Philosophy of Right* and Hannah Arendt's *The Origins of Totalitarianism*, approach a cluster of implications that are all bound up not only with the internal dynamics of the experience of consciousness but also with the modes of social organization within which what is understood to be those internal dynamics take form.[7] These questions are not meant to sanction the easy conflation of state and nation, even though they assume the intensity of their relation; rather they are meant to allow their more rigorous separation. Maybe they mark the spot where the nation-in-dispersion renders the state inoperable. Certainly they occasion another question: What forms do the nation-in-dispersion, the family in dispersion, the facticity of natality *as* alienation, take? This question, instantiating a kind of relay between Arendt's *The Human Condition* and Orlando Patterson's *Slavery and Social Death*, is, in turn, all bound up with the question of how enslavement delineates—in its attempt to regulate—an already given dispersion.[8] What if slavery is not the systematic relegation to natal alienation in/as/and dispersion but is, rather, the response to, and the attempt to regulate, them? What must be asserted here, with the greatest possible emphasis, is that the problem of the state emerges as a set of questions of travel that are immediately questions of study, as well, where we contemplate, while performing, the relation between dispersion and descent, descent and declivity, declivity and experiment, experiment and escape. It is not an accident that for the last two centuries all of the questions I have here been trying to approach have found their most fundamental articulation in and as the animated interval simultaneously linking and dividing pan-Africanism and black nationalism.[9]

Let's say that our study of and in displacement, in and through this interval, occurs in some region we are making and unmaking, the region of our making and unmaking, called the Atlantic World. The charting of this region under that name, in the name of some specific terms of order that naming instantiates, might be said to have begun with or in yet another relay, this one between *Slavery and Social Death* and Bernard Bailyn's *Voyagers to the West*.[10] Though the movement between tragedy and triumph these texts enact is constantly broken—emphatically, and in anticipation, by Peter Linebaugh, when he resounds the anoriginal forces that made all the Atlantic mountains shake; or by R. A. Judy when he shows how Euro-anthropological regulation (the failed protection of transcendental subjectivity's self-regard given in the racial projection of human life's self-dispossessive immanence) is solicited by an heterographic Afro-Arabic invitation to dance its way out of its constrictions—a paradigmatically exclusionary bipolarity to which Atlantic studies is susceptible and which Patterson and Bailyn jointly embody remains online.[11] The multiplicity of forces, voices, in the hold of the ship, which is a language lab, which fact does not lessen but rather intensifies the ship's and the shippers' brutality, precisely in its fantastic confirmation of it, is where transcendence and immanence move in constantly corrosive orbit of one another. There are those who act as if the only way to speak or fathom or measure the unspeakable, unfathomable, immeasurable venality of the slavers is by way of the absolute degradation of the enslaved. But such calculation is faulty from the start insofar as we are irreducible to what is done to us, that we were and remain present at our own making, even in the hold of the ship, and that this making, that presence, this presence in that void, this fugitive avoidance in and of and out of nothing, nowhere, everything, everywhere, is inseparable from fantasy.

The geography of the old-new world continues as an extension of one pole, one stanchion: over the last two decades Paul Gilroy—moving only slightly less depressively than Patterson but in mutual echo of a certain expansion of

Arendt, a certain reduction of Frantz Fanon, and the epiphenomenology of spirit that's laid down in their combination—misapprehends the void, the act of avoidance, as absence.[12] Cosmopolitanism is understood, in this annex to Arendt that is never quite errant enough, as having its origin and end in the claim of the citizen, the democratized sovereign, in such a way as to confirm the already given requirement that the relation of blackness to the nation-state be understood as analogous to that between a stubborn monolith and a finally irresistible solvent.[13] This problematic of mixture—of hybridity, if you will—is not at all to be reduced to a matter of miscegenation. What's at stake, rather, is how living outside or against the nation-state, when such an entity is understood to be the ground of a theory and practice of cosmopolitanism that simultaneously protects and undermines its sovereignty, is understood as the very form of deadly life. This is to say that insofar as such life, in its supposed fatality, is either posited, in being immeasurable and incalculable, as absence or slated for dissolution in being incorporated by the nation-state, it persists and subsists in a relation for and through which it can only signify nothing, sound and fury notwithstanding. Moreover, blackness, which is the name that has been assigned this *relative* nothingness, is often said now to have been given most fully, as it were, in the African American example, which is manifest in and as this simultaneously melancholic and celebratory tendency to remain in the hold, as Frank B. Wilderson III has said, in echo of Mackey's song.[14] The interplay of study and enactment, contemplation and performance, which is given in that tendency, that displacement, with(in) which we are preoccupied, continues to elude us even in our inhabitation of it. For those who wish to leave this constancy of leaving without origin— the ones who keep looking for a home or a national or even international identity—the African American example is often understood to be both hegemonic and degraded. Perhaps this is because it is a certain distillate of this example—and it is Nahum Chandler, in the inaugural attention that he pays to W. E. B. Du Bois, who makes it possible to think this exemplarity—that seems most emphatically to bear, with something that seems never quite close enough to embarrassment, the trace of the commodity and the weight of refusal, even when that trace disrupts commodification's valuative power, even when what is refused is what has been refused.[15] As Lindon Barrett brilliantly and rigorously shows, the critique of value and the refusal of national identity are desired even if the means and (musical) materiality by which they are achieved and refined are disavowed.[16] Certain blacks embody, somehow more than anyone, being on, which is to say subjection to, the market, which is given always in its contrapuntal relation to that braided, frayed refusal of what Bryan Wagner calls "being a party to exchange," within the context of an analysis that calls upon us precisely to consider how that refusal troubles the entire complex of subjection in the market that constitutes existence either in or out of exchange, either before or after "emancipation."[17] "Certain blacks [underneath the market] dig they freedom," tunneling through it in order to traffic in vindication and insurrection as if free movement were obligatory, as if exclusion were more desirable than power.[18] This is what Patterson figures as tragic, what Gilroy figures as moribund. Their investigation of the hold is always also a rejection of such sojourn, structured neither by fantasy nor flight but rather by something situated at the nexus of value and fact, phenomenology and positivism, personhood and the state. Gilroy advances what looks and sounds like the immigrant's embrace of citizenship, bringing the Bailyn pole online at its reinitialization in and as Black Atlantic studies. Recently, Kamari Maxine Clarke, in dialogue with a group of important contemporary scholars, including Michelle M. Wright, who move in "new directions for thinking diaspora," and in the service of a sharper analysis of the ways "diasporic humanitarianism" (in its genetic relation to military humanism, national humanism, and national cosmopolitanism) is mobilized in the service of the ongoing "plunder of Africa," extends Gilroy's unfortunate romance with the nation-state precisely by refusing altogether—or, at least, altogether more quickly—the hold that Gilroy has never quite been able either to relinquish or escape.[19]

In "New Spheres of Transnational Formations: Mobilizations of Humanitarian Diasporas," Clarke works "to advance a reframing of black diasporic formations that rethinks the relationship between diasporas centered on contemporary postcolonial African states and other conceptions of African diasporic linkage whose boundaries exceed, and often precede, the nation-state system itself."[20] In so doing, Clarke attends to postcolonial Afro-diasporic modes of being, thereby highlighting what Wright, in a response to and extension of Clarke titled "Black in Time: Exploring New Ontologies, New Dimensions, New Epistemologies of the African Diaspora," calls "key differences between different Black communities." Those differences are obscured, Wright claims, when scholars apply one "closed," narrowly conceived and constrained epistemology "time and time again" to the richly differentiated field of global black social life. Wright is, therefore, encouraged by what she sees as Clarke's "move to decouple . . . a 'Middle Passage Epistemology,' which . . . is the dominant formation imagining, justifying and celebrating what has been termed the 'African' diaspora in the 20th century."[21] The verb *decouple* is crucial in Wright's formation. On the one hand it appears to amplify Clarke's commitment to detaching "a new ontology of sub-Saharan Africa in crisis [from] African America"; on the other hand, what remains unclear in her interpretation and application of Clarke's work is not only what it is that "Middle Passage Epistemology" must be decoupled from but also how the reattachment of "sub-Saharan Africa in crisis to African America," which Clarke also seeks, is to be accomplished. There is something interesting and obscure about that which implies or evokes a decoupling whose partial object seems to instantiate its generality. It is as if that which must be decoupled from nothing in particular must, in fact, be decoupled from everything; or, deeper still, it is as if this particular call for the decoupling of "Middle Passage Epistemology" from, well, nothing, turns out to announce what it had meant to evoke. What work will this general decoupling have accomplished? And in whose service will such work have been done? Perhaps these questions concerning the general and already given decoupling that, according to Wright, corresponds to "Middle Passage Epistemology" can be addressed by returning to the precision of Clarke's investment in detachment and reattachment. Given in full, Clarke's desire is

> to reevaluate the centrality of both trans-Atlantic slavery and race as the single most important problem of the West in the 20th century, in order to detach and reattach a new ontology of sub-Saharan Africa in crisis to African America. In the twenty-first century, it is not the color line that summons our urgent attention, but the crisis of death and global complicity to live and let die. The dilemma of various weakened African state polities whose significant economic and political decisions are brokered outside of the country with international donors and institutions, must be seen alongside diasporic survivors of slavery in the Americas whose ontological formation emerged from a pre-Westphalian order.[22]

The crux of a problematic convergence occurs here, first, in Clarke's misprision of Du Bois's conception of the color line, which he understood to be a global problematic within which the general relay between life and death was framed and adjudicated, and second, in the refusal to attend to the massive theoretical energy that Du Bois poured into both the idea and the materiality of African American exemplarity within that global problematic. Fortunately, Chandler offers a painstakingly brilliant reading of Du Bois's engagement with and embodiment of the anhegemonic exemplar whose historical specificities distill "the relation of the darker to the lighter races of men in Asia and Africa, in America and the islands of the sea."[23] What Chandler shows, by way of the example of Du Bois's deployment of African American exemplarity, is precisely what Clarke's phrasing obscures: that African American reference to "our 'Africa' as the Africa of African American heritage without thinking about the 'Africa' of contemporary economic strife is part of the dialectic of things African" but not all of what African Americans contribute to that dialectic.[24] There is an open vision that is already given in Du Bois as antinational vantage. What is seen from and as this (dis)location lies beyond the paradoxes of national cosmopolitanism whose devolutionary update, diasporic humanitarianism, Clarke seeks to criticize, rightly, but from within the constraints of the very Westphalian order that the idea of national cosmopolitanism helps to found and seeks to regulate. This other beholding, given in what is beheld, implies an anarchic, anarchronic, earthly apposition that, among other things, exposes the fact that the analytic capacities that produce and accompany the simple distinction between pre-Westphalian and Westphalian orders are insufficient for the kind of analytic attention that Clarke and Wright desire.[25]

At stake is precisely what it is that the thought of middle passage, that remaining in the supposedly viewless confines of the hold, makes it possible to imagine and improvise. It's not just that there are flights of fantasy in the ship's hold but also that such fantasy calls into more refined and brutal existence every regulatory structure through which we identify the modernity of the world. The problem has to do, in the end, with the exhaustive deprivations—in their relation to the revolutionary forces—that mark the lived experience of statelessness, which is, before its exclusionary imposition, a general and inalienable sociopoetic insurgency. In other words, the operative distinction is neither between the postcolonial state and diaspora nor the (neo-)imperial state and diaspora; the problem is the relationship between the state, however it is conceived and instantiated, and statelessness. How do we inhabit and move in statelessness? How is statelessness not only an object but also a place of study? The address of this question requires brushing up against a problematic implication. That implication is not that African American studies bears the special responsibility of bracketing its own local concerns in the interest of a systemic analysis of the postcolonial state, an imperative that is underwritten by the assumption that certain kinds of attention paid to certain local conditions of black American social life not only imply but also enforce fixed notions of blackness that exclude some who would seek to claim blackness as (inter)national identity. Rather, the implication is that African American studies must ever more fully repress its own comportments toward the interplay of anticoloniality and statelessness in the interest of analytic devotion to the postcolonial (African) state. When questioning the value or necessity of attention to certain local conditions of and within the striated generativity of black social life in the United States (where the pitfalls of the consciousness of passage seem to have their greatest intensity) is given as a kind of methodological imperative for those in the advanced guard of professional Afro-diasporic intellectual life; when we are constrained to wonder how the most enduring modes and experience of statelessness, lived and enacted by those who are said now to have a pre-Westphalian ontology and epistemology, have come to signify not only the most powerful manifestation of the Westphalian state but, more generally, something that seems to show up for Clarke and Wright as a kind of willed, self-imposed, exclusionary form of identitarian stasis; perhaps it is because a choice has already been made, at the most general level, for political order over social insurgency.

The straight, deictically determined linearity implied by the distinction between pre-Westphalian and Westphalian delivers the brutal kick of a Hegelian historiographic and geographic cocktail, one designed to produce maximal effect by way of minimal flavor. This time, in the light of the state, which is manifest as deadly shade, Africa is a zone of relative advance. But what theoretical force is held in the ongoing generation of what is called the "pre-Westphalian"? What work does that force allow? Where did it come from? Is this a problematic of dialogue as J. Lorand Matory, or retention, as Melville J. Herskovitz, would have it?[26] Or is the real issue the preservation of "the ontological totality" that Cedric Robinson indexes to black radicalism, which is given in general as the enactment of the refusal of the state and which is, as Laura Harris argues, to be found in every instance of "the aesthetic sociality of blackness," in every exorbitant local inhabitance of the motley crew that is instantiated by those whom Michel Foucault might also have called "prisoners of the passage"?[27] Outside the history of sovereignty, self-determination, and their violent dispersion—that general and genocidal imposition of severalty, of the primacy and privacy of "home," that Theodore Roosevelt prescribed for the indigenous people of North America as if it held the pestilential increase of a Matherian blanket—blackness keeps moving in its Müntzerian way. It does so in honor of the ways that the Peasant's War continues to disrupt the Peace of Westphalia, which it anticipates, whose brutalities it brings online in the way that insurgency always brings regulation online. Such combinations of precedence and fracture—in addition to the simple fact that the slave trade continued two centuries after the series of treaties signed in 1648 that initialized the Westphalian system—call severely into question any historical calculus that places the middle passage and its modes of study (as opposed to its epistemology) under the rubric of the "pre-Westphalian." However, under a Hegelian influence whose strenuous critique she elsewhere studies and extends as a mode of becoming (black), statelessness and nonarrival are objects of correction for Wright even as Clarke implies that adherence to the peace of Westphalia, which is imagined to be applicable to Africa, whose pillage it foretells and propels, might guarantee the sovereignty of the postcolonial African state.[28]

Clarke calls for "a recognition of an ontology that is an extension of the modernity of state formation and the hierarchization of racial difference but that also represents a new node of shift in the formation of contemporary capitalism."[29] That new node has to do with the fact that "the reality on the ground is that a significant component of governance issues in Africa are integrally tied to the international community" and that, moreover, these ties or linkages are both cutting against the grain and more deeply entrenching the old slave routes and their brutally modernizing impacts.[30] And, just as in the time of the slave trade, black migrants, in complex disruption of voluntarity and its opposite (along with sailors and traders of every stripe in markets both real and virtual, in ensembles of social relations and configurations of production that bend the bodies/corporations they justify and trouble the states they instantiate), operationalize and administer the accumulations and dispersions of capital, labor, and resources that their flesh instantiates. This is an old new thing and the question is not only how to recognize but also how to overturn it. If a powerful and anticipatory countermovement emerges in/as passage, precisely as a theoretical practice of overturning, while "new regimes of supranational governance . . . cross-cut [and mirror] those of the earlier trans-Atlantic routes," then why would the proper response be further to displace that already given insurgency-in-displacement, particularly when it bears such rich resources for dealing with and in the dialectic of statelessness?[31] Perhaps the commitment to sovereignty, either as a bulwark against imperialism or as the basic form that diasporic identities take up, requires such displacement, which begins by positing the centrality of a range of anoriginal eccentricities. It is in this regard that it becomes possible and necessary to ask again how it is that within the Afro-diasporic frame blacks in the United States have come to stand in both for putatively pre-Westphalian statelessness and for the specifically and paradigmatically post-Westphalian potency of a particular state?

In order to address this question one must first acknowledge that in the case of the United States, in what many like to call the "post–civil rights era," not every black person bodies forth this seemingly impossible ante-state statism.[32] The ones who signify a statelessness that is infused with the American exception are the objects of a disavowal that is tellingly figured as expansion. In the interest of being "bigger than that," as filmmaker Thomas Allen Harris was once heard to put it, the black American intellectual field, by way of its own professional restraint, must singularly disregard itself and its own comportments and go on tour.[33] This process is predicated upon a model of the African diaspora that excludes and demonizes a certain figure of the African American whose precarity and supposedly preintellectual insistence on a supposedly preintellectual and anticosmopolitan "authenticity" elicits various combinations of pity and disgust that are packaged in the language of policy and correction. When certain black American particularities are serially enjoined to turn from themselves, questions concerning the implications of such a turn for the articulation and enactment of the theory and practice of stateless social life must be raised. There is, moreover, a corollary set of inquiries that is just as urgent given that the diasporic turn can so easily bear that alignment of identitarian expansion, imperial acquisition, and humanitarian intervention upon which Clarke rightly trains her analytic attention. In this alignment, disavowal, concern, and censure are projected upon a certain figure of the African, as well, which requires us to consider how it is that those who live in and under the administrative force of the state as an idea and an ideal in Africa come to symbolize the precarity of African states within the international order. How does attention paid to failures of governance in African states, figured in turn as products of a supposedly failed international order, both structure and limit the attention that is paid to the theoretical practice of resistance to governance within and underneath those states? Is there another model of diasporic studies that might move through these constraints, limitations, and modes of disregard in order to illuminate pan-African insurgency and, more generally, blackness as an international antinational force?

Statelessness, precisely in its relation to the paraontological arrangements of populations, is uncontained by the distinction between pre-Westphalian and Westphalian. Moreover, no appeal to physics in the interest of establishing the hierarchized copresence of (the "ontologies" and "epistemologies" that attend) these orders is sufficient to the disorder to which they respond. At stake is not only a conception of ontology whose vagueness complements its narrowness and whose application to the general field of the colonized and the shipped seems untroubled by the attention Fanon paid to a lived experience that "prohibits any ontological explanation," but also an appeal to a notion of epistemology that valorizes measurement over measure and political possibility over social poiesis.[34] This is to say, more precisely, that the narrowing of identitarian possibility within an already given political and cultural framework might not be as great a concern as the ongoing project of forming modes of general social organization that are compatible with what black folks already know and make. It still appears to be necessary, even within the field of black studies, to say that what those who remain in the hold know and make is not as simple as some would have us believe.

Once the problematic of statelessness comes into relief, it quickly becomes necessary at least to consider that compensation for the deprivations that are visited upon the stateless are given in its maintenance and not in its eradication. Such consideration is the motive force of educational theorist Annette Henry's work, to whose supposedly primitive physics and sociality Wright condescends insofar as that work can be said to represent, at the level of its objects and its methods, the tendency of "many of the books of the Black Studies/African Diaspora canon . . . to serve the . . . function of offering Africans and peoples of African descent an enabling rather than disabling interpellation, interestingly enough, using the Middle Passage and slavery as our interpellative events."[35] In fact, Henry, who Wright acknowledges is the first to coin the term "middle passage epistemology," offers an analytic that is insistently attuned to the problematic of the double—of the both/and—against the backdrop of which Wright's opposition of temporalities, as if the universe weren't complex enough to afford both classical and quantum mechanics each their own (un)folding, seems, at the very least, an unfortunate imprecision. Wright deploys this opposition to explain how it is that Henry's work is emblematic of a pervasive occlusion of "many other Black, diasporic identities" by those who are insufficiently advanced to relinquish middle passage epistemologies. Henry both studies and exemplifies this insufficiency, which I prefer to think of as something on the order of a superabundant exhaustion of normative conceptions of cultural and political identity. With the help of science journalist Dan Falk, Wright attempts to understand Henry's exhaustiveness by comparing it with Clarke's work. I quote her at some length.

> While Henry uses what physicists have called "A series time," "simply the everyday notion of time in terms of past, present and future," Clarke uses what they refer to as "B series time" [which] "refers to fixed labels that we attach to specific moments in time . . . this is sometimes called the 'tenseless' view of time. The difference is loaded: contemporary theoretical physicists such as Lee Smolin, Lisa Randall, but also those over a century back, such as John McTaggart view "A series time" as at least deeply problematic . . . and at the most illusory, a trick of the mind because experiments in particle physics seem to indicate that time does not flow and, therefore, tenses of time exist only in the linguistic and psychological register, not the physical world. . . . Simply put this is because "A series time" requires a fixed point of reference that allows one to then speak of the past, present and future, whereas "B series time" provides "exact coordinates," so to speak, which do not require a universal fixed point of reference.

I raise this distinction to link Henry's definition of the "Middle Passage Epistemology"—a counter epistemology to allow a less harmful interpellation of African American female subjecthood (or "consciousness," as Henry terms it)—to my own definition, in which I also question the MPE's fixity in "A series" time. Henry uses terms such as "African American," "rites of passage," "hybridized practices" that assume fixed meanings accorded by the MPE. A Somali-American for example, is quite literally an African American but has trouble being interpellated by the MPE even in Henry's brief quote above—she is not determined by the Middle Passage, and may understand herself and be understood by her community as a woman at the age of 13, but it is unlikely Henry means "girls" must be 12 and under, and "rites of passage" in the Chicago African American community Henry studies will likely be different from those in the Somali community. Yet the reliance on "A series time" implicitly locates this hypothetical Somali-American wholly outside Henry's discourse, regardless as to whether Henry seeks this exclusion. In Clarke's article, by contrast, the invocation of "pre-Westphalian" and other "B series time" markers, quickly and clearly invokes all black communities because there are several points of entry rather than the fixed timeline of the Middle Passage

Epistemology in which past, present and future can only be accessed by those willing and able to interpellate themselves through this epistemology.

The "brief quote above" to which Wright refers is a passage from an essay Henry wrote in which she analyzes the "'Middle Passage' epistemology" mobilized by two black mothers in what she and they call the "spiritual education of their daughters."[36]

> The narrative of Mavis and Samaya evoked tensions produced at the intersections of living in American society as Black mothers and practitioners seeking a home pedagogy that resonated with their African-American heritage and traditions. As educators and as former students in American educational institutions, they mistrusted the mainstream system for its poor record of producing competent Black citizens. Thus, they sought alternatives. Their hybridized practices carried the hope of developing their daughters academically, emotionally and spiritually. Their insistence on the church and rites-of-passage programs for girls rested on their desire for a larger set of formative experiences in their daughters' lives than the curricular and philosophical orientation espoused either in public schools or at Malcolm X School. And, as mothers of pre-teen girls, they expressed, in veiled tones, a hope that these practices would protect their daughters against violent or regrettable situations specific to girls.[37]

For Wright this kind of spiritual education exemplifies a mode of essentialist black study in the United States in which ideas of authenticity are mobilized in the service of "enabling rather than disabling interpellation."[38] The service it does explains, if not justifies, its simplicity, the purported fixity of its point of view. However, even in light of its invocation of "competent citizenship" as a goal, what is most striking, for me, is the alternative social cosmology that Henry illuminates (and Wright passes over in silence). The pedagogy Henry describes is one not only in which another world is prepared but also in which the already existing world is radically redescribed. Henry suggests, by way of the intellectual work of the women she studies, that the universe is "ambidextrous epistemological terrain" and, in fact, the maternal "progressive pedagogy" to which she attends acknowledges "reality as 'non-unitary,'" thereby practicing "a 'double agenda,' negotiating among societal contradictions."[39]

One such contradiction centers on the problematic of interpellation which, "interestingly enough," in the classic form within which Louis Althusser elaborates it, concerns the ways that state apparatuses produce, insofar as they position, subjects.[40] Wright argues for a level of voluntarity within the interpellative scene that Althusser wouldn't recognize. In Wright's formulations, people "interpellate themselves" or have "trouble being interpellated" by "epistemologies" that remain unanalyzed as ideological state apparatuses or, for that matter, by way of any alternative analytic. In *The Physics of Blackness: Beyond the Middle Passage Epistemology,* Wright more fully elaborates her understanding of becoming a subject/citizen as a process of elective naturalization. By way of James Baldwin, she might be said to advance a certain negotiation of inheritance and birthright that is imposed upon the "bastards of the west" that finally can't but be defined along the lines of Bailyn's triumphalist narrative of the "voyagers to the West" insofar as it allows the achievement of a kind of characterological "multidimensionality" that seems to accrue to those who have the wherewithal—as a function of an intense combination of deprivation and privilege—to take (or to have been taken on or by) "the grand tour."[41] The triumph is given in voyage's constant renewal, which is manifest as a kind of cosmopolitan choice that forgoes Clarke's deconstruction of the opposition of imposition and voluntarity. Consider, however, against the grain of both Clarke and Wright, that middle passage might be more accurately understood, as Du Bois knew and aggressively and ceaselessly maintained, as the interpellative event of modernity in general. Implicit in this is that to be interpellated, to be rendered subject, is to be put in profound existential trouble. Moreover, the anarchic epistemology of passage is the history of a general troubling, a general multiplication, of the voice, as Kamau Brathwaite asserts and affirms.[42] The cryptanalytic state voice is worried in the direction of the unheard while the cryptographic voice of the stateless is synthesized into the open secret that is Henry's object and method of study. The deictic force of the state's interpellative call, which is supposed to let you know who—in letting you know where—you are, is issued forth in and from the voice of the fixed coordinate. The sound of the teacher who functions as what Augusto Boal calls "the cop in the head," or the cop who functions as what Boal (or Paolo Freire) might have called the teacher/banker in the head, is precisely what black mothers like Mavis and Samaya—whose work in the field of black studies Henry approaches by way of a celebratory analytic and whose supposedly unsophisticated sense of time Wright critically laments—are not trying to hear.[43] They resonate with and in that anoriginary trouble that calls interpellative trouble into its own troubled being (where being is understood as the regulation of living). They are concerned with what other sounds and soundings are available to those who remain in passage, in the ship's hold, in the hole, in the brokered, broken, breaking whole. Wright's critique and Clarke's intervention, "interestingly enough," seem to be structured by the desire for another interpellative event; the one that remains readily available is precisely that which Althusser describes. We are left, again, to consider that "the crisis of death and global complicity to live and let die" is an effect of citizenship and not its absence or even its incompetence.[44]

With regard both to the pre-Westphalian and the Westphalian orders, it behooves us to contemplate the notion that the regulation of statelessness is the (primary and proper) function of states; that it is the interpellative work of state apparatuses, precisely in calling the citizen/subject into being, to regulate statelessness. The thought of the color line remains a potent instrument for thinking both the interplay and the divergence of statelessness and citizenship. The prophetic aspiration of "middle passage epistemology" is serially given in the radical contretemps of its (dis)articulations of stateless flesh and the bones of the citizen as they crack and crumble in the parched atmosphere of sovereignty's violent democratization. It's not enough to "insure that 'Africa' is more than a symbolic holding place for African American identities"; what's at stake is how the general interdiction of Afro-diasporic identity makes possible a social irruption through the fateful, fatal coupling of politics and identity that constitutes modernity, of which the middle passage is both the beginning and the end.[45] People might have trouble accepting their interpellation by the middle passage and its attendant modes of insurgent thought but the interpellation goes on apace and in general, whether one is Somali American or Swedish American or some combination of the two. Moreover, throughout Henry's long intellectual engagement with the teachers and students of the Malcolm X school in Chicago, and in her other work, which focuses on African American, African Canadian, and Caribbean immigrant teachers and students, whose interpellation by the epistemology of passage includes their own sojourns north into the United States and Canada, she makes it impossible for a careful reader not to consider that the simple distinction Wright makes between the African American community and the Somali community—directly after asserting that a Somali American is "quite literally an African American"—is another highly motivated imprecision. The time of the middle passage is not fixed; it is the brutal *ekstasis* of a global condition, as Henry and Dionne Brand, Gayl Jones and Julie Dash, M. Jacqui Alexander and Grace Nichols, M. NourbeSe Philip and Lorna Goodison, among a host of others, both in and out of the hemispheric configuration of the African American, constantly assert. The middle passage is and opens onto an alternative warp, enacting its own singular rupture of the space-time continuum, of a transcendental aesthetic that lays down the terms and conditions of possibility for the modern subject of knowledge and power. Having been abandoned to ceaseless passage the prisoner, the refugee, the black student is enjoined to enjoy that abandon wherein statelessness is imagined and enacted as a kind of aninterpellative shift where what it is to have been hailed is also always what it is to frustrate calculation in defiance of the state as ontological, epistemological, and political condition.

This experimental invagination, this slit or envelope in spacetime, is given not so much as multiple points of entry but rather as the division and collection of entry as such so that Anna Julia Cooper's resonant phrase "where and when I enter" is properly understood as a black feminist announcement and enunciation of quantum reality at both the cosmological and the subatomic levels, where and when both where and when are beside themselves, as intrications of compulsive, propulsive, percussive, percaressive, anarecursive, anaprogressive clearing; as no room, no place, amenity's absence, it's out of phase, nonstandard noncontemporaneity, "where" and "when" the laws of (meta)physics break down in hapticality's terrible, beautiful intensities. This syncopic feint and faked book, this unbooked, annotated, immanent praesthesis, does not impose the implication that physics is wrong to be concerned with the theory of everything; it's just that we must also be concerned with the theory of nothing. The interplay of physics and blackness is precisely at this intersection—this mutual sexual cut—of the theory of nothing and the theory of everything. And who are the theorists of everything and nothing, everywhere and nowhere? Refugees, flightlings, black things, whose dissident passage through understanding is often taken for a kind of lawless freedom.

It is precisely in the interest of such a theory that one happily engages Wright's address of this problematic in her work on the physics of blackness even as one considers that what's really at stake, here, is the blackness of physics. Black enlightenment, the dark *materiality of another way of thinking the universe, is how I understand this echoic anepistemology of passage, this "pedagogy of crossing" to which Clarke, at least, still manages to gesture.[46] It is the thought that emerges from the experience of time itself having been put in motion. As Wright knows, it is one of the very theoretical physicists she cites in her response to Clarke, Lee Smolin, whose account of quantum physics allows and asks us to consider that the cessation of historical movement to which Hegel consigns Africa is, in fact, nothing other than a belated and compensatory projection of the geometric and geographic seizure to which Descartes consigned not only European thought but Europe itself. Smolin appears, in my understanding, to resist that spatialization of time. He seeks to "*unfreeze time*—to represent time without turning it into space," a transformation the fixed coordinates of the graph imposed on the straight-ahead discontinuity of the timeline, whose minimalist suggestion of motion's arrowed, uncontained endlessness can at least be said to have figured an escape from the graph's exacting incarceration of curvature.[47] But this is not about preferring the latter to the former. Wright challenges what Heidegger calls the vulgar concept of time, and seemingly as a matter of course it is a certain figure of the African American, in the fallen, ordinary sociality of a quite popular configuration of her within some newly arisen subdivisions of "public" intellectual life, who constitutes the bad example; but what Smolin is trying to cut is what he calls "background dependent theories," such as the one that Kant, by way of Newton, codifies under the rubric of the transcendental aesthetic.[48] Einstein's general theory disrupts that background, disrupts its sanctioning of a highly restrictive mode of representation, precisely in the experience/performance of dynamic, interactive fields which I will call, by way of Darby English but against his grain, "black representational space," a field whose intricacies and intimacies even quantum mechanics has yet to approach.[49] Black representational space is the hold of the ship. Black representational space is a language lab. Strong and weak interaction not just in constraint but in exhaustion, where the submerged (if not subatomic) and the cosmological converge. That space is nowhere or is, at least, not there but elsewhere, accessible through flight and/or fantasy but not calculation. Not there is where we remain, in motion. An exact coordinate is, it seems to me, what Wright desires, a home in which (pre-)Westphalian has some universal meaning, defining our differential commonness by way of that putatively straight Euro-spatialization of time and Euro-temporalization of space that used to be known as imperialism. But "where we were wasn't there. The world was ever after elsewhere, no way where we were was there."[50] What if spacetime, the transcendental aesthetic, and the coherence/sovereignty it affords/imposes, is an effect rather than a condition of experience? This is the question that the submerged connector or conductor, that the interplay between nothing and everything, nowhere and everywhere, never and always, coalescence and differentiation, allows us to ask. B-series? B Sirius. Actually enter into the tortuous, torturous chamber of horrors and wonders that constitute serial form, the seriality of our formation, the brutally beautiful medley of carceral intrication, this patterning of holds and of what is held in the holds' phonic vicinity (as disappearance in/and expanse, hole, whole, blackness). So that a certain circling or spiraling Mackey speaks of suffers brokenness and crumpling, the imposition of irrational, terribly rationalized angles, compartments bearing nothing but breath and battery in hunted, haunted, ungendered intimacy. Is there a kind of propulsion, through compulsion, that ruptures both recursion and advance? What is the sound of this patterning? What does such apposition look like? What remains of eccentricity after the relay between loss and restoration has its say or song?

The atrocities of national cosmopolitanism, of Afro-diasporic military humanism, are terrible and to be feared and fought, as Clarke asserts, but neither by way of a disavowal, or even a redoubled displacement, of the middle passage and its already marginal modes of thought, nor by way of an embrace of the very Westphalian claims of and upon sovereignty that justify the ongoing exercise of neoimperial power. Nonstate thought is more crucial than ever and the question is this: Where is it held, most securely, in the open, in trust, as an undercommon resource? If the middle passage is a condition of its transport that is not just one among others, then it is the ongoing exercise of certain modes of statelessness that are its reservoir. What if what remains of value in Afro-American thought and life is the example of life in statelessness and not at all some supposedly triumphant emergence into citizenship? Exemplarity, here, does not bespeak exclusiveness. What emerges as decisive is an accident of history—the "unlikely" convergence of deprivation and privilege—that requires us to ask how we can think the centrality of a radical and irreducible eccentricity in and of black studies. Just as Clarke sometimes seems to repress the way that the color line organizes the sovereign operations that structured the violent "peace" of Westphalia and the viciousness of its current biopolitical permutations, so does Wright sometimes seem to join most of the modern world in forgetting that the middle passage is its condition of possibility. Moreover, the color line marks the immeasurable contours and incalculable duration of a global thing, a world event, which disrupts whatever dream of sovereignty that emerges in the opposition of, and in opposition to, things and events. Along and in constant transgression of that line, blackness places a kind of pressure on identity that identity cannot withstand. Passage, itself, moves through the narrow straits of epistemology and ontology. Epistemology and ontology are, at the same time, in a complex ensemble of times, in a radical dislocation of time, lost in passage. Out of joint, where the joint is jumpin', refugees study the sacred profanities and eloquent vulgarities of passage in order to articulate the Earth at the end of the world.[51]

In Clarke's critique of the structures of inclusion and imposition that mark the spread of the Westphalian system to Africa, she attempts to detach sovereignty from what appears to be the inconsistency of its founding paradigm. But what if the problem is not the Westphalian betrayal or curtailment of the sovereignty it instantiates and is supposed to defend? What if the problem is sovereignty as such? What if the problematic she investigates is best understood, along lines that Denise Ferreira da Silva brilliantly and rigorously explores, as the violent cunning, the brutal ruse, of self-determination?[52] What if, in turn, as she suggests, blackness, which is to say black study, is an ongoing and inaugural violence to or indetermination of self? What if what's at stake, finally, for Clarke is a way to think, in the necessity of thinking, the relation between what she calls the pre-Westphalian and what she appears to want but does not explicitly name the post-Westphalian? Then, the validity of Clarke's work will have been manifest most clearly in the demand to imagine with the utmost precision, within an absolute necessity of misunderstanding, the nature of this extra-Westphalian, paraontological, anaepistemological insovereignty in its movement in and as radical disarticulation, or even general decoupling, if Wright's grammar is correct in its implications. Clarke appears to believe that the current dimensions of black suffering in Africa preclude any attendance upon certain spooky actions at a distance that occur within the sub-Westphalian social field. But perhaps the imperative isn't to pay attention to blacks in Africa from their or its own standpoint rather than that of the self-absorbed and all-absorbing, insular but enveloping, blacks of the (non-)African diaspora, particularly as they are manifest in the prison of anarchic versioning that is called the United States, where diaspora is enacted and repressed with equal extremity. Perhaps the imperative is, rather, to pay attention to blackness in and by way of the displacement that it embraces and defies. I would agree, I hope, with Wright and Clarke, on the necessity of our centrifugitive task, which is to look for it everywhere.[53]

chapter 11

Here, There, and Everywhere

I

The justification of the boycott of Israeli academic and cultural institutions is quite simple and quite clear: the victims of a sovereign brutality instantiated in racial-military domination have come to an overwhelming consensus—in the rubbled, concrete shadow of the state that has come to exemplify The State and its exception—that boycott is the most immediate form of international support they require. To be in solidarity with the Palestinian people is to enact and support the boycott. However, the significance of the boycott is a slightly more complicated matter. Some of the arguments against it that go beyond the rejection of whatever form either of criticism of Israel or Palestinian resistance, or beyond the sometimes open/sometimes veiled assumption of Israeli exception and exemption, focus on the negative impact the presumed isolation and withdrawal of support for Israeli dissidents will have, already a morally obtuse emphasis insofar as it serves to preclude the possibility of a primary and necessary political and ethical concern for the direct victims of racial-military domination. At the same time, one of the most crucial possibilities (the call for) the boycott instantiates is support for the supporters of the Palestinians not only in Israel but all over the world and particularly in the United States, Israel's outsized and enabling evil twin. Here, support of the Palestinians denotes whatever operates in conjunction with, but also and necessarily in excess of, criticism of Israel. The critique of Israel, however necessary and justified, is not the equivalent of solidarity with Palestine, which, in the United States, can only ever augment and be augmented by our recognition of and resistance to the ongoing counterinsurgency in which *we* live. It is, therefore, of great significance that the boycott can help to refresh (the idea of) the alternative, both in the

United States and in Israel, even amid reaction's constant intensification. Such refreshment takes the form of an antinational (and anti-institutional) internationalism—the renewal of insurgent thought, insurgent planning, and insurgent feeling as a radical solvent, borne in radical insolvency (in the radical sociality of our promised and unpayable debt to one another), exchanged between those who refuse to be held by the regulatory force of an already extant, calcified two-state (United States/Israel) solution. Standing with the Palestinians gives us something to stand upon precisely so that we can stand against the horrifically interinanimate remains of state sovereignty and exceptionalism in its biopolitical, "democratic" form. We share an already given indebtedness with one another that remains as the very resource that will allow our absolutely needful understanding of it since there is no (two- or one-)state solution.

The idea and reality of racial-military domination, whose most vulgar and vicious protocols are in a kind of eclipse that is properly understood as a kind of dissemination, but whose effects—the very order that it brings into a retroactively conferred sacred existence—remain as the afterlife of sovereignty in the regime of biopolitics, is emphatically and boisterously alive in the state of Israel and in the territories it occupies. Reference to this idea and its continuing necessity for already existing structures of power helps us understand why Israel is called almost everything but the settler colony that it is in official media and intellectual culture. This discursive exception turns out to be a reservoir for the sovereign exception. It is as if the essence of sovereignty remains available as long as it is manifest somewhere, as a kind of exemplary remainder. Because the bad object of biopolitical containment is social rearrangement, it's important to note how the assertion of the right of death and the power over life still must make its presence felt as the precondition of a liquidation of the very possibility of an alternative. One way to think about all this is to begin with the axiom that Israel has been thrust into, only partly by way of its own having volunteered for, the role of the exemplary remainder of sovereignty after having taken the form of racial-military domination. The exemplary remainder of sovereignty is constrained, among other things, constantly to claim a kind of exemption that accompanies its enactment of exception. The state that constantly asserts its right to exist, and its right to insist that its right to exist be constantly recognized by the very ones upon whom that right is built and brutally exercised, is the one that bears the standard for the right of every other state so to exist and to behave. Insofar as the United States is also a settler colonial regime whose very essence and protocols are racial-military domination, it shares with Israel, in an extraordinarily visceral way, this tendency violently to insist on its right to exist and on the rightness of its existence no matter what forms that existence takes, no matter how much the everyday life of the state contradicts its stated principles. But this is also to say that the state form, in whatever materialization of its various stages of biopolitical development, always shares in this insistence. What's at stake, precisely, are the stakes any state shares in Israel's right to exist, in the residue of sovereignty in the biopolitical, and in the traces of sovereignty that will have been carried in any state, anywhere. In the most general sense, always already residual sovereignty must respond violently to what brings it into existence—the already given, constantly performed capacity for the alternative. The alternative is always under duress and must continually be refreshed and rediscovered.

I am speaking for the boycott, in solidarity with the Palestinians, because I am committed to the insurgent alternative, whose refreshment is (in) the antinational international. The terms of that commitment are nothing other than the terms of my commitment to the black radical tradition. In preparing myself not only to speak, but also to write and teach from that commitment, a particular question has become, for me, quite persistent: How might discourses of globalization and, more pointedly, of diaspora become more than just another mode of turning away from the very idea of the international? I've been dwelling—in a way that is possibly quite problematic—on this question, which is a particularly urgent question now for black studies and which is deeply and unavoidably concerned with what the boycott—which is to say solidarity with Palestine—might mean for black studies. There is a particular kind of subpolitical experience that emerges from having been the object of that mode of racial-military domination that is best described as incorporative exclusion that settler colonialism instantiates. It is not the experience of the conscious pariah, as Hannah Arendt would have it. Her misrecognition of this experience is at the root of her profound misunderstanding of black insurgency in the United States, which was not the unruly, sometimes beautiful, and ultimately unstable and pathological sociality of the ones who are not wanted, but was and is, rather, an unruly, always beautiful, sometimes beautifully ugly, destabilizing and autodestabilizing sociality-as-pathogen for the ones whose desire precisely for that pathogen and its life-forming, life-giving properties is obsessive and murderous. The more and less than political experience of the ones who are brutally and viciously wanted is something to which anyone who has any interest whatsoever in the very idea of another way of being in the world must constantly renew their own ethical and intellectual relation. This experience, in its incalculable variousness, in the richness of its social, aesthetic, and theoretical resources, is the very aim of black studies and the source of its significance. As someone whose intellectual orientation is defined by the study of that experience, I am interested in the refreshment of that orientation, for which I sometimes feel despair, in a moment that is so often misunderstood as victorious. I believe this boycott, as a mode of international solidarity and exchange, can bring that refreshment. I think that anyone who shares this orientation (for peace, justice, freedom of movement and association, freedom from want and domination), under whatever of its local habitations and names, in Palestine, in Israel, and most certainly in the United States, simply must be attuned to the necessity, and to this specific possibility, of refreshment. Selfishly, I am interested in how this boycott might provide some experiential and theoretical resources for the renewal of a certain affective, extrapolitical sociality—the new international of insurgent feeling. This is to say, finally, that these remarks have been nothing other than a long-winded preface to a declaration of my indebtedness to Palestinians for the fact that, in the end, the boycott might very well do more for me than it does for you, precisely in its allowing me to be in solidarity, which is to say consciously in a mutual indebtedness, with you and with the richness, impossibly developed in dispossession and deprivation as payment of a debt (or being subject to the violent imposition of a kind of credit) that was never promised and never owed. The imposition of credit, and its having been exceeded by an already given debt that is insofar as it is to come, is what constitutes Palestinian social life, for and to which thanks are in order since what is given and remains is the chance to join that social life, to be, as it were, pre-occupied with it. This is what the call for solidarity, which is itself an act of solidarity, provides.

Most folks who refuse to answer the Palestinian call for solidarity don't dispute the facts. A few do, but one generally feels it necessary to respond to them in the same way that you would respond to anyone who denies conquest. When I say anyone I'm not thinking of any imperial nation or corporate entity; I'm thinking of any child who blatantly takes something from another child they think of as other, or as weaker, or, simply, as someone who has something they want and think they should have. You may or may not listen to their arguments about how their conquest and theft isn't really that; you may or may not be disgusted when they don't even feel the need to make an argument; either way, in the end, you just make them give it back. The situation of Palestine, alas, isn't so easy. When things are more complicated, when the task of reversal and repair requires great intellectual and moral energy, rather than counter-coercion, you have to think a little bit. There is a general history of brutality and its various justifications to unravel and to begin that work requires the cessation of business as usual. Boycott divestment and sanctions, and the call for them, in the refusal to allow things to go on like this, provides the conditions and atmosphere for such thinking, which, in the end, is not about facts but about feeling.

II

I've been learning something recently about feeling and the lack and/or partition of it as the rhetorical energy surrounding the idea and actuality of BDS intensifies. Two ploys are of special import to antiboycott rhetoric: a radical refusal/inability to distinguish between individual and institution that emerges as essential to the defense of Israeli academic freedom; and a totalizing logic that suggests academic and cultural boycott of Israel is legitimate if and only if it is accompanied by similar action directed at every regime structured by the selective application of brutality upon populations under its control or, more specifically, at every settler colony including, and most specifically, the United States of America. These moves are revelatory precisely insofar as they say something about the relay within which fantasies of sovereignty operate. On the one hand, Israeli academic freedom, but more precisely, Israeli academic activity as such, is understood to be inseparable from those institutions that—admittedly, without debate—participate in and benefit from occupation, which is thus understood simply to be the condition of possibility of Israeli intellectuality. On the other hand, settler colonialism and racist brutality are implicitly acknowledged to be the structural foundations of Israeli and American sovereignty so that we are challenged with the necessity of a general critique of such authority lest, in singling out Israel for special notice and censure, we be unfair.

What if the vicious prevarication in which defenders of Israeli, and only Israeli, academic freedom are engaged inadvertently alerts us to something true? What if the charge of selective prosecution, brazen in its admission of the prosecution's factual basis, has the effect of exposing the general conditions and apparatuses of force and terror that must undergird the settler colonial state? Then perhaps we would do well to take note of what defenders of the terrible emergency that radiates beyond Israel's ever-expanding borders (as incorporative exclusion and purportedly self-protective aggression) admit with the cavalier thoughtlessness and self absorption that characterizes sovereignty's half-assed, pseudointellectual comportment. Then perhaps we would do even better to attend to the local conceptual field in which the state-sanctioned, institutionalized individual intellectual, the state-sanctioned intellectual institution, and the settler colonial state animate and support one another. Surely such inquiry would allow and require us to disavow the kind of regulated, regulatory cogitation that always and only extends the material effects of sovereignty's horrible immateriality in favor of a vast range of fugitive assertion. At stake, finally, in the opportunity that the current rhetorical situation affords, is the question of an- or sub-autonomous knowledge. Another way to put that question is this: What's academic freedom got to do with us?

If, by academic freedom, we mean the unfettered exercise and exchange of speech, thought, and research by every member of the global academic community, including both Israelis *and* Palestinians, then endorsement of the call for boycott and sanctions of Israeli academic institutions complicit in the administration of the illegal occupation of Palestinian lands is a significant advance in our assertion and protection of it. The responsibility of intellectuals will have been affirmed not only in exercising academic freedom but also in working to enact the conditions that make it possible, meaningful, and universal. Thought is irreducibly social. When we callously accede to the exclusion of so many from the conditions that foster its flowering, enactment, and constant differentiation we violate our own commitment to fulfill its responsibilities. The global history of settler colonialism is the history of the administration of such exclusion. Those of us who study the history and culture of the United States of America know that it has played and continues to play a major part in this tragic and brutal history, both within its own borders and everywhere it seeks to extend, consolidate, and instrumentalize its power. In endorsing the call for boycott that first emanated from Palestinian civil society but is increasingly echoed by Israeli activists and intellectuals concerned with the moral and political sustainability of their collective life, we recognize that what it is to be a friend of the state of Israel—a polity whose status as an artifact of colonialism and racism is not in dispute either for those who refuse or those who assume colonialism's and racism's legitimacy—and what it is to insist upon the right of the Jewish people to live and thrive in justice are two entirely different things. Insistence upon this right, whether seen in its impossible particularity or

understood in its irreducible entanglement, especially, with the rights of Palestinians, requires resistance to the state and its idea, especially when that
idea and its claim to right is imposed upon and embraced by those who were
so recently, so consistently, and so brutally said to stand in for the stateless.
Thinking demands suspicion of the condition in which Israel is required to
lead the assertion of the state's right to exist in general in the constant renewal of its own right to exist, thereby undergoing the unsustainable process of rehabilitating the very idea of the state. Thinking can't exclude the
consideration that the establishment of Israel—as effect and extension of the
noxious history of exclusionary ideas and realities—and its subsequent and
ongoing attachment to the moral burden of the state, its rights, and its claim
to right is antisemitism's residue. Thinking must engage the notion that the
rights of the Jewish people and the rights of the Jewish state are a geopolitical and politico-theological incompatibility whose terrible, and eventually
uncontainable, effects Palestinians are now forced to endure.

States are effects of racism and colonialism. They have no right to exist and
Israel is no exception. States have no rights, and ought not have rights, but
if they did surely those rights would be contingent upon the state's capacity
to do what liberal political theorists tell us states are supposed to do, namely
protect the rights not only of all their citizens but of all the citizens of the
world. The assertion of this simple but irreducible cosmopolitan imperative
is supposed to justify the state's existence; but states have never been either
capable or desirous of its execution. States don't have rights and the assertion
that they do is almost always the discursive residue of apartheid, in which
contingency is externalized and security internalized through acts of aggression and regulation designed to protect racial, religious, or national character
and the regular renewal of modes of hostility most efficiently and duplici-
tously carried out under the cover of "peace process" or "cease-fire." Commitment to the administered world's inveterate statism, which is imposed upon
and embraced by the state of Israel, is a commitment to the refusal of justice.
At stake, here, is a kind of undercommon, counter-Kantian cosmopolitanism
that seeks after justice against the grain of its administration in and by the
state. The necessity of such theory and such sentiment becomes clear in the
examination of what Ariella Azoulay and Adi Ophir call the "one-state condition."[1] We must be concerned with the fate of thinking, in and against its
reduction to academic freedom, within and under that condition.

Consider that some of those who organize and agitate for BDS—whether
within academic organizations such as the American Studies Association

and the Modern Language Association or outside of them—rightly remark that arguments against BDS in the name of Israeli academic freedom exhibit no concern whatsoever for the far more debilitating and absolute assault on Palestinian academic freedom that Israel has carried out, as a matter of policy, for six decades. (Even those who argue against the very idea of free speech speak in defense of [Israeli] academic freedom as if inhabiting such a contradiction required neither thought nor comment, perhaps in the recognition that none of the various reconciliations of these positions that one might imagine can be very comforting.) Supporters of the boycott note the immorality of this position even while taking pains to assure those who take it that, in any case, BDS in no way infringes upon Israeli academic freedom as it is narrowly and exclusionarily defined. But this raises the question of whether Israeli academic freedom—or, for that matter, any state-sanctioned, state-protected academic freedom but also the very idea of academic freedom insofar as it must be state-sanctioned and state-protected if it is to exist—should be subject not simply to the constraints that must accompany narrowly defined and selectively enjoyed freedom but to a radically liberatory critique of freedom so defined and so enjoyed. If academic freedom is defined precisely by the fact that it is a thing that can be enjoyed by peoples such as the Israelis and not by peoples such as the Palestinians why should we defend it? What is academic freedom that it can be exercised by Israelis and not by Palestinians and why would Palestinians, and those in solidarity with them, want it? What does Israeli academic freedom cost the Palestinians? Corollary, but absolutely subordinate, to that question is the question concerning the cost of academic freedom that Israelis themselves are asked to pay. Like the evil song says, freedom isn't free. This problematic of cost is, of course, inseparable from the question concerning benefit. We assume the benefits that accrue to academic freedom without considering the benefits that accrue to intellectual fugitivity. Academic freedom is an affair of state. It's unclear what business it is of those of us who are, and/or may choose to be, stateless.

Perhaps we should be moving and thinking against state-sanctioned, terror-defined academic freedom, intellectual normativity's oxymoronic mode of being, which is only instantiated by way of exclusion and honored always and only in its nonobservance, which liberal defenders of it administer constantly through any number of vicious and brutal forms of evaluative regulation. Consider the profound structures of unfreedom within which students everywhere, and of every age, must operate. Academic freedom is the condition under which the intellectual submits herself to the normative model of the settler. Academic freedom is a form of violence perpetrated by academic bosses who operate under the protection and in the interest of racial state capitalism. Recognize that as a form of violence it is reactive and reactionary in its brutality. It responds to the anoriginary counterviolence of thought and of imagination. It seeks to regulate thought's capacity and imperative to (over)turn. It is left to us not only *not* to assert a right to this irreducible violence of thought and poiesis but also, and rather, *to* assert that its existence is before rights, before the state that constructs and guarantees rights by way of a range of modalities of exclusion that can only be ours to refuse.

III

It is, of course, entirely possible to understand the tactical necessity of asserting that BDS doesn't violate (Israeli) academic freedom; but such understanding doesn't negate the importance of pointing out what might be seen as the strategic legitimacy of recognizing the limits of academic freedom and of recognizing what might emerge from violating its pieties not only at the level of how we relate or don't relate to Israeli academic institutions but, more importantly, in how we relate to one another in our common struggle against settler colonialism. To be more emphatic: How do we relate to one another? Do we relate to one another? If we don't—or if those attenuated relations are the artifacts of an intransigent combination of misperceived tactical necessity and uncriticized ideological and metaphysical assumption—then how does that impact our struggles and aspirations? This is not a call for a suspension of the tactical; it does not come at the end of either ideology or metaphysics; it is, rather, a gesture toward a strategic discussion grounded in an already lived alternative. It is admittedly self-serving since I am more given to the strategic and, more pointedly, because I find myself sometimes at odds with initiatives that are made as a function of perceived tactical necessity—as, for instance, the shaming of black people who defy the call for boycott as if black people bear some special obligation to adhere to the boycott that others don't share; as if black (American) radicalism hasn't been emphatic in its solidarity with the Palestinians for many decades (so that we refer not just to a need to forge such solidarity but also to its historic presence and precedence); and as if, more fundamentally, shaming were an effective organizing tool, a more efficacious way of realizing the general antagonism, which moves by way of insovereign consent as opposed to national character or, more problematic still, genetic predisposition. This example leads to the third rhetorical ploy I'd like to examine and, I hope, to an instantiation of the differences between shaming and criticism, predisposition and consent.

> Though highly unlikely, let's say my audience in Eilat would be comprised of nothing but Zionist oppressors: Has anyone thought that perhaps those who most need to hear love in action through music are the people who think it's cool to fuck over others? Why should all attendees of the festival be punished for the actions of a few assholes in power? Sometimes you've got to go into the belly of the beast to make progress. If you always boycott and refuse to use your art to heal those most in need, what's the point? Not only am I an artist, but I'm a cultural diplomat. It is my job to open people's hearts and minds all over the world through the power of art.
>
> By your way of thinking, I would never play another jazz festival or club again. Jazz itself is musical apartheid. It's the whitewashing of Black music. It was stolen from Black people who aren't still fully credited, and to this day, is not controlled by Blacks. White people make most of the money and the very existence of the White race—which enables White supremacy and privilege—is apartheid to all people of color. So any time I play a gig anywhere, I am serving The Colony. It's all dirty money. If I refused to play jazz venues or refused to teach at jazz schools, I would be doing the ancestors and the music a disservice. So whereas for you, "Eilat" may be a name that has an oppressive connotation, to me, the name "JAZZ" has the same effect.
>
> I refuse to boycott Eilat and I refuse to boycott jazz venues, for your reasons, so those of you who are trolling me online about my decision to play the Red Sea Jazz Festival are just wasting your time trying to call me out. How much do any of you know about who I am, anyways? How many of my recordings do you own? How many of my shows have you attended? You appear to only be interested in using Nicholas Payton for your own personal, political narrative. I write my own stories. I don't allow others to define me and will not be pressured into feeling guilty about using my life passion to instill more beauty in the world.[2]

Fortunately, in his self-important and self-obsessed defense of his decision to perform at the Red Sea Jazz Festival in Eilat, Israel, and hence not to respond to the call for BDS, musician Nicholas Payton offers black artists and scholars who wish to think and live in solidarity with the Palestinian struggle against settler-colonialism an opportunity to clarify their own positions regarding not only the cultural and intellectual boycott of Israel but also black radicalism's displacement of, rather than place in, world affairs. He does so not by rejecting such solidarity but rather by declaring it, rendering solidarity a matter of assumption rather than enactment. To assume that one's solidarity is a given, that it exists as a function of an identity that is supposed to have been forged in past suffering rather than one that is continually reconfigured in present struggle, is to justify the conduct of business as usual, which is given in the drone-like combination of activity and inactivity. Payton seems to imagine himself part of a movement that exists only insofar as it does not move. In this respect his "music" and his "politics" can be said to share a certain narcotic quality characterized by the mixture of nervous stasis and dulled agitation. Pained self-assertion seems to be the proper idiom for this unfortunate and degraded interplay—it is as if he can't stop thinking about the way he's stopped thinking about music and politics. To be preoccupied with this condition of arrest is, quite literally, to have one's mind settled, colonized. The sound of this malady and the content of its expression are a mixture of self-aggrandizement and self-assertion. And if I return to the word "self" too much or too conspicuously it is because self is precisely what one is left to think about when a supposedly political musician stops actually thinking about music and politics; another way to put it is that self— its freedom, its discreteness, its sovereignty—is and must be the constant study of the settler as he engages that object at the intersection of the impossible personhood and the impossible nationhood whose establishment he is constrained to perform. What fascinates in Payton's screed, even to the point of outweighing what disgusts, is the intensity with which he also attempts to justify his position with a theory of sovereignty; moreover, his music sounds (like) his political theory, a phenomenon that might be worth some attention in another venue or in another life.

What also becomes clear as a function of Payton's eruption is that against the grain of whatever possible assertion of historical determination, black people in general, and Payton in particular, have neither some special talent for such solidarity (that he ought not betray) or some special obligation to show such solidarity (by which others are not burdened), a fact that requires us now to think the relationship between black struggle and Palestinian struggle. To my mind, solidarity with the Palestinians implies, first and foremost, an imperative to follow their lead and example in their own struggle. If they require us to disavow institutions that directly or indirectly support or benefit from their dispossession solidarity dictates that we boycott; but more than this, the way they live, the way they struggle, the way they intertwine living and struggle, bears some lessons for us regarding how we must live struggle in our own fight against the interplay of settler colonialism, racial capitalism, antiblackness, and ecocide that constitutes the modern world. Moreover, solidarity with the Palestinians demands but also makes possible a theoretically informed and principled stand against a range of national and personal maladies that can best be characterized as the structures and effects of sovereignty insofar as settler colonialism is, at once, the most simple and the most extreme form that sovereignty takes, now, in the era of its democratization, which is to say its imperial imposition on those who retain the resources to imagine and enact modes of life that aren't determined by the brutal fictions of self-determination, a term whose usefulness for anticolonial struggle turns out never to have arrived, as the current condition of what is call the "post-colonial" tragically confirms. If there is a stateless antinationalism that is the surreptitious essence of black radicalism then it bears lessons for Palestinian struggle, too.

This point, again, is given special clarity in the occasion Payton provides since the music he purports to play, and which is supposed by him to constitute his politics, is nothing other than a long, communal experiment in modes of life characterized by exchange in study. There's a special link between the two situations (exacerbated by U.S. funding of the practical/material manifestation of this ideological convergence) that requires and allows a redoubling of the very solidarity whose pantomime Payton claims and deploys as a justification for business as usual. But this is to say, again, that this solidarity must be enacted, not assumed, from every possible position on the spectrum that is defined by its declaration, including those who are organizing the boycott that Payton declines to join. If the struggle against Israeli apartheid not only joins but also helps to renew the struggle against American apartheid in both its international and intranational dimensions, it is also the case that recognizing and joining that struggle (at the level not only of its social but also of its theoretical demands and resources) is essential for those who wish to enact solidarity with the Palestinians.

What does the history and force of black radicalism allow and require of those who would deploy that history in the name of Palestinian struggle? Payton's assumptions are given in his attempt to mobilize the intertwined histories of the oppression of black people and the making of black art to justify his assertion of the refusal of the boycott as an act of solidarity with oppressed people everywhere. Payton's argument is pseudo-ontological: I am a black man and therefore I must always already be in solidarity with the Palestinians insofar as I must always already be in solidarity with oppressed people everywhere. Consider, on the other hand, that black radicalism's diverse theorization of struggle actually requires something other than the assertion of an identity and the smooth carrying out of one's daily business (in his case, playing his horn in the retrograde and regressive manner that has marked his career). This is to say that what is so venal in his response, and what manifests itself so thoroughly in and as the convolution and arrogance of his "argument," is the depth of his commitment to his own putative sovereignty. Payton is going to do what he wants; he is not going to be put in anybody's box. Moreover, it appears that he believes that the necessary precursor to any dispute with his political reasoning is that we submit ourselves to the nausea and boredom of listening to his entire recorded output. To speak against his political reason, which is manifest so clearly in his decision to play in Israel, we must "know about him" or "know him." What's implied in Payton's personal categorical imperative is that to know him is automatically not only to accede to the logic of his political reason, not only to acknowledge that he is in fact in solidarity with the Palestinians precisely in refusing their request for solidarity, but also to recognize that he has discerned and is now acting out the only possible legitimate response to those contradictions of modern life that locate us in what he calls "the belly of the beast." In Payton's logic to play jazz is to live (in) and accede to apartheid and what's deep about this formulation is how neatly it follows from Ralph Ellison's (in)famous insinuation that jazz is the music of American democracy, a bit of dogma that is oft-repeated in the discourse of jazz reaction that is most often associated with the work of folks such as Ellison, Albert Murray, Stanley Crouch, and Wynton Marsalis, a group whose considerable talents have been sadly devoted to an ideology that the music constantly undermines and contests.

Again, we could ask some questions about how Payton's music is organized. How sovereignty is assumed, how its fiction is served, at the level of form in his music. But it's better to ask how sovereignty is assumed and served in the way we organize. In both instances, perhaps, a rejection of the fetishization of the soloist is needed. In Payton's case, that fetishization plays itself out at the level of the intensity of his own self-regard. Payton cries out his autonomy and independence, demands that these be recognized, thereby revealing the weird relation between the assertion of the black man's humanity and the assertion of the Jewish state's right to exist, where historically, and continually, humanity is established by way of its exclusion of blackness and the state is established by way of the assertion and imposition of Jewish statelessness. What remains necessary are the ongoing imperatives of exodus from the genocidal construct of human sovereignty that ceaselessly consumes what it is meant to protect. Those imperatives are the antinational, international, antepolitical refuge of the refugee. They constitute the resistance to every state, the disavowal of every homeland, the destruction of every wall, the obliteration of every checkpoint, and the refusal of every exclusionary and merely artistic or academic freedom. And though it's unclear if Payton really cares or really means for this question to be asked, beyond expressions of support for struggles here that are made by people who are, in fact, *here*, how do we organize ourselves so that we are actually part of a revolutionary struggle against settler colonialism and antiblackness here, there, and everywhere. Maybe my justification for paying Payton a little bit of attention is the fantasy I keep having about the transition from boycott to general strike. I've thought or imagined or hoped for such insofar as the force of what we do for them over there is directly tied to what we do for ourselves here. Again, it's unclear if this is Payton's concern since he gestures toward it with such insidious and dishonest vulgarity; nevertheless, if we ask that question, taking its trace from his hands, we advance both specific struggles, in their interinanimation, as well as the general struggle to see the earth, as Ed Roberson says, before the end of the world.

chapter 12

Anassignment Letters

I

I think I figured out what my job is: to support you in the development and refinement of your own intellectual practice. (But maybe development, and certainly refinement, are not quite right: change is better than development; think of this as a change that can be out in turning in on itself—a knotty, folded kinda thing, a multiplication of curve, edge, edginess, which corresponds to that combination of sharpening and serration that displaces refinement; or maybe, scarier, an ovarian, Octavian, hyper[re/de]generative dangerously salvific potentiality, change become a change bearing nothing, differentially, in particular.) This is not about the inculcation of the skills you'll need to be a good citizen or a normal subject or a responsible professional. What I'm talking about is a profoundly unprofessional imperative though; interestingly, cultivating an intellectual practice will help you to achieve precisely that professional status for which it will also make you unsuitable.

This is the disavowal of the very idea of an endpoint; the task at hand, the activity in question, is aleatory. This is not about achievement; more specifically, and more generally, as we move in the weighted, weighty air of enlightenment, this is not about the achievement of freedom. This is about escape. Intellectuality is fugitivity, as a mode, and as a quality, of life. And this is precisely where the subject matter of our class places an ethical demand upon us to think our class's form and structure and, more generally, to consider the form and structure of The Class. Consider, by way of Phillis Wheatley, Solomon Northup, and Harriet Jacobs that freedom is not a place that one occupies. It's not a fort or a house. It's not the woods or a crawlspace. It's not across the ocean or the river or the stage you walk on when you graduate. It's not up north or out west. It's not a point of arrival. It's not some mythological land with a big statue of a woman in front of it holding up a lamp so you can see how to get there. The much more accurate image is of a border, with an electrified fence, patrolled by vigilantes who dream a vested interest both in whatever you might bring to the place whose border they patrol and whatever might be derived from your exclusion. This brutal logic, by way of which you are subject both to disavowal and incorporation, is deeply bound up with the idea of freedom as endpoint or, more precisely, as an infinite series of endpoints, each one prefatory to the next one which substitutes for it. Consider that the best way to monopolize and accumulate whatever it is that emerges in and as the radical inconclusiveness of earthly endeavor is constantly to reproduce the illusion of the end and brutally to impose upon the earth and its inhabitants a logic based on that illusion. If there is such a thing as freedom whatever it is is much more accurately denoted, precisely because it is emphatically deferred/displaced/deconstructed, by the term/activity of escape. That which is called freedom is not, nor could it ever correspond to, the completion or the achievement of an assignment. Freedom is a practice—a fugitive act—of its own (un)making, a structure that is the very apotheosis of the terribly redoubled double edge (freedom's articulation in bondage; its dearticulation and rearticulation in flight). And so, in order to comport ourselves in some relation to it, initially we move by way of disorganization—more specifically, the disorganization of the assignment, of the end point, of, more emphatically, the end or the idea of the end. The disorganizational impulse is preliminary to a mode of organizing the class that is not predicated on the necessity of punishment and management. What is required is not only a critique but also a disavowal of whatever benefits seem to accrue to doing what somebody tells you to do.

The particular assignment that I gave you early on in the quarter had three primary functions. The first was coercive. It was meant to force you to do the reading, an imperative that assumes force is required in order to get many, if not most, of you to do the reading, an assumption totally independent of the question of whether or not it's actually worthwhile to do it. (The imperative, in other words, is read X because I said so. How often do we make an argument for why we think it would be good for you to read X? How often do we ever make an argument for the reading of X that is predicated upon the fact that we like X? Meanwhile, in the wake of these questions we're also called upon to consider what the impact of coercion is on intellectual experience. What if coercion is not subordinate to intellectual practice? What if the academic administration of intellectual practice is an occasion/platform for coercion, regulation, and the particular sociopsychic affects they produce?) The second function was to prepare you for the next assignment, which would then, in turn, help to prepare you for the final assignment. (We are immediately called upon to consider what the impact of the telic achievement of the assignment is on intellectual practice. What if the assignment is not subordinate to intellectual practice? What if the assignment lends itself, rather, to a set of sociopsychic affects that are incompatible with intellectual practice?) The completion of the assignment only ever prepares you for the next assignment, which requires one to consider the purpose of the neverending proliferation of assignments. The logic of the assignment is a logic of calculation. It makes it possible to construct a mode of quantification that imposes value upon human endeavor. The third function of our assignment was more general and more complex. It linked the local concerns of our class with this general, global logic of The Assignment, whose purpose, given in its hyperproliferation, is the maintenance of a regime of (e)valuation which, in turn, instantiates and supports the exclusionary accumulation (as opposed to the nonexclusionary dispersal/disbursal) of wealth and the maintenance of an already existing hierarchical political order. Insofar as I am constrained or choose to give you assignments, and to submit our class to the logic of the assignment/(e)valuation, which subordinates ongoing intellectual practice to quantifiable, (e)valuable units, I am servant of and subservient to the already existing order. My function is, at that point, intellectual in name only since the actual academic/administrative function that I have overwhelms any other possible function. I am, at that moment, nothing other than an overseer even if what I teach appears, at the level of its content, to resist the actually existing political-economic order. I administer your placement in the already existing order by way of the assignment, by way of the fact that the assignment must be graded, by way of the fact that the assignment always and only leads to the next assignment, by way of an addiction to grading that is operative for the one who gives it and for the one who receives it. (Professors love to be graded, too; we serially violate the slinger's golden rule—we get high on our own supply.) Another way to put it is this: grading degrades intellectual practice and what we must consider, again immediately, is what the relation is between the degradation of intellectual practice and the maintenance of the already existing order of things. What I am trying to do, as emphatically and absolutely as I can, is refuse the administrative function. This refusal is manifest as the disorganization of the logic of the assignment/(e)valuation but that's only the first step. What has to follow is the formation of another mode of organization—a reorganization.

What I'm talking about, what's in the offing, is a devotional, sacramental, anamonastic (or maybe animagnostic) kind of intellectual practice. This out, other, undermonasticism we're after is fleshly, unruly, flawed. It requires us to consider our relation—however tenuous and warped it is and ought and ought not to be—to the university's origin in contemplative life, whose remainder is probably much more emphatically present outside the university, in social/aesthetic/intellectual modalities that have never really been safe in the normative university, or which sustained themselves—or tried to against the grain of a range of brilliantly charismatic authoritarianisms—for a time in alternatives such as Black Mountain College or The Institute of the Black World, or around a whole bunch of various kitchen tables, or in the sonic relay between juke joints and storefront churches. We have to support one another in the care of intellectual practice/s. This is a social imperative. It's all about how we organize ourselves in the face not only of the twin logics of assignment/(e)valuation but even in the face of the chairs in our classroom being bolted down (to assign is to fix, to determine, to allot—it's a way of administering property and, more generally, the proper; the bolting down of the chairs is indicative, is a sign as well as an enactment, of this function). Because what if intellectual practice is irreducibly chor(e)ographic? What if you have to move in order to map? What if reflection is also a matter of reflex? What if the animation of flesh is fundamental to reflection? What if reflection and reflexion and refleshment and refreshment are one in the same? Deeper still, what if the movement in question is, at once, collective and in concert, but also disruptive or deconstructive of the idea of a certain coherence or integrity of the single body/being? I'm thinking of Édouard Glissant and Hortense Spillers here. But also of cultural critic and musician Greg Tate who once wrote, in a newspaper called the *Village Voice*, about a kind of (black) social dance in which it seemed almost as if the dancers were trying to fling their hands off of their own arms. You know what I mean? It's that thing when aesthetic experience/desire results in the breakdown of individual bodies and their anacorporeal recomportment in and as the mass + energy of social flesh. If you've been to a club or been to church you know what I mean. Maybe getting down, or getting happy, or getting haptical, are just some other names for this breakdown. Meanwhile, school has become the place where people read Shakespeare or listen to James Brown while staying in their bolted seats. On the other hand, the kind of ana*monastic*/*anima*nastic practice I'm talking about happens in/as some small recess, a temporary palestra as in Plato's *Lysis*. I'm not saying we're all totally divorced from this. I truly believe it is, actually, at hand. But we have to activate it, rather than suspend it, in the place that is supposed to have been set aside for intellectual practice. This means resisting the setting aside of that place. The university has to be not only open but overrun; it has to be dispersed so that it can disappear; so that when it's nowhere, which is to say everywhere, its general displacement can't be set aside. Anyway, what if in the interest of movement, of passage, we organize ourselves in relation to movements and passages? Let's luxuriate in that term, *passage*, even in the context of a course that takes up its absolute horror. What if we elect to remain in passage by way of the attention we pay to a passage that you read, or a passage that you wrote? If we pay some devoted attention to a movement that you see or hear, something that requires you to see and hear it again, to abide with it, to tarry with it, we might actually place ourselves in motion.

On a practical level, here's what's at stake: to take note of your intellectual movement/passage/practice. Open a file. You can call it your journal but let it also be your missal. Let it be a liturgical book prepared in/for celebration. Let it be your plan, your project, your projectile, your missile. It would not only be a record of but also a set of protocols for your intellectual practice. Here's a way to start: Find, take note of, an object—a movement, a passage, from a song, a movie, a memory, a dance, a sculpture, a word or phrase or sentence or paragraph from one of the books that we've been reading, something you heard on the bus, a billboard, a flash of unexpected color that falls into the corner of your eye. Copy it into your file then write your relation to that object informally. Then, through a (devotional/sacramental/ritual) practice of revision, let a form begin to emerge. Consider the relation between revising and remaining, between revision and the refrain (of a song), between revision and the break (the musical unit out of which hip-hop flows). To write your relation is not to make a report at the end of your thinking. It is not to offer a conclusion. It is, rather, an extension of your thinking, one that constitutes another method in disavowing the conclusion. Don't try to close it down; try to keep it open. Let your relation; let your relation change; let your relation fade into an entanglement that lets difference run even faster. Revision is keeping it open, seeing it again, letting it see, remaining at sea, in passage. Revision is rehearsal, hearing it again, playing it again. Practicing. Practice thinking because that is the practice of thinking. So let's share our files, share our objects and some moments of our ongoing, revisionary relations to them. Then our class will remain open in defiant refusal of the (final) assignment, which administration designates as the end of our class but which is always only an assigned preface to the (next) assignment, which will have been the regulatory deferral of our class, our set, our jam.

II

This is a note to everybody in both English 23 and English 117A. In writing to all of you in this way I am implying what I have been saying more explicitly all quarter: that the questions we have been discussing in our class on African American autobiography are inseparable from the questions we have been discussing in our class on Shakespeare. Your assignment, or, more precisely, my refusal to give you one, is entangled with how I have tried to approach those questions. So, in lieu of telling you what to do I am going to tell you why I won't tell you what to do. For those of you who attended class regularly, and who actually attended to what was discussed in class when you were there, this will all seem very familiar. I apologize for repeating myself yet again.

In focusing on *Richard II*, *Henry IV* (*I* and *II*), and *Henry V* we were trying to look at the birth or early history of the modern subject/person. Sometimes Shakespeare is seen as the literary midwife attending that birth; sometimes he is seen as the mother. Either way, a lot of what's interesting and important is that the modern person is presented to us in the figure of the king. Now, there's a tangent I want to go off on right now about the tension between midwifery/maternity and sovereignty but I will refrain. Instead, I just want to suggest that the way sovereignty is figured in these plays—as a kind of constantly violated invulnerability; as the constant self-assertion of constantly disrupted self-possession and self-control; as a developmental trajectory in which the sovereign/subject is embedded in the paradoxical process of becoming itself or being more (like) itself—is often best understood from the perspective of those who have been denied access to it. Well, in our African American autobiography class that's precisely what we studied: the work of those who have been denied that access and who speak from the position of having been denied it. That's why those of you in my Shakespeare class kept hearing me say that I teach Shakespeare from the perspective of black studies. What I would say now, a little bit more precisely, is that I was trying to read Shakespeare as a mode of, and also within the context of, black study. This is an important distinction and I will try to explain why.

Black studies is an academic discipline. It works by way of certain rules and protocols.[1] Think of it as a way of dwelling in a deep and fundamental paradox where you try to tell the story of the denial of access to subjectivity by way of exemplary assertions of subjectivity. Autobiography is a privileged mode of such assertion but you can see how this presents a problem: the African American autobiographer might be heard to say, "In telling you the story of how my personhood is thwarted maybe my personhood can be established." One of the reasons I was so interested in, and so happy to have the English 23 students read, Saidiya Hartman's *Lose Your Mother* and Frank B. Wilderson III's *Incognegro* is that they not only are saying/doing that but are also saying/doing something else. It's as if underneath that interplay of narrating the denial and enacting the assertion of personhood/subjectivity they are also intimating that personhood/subjectivity ain't all that and that there might be something else that's even better. This is especially important because they are also constantly attuned to the ways that the supposedly successful assertion and establishment of subjectivity/personhood is carried out, literally, on the backs of those to whom it is denied. It is established *in* that denial. Now the cool thing is that you Shakespeareans have seen just as clearly as you students of African American autobiography that this is so. The king is king, his subjectivity is given, in relation to those whom he subjects. To be subjected is to be unkinged or, as Richard II puts it, "Subjected thus / How can you say to me I am a king?" Richard, the king, the sovereign, the ultimate subject, the one who is supposed to remain unsubjected, is unmade when he finds out that he is subject to his subjects and, just as terribly, to his own body. This is a condition of his birth and of his rebirth (given in the previous king's death and confirmed in his own tragicomic crowning of the future king, both events being both belated and premature). He finds out, in being off or out of time, that one is never really king; rather one is always pretending to be so, even/especially when that pretense takes the form of theft, even the theft of life. And this pretense always ends in a kind of failure, and in the so-called king's recognition of that failure. What I've written may seem confusing, but try to remember what we have been working through all along: this weird and arrhythmic doubleness of the term *subject*. Somehow, it's offbeat blurriness implies what it is to be both ashamed and exalted, both vulnerable and invulnerable. Even *Henry V*, which ends in triumph, is constantly dealing with this problem of the sovereign/subject being forced to pretend, being subject to another, being unable to face the responsibility that goes with his privilege. The thing about Henry V, what makes him more successful than his immediate predecessors, is that he sort of knows this, and figures out a way to deal with it and not exist in a constant state of melancholy with regard to it. He can be more like a king than his father because he knows that to be a king is to be like a king. At the same time, the one who says "presume not that I am the thing I was" figures out that to be (like) what he is now requires constantly bearing, even if in reserve, the ghost of his minority, which sovereign presence is supposed to bury. Henry V, because he's always also Prince Hal, figures out a way to more effectively approach the royal normativity he desires. In a different vein, what's cool about Wilderson and Hartman is that they want something else. Rather than desiring a more successful way to approach a necessarily failed/thwarted/limited sovereign/subject they want to be with other people. But those of you in English 23 know that at the end of their memoirs this being with other people, this being a part of something that is larger than sovereignty and subjectivity, is just not quite available. It is as if being a part and being apart are inseparable. And the thing is, this inability to get at or become this other thing, this *social* thing, may be given in the very form of autobiography. To tell one's own unique story is, in some way, to respond to an unbearable duress whose final and ineluctable requirement is to relinquish the capacity to be social, to sit and talk with your mom and dad, say (who tragical-historically, Poloniusly, are and have, while never really being or having, stories of their own), or join a circle of little girls singing and dancing the theft of your ability to sing and dance with them. And see, for me, this is a problem of *study*.

I guess I think of black studies or, for that matter, traditional literary studies as rule-based and essentially individual activities. The rules are designed to impose upon you the necessity of simulating, in your intellectual activity, the achievement of the very subjectivity that our classes have been calling into question. What you're supposed to be doing, by yourself, so you can be (de)graded, accounted for, and properly separated from one another, is showing that you have become a self-possessed and self-contained intellectual subject. The fact that we have classes, or conferences, or whatever—that we carry out our proper individuation in groups—doesn't negate that. In the end the work we do, the assignments we are given, are individuating and, I think, isolating and alienating. And this is written into the form of the assignment, which implies a particular trajectory. You start with notes or with an idea and then you are supposed to polish that idea into a kind of coherent argument or some clear presentation of yourself having thought about a thing and brought that thinking to a proper conclusion. I hate assignments because they are designed to show how you have come to a conclusion and they are designed to allow me to judge the legitimacy and value of that conclusion. But the thing is, when it comes to the stuff we've been reading and thinking about there is no conclusion! This thinking is not supposed to come to an end and, moreover, this thinking is supposed to be something shared. Your writing is not supposed to be the establishment of your intellectual propriety and it is not, at least in my view, some piece of intellectual property. Thinking is in process and it is in common. It is inseparable from reading and writing. Thinking, reading, and writing—in process and in common—is the work you are supposed to have been doing for this class. One of the things I fucking hate about assignments is that they allow you not to pay attention. It's like if you know what you are supposed to do, or to have done, in the end then you can organize your time around achieving that end, which is always only a form of pretending to know or to have come to some conclusion. You get to move in the organized safety, which is to say brutal surveillance, of having been told what to do rather than the complexity and danger, but also fun and pleasure, of paying attention to what you are doing, which is an activity that is given in process and in practice and in common.

When I say "in common," I mean the commonality of listening to and paying attention to what the other members of the class (including me) say—but also the commonality of consulting other texts. Above all this means the primary texts of the class but it also means the introductions of the Shakespeare texts, or the supplemental readings I made available for English 23, or what you're reading or have read in your other classes, or something you saw on the Internet or the song you can't get out of your head, or something crazy your brilliant Uncle Jake, or something brilliant your crazy cousin Ella, said. It's what it is to be thinking in the world with other people. And whoever wants this thinking to come to, or have been brought to, a conclusion must not be our friend. So, again, what I want is for you to turn in the work you have been doing for this class insofar as that work can be translated into writing and into what might be called an open form of scholarship. And the thing is, even if you haven't really been doing that work all along—if you were waiting for me to make it worth your while to do the reading, or to figure out some way of surveillance and punishment and policing that will have essentially made you do the reading under threat—you still have time to do it now. Again, I want to see the written form your reading and thinking has taken. I'm not interested in its being polished or having been brought to a proper conclusion. But I am interested in what you think about that written form. This means you should have been reading what *you* have been writing all along, or that you need to go back and read your own writing now, commenting upon it, revising it, treating it, too, as one of the primary texts of the class. If this were a math class you would get credit for "showing your work" in this way, even if you didn't get the right answer or come to the proper conclusion. Here, showing your work is all about acknowledging and even celebrating the absence of the proper conclusion. I won't give you partial credit for it but I will be in your debt.

chapter 13

The Animaternalizing Call

I brought something to show and tell and to hand around; something for you to lay your hands on—the copy of *The Telephone Book* that Avital Ronell signed for me twenty-four years ago today. Her inscription reads:

> For Fred
> and all the close calls we
> were meant to have.
> admiringly,
> Avital Ronell
>
> 10.30.90, Berkeley

At first glance it will appear as if we missed each other, as if we missed just missing each other, as if articulation's asymptotic brush just missed us; but an encountering was already occurring, had already come on (the) line, a three-way conference call spurred by my big brother—which is to say that I am his big, belated double—Akira Lippit, who's here right now, even though he's not here right now, in being just a phone call away. Avital had already been taking care of me in Berkeley, the capital of carelessness. I was in a different department, the English one, the department of a kind of literary study that was beneath comparison insofar as it always thought itself to be above compare. The space between Wheeler and Dwinelle wasn't untraversable but to feel the transversal, to enact a reverse, you had to be taken care of, you had to be taken, you had to be smuggled, you had to be carried while also being welcomed. Who is it, or deeper still what is it, what is the mechanism, what is the function, that can not only carry and welcome but also, and in and at the same distended time, release? The maternal calls us, carries us, sends us away, always one last throw into the community sing. In the last real conversation I keep having with my mom, she'd come to New York to hear me read; it was a raucous, New York Schoolish, Black Mountainous kind of thing and she'd been so particularly impressed by a Joe Torra poem about or inflected with masturbation that she looked at me with a certain A.M.E/Arkansas/school teacherly primness and said, "I see, now, I'm gon' have to let you go." I was thirty-seven. A few days later she died on her sixty-sixth birthday. Let me go where, mama? Let me go to whom? I wish I could call her right now so she could tell me. But she already told me. She's telling me right now. She began letting me go the instant she began to carry me; the instant she began to bid me welcome, telling the fucked-up world it was welcome to me, holding me in her hands, holding me out, handing me. Anybody who knows me knows that I'm a mama's boy. They are responsible for me and so they have to take responsibility for me.

It's embarrassing to talk about myself when I should be talking about Avital—her address, her call, the severe discipline of her antidisciplinary, antidissertational directory assistance—but I'm incapable of that separation in the infinitesimal but unbridgeable distance between us, our inseparable distance and difference from one another, our ongoing near miss, our incessant close call. I know it's a little strange in being too unestranged; it's a little too close for comfort. It's not easy. I'm uneasy about it. Surely, we all have to feel a bit uneasy. My embarrassment is pregnancy's false friend but I am full with, and full of, something other than myself, having been made responsible for carrying this other thing around, having been made responsible by having serially been carried and lovingly handed on. I'm deeply, incalculably embarrassed but I'm not ashamed. With regard to this embarrassment I have no conscience, am not a coward, have not been rendered subject. The call I keep trying to answer bespeaks the infusion, the insistently previous insemination, of the politics of technological modernity with the sociality of ec(h)otechnographic maternity. It's another and an uncertain type of call of conscience, an imperative to answer and so to acknowledge an irregular kind of hard-rock catastrophic fluidity drowning out the telephonic connection to "the paternal belly of the state," an anumbilically radical incontinence, the thing of darkness and its submarine feel, the black thing, because the impossible mother is always black, because blackness is impossible maternity, is the shadow whisper in your ear that comps every call, like Glenn Gould humming through the interplay of practice and performance and mechanical reproduction both to drown out and replicate the substitutive maternal hum of unaligned and impossible domestic service. The incessant substitution that comprises the maternal ecology: what it is continually to be handed, as Hortense Spillers would say; the fugal, fugitive seriality of maternal lesson and lesion, of the oedipedagogical set or jam, the jammed lines of the ongoing maternal lecture. I have been continually introduced to, and in, this folded circle by Spillers, by Toni Morrison, and, more immediately, in a more hands-on modality of being handed, by B Jenkins and Avital Ronell. It makes me wanna fill Deutches Haus up with country music: Mama tried, I've heard the sound of my dear ol' mama crying, my baby goes from (hand to hand), until Merle Haggard, George Jones, and Lefty Frizell are rightly taken for Craig Mack's true, otographic opening, as he arrives to put some flava in ya ear.

All that was just to say that I never have been and never will be either willing or able to separate myself from this paragraph:

> In this light, one of the things that we shall need to ponder concerns a tranquil assertion such as one finds in *Being and Time*: "Being towards Others is ontologically different from Being towards Things which are present-at-hand" (*Being and Time*, 124). While this articulation involves a complex series of designations whose elaborations would require a patient tapping of each term ("being towards . . . ," "present-at-hand"), it nonetheless can be seen to assume a clean ontological separation of Others and Things wherein the Other, as Heidegger states in the same passage, would be a duplicate (*Dublette*) of the Self. The question that we raise before any approach can be made toward this passage or the locality of the Other suggests a disposition other than the one disclosed in Heidegger's assertion. The mood we wish to establish is not one of reactivity but of genuine wonder and bewilderment before the statement. At first sight the statement asserts itself as constatively unproblematic: Being towards Others is ontologically different from Being towards Things which are present-at-hand. What is supposed, however, regards not only the difference between modes of "Being towards" but the aim or destination which would know the gap separating Others from Things. Now, what if Others were encapsulated in Things, in a way that Being towards Things were not ontologically severable, in Heidegger's terms, from Being towards Others? What if the mode of Dasein of Others were to dwell in Things, and so forth? In the same light, then, what if the Thing were a *Dublette* of the Self, and not what is called Other? Or more radically still, what

if the Self were in some fundamental way becoming a Xerox copy, a duplicate, of the Thing, in its assumed essence? This perspective may duplicate a movement in Freud's reading of the uncanny, and the confusion whirling about Olympia as regards her Thingness. Perhaps this might be borne in mind, as both Freud and Heidegger situate arguments on the Other's thingification within a notion of *Unheimlichkeit*, the primordial being not-at-home, and of doublings.[1]

The primordial being not-at-home, the paraontological difference, is our animaterial, animaternal home-in-homelessness, where mutual aid and mutual estrangement fold into and out of one another, where maternal ecology is the constant erasure and ungendering of, the endless differentiation and distancing from, whatever figure of the mother in whatever proximity that figuration might breathe and bear. Being present at one another's hands, and ears, and mouths, we strive to be held and handed and kissed goodbye. We strive to disappear into anaxeroxic nothingness, to be at ease in the general and generative unease of social call, social rub, social hum, social mmmmm, social muah, social music.

Avital, are you my mother? No. Moreover, you are neither a mother nor the mother. No one is, or was. That would have been impossible. At the same time, we are taught to speak irregular, irreducible impersonation and in the general socialization of the impossible maternity that bears and hands and gives its signs. This is our music, discomposed. Impersonation makes it so you just can't help but get personal. I'm sorry. But, Avital, will you sign your undrownable book for me again?

chapter 14

Erotics of Fugitivity

Blackness is enthusiastic social vision, given in non-performed performance, as the surrealization of space and time. Anticipating originary correction with the self-defensive care of division and (re)collection, it goes way back, long before the violent norm, as an impure informality to come. Its open and initiatory counter-pleasures reveal the internal, public resource of our common sense/s, where flavorful touch is all bound up with falling into the general antagonistic embrace. That autonomous song and dance is our intellectual descent; it neither opposes nor follows from dissent but, rather, gives it a chance. Consent to that submergence is terrible and beautiful. Moreover, the apparent (racial) exclusivity of the (under)privilege of claiming this dis/ability serially impairs—though it can never foreclose—the discovery that the priority of sovereign regulation is false. In order to get the plain sense of this you have to use your imagination.

The paraontological distinction between blackness and black people is crucial but this is so only insofar as it is the case that blackness cuts the distinction between essence and instance. It might seem, and I used to think, that this is the importance of always beginning with performance. At such beginning, or within the context of this particular way of assuming the very possibility of a beginning, a simultaneously real and virtual complex of issues arises between blackness and a certain dominant and normative formulation within performance studies. If, virtually, what is at issue is the problematic of liveness and nonliveness in performance, then actually, what is at issue is the emergence of nonperformance in the field in which the interplay of performance and performances is assumed. If blackness cuts the distinction between essence and instance, between performance and performances, it is in and as nonperformance, where both the thing and its activity fade from the (mis)understanding into differential, inseparable blackness. If the performances I have most usually invoked are not live, this has been a function of my preference for how blackness displaces the particular (and sclerotic) notion of presence that liveness is supposed to instantiate. At stake, finally, is emphatic, surreal, nonperformative presence in the making of a living: at stake is "the presence of the flesh" that emerges at the intersection of Hortense Spillers and Andre Lepecki.

Blackness comes into relief against the backdrop of its negation, which takes the form of epidermalization, of a reduction of some to flesh, and to the status of no-bodies, so that some others can stake their impossible claim upon bodies and soul. This reduction has profound politicoeconomic consequences but it's also right to say that it's a function of the violent profundity of the very idea of the political, the very idea of the economic, which we can think of as the systemic operation/oscillation of the public/private. Public and private are both bound up with a metaphysics of possession, of the self-possessed/possessive individual, his discreteness given in the sense and in the assumption of a body. Blackness is consent not to be one: not just to be more + less than one but the mobilization of that indiscretion and incompleteness against or "otherwise than being" (which is to say that Levinas's great mistake, so to speak, is his failure to dislodge ethics from the regulation of the one in the form of the distinction between self and Other, a failure that is emphatically shown in the intensity of his antiblackness, whose structural force is shared by Arendt and even by Fanon, manifest as a residual of phenomenology's self-concern, its focus on discrete singularity as both subject and object).

Kant's fear of and his subsequent attempts to regulate *Phantasie*; his anti-ante-normative, anti-anabaptist distaste for the swarm, for the profligate, for unchecked generativity is crystallized in his invention of race as a philosophical assertion and instrument of antiblackness. When Kant equates blackness with ugliness and with stupidity, this can't be separated from his understanding of the intensity of the relation between beauty, morality, and reason, which is given in the subject, and also in the nation/state, as an uneasy confluence of sovereignty and self-determination. The philosophical disavowal of blackness, along with the politicoeconomic accumulation of blackness (given in the accumulative, genocidal, and patriarchal operations of the transatlantic slave trade and the epidermal racialization of settler-colonialism), constitute the modern world as socioecological disaster.

The fact(s) of antiblackness, its specific operation/s, reveal, though, that a distinction exists and must continually be asserted between blackness and the people who are called black. At the same time, the preservation of blackness, which more and more is revealed to be tantamount to the preservation of Earth (in its paraontological totality), remains for us now as a chance only insofar as the people who are called black operate as a thoughtful sensuality, in the interplay of the refusal of what has been refused them and the consent to what has been imposed on them. To refuse what is normatively desired and to claim what is normatively disavowed is our lot, our anteperformative repertoire, our violently studious animation. What it is to enact and to inhabit that repertoire is all but unfathomable. It falls outside the purview of any analytic that has been devised to understand whatever delusions exist under the rubrics of behavior, however many times it is behaved, or decision; it defies those dominant modes of description that are paradoxically subordinate to an assumed natural history that understands deviance as derivative positioning rather than what Nahum Chandler calls "anoriginal displacement."[1] Deviance is not opposed to the norm; it comes before it, bears it, must take responsibility for explaining, in defying, how the brutal ensemble of differences under which we now live became the same.

We are a message-effect regarding the theory of blackness, which parallels but also instantiates the simultaneous theorization and deconstruction of the subject. Modern philosophy critiques the subject, operates (within) that dis/enchantment of the subject's value (the valuative oscillation between exaltation and shame; the operational im/possibility of sovereignty and self-determination). Blackness, which is to say black study—the undercommon, underground monastic attitude of the quarters, the field, the refuge, the territory, the church, the joint, the (sound barrier) club—is the refusal, by way of black and fugal operations, of the subject's long, developmental nightmare. The contrafantastical trauma of self-obsessional *Bildung* has been—as a matter of law (both supposedly natural and juridical)—refused to the people who are called black, the people to whom blackness has been ascribed (within the operations of a certain racial-human declension, an assumed chain of being that declines from whiteness to blackness and their presumed sexualization and engendering). To have been refused this traumatic development is, at the same time, to have been drafted into its operations as apparatus. So that to refuse what has been refused is a combination of disavowing, of not wanting, of withholding consent to be a subject and also of refusing the work, of withholding consent to do the work, that is supposed to bring the would-be subject online. It is to prefer not to, in stuttered, melismatic, gestural withdrawal from that subjectivity which is not itself, which is not one, which only shows up as a thwarted desire for itself, as the lurid auto-cathectic lure of an airy fiend that walks beside you in a storefront window. The experience of subjectivity is the would-be subject's thwarted desire for subjectivity, which we must keep on learning not to want, which we have to keep on practicing not wanting, as if in endless preparation for a recital that, insofar as it never comes, is always surreally present. Meanwhile, the subject, which was never here, cannot then disappear; it can only haunt. This is what one might call the unholy ghostliness of liveness and it has to do, paradoxically, with the fact that the body requires but has no soul, that the soul requires but doesn't want a body. This is the incommensurable twoness of the one, which renders it relatively nothing, in contradistinction to the absolute and general no-thing-ness that is given in/as blackness. Meanwhile, this deficit-driven enclosure, this paradoxically triadic binarity (the two/zero/one beat) is the field in which—with all respect and reverence—Richard Schechner's and Joseph Roach's and Peggy Phelan's theories of performance operate. Liveness (even in/as restored behavior; even in/as surrogation; even as insubstantial avoidance of reproduction) is compensation for withheld consent. The here and now is meant to compensate for the surreal presence in/and the materiality of its persistence. Or, we could say that what we're after is a move from the metaphysics of presence, given in the figure of the one, to the physics of presence, given in transubstantial no-thing-ness, in consent not to be (single), in differential inseparability, in the nearness and distance of the making of a living and its spooky, *anima*terial actions.

Our actions are not twice behaved and disapparent stand-ins for standing; rather, they are ani*mater*ially out and gone. They are neither the resistance of the object nor the insistence of the thing but something like a kind of negative relay between thingliness and nothingness that is given as an assertion, and in defense, of difference without separation, of consent not to be a single being. Our fate is not to become one and yet many; it is, rather, to become the *mu*ni bird. To become bird. To become mu. Implicit here is a kind of communicability that is or that marks a presence that is more + less than here and now: an aesthetic whose immanence makes it more + less than transcendental, as Nathaniel Mackey says.[2] A presence of flesh rather than a presence of the body, which, as Gayle Salamon says, cannot, in its transit, be assumed.[3] (Not that being in transit reduces the body to flesh, which is a formulation one could derive from some combination of Salamon and Spillers, but rather that being in transit enacts a kind of ante-phenomenological reduction to flesh that is before the body as empathy, as general and prior consent, as insistent previousness. Flesh is before the body, just as blackness is before whiteness, as Aldon Nielsen has intimated.[4] From body to flesh, from world to earth, the study of blackness is inseparable from the study of (non) performance. A declension could be said to have occurred, from subject to object to thing to nothing, that hopefully constitutes a way back into the ground of this physics. (Heidegger, by way of a certain work of critique/ negation, called it, or something like it, "the way back into the ground of metaphysics.")

Someday it will be really important to get at that the precisely unlocatable difference between skin and flesh, Fanon and Spillers. For now we have to ask some other questions. Can there be an authentic anti- or ante-epidermal consent? How can the ones who are not called black make a claim upon and consent to that calling, which both holds and projects? How might we move from an ontotheology of performance to a paraonto-theology of performances to a physical sociology of anaperformative differences? Ontotheology attempts to get at the divine, to get at an original or originary being, by way of concepts, independent of experience. Ontotheological aspiration is embarrassed by the instance. In this regard, performance studies is embarrassed by performances, particularly if the ontology of performance is understood to have been given in performances' serial disappearances, their supposed distance from any economy of representation or reproduction. But what if further embarrassment, which might be thought in its false but faithful translinguistic friendship with fertility, lies in the fact that when performances disappear they go to a nonperformative or anteperfomative social field? If what it is even merely to describe a performance is, as it were, to record and therefore violate the ontological integrity of (a) performance, so that the "bare" materiality and sensuality of a performance is always constituted as the embarrassment of the essence of performance, then what do we make of a description that more or less refuses the chance even to get at the matter, as if in avoidance of an embarrassment that is given in unruly, undesirable sociality's avoidance of the terrible paradox of single being? At stake here is an irreducible relation between sensuality and representation to which I must return. Meanwhile, the degeneration and generativity of differences are in concert, so that what remains is nonperformance, where a way is made out of no way into nothing and a table is prepared but without amenities. An indentation, a recess; a caesura through seizure; that's what is opened, into negation's affirmative space—and she doesn't open it, being the soloist who is not one: sent and gone like a comet, or its rumor. Transcript's fugitive subscript defies narration and phenomenological description. It's not that she didn't return to a brutal lifeworld; it's that in so doing she turned to something else so that we might keep turning into something else.

All that is the case of blackness comes to us by way of antislavery's liberal brutalities, which take the form of an ancient and persistently significant noncorrespondence of what it is to be antislavery and what it might be to be abolitionist, and an anteinterpellative militancy whose lower frequency might easily be mistaken for quietude. Lower frequency is, here and as usual, a black woman's homeless, stateless imperative. Softly against the grain of a metaphysical presumption of a right to perform or not to perform (a knowledge, one might say, of the freedom to be or not to be), which undergirds performance even at its most critically and theoretically sophisticated, here are some notes, both belated and preliminary, on blackness as nonperformance. They are merely prefatory to a response to a powerful insistence given in Sora Han's extraordinary essay, "Slavery as Contract: Betty's Case and the Question of Freedom," where she beautifully and rigorously undertakes to apprehend what description and narration cannot comprehend.

> In 1857, Chief Justice Lemuel Shaw of the Supreme Court of Massachusetts declared Betty to be free. Betty, a slave woman, had been brought from Tennessee into Massachusetts by her owners, the Sweets and by virtue of their travel and stay in Massachusetts, the Sweets' relation with Betty had been legally converted from one of enslavement to one of labor. It was within this latter context that Shaw determined Betty to be a contractual agent with free will. This case, driven in its ruling and circumstances by a question about the legal personality of a slave, would come to be called *Betty's Case*.
>
> . . . As matter of the legal issue of contract at the heart of the case, the law recognized Betty's free will. But as a matter of the facts surrounding the case, Betty curiously, even unthinkably, asserted and exceeded this legal freedom. For against the disapprobation and outright hostility of the abolitionists who had successfully brought the case before Shaw in her name, and immediately after Shaw's declaration of her freedom, Betty decided to return to Tennessee with her owners. In *Betty's Case* we find the crucible of mounting national tensions around the issue of slavery, the particular legal issues of contract and property at stake for the parties involved in the case, and the scandal of Betty's decision to return to slavery.[5]

If *Betty's Case* recognized Betty as party to the social contract, it is nonetheless unclear what, if any, kind of promise Betty made to whom as an exercise of legal freedom. The recognition of Betty's freedom by virtue of finding in her "free will" neither implies a mutual promissory relationship, nor the possibility of finding some form of breach of that promissory relationship by either party. Herein lies the ultimate stake of my reading of the private law of slavery: How, as a matter of the law's language, to rethink the relation between promise, breach, and freedom raised by the slave as a figure of contract? While it is accurate that the law's facilitation of the historical shift from slavery to segregation worked through innovations of contractual relationships (not only of labor, but also of kinship, citizenship, and selfhood), my reading of the intellectual history of modern contract law suggests that this legal development is symptomatic of a deeper jurisprudential problem rather than a moment of progressive reforms to the laws of chattel slavery.

In this sense, Betty's act faces another order of ethics what we might call an ethics of the obscene. Her decision is neither her submission to slavery, nor her permission to the state to enforce her legal freedom. It is a remnant legal act, or an unconditional responsibility to freedom a redoubled and redoubtable materialization of freedom that is otherwise known only in its relationship to the transcendent right of freedom driving modern law. The decision of unconditional responsibility shows up, at least on my reading, as a reveling in an enacted threat of a freedom against freedom that haunts any and every promise of freedom the law both makes and guards. Her decision is an a priori fugitivity to becoming a fugitive of the law of slave and free states.

The force of this fugitivity is what we might reference as blackness, a performative against all performances of freedom and unfreedom dependent on the historical dilemma of a lack of meaningful distinction between freedom and slavery. The distinction here between performances of (un)freedom and a form of freedom in and as the performative of blackness is crucial. The latter arrives at a form of freedom dependent on, but in excess of, not only rules distributing the right to freedom of contract (which is contract law's primary occupation), but also, on the radical adherence of the law's language to the transcendent idea of freedom through the case of the slave. And while this performative is displayed in plain sight with *Betty's Case*, it is buried, but no less present, in contract law.

In what is perhaps the irony of all legal ironies raised by *Betty's Case*, we find that the formalization of what I am calling the performative of blackness is generally referred to in contract doctrine as "nonperformance."[6]

Han shows us that against the backdrop of nonperformance a paradox emerges and recedes in the black light of general antagonism:

> The unthinkable question *Betty's Case* presents (and, again, this is not because of Shaw's ruling, but rather because of Betty's act in relationship to the ruling) is whether freedom, as constituted by the law's language of contract, must include *the freedom to be a slave*.[7]

> Contract law today, in practice and as conceptual metaphor for social relations, marks the law's impossible attempt to harmonize principles of regulated and regulatory exchange *and* a categorically abstract realm of freedom.

> In this precise differentiation, we should attempt to account for how personal sovereignty, recognized by contract law in the legal personality of the individual, is haunted materially at the level of formal legal reasoning by a notion of "free will" that is free precisely because this freedom can be given away.[8]

Han's analytic of freedom's brutal necessity allows us to ask some questions that it also requires. What if the paradox fades as a function of refinement? What if absolute and inalienable freedom—what if freedom's generality, its universality and universal applicability—turns out to be both instantiated in and eclipsed by a particular freedom? What if it's not freedom but the freedom to give freedom away that is inalienable and absolute and constitutes the ground of freedom's *virtual* generality? To think these questions requires taking a turn with Han. I want to take turns with Han. The pivot, which she has established, is blackness and nonperformance, toward which she proceeds by way of Shaw's recollection of the public/private scene of judgement that he stages:

> Whereupon, I proposed and had an examination of the said Betty apart from the said Sweet and wife, and all other persons—upon which it appeared to me, that she is twenty-five years old, intelligent and

capable of judging for herself; that she has a husband in Tennessee and other relatives; that she is much attached to Mr. and Mrs. Sweet; is very well treated by them, and desires to remain and return with them, and this desire she expressed decisively and upon repeated inquiries. I explained to her right to freedom and protection here, and that she could not lawfully be taken away against her will.[9]

It is well to acknowledge Robert Cover's reminder that Lemuel Shaw was Herman Melville's father-in-law, and to speculate along with and in excess of Cover that he is, at least in part, serially fictionalized as Bartleby the Scrivener's narrator and boss and as Captain Vere, Billy Budd's admiring captain and judge, who sentences him to death.[10] Melville's abiding concern with mutiny is played out in relation to these figurations of the position and activity of judgment and mutiny is, in these two tales, given in a certain kind of pathological speech, instances of something Adrian Heathfield might call and recall within "a short and stuttering piece" that will have amounted to a story: Billy Budd's stutter turned to murderous blow or Bartleby's emphatically nonexpressive mantra, which is given as a radical and mysterious preference for something (else) held in or hidden by nothing.[11] Something is both held and poured forth in his preferring not to work and not to leave that tempts one to think of them, as well as Billy Budd's worried talk and violent reflex, as mutations of Betty's muted operations. Shaw's decisions, which embody the ambivalence of the figure of judgment whose antislavery tendencies are constrained by an antiabolitionist commitment to private property—which is to say to the very idea of the private, the very idea of the proper—are extensively analyzed by Cover, who is concerned with the conflict between a commitment to the principle of legal formalism and the commitment to the principle of freedom, a conflict laid bare as a peculiar kind of nonexistence in *Betty's Case* and, more generally, in the case of blackness. The conflict/contradiction turns out not to be destructive in turning out not quite really to *be*. Things go on apace and that's the rub. This conflict which is not one is not an autodestruct mechanism but an engine.

Of course, while we have Bartleby's and Billy Budd's voices, and actions, however attenuated, we don't know what Betty said in her interview with Shaw and we don't know what else she did or what else happened to her. She disappears, as does her fate, perhaps in a way that Phelan might attribute to the particular ontology of performance.[12] And certainly her purported declaration of affection for her owners might very well be best understood as twice-behaved. But here we might also begin to speak of her nonperformance's afterlife, which will have been inseparable from the ongoing and interminable afterlife of slavery, as Saidiya Hartman has described and analyzed it. So what I'm interested in, against the backdrop of Phelan's and Hartman's powerful interventions, by way of Han's rediscovery, is to imagine something on the other side either of the freedom to perform or not to perform (or even to be or not to be), which might open up the possibility of another kind of examination of the metaphysics of "behavior" and "decision." What if disappearance is, itself, best understood as a return to the exhausted, futurial sociality by which the one who is not one—as a matter of law, custom, and theory but, before these, as a matter of a rich entanglement of refusal and consent—has been sent?

Clearly, Shaw saw enough in Betty's performance, and had faith enough in his own power to explain, that he was able to judge her competent. In the courtroom, Shaw adds, "the attendance of colored people was very numerous, but strict order and decorum were observed throughout the proceedings." In the judge's chambers, however "bound to appear" (to use Huey Copeland's apt phrase), colored people refused to do so.[13] Betty does not attend. There is no one to attend. There's no way to read such nonattendance as freedom; there's no way not to read such (con)strained inattention as flight. There's no way to read the abyss as haven. There's no way not to read the hole (the whole, the hold) as haven. Born into the dominion of will as its exile, attached to Mr. and Mrs. Sweet, chained to their freedom as the very principle of its operation but unknown by it, Betty remains, in thwarted and imposed mobility, and we are left to discover what is left of what still sends her.

Nonperformance is a problematic of décor, of a refusal to decorate, to embellish tastefully. Uncollected, incollectible, Betty's nonperformance is radically inappropriate; her refusal to (re)behave is given as if she has no interests. Can we recover what she did not say to Shaw; can we excavate what is held in her having been withheld from their exchange, in her refusal to be party to it, in the obscenity of her objection to the objectifying encounter with otherness? What sociality is concealed from him in whatever what he thought of as her "face" revealed to him? Her face was not her own but it was a face, and it could be read, he must have thought. Wasn't it a face? Couldn't it be read? Couldn't it reveal? Didn't it unconceal? What material amazement is held in the difference that giving and showing embrace? And what do giving and showing withhold? What is withheld in and as their nonperformance? What remains unowned? What if to be free from slavery is to be free of slavery? What if freedom is (a condition) of slavery? What if the condition of the slave in general, or "generally speaking," is that she is chained to a war for freedom, chained to the war of freedom, to the prosecution of freedom as war, to the necessity, in freedom, that freedom imposes, of the breaking of affective bonds, the disavowal, in entanglement, of entanglement? What if freedom is nothing more than vernacular loneliness?

The paradox (if freedom is inalienable then the freedom to relinquish freedom must also be so) disappears when it is discovered that slavery and freedom are not opposed to one another. Han requires us to deal with the fact that the relation between freedom and slavery is not mutually exclusive but mutually metonymic. Things become a bit clearer in reverse, at the broken rendezvous of attenuated victory. There, we consider what it is to be enslaved to freedom rather than to be free from slavery. From there, we might follow Han, while taking some notes on the erotics of fugitivity.

The clear, expressly abolitionist expression and enactment of Betty's repudiation of antislavery's abolitionist appearance, to whose nonperformance, which Han teaches us to understand as such, we have no access, is reconfigured in Harriet Jacobs's various self-denials or self-enclosures, her variously performed givings-away of herself and her freedom. Further, and in furtherance of a set of lessons given by Hurston, Hartman, Spillers and Daphne Brooks, Han teaches us not to misread these disavowals of individual freedom as some transcendent achievement/enactment of absolute freedom but rather to read them as refusal of any such transcendence or abstraction or formalism in the interest of immanence, materiality, and what we might call a certain (il)legal (sur)realism. Denise Ferreira da Silva might call it the jurisgenerativity of no-bodies, which will have existed, as it were, only in the absence of the story, as resistance to or abstention from narration. Against the grain of Cover's juridical commitment to narrative, Betty's story, which is not one, which she neither owns nor tells, in the very fact of its having been withheld from the court, obliterates the court. At stake here, in general, is the withholding of, the withdrawal from, the antagonism toward, story. In this respect, Betty goes against Jacobs's grain as well, even if the veiled shadow of something like what one wants to call Betty's face is glimpsed, before the mirror that *Incidents in the Life of a Slave Girl* is supposed to constitute is shattered in nonperformance.

What's the relationship between the scene (of subjection) and Betty's obscene act of nonperformance? Betty's case, her revelry, her nonperformance of the freedom to perform, is an obscenity of objection. It lets us know that the obscene is the scene's origins: the Greek scene of politics, the democratic staging of statecraft, is given in the messy, filthy, smelly hapticality that Shaw represses in the proper antiabolitionist's proper antislavery narration. Betty holds, and is held within, another promise, an anti- and anteontological plain of consent. She remains in the hold, in flight's rubbed, strummed, hummed, arkestral fantasy. She holds and is held in the promise of sociality, which is given in nonperformance. What if we said "compact" instead of "contract"? Or if we just cleave to that old sense of concentration that both terms bear? Then there is openness in the compact. Then the contract is (in) (the) open, broken, shattered in imagination, crazy in love.

Judges and legislators cannot and will not understand her. Ob-scene, ab-heard, her nonperformance is a refusal of the solo. She refuses the individuation that is refused her and claims the monstrosity of obscene social life that is imposed upon/ascribed to her. Tongue-tried, her silence softly speaks anaperformative, degenerative, and regenerative density, in deviance both from and within the grammar and diction of the administered world. What would a general strike against the solo be? A superimposition of the wor(l)d on or over itself. A bold, shadowy, ob-scene, anafoundationally overflowing font. Betty's ascriptive superimposition is what Han reenacts, writing all over and under the law, sounding Betty out, shattering, unmasking even the questions she requires and allows as if they were the rungs of a tractatarian ladder. A poetics of property's radical, dispossessive impropriety is announced:

> Betty's act within and against the law's language of freedom is an ob-scene sign of "free will" that irrupts like the Real on the development of personal sovereignty in contract law.
>
> This catastrophic nuance retained by Betty's act in the formal structure of legal reasoning in *Betty's Case* holds open the question of a subterranean realm of legal thought about freedom that precedes property understandings of the legal personality of the slave.[14]

Han is not interested, here, in promoting "a voluntaristic theory of enslavement." She would, instead, "present a certain rebus-like territory of law where distinctions between freedom and enslavement appear as effects of a freedom that is there in the law, but not *of* the law, and thus, obscene."[15] Han allows and requires us to see that Betty's deferral, whose profound impatience is impossible to grasp, not only reveals bondage to have thoroughly infused the voluntarity that it also constitutes but also intimates an extralegal fugitivity that is, to use B. F. Skinner's phrase against his brutal and behaviorist grain, "beyond freedom and dignity."

And so we get down in(to) the archive of the law of slavery, which is, as Hortense Spillers says and Han echoes, "riddled," motley, and impure.[16] Then, in that thickness, we get to think the relation between what it is to be riddled and what it is to be protean. There's a relation between being protean and being permeable, open (to change) in ways that are generative as opposed to creative. Here we could think of what the conceptualists might call M. NourbeSe Philip's "uncreative" writing in the term, *generative*, she'd already established and within the antagonism she'd already acknowledged. Her sliding, glissed, Glissantian, superimposition, her ex-solicitor's solicitation of the words of the case, her jurisgenerative obliteration of the false alternatives "positive" and "natural," of their juris*diction*al trace, given in recitations that are not recitations but more and less than that, given in withdrawal into the deep plane and submarine plain of our history, is the nonperformative activity that Han echoes, as a matter of law laid down in mutation, stutter, muted whisper and in lifework's genocidally regulated irregularities.[17]

What if slavery and freedom are each the other's condition of possibility? What if the distinction between life and death is just a way of naming the distinction between life and lives? What if the irreducible mutuality of slavery and freedom occurs in the realm of lives, which is the zone in which life and death are made to (seem to) negotiate? What if the right of death and power over life that is given in and as sovereignty (i.e., in and as the sovereign's absolute omnicreative/omnidestructive/autocreative/autodestructive power), is given and held in the fantastic domain of individuated lives, wherein "the subjugation of bodies and the control of populations" takes place as a modality of arithmetical calculation? What if biopower is the right of death in and as the power over lives and contractual relation is a biopolitical innovation? Isn't this what Hartman, and now Han, teach us?

As I discussed earlier, *Betty's Case* suggests not that contract law is one legal mode of domination among others available to the master, but that contract is the condition of possibility for the slave's property status. It is not because the slave is a priori property that the master uses contractual relations to exercise his power over the slave; but rather, the development of legal freedom is dependent upon on the slave as a passage between a fundamental split between radically heterogeneous exercises of individual contract rights (within both public and private realms) and a transcendent idea of the free will at the heart of contract freedom. Far from valorizing transcendentalism, contract law reveals a curious moment in which the protection of the transcendental right to freedom of contract is formally bound to the singularity of the case of the slave. Legal freedom, on this view, is not only the operationalization of universal individual freedom; it is also a limitless horizon of the limits of contracts brought into view by a certain transcendental register the slave's emancipation must work through. At this register, the obscene legal effects of contracts made and broken between master and slave in both market and domestic contexts are factual predicates through which a transcendent freedom in law is materialized. Of course, those effects give rise to relatively empowered or disempowered claims of injury. But continuing to follow Spillers and [Christopher] Tomlins, those positive claims are always already translations, which require literacy in more than one idiom of representational forms if we are to mobilize them toward a knowledge of the law of slavery.

The jurisprudential language of contract is one such idiom heretofore missing from predominantly historical, literary, and anthropological approaches to the law of slavery. In fact, legal philosopher and jurist Theophilus Parsons observed something similar about the production of American law through an internal structure of translation in his treatise, *The Law of Contracts* (1853). In the opening chapter, which remained unchanged for the most part across the nine subsequent editions, he observed, "The law of contract, in its widest sense, may be regarded as including nearly all the law which regulates the relations of human life." He elaborated further, "All social life presumes it, and rests upon it; for out of contracts, express or implied, declared or understood, grow all rights, all duties, all obligations, and all law."

Parsons' idea of contract as the common denominator of legal relations and conflict is accessible from a lay understanding of the law. Without first finding some form of contractual relation between two parties, there is no legal basis to judge a claim, no matter what the conflict or injury is, or who or what the parties are. A natural or corporate person can sue a government entity because citizenship establishes a contractual relationship between them. One governmental agency can sue another because federal republicanism establishes a contractual relationship between them. A criminal defendant can sue state agencies because due process establishes a contractual relationship between them. And an individual can sue another individual because the social norm not to cause harm to others establishes a contractual relationship between them. These forms of contractual relation are variations of the social contract as a theory of modern political life, but their legal forms (and there are many more like examples of contractual relations that we might reference) are hardly uniform or rational as expressions of the social contract put in action by the law's language of contract.[18]

Contractual relation implies that there are lives, that there are parties, individuated natural or corporate persons, i.e., that there is individuation, and it is that implication which the law of contract simultaneously assumes and enforces and which, as Han shows, Betty's nonperformance not only refuses but gives over to the severest solicitation.

If individuation is the regulation of social life, then the law of contract is one of its most essential formal mechanisms. Contractual relation is a polite way of naming what Orlando Patterson calls "the game of honor,"[19] and what is implied in that naming is not only the irreducible fact of power in "social relation" but also individuation as relation's condition of possibility. The law of contract regulates social life precisely by positing it as the domain of social lives, which is understood as an arena of competing solo performances. It's as if the actual fight is shadow boxing's degraded materialization. What Patterson calls social support is simply antisocial sociality, nothing but a platform upon which individuation can be staged. This is how Edward Covey and Frederick Douglass are one another's social support: it is only through their conflict, the contractual noncontact of the endless struggle to which they are both chained, in a fucked-up kind of hostile parallel play, that Douglass can become "the most articulate slave who ever lived." Implicit in all this is that Édouard Glissant's notion of consent is actually in excess of his poetics of relation! Maybe the way it works is that the law of contract, in its death drive/regulatory function, assumes the individuation that it then seeks to instantiate. Betty's non(solo)performance is against that law, precisely by way of a fugitive erotics that is performed in and by and as the anarchic "fecundity of the jurisgenerative principle."[20] Here's the most brutal irony that can be imagined: that in going back to Tennessee she was going back to (social) life, i.e., refusing the return to/of the inorganic. "Social relation" is an oxymoron that social entanglement causes to tremble.

The modern will-based approach, emergent in Parson's treatise, finds contractual obligations where there is mutual consent to obligations freely given between individuals. And to the extent that Parson's treatise, according to [Lawrence] Kreitner, exemplifies an attempt to narrate the emergence of this will-based approach of contract law from status-based approaches, it marks an "intermediate" point at which the universalization of the individual from status-based social groups is as yet incomplete.

But perhaps there is a way in which we might read Parsons's treatise not as a stage in the teleological development of contract law, but as a fundamental articulation of an ongoing process of transplantation and supplementation of various sources of law at the core of American legal modernity. On this view, the dominance of one theory of contract law over another signals the broaching of some internal limit within contract law that is carried along and given new form through varying arrangements and applications of fundamental legal concepts, such as the right to freedom of contract we read across *Betty's Case* and *Frisbie [v. United States]*. The expansive and categorically *abstract* idea of freedom of contract might be read, then, to have always been the foundation for various applications of theories of contract—from status-based approaches characteristic of early modern legal regimes, to consent-based approaches characteristic of today's late capitalist legal regimes.[21]

And it will always be incomplete; and the phenomenon of the status-based (anti-)social group is part of that incompletion, is already on a continuum with the necessarily incomplete individual. This general trajectory, though, is called "the democratization of sovereignty," which is constantly betrayed in its transplantation, supplementation, riddling, stuttering, and proteanization. This piercing leaves in its wake a myriad of holes, which we call individual lives. These holes are then taken for both agent and apparatus; freedom is their articulation. The abstract free individual, the hole, is both assumed and residual.

Contract law is both an abstract totality *and* an empirically residual legal relation, and thus any perception of change in its substantive rules for finding an enforceable contract is only ever a function of historically contingent inclusions and exclusions of other areas of law from an essentially empty legal core.

Further, because of contract's essential abstractness, [Grant] Gilmore observes, "it resisted, and continues to resist, codification long after most, if not all, of the fields of law apparently most closely related to it had passed under the statutory yoke." The crystallization in the late 19th century of this legal terrain of general legal abstraction through the construct of individual will was "a revolution in private law," to use Kreitner's words. That revolution, captured by Parsons's theory, posits a form of private law that is the ground from which social relations are translated into specialized rights, duties, obligations and various genres of doctrine (including administrative law, corporate law, labor law, sexual harassment law, environmental law, animal rights law, maritime law, etc.). What is important to emphasize here is that contract law appears as law's glance toward that which is anterior to socio-legality, and by this glance, we are reminded that positive law as the spatio-temporal mapping of rules and judgments can only ever be an approximation of the totality of law.[22]

In other words, contract law, in its innovative continuances and refinements, which bring online the abstract free individual in all his (un)holiness, is the death drive whereby law attempts to return to the inorganic, to a moment before sociolegality, in the interest and in search of a private law that Han shows to be inextricable from slavery.

> The private law of slavery . . . must be grasped as a "residual" legal practice that endures after all of the social (and necessarily politically contested) practices of slavery have been institutionalized and abolished by law in various areas of property, commercial, criminal, constitutional, etc. doctrines. For these specialized legal doctrines are cannibalized from the essentially empty core of contract in the private law of slavery, which is always there as relatively fragile or relatively robust in the law's language of contract. Consequently, the slave, as an enigmatic party to various kinds of contractual relations that make up private practice, remains after the various kinds of positive law institutionalizing slavery have been abolished.

> While we are accustomed to condemning contract law as state legitimization of social Darwinism, my reading of contract law thus far suggests a crucial point that goes unnoticed by reductive approaches to legal discourse. This point is that legal formalism's dependence on contract law's circling around a transcendent freedom is also a

dependence on the immeasurable presence of the singular case of the slave, irrupting in the legal archive as an obscene form of freedom through which the transcendent right to freedom of contract is spectrally materialized.[23]

Listen to the ghost of all these words, the ghost of the enslaved haunting these words, the enslaved as afterlife bearing a tremor, a solicitation, a black-and-blue blur of legal reason. It's Betty's blur, a promise kept and given in the contract's nonperformance. The dependence Han delineates is on the incalculable presence of the case of the slave when both the case and the slave are always and emphatically both more and less than singular, more and less than one; and what irrupts into the legal archive—from or as one of those fissure vents, an irruptive flatness disruptive of peaks and valleys—is obscenity, the nonperformance of freedom and unfreedom, consent not to be a single being, and the claiming of an erotics of fugitivity of which the hole, the soloist, is a kind of virtual emanation, an anaperformative effect of social life or, in the impossibility of a better word, blackness, as Han teaches us.

In what is perhaps the irony of all legal ironies raised by *Betty's Case*, we find the formalization of what I am calling the performative of blackness is generally referred to in contract doctrine as "nonperformance." Nonperformance in contract doctrine generally designates the failure of one party to a legally enforceable promise to fulfill her obligation to the other party. *Black's Law Dictionary* defines nonperformance as "the breach of a contract and the failing to carry out the terms of the agreement." Nonperformance takes many legally actionable forms, including intentionally or unintentionally failing to keep a promise, or the judicial disposition of the excesses of promising as either "material breach" or "gift." Stated another way, nonperformance claims are based both on omissions of acts expected to fulfill a promise, *and* positive acts which reveal the impossibility of meeting the expectations arising from what was a foreseeable future when the promise was made. This scene of contract encompasses nonperforming parties performing willed refusal, fraud, bad faith, or protest. But even more complicated than these performances, contract law also addresses nonperforming parties performing assent, good faith, accommodation, and commitment after any practicable conditions or moral justifications for the enforcement of the contract cease to exist by virtue of the fact of the future's unforeseeability.

This second form of nonperformance pokes a permanent hole in contract law's disciplinary function. Here perhaps is the jurisprudential analog to Spillers' and Tomlins' notations of a "riddled" and "protean" law of slavery. For while we can imagine a contract law so punitive it might manage to effectively deter intentional breaches of contract obligations, it is harder to imagine a contract law unburdened by nonperformance resulting from wholly unforeseeable changes in conditions that render the expectations and enforceability of the contract impossible. "Nonperformance" is the promise of the material threat of chance that appears obscene only to the extent that the delusion of contract enforceability is maintained against the totality of circumstances in any given situation. It is a futurity that is radically indeterminable, and that is formally and uniquely structured into the temporality of the promise. Nonperformances of acts or intent make of contracting parties either competitors or crooks, but the legal idea of nonperformance also makes of the contract a way out for the contracting parties from their expectations' hold on the future. This way out, an always present fugitivity, or the performative of blackness as nonperformance, is the horizon of slavery as contract.

The idea of blackness as a performative in and against law then, is nonperformance, in this precise legal sense of a form of pure performativity . . . [called] "improvisation." Improvisation, notably, is that which cannot be contracted, nor performed against a contract, but is nonetheless a legal form of being that contract law might refer to as nonperformance. We might say that improvisation is the kernel around which contract law's recognition of nonperformance circles, and that which it attempts to defend the promise against, and contains as its other question of freedom.[24]

In teaching us that nonperformance is fugitivity's irreducible futurity, Han sees improvisation with improvisational clarity. She knows there is a foresight that is somehow given in and as the unforeseen. Change *is* the anticipation—the unanticipated that anticipates us, the consentual/consensual ensemble that lies before us, as vestibular, dispossessive kinship, the promise from which/as which we emerge, what we owe, the promise that we never promised, "the (bad—in the James Brown sense of the word) debt we never promiséd." Promise: *promittere*: pro (forth) mitt (send): to send forth: to have been sent forth: to have been sent, as Lorna Goodison says, by history. We are sent in history, pour out of its confinements. We send history. History comes for us, to send us to history and to ourselves. We come, as history, to history. We are, almost as Kamau Brathwaite says, the arrivance. Here Han cites Spillers's explication of the terror of our birth: "In the context of the United States, we could not say that the enslaved offspring was 'orphaned,' but the child does become, under the press of a patronymic, patrifocal, patrilineal, and patriarchal order, the man/woman on the boundary, whose human and familial status, by the very nature of the case, had yet to be defined. I would call this enforced state of breach another instance of vestibular cultural formation where 'kinship' loses meaning, since it can be invaded at any given and arbitrary moment by the property relations."[25]

Spillers brushes up against nonperformance in contract law here in two ways. First, the processes by which property relations "invaded" forms of black kinship, forged despite the law's refusal to recognize and protect them, occurred through what I have called the private law of slavery. The most common example is the slave family that is broken up by financial and disciplinary imperatives of the master to sell away a family member. However, Spillers's specific reference to black kinship as an "enforced state of breach" gestures to the private law of slavery where all the conjugations of the abstract realm of contract law (what Parsons identified as "all rights, all duties, all obligations, and all law") could be enforced against black kinship. In this particular example, the "property relations" are invasions cum conjugations of contract: to be more precise, changes in the name of the master with title to the exchanged slave. The invasive property relation is a mere example of a general condition of slavery as contract, which must include all variable obscene forms of unfulfilled promises. Notably, though Spillers references specifically the "property relation" as that which interferes with otherwise established (however precarious) legal relations of black kinship, in *Betty's Case*, it is not the property relation, but the legal freedom of contract, that invades.

Second, and more important for my discussion, this "enforced state of breach" is itself a reference to contract, but by promises that are known only by their inherent brokenness. The temporality of the promise represented by Spillers's phrase, "enforced state of breach," here is not of future satisfaction or fulfillment foreclosed, but a condition in which compromise with any future called forth by the promise of human kinship is impossible (which is not to say that promises of some other kind of relation are not forged). We must retain this nuance. On my reading of it, Spillers is not arguing that the law of property denies the slave the capacity to promise, for some form of contractual relation (kinship) must exist in order to be *"invaded."* Instead, she is arguing the reality of a "state of breach," which through its phrasing, implicitly introduces the need for a specific understanding of the nature of the promise, on the side of the slave, in a context where both legal unfreedom *and* freedom are enforcements against the radically indeterminable future invited by the legal idea of nonperformance. Thus, as she states, the contractual relation of "'kinship' loses meaning," which is to say neither that whatever Betty might have promised no longer exists, nor that the reality of unkeepable promises forecloses the radical undeterminable futurity contained in those promises. Rather, we are on the terrain of a relationality based in an unnotarizable promissory note, already breached because unfulfillable. The performative of blackness as nonperformance opens up onto a form of intimacy that registers only in an obscene form of consent to being bound through such promises.

Black kinship is the exception that proves the rule of the exception. Blackness is a showing of invaded, wounded kinship, in general, which is given in and to entanglement when the proper is constituted as a dominant possibility. Kinship is on the continuum (not-in-)between entanglement and fixity/separation. Kinship is on the way to the normalization and naturalization of blackness; but what is called black kinship shows both a particular and the general inability to arrive as both always already invaded as well as that which invades. Kinship is an emanation of the unsettled, surrounded settler. So that if (the nightmare of) normative kinship is always already invaded by property, then black kinship remains fantastically to claim the breach that is imposed on it when blackness is conceived of as property without property. In other words, we claim the monstrosity of being property without property so that we can bring the disruptive noise of the improper to bear in and on and out of the world. The flipside of refusing what has been refused is claiming what has been imposed. Breach recognizes this absolutely irreducible and monstrous dispossessiveness in kinship—the alienation that constitutes and is constituted by natality. This is what it is to unown, which is underived from normative agency, which moves neither as act nor enactment, which is consent to entanglement's habitation in relationality's void. Consent bespeaks a noncontractual nonrelationality that is underived from individuation. Perhaps it would be more precise—in a precision that Han makes both necessary and possible—to say that we are on the terrain of anti- and anterelational promise, (venereal, funereal, futurial) (under)ground made visible by the seismic disruption of Betty's nonperformance (of the solo) in the breach.

If slavery's "afterlife" is law's original historical time, the law cannot be read as an archive that will take us back to slavery, or more precisely, cannot be read primarily through a desire that it might contain a written path to the experience of the slave so that we might be able to deliver to her something called justice. "The story of progress up from slavery is a lie, the longest lie," finally, to return to the epigraph from Anthony Farley I open this article with. In this way, it is a continuing presence of the most horrific and most liberatory kind imaginable.

The law of slavery cannot be interpreted into historical evidence against itself as democracy's native tongue. Slavery remains law's accent. The law of slavery cannot be marshaled as an argument against itself by convicting its agents for crimes against humanity or sanctioning remedies for histories of oppression. Slavery's prosecution and remedy is the law's infinite jurisdiction of calculating promises kept and unkept. And though we might hear law as recordings of failed justice on repeat, that recording cannot be the slave's memorial. For the slave's freedom, as in *Betty's Case*, is what becomes not in memoriam but in the inventions of decision in a general condition of forced choice.

This is the terrible truth we know by Betty's act. The law's universal promise of freedom is not false, as Shaw demonstrated upon his emergence with Betty from his chambers. The law's universal promise of freedom is a perverse wish. We domesticate this insight when we treat the case as an artifact, instead of as law on the perverse order of drives, that is, what [Fred] Moten gestures toward as "a freedom drive that is expressed always and everywhere." Thus, the slave's "strange arrival" in whatever may be the case before us.[26]

"Decision in a general condition of forced choice" is American Democracy. Meanwhile, Betty revels in nonperformance, is revelation as nonperformance. Her revelry, revelation, and refusal, her fugal, erotic fugitivity flies into existence that from which it flees. Betty's case—within which her "decision" lies hidden and unrecoverable, as if the case then constitutes a refusal of decision and its accompanying metaphysics; and which, therefore, bears the clearest expression of the case of blackness as the debt that can neither be finally paid nor officially promised—is way over the edge of any kind of knowledge of freedom. As Han says, it is an a priori fugitivity, and blackness is, as Han says, "a [non]performative against all performances of freedom and unfreedom dependent on the historical dilemma of a lack [and not just a lack but the very idea, which is only articulable as lack] of meaningful distinction between freedom and slavery." Blackness is unchained to the struggle for freedom to which it appears that black bodies, insofar as it seems to be the case that there are such things, have been relegated.

The freedom drive is a death drive, sovereignty's continual (dis)establishment, the repetition of subjection, the repetition rather than remembering of subjectivity's failure to launch, which almost always takes the form of a disavowal of individuation, a submission, let's say, to being held, but which, because it is valued as failure, is repeated as distress. The memory of impossible individuation's disavowal becomes the repetition of a failure to individuate. And so, as Oscar Zeta Acosta says, we are chained to (the struggle for) freedom.[27] Betty and Oscar Zeta Acosta, Spillers, Hartman, and Han bring the freedom drive as death drive into relief, and this teaches us to be emphatic in the movement from the freedom drive to an erotics of fugitivity. The freedom drive is a death drive; and fugitivity is the realm of the (always anticipatory) afterlife. Black life is anticipatory afterlife. The social life that now we know as Betty is neither slave nor free but fugitive.

The erotics of fugitivity is all bound up with the distinction between creation (out of nothing) and anoriginal generativity. The death drive tries to get back to the inorganic, where private life is given in the imposition of slavery as political and juridical death, the relative nothingness from which a certain fatal procreation emerges or is extracted. The freedom drive is where the failed imitation of sovereignty, of the simultaneously omnicreative, autocreative, uncreative power that sovereignty is supposed to have, takes that self-destructive social turn, which is then aligned with or is conceived of as failure rather than the interinanimation of refusal and (alternative) claim. The erotics of fugitivity are obscene. We either remember (and memorialize and differentially ceremonialize—the more precise term would be *remember with a difference*, or *rememory*, the memory of [no]things) our consent to that (nonsingle, paraontic) sociality, or we repeat what will have then shown up as our failure to defeat it.

The (give me liberty or give me) death drive is, literally, an attempt to "return" to social death (the imprecise name that has been given, or concept/

metaphor that has been applied, to the inorganic realm of political lives). If freedom is the inorganic state to which the sovereign subject is supposed to return, then the erotics of fugitivity is anoriginal, organic fecundity—the nonperformance, the unmade promise, the terrible, beautiful, irreducible futurity that sent us and that sends us every day.

A contract is imposed the moment you have standing; that's the moment of death, which is the regulation of nonbehaved or misbehaved behavior, which resides before the subject/citizen, before the national unit's being before the law, not as crime but as the essential, jurisgenerative criminality that undermines the very idea of decision. Freedom is very sweet, perhaps Betty thought. Perhaps she thought it is already given in what it is to belong to the Sweets. Or in what it is to belong. Or in what it is to be, that mortal coil. The freedom that belongs to the Sweets is inseparable from what it is to belong to the Sweets, which is the condition in which she would have remained had she remained and not returned. In returning with the Sweets, Betty submits belonging to a nonperformance that neither exercises self-possessive freedom nor confirms being possessed. In returning, she refuses to perform the terms of the contract she had been forced to enter, the contract of the mere petitioner. A paradox is pierced by Betty's unspoken, or perhaps more precisely unheard, or perhaps more precisely unrecited, nonsequitur. I wonder what it is to stand or to have stood, right before the instance of one's death, before the law. Hers is a nonperformance of performance in the guise of an unspeakable, unrecitable vacation of decision and its metaphysics. Betty's decision was and is impossible; her nonperformance of it is decision's exhaust(ion). In this regard, given as she is to the renewal of a maternal ecology, she cannot be our mother. Can Betty be seen and heard in the absolute agony of her passion? That might not even be the question. But there is a broken window we can see through her, our idea of ancestry and flight, our militant descent, our style. We are farmers by nature, natural-born thieves, erotic fugitivity in love. There is no space between. There's just this continual problematic of singularity, in deictic isolation.

In order to understand this, and everything else, we must turn again to Hartman so that we can return with her. She guides our confrontation with "the impossibility of instituting a definitive break between slavery and freedom" so that we can try to understand "the forms of subjection engendered by the narrative of emancipation and the constitution of the burdened individuality of freedom."[28] Here, Hartman lays out the importance of the task that Han has taken up with such devotion.

By examining the metamorphosis of "chattel into man" and the strategies of individuation constitutive of the liberal individual and the rights-bearing subject, I hope to underscore the ways in which freedom and slavery presuppose one another, not only as modes of production and discipline or through contiguous forms of subjection but as founding narratives of the liberal subject revisited and revisioned in the context of Reconstruction and the sweeping changes wrought by the abolition of slavery. At issue are the contending articulations of freedom and the forms of subjection they beget. It is not my intention to argue that the differences between slavery and freedom were negligible; certainly such an assertion would be ridiculous. Rather, it is to examine the shifting and transformed relations of power that brought about the resubordination of the emancipated, the control and domination of the free black population, and the persistent production of blackness as abject, threatening, servile, dangerous, dependent, irrational, and infectious. In short, the advent of freedom marked the transition from the pained and minimally sensate existence of the slave to the burdened individuality of the responsible and encumbered freedperson.[29]

Hartman shows not only that the definitive break between slavery and freedom is impossible but also that insofar as we remain within the discourse of self-improvement, or in mourning for individuated exaltation, we extend the peculiar institutions of this interminable interplay between slavery and freedom. We move in this wake, as a function of its imperative and path, if we are concerned with the study of what exceeds subjection/individuation in black art and black social life, where terror and enjoyment, the mundane and the spectacular, are interinanimate.

At the same time, Hartman teaches us that we must also move through a certain recrudescence of the impulse to self improvement that provides the intellectual strain from which she and all her current students, including myself, emerge with cold animation—that tendency toward the production of anti-anti-blackness that will have been activated by way of the liberal subject's capacity to imagine some combination of uplift and overturning. Improvement, here, operates by way of the formulation we are not what they say we are, whose normative circuits of transformation will have avoided what is given in that we are not, as they say we are. What if blackness is, in fact, abject, threatening, servile, dangerous, dependent, irrational, and infectious precisely insofar as it is the continual refusal of normative individuation, which is supposed to be the enactment of everything opposite to these qualities? Moreover, if Hartman's critique of the simultaneously illusory transition from freedom to slavery must bear a remainder of that transition insofar as it is also the real from which she speaks, here in the movement from the pained and minimally sensate existence of the slave to the burdened individuality of the responsible and encumbered freedperson, then her critique also gestures toward the maximally sensate and sensible flesh of the enslaved, which exists in excess of a burdened individuality that turns out also to have been the slave's estate, under a regime of brutally enforced individuation whose viciousness is given in that what was enforced was also denied. What if pain is the modality of sensate experience that is, in fact, the primary conduit through which individuation is imposed? There is a realm and a range of modalities of torture whose effectiveness is possible because animated flesh feels. And what if the resistance to subjection, the objection to it, the eradication of it, is borne in such feeling and in its transgenerational transmission? This feeling, its feeling, bends toward apposition; it is given in and from and to no standpoint and it can neither stand nor bear nor approach any aim but the exhaustion of redress and, more generally, the regime of subjection that Hartman delineates and identifies. This feeling exhausts the subject and his world in the absolute deprivation, held in what it is to return rather than remain, that constitutes renewal of the maternal ecology from which world and self emanate as separable defects of a certain metaphysics of birth.

The terror of return and renewal are ours to join and to enjoy, as an irresistible violence to narration. Aunt Hester's scream stands mute in Betty's silence, where each undoes being-narrated with stories "too terrible to pass on" that are, nevertheless, given in exhaustive, interminable passage. It is as if one is infused with the other until one and other are no thing at all. That we are emanations of no thing is more terrible than any fact of antiblackness. Still more terrible is that without will, we will this circle be unbroken. Only no thing can pass through this blood stain'd, gateless gate; in terrible return and renewal, no thing is all we can enjoy. This is the facticity of blackness, which we might begin to think of as its nonperformance. When Heathfield describes the "lifeworks" of Tehching Hsieh as "out of now," that hold in which the evilly emphatic, self-assertive "I" oscillates with its own relative nothingness, it is as if time has been told to go off, or step off in and by an absolute commitment to abide. Out of here and now is the very displacement of place, in refusal of its egocentric particularities, in favor of absolute nothingness, the inseparable differences of consent not to be single, where the break between the transcendent and the immanent bears nonfull sound with nonsimple fury. This is the realm of what Baraka called funk/lore, where data gathered under the concept of social death, which operates as simultaneous abandonment and protection, is shown to be insufficient to blackness's unsettled and untimely inexperience, its stolen life.

NOTES

Preface

1 See LeRoi Jones (Amiri Baraka), *Home: Social Essays* (New York: William Morrow, 1966).

Chapter 1. Knowledge of Freedom

1 Winfried Menninghaus, *In Praise of Nonsense: Kant and Bluebeard*, trans. Henry Pickford (Stanford, CA: Stanford University Press, 1999). My concern with Kant, and with the claims of blackness in Kant, moves by way of Menninghaus whose work has been, for me, a kind of rebeginning. Of course, I deviate from that rebeginning from the beginning. This deviation is, in part, a function of Pickford's translations of Menninghaus's interpellations of Kant. Pickford uses Werner Pluhar's translation of *Kritik der Urteilskraft* exclusively; sometimes I refer to that of Paul Guyer and Eric Matthews. See Kant, *Critique of Judgment*, trans. Werner S. Pluhar (Indianapolis: Hackett, 1987), 188; and *Critique of the Power of Judgment*, ed. Eric Matthews, trans. Paul Guyer and Eric Matthews (Cambridge: Cambridge University Press, 2000), 197. More deviance, and even some actual attention to what might emerge in the interplay of divergent translations, follows.

2 Hannah Arendt, *The Origins of Totalitarianism* (San Diego, CA: Harcourt Brace, 1973), 301, 302. I am grateful that Anne Norton alerts us to these phrases so that it is possible to deeply consider the trouble, in mind, they bear. See her "Hearts of Darkness: Africa and African Americans in the Writings of Hannah Arendt," in *Feminist Interpretations of Hannah Arendt*, ed. Bonnie Honig (University Park: Penn State University Press, 1995), 257.

3 This is Guyer and Matthews's rendering of the original *gesittet*. Pluhar translates it as "civilized."

4 Menninghaus, *In Praise of Nonsense*, 2. See also Immanuel Kant, *Anthropologie in Pragmatischer Hinsicht* (Hamburg: Felix Meiner Verlag, 2000), 122. The translation Pickford consults is *Anthropology from a Pragmatic Point of View*, trans. Victor Lyle Dowdell (Carbondale: Southern Illinois University Press, 1978), 112.

5 Menninghaus, *In Praise of Nonsense*, 1.

6 This attunement to Kant's ambivalence is a common. See Robert Bernasconi, ed., "Who Invented the Concept of Race? Kant's Role in the Enlightenment

Construction of Race," in *Race* (London: Blackwell, 2001); Gilles Deleuze, *Kant's Critical Philosophy*, trans. Hugh Tomlinson (New York: Columbia University Press, 1993); Jacques Derrida, *The Truth in Painting*, trans. Geoff Bennington and Ian McLeod (Chicago: University of Chicago Press, 1987); Elaine P. Miller, *The Vegetative Soul: From Philosophy of Nature to Subjectivity in the Feminine* (Albany: State University of New York Press, 2002); Diane Morgan, *Kant Trouble: The Obscurities of the Enlightenment* (London: Routledge, 2002); John Llewelyn, *The HypoCritical Imagination: Between Kant and Levinas* (New York: Routledge, 2000); Jean-François Lyotard, *Lessons on the Analytic of the Sublime*, trans. Elizabeth Rottenberg (Stanford, CA: Stanford University Press, 1994), and *Enthusiasm: The Kantian Critique of History*, trans. Georges Van Den Abbeele (Stanford, CA: Stanford University Press, 2009); and Gayatri Chakravorty Spivak, *A Critique of Postcolonial Reason* (Cambridge, MA: Harvard University Press, 1999). Great benefit is also to be derived from the work of a couple of scholars who are deeply committed to what they take to be Kant's clear-sightedness. See Paul Guyer, *Kant and the Claims of Taste*, 2nd ed. (Cambridge: Cambridge University Press, 1997); and Adrian M. S. Piper, *Rationality and the Structure of the Self, Volume II: A Kantian Conception*, 2nd ed. (Berlin: Adrian Piper Research Archive Foundation, accessed June 10, 2010, www.adrianpiper.com/rss/index.shtml. Finally, pay the closest possible attention to Ronald A. T. Judy, *(Dis)Forming the American Canon: African-Arabic Slave Narrative and the Vernacular* (Minneapolis: University of Minnesota Press, 1993).

7   Denise Ferreira da Silva, *Toward a Global Idea of Race* (Minneapolis: University of Minnesota Press, 2007).

8   Menninghaus, *In Praise of Nonsense*, 2–3. See also Friedrich A. Kittler, *Discourse Networks 1800–1900*, trans. Michael Metteer and Chris Cullens (Stanford, CA: Stanford University Press, 1990).

9   Menninghaus, *In Praise of Nonsense*, 1.

10 In his *Anthropologie*, in a section on the faculty of foresight, Kant mentions "the joyous and bold premonitions of enthusiasts who scent the imminent revelation of a mystery for which the human being has no such receptivity of sense, and believe they see the unveiling of the presentiment of what, like the Epoptes, they await in mystical intuition. The second sight of the Scottish Highlanders also belongs to this class of enchantments. Several of them believed they saw a man strung upon a mast, the news of whose death they pretended to have received when they actually entered a distant port." What if Kant, having never left home, heard or savored the faint, irregular undertone in his own text, of his own afterlife, on another distant port? See Kant, "Anthropology from a Pragmatic Point of View," trans. Robert B. Louden, in *Anthropology, History and Education* (Cambridge: Cambridge University Press, 2007), 295; and Kant, *Anthropologie*, 87.

11 I also want to consider that second sight or seeing double is an effect of surveillance whose primary impact is visited upon the ones who survey. See W. E. B. Du Bois, *The Souls of Black Folk*, in *Writings*, ed. Nathan Huggins (New York:

Library of America, 1986); and Lindon Barrett, *Blackness and Value: Seeing Double* (Cambridge: Cambridge University Press, 1998). Their work prepares and allows that consideration.

12 Laura Harris, "Whatever Happened to the Motley Crew? C. L. R. James, Helio Oiticica, and the Aesthetic Sociality of Blackness," *Social Text* 30, no. 3 (2012): 49–75.

13 Robert M. Cover, "The Supreme Court, 1982 Term—*Nomos* and Narrative," *Harvard Law Review* 97, no. 1 (1983): 40.

14 Robert M. Cover, "The Bonds of Constitutional Interpretation: Of the Word, the Deed, and the Role," *Georgia Law Review* 20 (summer 1986): 833.

15 Samuel Beckett, *The Unnameable*, in *Three Novels by Samuel Beckett* (New York: Grove Press, 1965), 292.

16 For more on Holmes's response to jurisgenerative fecundity, see Richard Maxwell Brown, *No Duty to Retreat: Violence and Values in American History and Society* (Norman: University of Oklahoma Press, 1994), 3–37; and Louis Menand, *The Metaphysical Club: A Story of Ideas in America* (New York: Farrar, Straus, and Giroux, 2001), 3–69. I thank Ruth Wilson Gilmore for alerting me to Brown's work.

17 Bernasconi, "Who Invented the Concept of Race?," 25–26.

18 Achille Mbembe, "Subject and Experience," trans. Robert Bononno, in *Keywords/Experience*, ed. Nadia Tazi (New York: Other Press, 2004), 11–12.

19 Nahum Dimitri Chandler, "The Problem of the Centuries: A Contemporary Elaboration of 'The Present Outlook for the Dark Races of Mankind' circa the 27th of December 1899," unpublished manuscript, 2007, 41.

20 Here I should acknowledge that, though I hope to move along a different track than the ones he takes, I am propelled by Houston Baker's work. See, in particular, the final chapter of his *Blues, Ideology, and Afro-American Literature: A Vernacular Theory* (Chicago: University of Chicago Press, 1985).

21 Kant, *Critique of the Power of Judgment*, 19, 20, 55.

22 Guyer, *Kant and the Claims of Taste*, 3.

23 Stevie Wonder, "Too Shy to Say," *Fullfillingness' First Finale*, Tamla т6-332s1, 1974.

24 See Adrian M. S. Piper, "Critical Hegemony and Aesthetic Acculturation," *Noûs* 19, no. 1 (1985): 29–40.

25 Here I both follow and deviate from Guyer. See *Kant and the Claims of Taste*, 1–11.

26 David Kazanjian's analysis of this ruse is especially clear and brilliant. See his *The Colonizing Trick: National Culture and Imperial Citizenship in Early America* (Minneapolis: University of Minnesota Press, 2003).

27 Cedric J. Robinson, *Black Marxism: The Making of the Black Radical Tradition*, 2nd ed. (Chapel Hill: University of North Carolina Press, 2000).

28 Bryan Wagner, *Disturbing the Peace: Black Culture and the Police Power after Slavery* (Durham, NC: Duke University Press, 2009), 1.

29 Wagner, *Disturbing the Peace*, 21.

30 Wagner, *Disturbing the Peace*, 21.

31 Wagner, *Disturbing the Peace*, 21.

32 Nahum Dimitri Chandler, "Originary Displacement." *boundary 2* 27, no. 3 (2000): 249–86.

33 Wagner, *Disturbing the Peace*, 1–2.

34 Frank B. Wilderson III, *Red, White and Black: Cinema and the Structure of US Antagonisms* (Durham, NC: Duke University Press, 2010).

35 Cecil Taylor, *Dark to Themselves*, Enja Records 2084 LP, 1976.

36 This formulation emerges from and in long collaboration with Stefano Harney. See Stefano Harney and Fred Moten, *The Undercommons: Fugitive Planning and Black Study* (Wivenhoe, UK: Minor Compositions, 2013).

37 Wagner, *Disturbing the Peace*, 2.

38 Wagner, *Disturbing the Peace*, 2–3.

39 Hannah Arendt, *Lectures on Kant's Political Philosophy*, ed. Ronald Beiner (Chicago: University of Chicago Press, 1982), 58–65.

40 See Guyer, *Kant and the Claims of Taste*, 106–47.

41 Charles Mingus, "Scenes in the City," *A Modern Jazz Symposium of Music and Poetry*, Bethlehem Records BCP 6026 LP, 1957.

42 This is Nathaniel Mackey's constant announcement. See *Splay Anthem* (New York: New Directions, 2006).

43 J. L. Austin, *How to Do Things with Words*, 2nd ed., ed. J. O. Urmson and Marina Sbisá (Cambridge, MA: Harvard University Press, 1975), 95.

44 Michel Foucault, *The History of Sexuality, Volume I: An Introduction*, trans. Robert Hurley (New York: Vintage Books, 1978), 143.

45 Ed Roberson, "On the Calligraphy of Black Chant." In *When Thy King Is a Boy* (Pittsburgh: University of Pittsburgh Press, 1970), 74. See also Aldon Lynn Nielsen, *Black Chant: Languages of African-American Postmodernism* (Cambridge: Cambridge University Press, 1997).

46 Nathaniel Mackey, *Bedouin Hornbook*. Callaloo Fiction Series, Volume 2 (Lexington: University Press of Kentucky, 1986), 34–35.

47 N. H. Pritchard, *The Matrix: Poems 1960–1970* (Garden City, NY: Doubleday, 1970) 46–50. Hear also Pritchard's performance of the poem on *New Jazz Poets*, ed. Walter Lowenfels, Smithsonian Folkways FW-09751-CCD, 2004.

48 Consider Norman H. Pritchard's rupturing of sense precisely at the point where the play of sensation and the play of ideas confound one another, where poetry breaks down at its own instantiation in a way that is reminiscent of the simultaneous foundation and destruction of the critical philosophy, in a canted, black chanted, racial underground that is beneath (en)light(enment) and beneath literature, an underground that is their ground and the disestablishment of their ground, "sound variegated through beneath lit." See Pritchard, *The Matrix*, 46–50. Hear also Pritchard's performance of "Gyre's Galax" on *New Jazz Poets*, ed. Walter Lowenfels, Smithsonian Folkways FW-09751-CCD, 2004.

49 Du Bois, *The Souls of Black Folk*, in *Writings*, 359.

50 Nahum Dimitri Chandler, "Introduction: Toward a New History of the Centuries: On the Early Writings of W. E. B. Du Bois," in W. E. B. Du Bois, *The*

Problem of the Color Line at the Turn of the Twentieth Century: The Essential Early Essays, ed. Nahum Dimitri Chandler (New York: Fordham University Press, 2014), 1–32.

51 Mackey, *Bedouin Hornbook*, 34; Jacques Derrida, *Margins of Philosophy*, trans. Allan Bass (Chicago: University of Chicago Press, 1982), 11.

52 Chandler, *X: The Problem of the Negro as a Problem for Thought* (New York: Fordham University Press, 2013), 1.

53 Chandler, *X*, 184n10.

54 Chandler, *X*, 71.

55 See Andrew Benjamin, *Translation and the Nature of Philosophy: A New Theory of Words* (New York: Routledge, 1989).

56 Jacques Derrida, "In Discussion with Christopher Norris," in *Deconstruction: Omnibus Volume*, ed. Andreas Papadakis, Catherine Cooke, and Andrew E. Benjamin (New York: Rizzoli, 1989), 75.

57 See Jacques Derrida, "The Law of Genre," trans. Avital Ronell, in *On Narrative*, ed. W. J. T. Mitchell (Chicago: University of Chicago Press, 1980), 51–77.

58 See Derrida, "The Law of Genre," 52.

59 Ralph Ellison, *Invisible Man*, 2nd ed. (New York: Vintage International, 1995), 577.

60 Noam Chomsky, *Knowledge of Language: Its Nature, Origin and Use* (New York: Praeger, 1986), xxv–xxvi.

61 "Passage: the emergent lingering (in descent, not suspension) of a rupture, *syncope*, rhythmic break or cut; a *middle* passage to another action, to another subjectivity, to the improvisation of ensemble" (Leon Litwak, *Been in the Storm So Long* [New York: Vintage, 1979], 30).

62 It is, in this sense, an echoic but full articulation of what Jameson problematically points toward with the phrase *national allegory*: one can trace here without too much stretching the ways in which this tale works like that; the congruence of description and prescription, individual and society, a highly localized yet broadly focused grasp of social totality and, most importantly, a mode of resistance—a kind of resonance before resistance—that operates at the site of an improvisation through the opposition of interpretation and change. There's more to be said here, at the point where the question of enlightenment slips into the question of modernity. One thinks of Fredric Jameson's reading of Stéphane Mallarmé, of what is read by him and others as the emergence of a certain written modernity in which the kind of intuitive holism that is implied by the constellation of terms like *allegorical, mnemonic, iconic* is rendered unavailable by the assertion of a notion of Literature which, in a paraphrase of Barbara Johnson's paraphrase of Barthes, is constructed at the very moment its death is announced. Jameson's idea of national allegory betrays both nostalgia and hope for a Literature which allows some grasp of the whole, a Literature in which, as Fritz W. Kramer says about Stendahl and Honoré de Balzac (who might be seen as substitutes for the one whom Johnson implies is Mallarmé's mirror image, namely, Gustave Flaubert), in a kind of complementary apposition to *The Political Unconscious*, "the whole of society, with all its varying milieux, could be shown through one

individual fate." This Jamesonian nostalgia and hope is complemented by a rigorous critique of that universal flattening of difference which exists as a function of late capitalism and its cultural logic, postmodernism. Unfortunately, the constellation of nostalgia, hope, and critique must always leave open the possibility of a certain Third World messianism, a waiting on the event/advent of the Other, which is, in itself, perhaps a constitutive feature of postmodernist and postcolonialist critical discourse. I, too, hope to make a case for the possibility of prescriptive and descriptive attitudes toward social totality. I would do so by way of a certain iconographic—if not iconoclastic—reading practice; however, I also would do so by way of a critique of any formulation that subjects that possibility to a restrictive location. That possibility, and the further possibilities it engenders, exists always and everywhere. See Fredric Jameson, "Third World Literature in the Age of Multinational Capitalism," *Social Text* 15 (autumn 1986): 65–88. The most prominent—and problematic—critique of some of what's problematic in Jameson's essay is that of Aijaz Ahmad (*In Theory: Classes, Nations, Literature* [London: Verso, 1992], 95–122). See also Jameson, *The Political Unconscious* (Ithaca, NY: Cornell University Press, 1981); Fritz W. Kramer, *The Red Fez: Art and Spirit Possession in Africa*, trans. Malcom R. Green (London: Verso, 1993), 254; and Barbara Johnson, "Writing," in *Critical Terms for Literary Study*, 2nd ed., ed. Frank Lentricchia and Thomas McLaughlin (Chicago: University of Chicago Press, 1995), 39–49. Please note that this echo is heard only by way of the work Margaret Bass is doing on Caribbean autobiography, the work Rosemarie Scullion is doing on Orientalism in twentieth-century French intellectual discourse, and an astute and suggestive review of Jameson's *The Seeds of Time*, by Barry Schwabsky ("Review of Fredric Jameson, *The Seeds of Time*," *The Nation* 260, no. 21 [1994]: 762–64).

63 Jacques Derrida, "'This Strange Institution Called Literature': An Interview with Jacques Derrida," in *Acts of Literature*, ed. Derek Attridge (New York: Routledge, 1992), 34.

64 Derrida, "'This Strange Institution Called Literature,'" 35.

65 Derrida, "'This Strange Institution Called Literature,'" 36.

66 Derrida, "The Law of Genre," 55.

67 Olaudah Equiano, *The Interesting Narrative and Other Writings: Revised Edition*, ed. Vincent Caretta (New York: Penguin, 2003), 7; emphasis added.

68 Vincent Caretta, "Explanatory and Textual Notes," in Equiano, *The Interesting Narrative and Other Writings*, 237.

69 Equiano, "To the Reader," in *The Interesting Narrative and Other Writings*, 5.

70 Frantz Fanon, *The Wretched of the Earth*, trans. Constance Farrington (New York: Grove Press, 1965), 220.

71 Fanon, *Wretched*, 227.

72 Fanon, *Wretched*, 241.

73 Fanon, *Wretched*, 240.

74 Jonathan Cott, "Chinua Achebe: At the Crossroads," in *Conversations with Chinua Achebe*, ed. Bernth Lindfors (Jackson: University Press of Mississippi, 1997), 80. Quoted in Kurt Thometz, "High Life, Useful Advice and Mad English,"

in *Life Turns Man Up and Down: African Market Literature*, ed. Kurt Thometz (New York: Pantheon, 2001), xiv.

75 This is a distorted, Kaprovian echo of Achebe's invocation of Fanon: "This has been the problem of the African Artist: he has been left far behind the people who make culture, and he must now hurry and catch up with them—to borrow the beautiful expression of Fanon—in that zone of occult instability where the people dwell." See Bernth Lindfors, Ian Monro, Richard Priebe, and Reinhard Sander, "Interview with Chinua Achebe," in *Conversations with Chinua Achebe*, ed. Lindfors, 28. See also Allen Kaprow, *Essays on the Blurring of Art and Life*, ed. Jeff Kelly (Berkeley: University of California Press, 1993).

76 Wole Soyinka, "The Autistic Hunt," in *Art, Dialogue, and Outrage: Essays on Literature and Culture* (London: Methuen, 1993), 267. Quoted in Thometz, "High Life, Useful Advice, and Mad English," xvi–xvii. Soyinka's dismissal of "Onitsha Market literature . . . [as] yet another opportunity for the Ph.D aspirant" bears a special resonance in his linking of the paraliterary to nonneurotypicality. In this instance, the pathway from insult to injury is subject to a diversion that might suspend the forced, endless march toward a more refined literary-mercantile subjectivity if we tarry with a range of differences that emerge from new capacities heretofore understood as mere incapacity.

77 See Dipesh Chakrabarty, *Re-thinking Working Class India* (Princeton, NJ: Princeton University Press, 1989).

78 Lindon Barrett, *Racial Blackness and the Discontinuity of Western Modernity*, ed. Justin A. Joyce, Dwight A. McBride, and John Carlos Rowe (Urbana: University of Illinois Press, 2014), 8.

79 This radical immanence ought to be thought of in terms of diaspora, more specifically in that special kind of (Brent Hayes) Edwardsian sense of the term where the convergence of roots and outness is articulated (in the sense of that term that moves from *The Grundrisse* of Karl Marx through Louis Althusser's and Etienne Balibar's *Reading Capital* through Stuart Hall's "Race, Articulation and Societies Structured in Dominance" to Edwards's *The Practice of Diaspora*) by and through a decalage that is at once infinitesimal and unbridgeable. While Edwards understands diaspora as articulation, Kazanjian understands the interplay of race, culture, and citizenship in early, imperial America as articulation as well and takes special note of Equiano's work in this regard. I am greatly indebted to both of them. See Brent Hayes Edwards, *The Practice of Diaspora: Literature, Translation, and the Rise of Black Internationalism* (Cambridge, MA: Harvard University Press, 2003), 13–15; and Kazanjian, *The Colonizing Trick*, 35–88.

80 I take this phrase from *Material Events: Paul de Man and the Afterlife of Theory*, ed. Tom Cohen, Barbara Cohen, J. Hillis Miller, and Andrzej Warminski (Minneapolis: University of Minnesota Press, 2001).

81 See Nathaniel Mackey, *Discrepant Engagement: Dissonance, Cross-Culturality, and Experimental Writing*, Cambridge Studies in American Literature and Culture 71 (Cambridge: Cambridge University Press, 1993).

82 For more on this interplay, see Fred Moten, *Black and Blur (consent not to be a single being)* (Durham, NC: Duke University Press, 2017).

83 Olaudah Equiano, *The Interesting Narrative of the Life of Olaudah Equiano or Gustavas Vassa, the African, Written by Himself* (Leeds, UK: James Nichols, 1814). Republished in *The Classic Slave Narratives*, ed. Henry Louis Gates Jr. (New York: Mentor, 1987), 32–33. Referred to, hereafter, as Equiano, *Interesting Narrative*.

84 Equiano, *Interesting Narrative*, 33–34.

85 Abjection is a break or arrest or suspension of the dialectic of recognition which occurs as a function of the rupturing of ego; a fascination that exists as a function not of the gaze-in-return of the other but of the radical absence of that gaze; the absence of a certain dialectical resonance in the object. Abjection occurs, then, as a certain derailment or cessation of the interplay between self and Other, the injection of a negative third term, a slippage from the Other-object to the Other as abject. Abjection is often formulated as if it were always articulated in some special and specific way in "the Jew." Think of Job and think of the way in which abjection is internalized as a kind of accepted humiliation and, also, how it is internalized or redeemed to the extent that the affect of the Same-subject is rearticulated dialectically in the interiority of the abject. This is, for instance, Sartre's formulation and Fanon appropriates it in order to articulate a difference internal to abjection between blacks and Jews. For if Jews internalize abjection, blacks' abjection is always externally generated and maintained. It will have always been outside given the paradoxical recognizability of the black, the immediate fact of the affect that is untransformable no matter what or who black does or is. What we have, then, is a kind of absolute abjection that is absolute precisely because it is a function of a kind of recognition: but it is a recognition that is not one, given that it is a recognition of an entirely featureless, faceless, deindividuated blackness. What I'm interested in, as you shall see, is thinking the rhythm of this absolute abjection and what it is that Fanon thinks that it opens. What happens or occurs in the rhythmic break that is abjection? Finally, it seems to me, nothing other than the oscillation within the always already prior connection between self and Other (be that other object or abject), an oscillation driven by the trace of an insistently originative sense of continuity, a syntagmatic phantasm that is the eternal return, rather than the deconstruction, of the sententious. It is a break that maintains the rhythm that it breaks by virtue of its maintenance of the duplicative unity embedded in the form of difference, of self/Other, of, finally, singularity. The radical break of the Other from the self is, then, never not contained by the continuity that it would sever; and there is, indeed, no possibility of the formation of a wholly internally generated identity that would somehow come as a function of such a break. There is no identity of the black man in the separation of the black man, and this is the meaning that is iconically given in Fanon's famous aphorism: *The black man is not. Any more than the white man.* No authentic upheaval is born in this phrase or in the radically differentiating encounter as which this phrase is often read (even by Fanon to the extent that he claims the black man wants such a radically differentiating encounter). Rather, authentic upheaval is born in the improvisation through succession and continuity, caesura, and sentence. This is the generative cut that

is embedded in the sense of the whole that, finally, is that which infuses Fanon's phrasing, his double and redoubled negation—of blackness, whiteness, man—in the name of ensemble. The thing to be enacted—the upheaval—is the aeffect of the generative cut that moves in the anarch(ron)ic, improvisational encounter with/as ensemble, the cut and rhythmic energy held within the sense of the whole. For this understanding of abjection, which proceeds, I hope, not from a misunderstanding of his, I must acknowledge the comradely guidance of Herman Rapaport. See also Frantz Fanon, *Black Skins, White Masks*, trans. Charles Lam Markmann (London: Paladin, 1970).

86 "The natives are extremely cautious about poison. When they buy any eatable, the seller kisses it all around before the buyer, to shew him it is not poisoned; and the same is done when meat and drink are presented, particularly to a stranger" (Equiano, *Interesting Narrative*, 22).

87 Equiano, *Interesting Narrative*, 51–52.

88 Equiano, *Interesting Narrative*, 63–64.

89 See Jacques Derrida, *Dissemination*, trans. Barbara Johnson (Chicago: University of Chicago Press, 1981).

90 Equiano, *Interesting Narrative*, 20.

91 See Equiano, *Interesting Narrative*, 5.

92 Equiano is both witness to and participant in this spectacle: "I used frequently to have different cargoes of new negroes in my care for sale; and it was almost a constant practice with our clerks, and other whites, to commit violent depredations on the chastity of the female slaves; and to these atrocities I was, though with reluctance, obliged to submit at all times, being unable to help them." This conflation of his identity and forced submission with that of the female slaves, this conflation of seeing and being, foreshadows the famous entry into the "blood stain'd gate of slavery" of Frederick Douglass and reveals the constitutive interinanimation of commerce and sexuality which shadows that of knowledge, language, and freedom with which this book is primarily concerned. Part of what I'm interested in is the emergence of a voice from the depredation of chastity that turns all of what is located at the intersection of lord and bonds(wo)man on its head. See Equiano, *Interesting Narrative*, 74.

93 Equiano, *Interesting Narrative*, 64–65.

94 Equiano, *Interesting Narrative*, 65.

95 Equiano, *Interesting Narrative*, 66.

96 Equiano, *Interesting Narrative*, 67.

97 This interinanimation of negative and positive forms of unmediated emotional expression remains to be thought and worked through, but its importance is superseded by another interarticulation, that between a general notion of expression and reflection. This synthesis was a feature of a certain moment in English literature (the eighteenth century) that was situated around the synthesis of the figure of the "man of feeling" (this very expression is used by Equiano to describe his third master, Mr. King; see Equiano, *Interesting Narrative*, 72) and the figure of the "man of reason." Part of what I want to suggest here is that many of the early slave narratives were also situated within this dialectic and, in this

sense, they, too, were part of the transition from enlightenment to romanticism, prefiguring the reflection on feeling that is the hallmark, for instance, of William Wordsworth. The move, then, is toward a literature of reflection, a literature of mediated experience and emotion. One begins to think again, unavoidably, of editing, prefacing, introduction, the figure of the "round, unvarnished tale" or that of "the learned curse."

98 Equiano, *Interesting Narrative*, 108.

99 Equiano, *Interesting Narrative*, 109.

100 Equiano, *Interesting Narrative*, 122.

101 Kazanjian, *The Colonizing Trick*, 38.

102 Kazanjian, *The Colonizing Trick*, 38.

103 Kazanjian, *The Colonizing Trick*, 35.

104 Kazanjian, *The Colonizing Trick*, 36.

105 Kazanjian, *The Colonizing Trick*, 36.

106 Kazanjian, *The Colonizing Trick*, 37.

107 Cedric J. Robinson, *The Terms of Order: Political Science and the Myth of Leadership* (Albany: SUNY Press, 1980).

108 See Judith Butler, *The Psychic Life of Power: Theories in Subjection* (Stanford, CA: Stanford University Press, 1997), 107; and Saidiya V. Hartman, *Scenes of Subjection: Terror, Slavery and Self-Making in Nineteenth-Century America* (Oxford: Oxford University Press, 1997), 117.

109 Kazanjian, *The Colonizing Trick*, 39.

110 Denise Ferreira da Silva, "On Difference without Separability," *32nd Bienal de São Paulo—Incerteza Viva*, ed. Jochen Volz and Júlia Rebouças (São Paulo: Fundação Bienal de São Paulo, 2016), 57–65.

111 See Kazanjian, *The Colonizing Trick*, 20.

112 Kazanjian, *The Colonizing Trick*, 17.

113 Kazanjian, *The Colonizing Trick*, 17.

114 Kazanjian, *The Colonizing Trick*, 18.

115 Kazanjian, *The Colonizing Trick*, 19.

116 See Kazanjian, *The Colonizing Trick*, 19.

117 Dipesh Chakrabarty, "The Two Histories of Capital," in *Provincializing Europe: Postcolonial Thought and Historical Difference* (Princeton, NJ: Princeton University Press, 2000), 47–71.

118 Theodor W. Adorno, *Negative Dialectics*, trans. E. B. Ashton (New York: Continuum, 1973), 183.

119 Kazanjian, *The Colonizing Trick*, 85.

120 I wish to acknowledge, here, the work of Michael Marder. See his *The Event of the Thing: Derrida's Post-Deconstructive Realism* (Toronto: Toronto University Press, 2009).

121 Karl Marx, *Grundrisse*, trans. Martin Nicolaus (New York: Vintage, 1973), 497.

122 See Hortense J. Spillers, "Mama's Baby, Papa's Maybe: An American Grammar Book," *Diacritics* 17, no. 2 (1987), 64–81; and Alexander Weheliye, *Habeas Viscus: Racializing Assemblages, Biopolitics, and Black Feminist Theories of the Human* (Durham, NC: Duke University Press, 2014).

123 For a thorough and caring inhabitation of these cartographical, topographical, geological matters, see Katherine McKittrick, *Demonic Grounds: Black Women and the Cartographies of Struggle* (Minneapolis: University of Minnesota Press, 2006).

124 Equiano, *Interesting Narrative*, 140; emphasis added.

125 Equiano, *Interesting Narrative*, 52, 53.

126 Equiano, *Interesting Narrative*, 143.

127 Mary Prince, *The History of Mary Prince, A West Indian Slave, Related by Herself, with a Supplement by the Editor* (London: F. Westley and A. H. Davis, 1831), in *The Classic Slave Narratives*, ed. Gates, 208.

128 Ellen Butler, quoted in *Bullwhip Days: The Slaves Remember*, ed. John Mellon (New York: Avon Books, 1988), 190.

129 See Prince, *History of Mary Prince*, in *The Classic Slave Narratives*, ed. Gates, 214. Thanks to John Nelson for calling my attention to this nuance in Prince's rhetoric of sweetness.

130 See Chomsky, *Knowledge of Language*, xxv.

131 *The Negro in Virginia*, compiled by Workers of the Writers' Program of the Works Project Administration in the State of Virginia (Winston-Salem, NC: John F. Blair, 1994).

Chapter 2: Gestural Critique of Judgment

1 Stephen Jay Gould, *The Mismeasure of Man*, rev. ed. (New York: W. W. Norton, 1996), 76–77; Louis Menand, *The Metaphysical Club: A Story of Ideas in America* (New York: Farrar, Straus and Giroux, 2001), 105.

2 Linda Williams, *Playing the Race Card: Melodramas of Black and White from Uncle Tom to O. J. Simpson* (Princeton, NJ: Princeton University Press, 2001).

3 Williams, *Playing the Race Card*, xiii–xiv.

4 Williams, *Playing the Race Card*, 283.

5 Williams, *Playing the Race Card*, 8.

6 Cedric J. Robinson, *Black Marxism: The Making of the Black Radical Tradition*, 2nd ed. (Chapel Hill: University of North Carolina Press, 2000).

7 Williams, *Playing the Race Card*, 8–9.

8 Richard Rorty, "Postmodernist Bourgeois Liberalism," in *Objectivity, Relativism, and Truth: Philosophical Papers, Volume 1* (Cambridge: Cambridge University Press, 1991), 197–202, and *Achieving Our Country: Leftist Thought in Twentieth-Century America* (Cambridge, MA: Harvard University Press, 1998). For an anticipatory critique of Rorty's published dismissal of American academic leftists' descent into "cultural" politics from "real" politics, see Judith Butler, "Merely Cultural," *Social Text* 52–53 (1997): 265–77.

9 Williams, *Playing the Race Card*, 293. See also Wendy Brown, *States of Injury: Power and Freedom in Late Modernity* (Princeton, NJ: Princeton University Press, 1995); Lauren Berlant, "The Subject of True Feeling: Pain, Privacy and Politics," in *Cultural Studies and Political Theory*, ed. Jodi Dean (Ithaca, NY: Cornell University Press, 2000), 42–62; and Robyn Wiegman, *American Anatomies:*

Theorizing Race and Gender (Durham, NC: Duke University Press, 1995). My contention that blackness (internationally and antinationally conceived) is the initial target of a certain critique of the relation between oppositional politicocultural identity and injury stems from my placement of Fanon at this critique's nodal point. See Frantz Fanon, *Black Skin, White Masks*, trans. Charles Lam Markmann (London: Paladin, 1970).

10 Williams, *Playing the Race Card*, 293.

11 Williams, *Playing the Race Card*, 293.

12 Peter Brooks, *The Melodramatic Imagination: Balzac, Henry James, Melodrama, and the Mode of Excess* (New Haven, CT: Yale University Press, 1976).

13 Brooks, *The Melodramatic Imagination*, 1.

14 For more on Morton and Lombroso, see Gould, *The Mismeasure of Man*, 82–101 and 152–73. See also James Q. Wilson and Richard J. Herrnstein, *Crime and Human Nature: The Definitive Study of the Causes of Crime* (New York: Simon and Schuster, 1985).

15 Brooks, *The Melodramatic Imagination*, 22.

16 Denis Diderot, "In Praise of Richardson," in *Selected Writings on Art and Literature*, trans. Geoffrey Bremner (New York: Penguin, 1994).

17 Brooks, *The Melodramatic Imagination*, 19.

18 Brooks, *The Melodramatic Imagination*, 10.

19 James, "Preface," *The Portrait of a Lady*, ed. Nicola Bradbury (Oxford: Oxford University Press, 1981), xl. Quoted in Brooks, *The Melodramatic Imagination*, 6.

20 Brooks, *The Melodramatic Imagination*, 18.

21 Williams, *Playing the Race Card*, 296.

22 Louis Menand, *The Metaphysical Club: A Story of Ideas in America* (New York: Farrar, Straus and Giroux, 2001), xii.

23 Daniel Bell, *The End of Ideology: On the Exhaustion of Political Ideas in the Fifties* (Cambridge, MA: Harvard University Press, 1960).

24 Oliver Wendell Holmes, "Letter to Harold Laski, May 12, 1921," in *Holmes-Laski Letters*, ed. Mark De Wolfe Howe, abridged by Alger Hiss (New York: Atheneum, 1963), 262. Quoted in Richard Maxwell Brown, *No Duty to Retreat: Violence and Values in American History and Society* (Norman: University of Oklahoma Press, 1991), 34. I thank Ruth Wilson Gilmore for this reference.

25 Zora Neale Hurston, "Characteristics of Negro Expression," in *The Sanctified Church* (Berkeley, CA: Turtle Island, 1981), 49.

26 See Susan Martin and Alma Ruiz, eds., *The Experimental Exercise of Freedom* (Los Angeles: Museum of Contemporary Art, Los Angeles, 1999).

27 Joan Dayan, "Cruel and Unusual: The End of the Eighth Amendment," *Boston Review* 15, no. 3 (2004), bostonreview.net/dayan-cruel-and-unusual.

28 Gayatri Chakravorty Spivak, "Righting Wrongs," *South Atlantic Quarterly* 103, nos. 2/3 (2004): 523–81.

29 Richard Ford, *Racial Culture: A Critique* (Princeton, NJ: Princeton University Press, 2004).

Chapter 3: Uplift and Criminality

1   Nahum D. Chandler, "Delimitations: The Positions of W. E. B. Du Bois in the History of Thought" (unpublished manuscript, 2002).

2   W. E. B. Du Bois, "Sociology Hesitant," *boundary 2* 27, no. 3 (2000): 37–44. In that volume, see also Ronald A. T. Judy, "Introduction: On W. E. B. Du Bois and Hyperbolic Thinking," 1–35; and Nahum Dmitri Chandler, "Originary Displacement," 249–86. The essay, along with Chandler's significant and illuminating annotations, has been collected in Du Bois, *The Problem of the Color-Line at the Turn of the Twentieth Century: The Essential Early Essays*, ed. Nahum Dimitri Chandler (New York: Fordham University Press, 2015), 271–84. While the essay should be read as Du Bois's call for sociology to escape its hesitancy in thinking black life as a matter for thought, it is necessary to recognize that hesitation will have been, in fact, the method of such movement. This abiding, (loco)motive immanence (an out, trane-like seriality of mantra or vamp) in the pause, in the delay, in the interval, in the break, is understood by Du Bois as confounding the "two sorts of human uniformity," chance and law. He therefore advocates inhabiting a polyrhythmic caesura that will have been the precise point of an interruptive conjunction of, say, the death rate and the women's club. But you'd have to get so into the deaths that both make up and disturb the rate, the measurement, of death, as well as so faithfully attend the activity of women that both makes up and disrupts the club, as to actually enact a recalibration of fugitivity as the traversal of the bridge between things and the whole they (de)form.

3   C. L. R. James, *The Black Jacobins: Toussaint L'Ouverture and the San Domingo Revolution*, 2nd ed., revised (New York: Vintage Books, 1989), 18.

4   LeRoi Jones (Amiri Baraka), *Blues People: Negro Music in White America* (New York: William Morrow, 1963), 20–21.

5   Baraka, *Blues People*, 21–22.

6   Du Bois, *The Souls of Black Folk*, in *Writings*, ed. Nathan Huggins (New York: Library of America, 1986), 538–39.

7   David Levering Lewis, *W. E. B. Du Bois: Biography of a Race, 1868–1919* (New York: Henry Holt, 1993), 14–15. Brent Hayes Edwards discusses the series of recordings of this song that Du Bois offers throughout his long autobiographical career in relation to Guadeloupean Suzanne Lacascade's 1924 novel *Claire-Solange, âme Africaine*. Lacascade's (writing of) music, Edwards forcefully argues, bears the cultural difference, mix, and transport that mark the necessary articulation of blackness and internationalism. Through the character whose name is also given to the novel, Lacascade indexes yet another song that lingers in the gap between transcription and translation: a song the figure of Claire-Solange describes as both "savage revolt" and the echo or trace of "the blow of the lash on the naked back of negro slaves"; a song of (dis)possession, contortion, and suspension (of traffic, of the bridge in Zanzibar where Claire-Solange first encounters its performance); a song of repetitive, even recidivist, insistence. In its resistance to, if not flight from, meaning and its regulations—whose manifestation in the novel's apparatus occurs at and as the convergence of fiction and fieldwork as

Edwards illuminates—Lacascade joins Du Bois and others before and after him in a certain phonographic insurgency; in my attendance to this insurgency, where blackness and internationalism must now be seen as interarticulate with vaga/bondage, I'm attempting to follow the example of Edwards. For the real thing, see Edwards, *The Practice of Diaspora: Literature, Translation, and the Rise of Black Internationalism* (Cambridge, MA: Harvard University Press, 2003). Take note, especially, of Edwards's discussion of Claude McKay's *Banjo* (187–233) as well as his discussion of *Claire-Solange, âme Africaine* (51–58).

8   Lewis, *W. E. B. Du Bois*, 585n7.

9   Lewis, *W. E. B. Du Bois*, 585n7.

10   Hortense J. Spillers, "*The Crisis of the Negro Intellectual*: A Post-Date," in Spillers, *Black, White, and in Color: Essays on American Literature and Culture* (Chicago: University of Chicago Press, 2003), 382.

11   See Cedric Robinson, *Black Marxism: The Making of the Black Radical Tradition*, 2nd ed. (Chapel Hill: University of North Carolina Press, 2000), 73.

12   Kevin K. Gaines, *Uplifting the Race: Black Leadership, Politics, and Culture in the Twentieth Century* (Chapel Hill: University of North Carolina Press, 1996), xv.

13   Gaines, *Uplifting the Race*, xv.

14   Du Bois, *Souls*, 467.

15   Gaines, *Uplifting the Race*, 176.

16   Du Bois, *Souls*, 466.

17   Du Bois, *Souls*, 466–67; emphasis in original.

18   I am thinking of the following passage by Louis Althusser and Etienne Balibar from an exegesis of a few sentences of Marx's *Grundrisse*: "It is precisely this *Gliederung*, this articulated-thought-totality [or 'articulated combination'/'*combinaison articulée*'] which has to be produced in knowledge as an object of knowledge in order to treat a knowledge of the real *Gliederung*, of the real articulated-totality which constitutes the existence of bourgeois society. The order in which the thought *Gliederung* is produced is a specific order, precisely the order of the theoretical *analysis* Marx performed in *Capital*, the order of the liaison and 'synthesis' of the concepts necessary for the production of a thought-whole, a thought-concrete, the theory of *Capital*" (*Reading Capital*, trans. Ben Brewster [London: Verso, 1979], 48). Perhaps the articulated combination of blackness and criminality makes possible a thought of another totality, a futurity given every day in our everyday. Edwards offers his own (thinking on) articulation, his own conceptualization of *decalage*, translation, and the enactment of diaspora, in a way that anticipates the line I am trying to trace or, better yet, follow. He moves by way of Stuart Hall's engagement with Althusser. See *Reading Capital*, 108, where the notion of "structure in dominance" is derived from an analysis of "articulated combination." See also Edwards, *The Practice of Diaspora*, 11–15. And for another, deeper engagement with Althusser that thinks the relation between the protocols of reading and the necessity of a conceptualization of the object in/of black studies, see Part III of Spillers, "*The Crisis of the Negro Intellectual*: A Post-Date," *Black and White and in Color*, 444–58.

19 Gaines, *Uplifting the Race*, 177.

20 Saidiya V. Hartman, *Scenes of Subjection: Terror, Slavery, and Self-Making in Nineteenth Century America* (Oxford. Oxford University Press, 1997).

21 See Jacques Derrida, "Force of Law: The 'Mystical Foundation of Authority,'" in *Deconstruction and the Possibility of Justice*, ed. Drucilla Cornell, Michael Rosenfeld, and David Gray Carlson (New York: Routledge, 1992), 3–68.

22 See Daniel P. Moynihan, *The Negro Family: The Case for National Action* (Washington, DC: U.S. Department of Labor, 1965). Spillers's exposure of the historical and theoretical conditions of possibility of Moynihan's argument is definitive. See her "Mama's Baby, Papa's Maybe: An American Grammar Book," *Diacritics* 17, no. 2 (1987): 64–81.

23 Ulrich B. Phillips, *American Negro Slavery* (Baton Rouge: Louisiana State University Press, 1966), 454.

24 Phillips, *American Negro Slavery*, 463.

25 I am indebted here to the valuable work of Steven Hahn. In his *A Nation under Our Feet: Black Political Struggles in the Rural South from Slavery to the Great Migration* (Cambridge, MA: Harvard University Press, 2003), Hahn exhaustively records the very kind of black political activity that Phillips represses, noting that "Southern slaveholders and their representatives (and, we might add, their historiographical apologists) . . . could scarcely acknowledge, let alone dignify, the disruptive or communal behaviours of their slaves as worthy of the name political" (15). Hahn's work does much to rectify this problem even as it might also be said to reify it, not only in its insistence on a distinction between resistance and politics that deeper consideration of the very idea of organization requires us to challenge, but also in its adherence to a notion of political subjectivity that forecloses further investigation into the possibilities of the slaves having produced new modes of agency that will have strained against the very modes of disciplinary citizenship they might be said to have called into being. In this respect, however problematic Phillips's discourse on slave crime may be, it bears the trace of political modes to which Hahn's brilliant corrective is not fully attuned even though it prepares us for a more faithful listening.

26 W. E. B. Du Bois, *The Philadelphia Negro: A Social Study*, rev. ed. (Philadelphia: University of Pennsylvania Press, 1996), 235.

27 Du Bois, *The Philadelphia Negro*, 411.

28 Such domesticity has its own music, as Du Bois's colleague Max Weber shows in his discourse on the piano in *The Rational and Social Foundations of Music*, trans. and ed. Don Martindale, Johannes Riedel, and Gertrude Neuwirth (Carbondale: Southern Illinois University Press, 1958). The "instrumental rationality" of the piano's harmonic construction is inseparable from its iconic position in the bourgeois drawing room and its symbolic relation to proper (feminine) accomplishment and proper (feminized) domesticity. For Adorno, the history of the piano is, in some ways, the history of a certain rebellion against the resolutions that are all but determined in and by its rational organization of sonic multiplicity. Beethoven's music, for instance—his piano sonatas in particular although his orchestral music also must move in this way as the

liberation of musical difference within musical collectivity—is understood to exemplify the glories of the seemingly impossible possibility of freedom. (Adorno will, of course, have no use for *this* braided line of tumultuous piano: Willie "The Lion" Smith, Duke Ellington, Thelonious Monk, Cecil Taylor; Earl Hines, Art Tatum, Mary Lou Williams, Bud Powell; or for the vast and unnamed maternal line of the organizers of frenzy who throw up their own sacred and profane strain—one thinks of Thomas Dorsey's complex relation to the mother, only partially enacted and in relation to the figure of Ma [Rainey].) What I can only point to here is the presence of another musicopolitical reason that animates Du Bois both in his etiolated attempts to recognize it and in his truncated attempts to eclipse it.

29 Robinson, *Black Marxism*, 171.

30 For more on the question of sexuality, labor, and the challenge to bourgeois domesticity and Du Bois's problematic attitudes toward working-class black women's autonomy, see Tera W. Hunter, "'The "Brotherly Love" for Which This City Is Proverbial Should Extend to All': The Everyday Lives of Working-Class Women in Philadelphia and Atlanta in the 1890s," in *W. E. B. Du Bois, Race, and the City: The Philadelphia Negro and Its Legacy*, ed. Michael B. Katz and Thomas J. Sugrue (Philadelphia: University of Pennsylvania Press, 1998), 127–51. Also see Hunter's extraordinary *To 'Joy My Freedom* (Cambridge, MA: Harvard University Press, 1997). For a striking analysis of the constitutive trace of "resistant orality" (a verbal, that is inseparable from a sexual, impudence) in black women's writing, see Harryette Mullen, "Runaway Tongue: Resistant Orality in *Uncle Tom's Cabin, Our Nig, Incidents in the Life of a Slave Girl*, and *Beloved*," in *The Culture of Sentiment: Race, Gender, and Sentimentality in Nineteenth-Century America*, ed. Shirley Samuels (New York: Oxford University Press, 1992), 244–64. For more on Hester's resistant aurality, see my *In the Break: The Aesthetics of the Black Radical Tradition* (Minneapolis: University of Minnesota Press, 2003). My formulations attempt, weakly, to enact what would have been infinitely more adequately given under Spillers's hand. On page 15 of *In the Break*, you'll see that here, now, I am late in imagining the incalculable difference between *handled* and *handed* to which Spillers gestures ("The African-American male has been touched, therefore, by the mother, *handed by* her in ways that he cannot escape"). What's at stake is some more efficacious approach to inheritance-in-dispossession; the hand-me-down im/possibility embedded in passing on and in what inheres outside and against grasping. See Spillers, "Mama's Baby, Papa's Maybe," 80. Finally, for a bracing challenge to the anthropological overinvestment in the phonic mode, one that helps to ground a brilliant reading of the force of the anthropological in black literature in general, see Gina Dent, *Anchored to the Real: Black Literature in the Wake of Anthropology* (Durham, NC: Duke University Press), forthcoming.

31 See Akira Lippit, *Electric Animal: Toward a Rhetoric of Wildlife* (Minneapolis: University of Minnesota Press, 2000).

32 Nathaniel Mackey, "Cante Moro," in *Sound States: Innovative Poetics and Acoustical Technologies*, ed. Adalaide Morris (Chapel Hill: University of North Carolina Press, 1997), 199–200.

33　Roland Kirk, *I Talk with the Spirits* (New York: Verve Records CD 558 076-2, 1965).

34　W. E. B. Du Bois and Moses Asch. *W. E. B. Du Bois: A Recorded Autobiography* (New York: Folkways Records FH-5511 LP, 1961).

35　I'm thinking of two passages in Adorno's late work. In the first, Adorno writes, "Brecht said once that the [Lenin] book on empirio-criticism obviated any further need to criticize the philosophy of immanence. It was a shortsighted remark. Materialist theory is subject to philosophical desiderata if it is not to succumb to the same provincialism that disfigures art in Eastern countries. The object of theory is not something immediate, of which theory might carry home a replica. Knowledge has not, like the state police, a rogues' gallery of its objects. Rather, it conceives them as it conveys them; else it would be content to describe the façade. As Brecht did admit, after all, the criterion of sense perception—overstretched and problematic even in its proper place—is not applicable to radically indirect society. What immigrated into the object as the law of its motion [*Bewegungsgesetz*], inevitably concealed by the ideological form of the phenomenon, eludes that criterion" (*Negative Dialectics*, trans. E. B. Ashton [New York: Continuum, 1973], 206).

In the second passage, Adorno argues, "The semblance character of artworks, the illusion of their being-in-itself, refers back to the fact that in the totality of their subjective mediatedness they take part in the universal delusional context of reification, and, that, in Marxist terms, they need to reflect a relation of living labor as if it were a thing. The inner consistency through which artworks participate in truth always involves their untruth; in its most unguarded manifestations art has always revolted against this, and today this revolt has become art's own law of movement [*Bewegungsgesetz*]. The antinomy of the truth and untruth of art may have moved Hegel to foretell its end. Traditional aesthetics possessed the insight that the primacy of the whole over the parts has constitutive need of the diverse and that this primacy misfires when it is simply imposed from above" (*Aesthetic Theory*, trans. Robert Hullot-Kentor [Minneapolis: University of Minnesota Press, 1997], 168–69).

36　It might appear that I risk privileging the ontological over the historical. I hope that the passages from Adorno that I quoted above would be the ground of my justification for the direction I have taken. Those passages contain what Herman Rapaport might call transcendental clues regarding the relation between blackness and radicalism, the politics and aesthetics, the history and ontology of criminality, which has everything to do with the *Bewegungsgesetz*, the (im) migrant law irrupting into and thereby constituting the object from outside. The methodological point, for me, is this: that the reemergence of the aesthetic and the ontological allow a more rigorous engagement with the political and the historical. These fields are no more to be divided, their terms no more to be fixed or hypostasized, than law and criminality or the *polis* and its *metoikoi*. Of course, the self-described criminal's self-description is mediated by the state; at the same time, the state is constituted by the very criminal/ity that it constructs and defines. This paradoxically contingent priority is what Cedric Robinson is already after when he says that black radicalism cannot be understood within the context of its genesis; and this is not negated but invaginated and augmented by the assertion that the priority of such radicalism, its broken and scarred ontological totality, is inseparable from a definable historical constitution. It's like what E. P. Thompson says in the preface to his masterpiece: "The working class was present at its own making."

It is important, then, not only to exhume the ontological in contexts or in relations to things that are thought only to defy it but also, and more specifically, to begin to consider a certain ontological notion of the city and of wealth that animates the middle and later Marx and which is tied to his formulations on the modes of primitive accumulation that have traditionally been linked to economies of the outskirts or the underground, to broken homes or black markets. This notion of The City/wealth that is operative in Marx is crucially tied to his analysis of enclosure. The two types of enclosure that I cite in this essay—in a way that certainly requires further development—are mirror images of one another that are important to my attempts to consider the relationship between blackness, radicalism, and the City. That they are mirror images of one another and need to be understood in their difference from one another is not at all to suggest that they are not continuous (though my quick treatment of them may give that impression). I just want to maintain the tension between them so that I can explore it elsewhere (i.e., consider enclosure within the context of a more general ontological history of the City). In the end, it just seems to me that the most concrete levels of historical analysis either require or, more modestly, are improved by the raising of precisely those ontological questions that always animate Du Bois's long historical and sociological engagement with the black ordinary.

37 See Robin D. G. Kelley, *Freedom Dreams: The Black Radical Imagination* (New York: Beacon, 2002), 157–94.

38 Karl Marx, *Grundrisse: Foundations of the Critique of Political Economy*, trans. Martin Nicolaus (New York: Vintage, 1973), 487–88; emphasis in original.

39 See Gilles Deleuze and Félix Guattari, *A Thousand Plateaus* (Minneapolis: University of Minnesota Press, 1987), 11–12.

40 See Audre Lorde, "The Master's Tools Will Never Dismantle the Master's House," in *Sister Outsider: Essays and Speeches* (Freedom, CA: Crossing Press, 1984), 110–13.

41 See Henry Louis Gates Jr., "The Master's Pieces: On Canon Formation and the Afro-American Tradition," in *The Bounds of Race*, ed. Dominick LaCapra (Ithaca, NY: Cornell University Press, 1991), 34.

Chapter 4: The New International of Decent Feelings

1 Louis Althusser, "The International of Decent Feelings," in *The Spectre of Hegel*, trans. G. M. Goshgarian (New York: Verso, 1997), 23.

2 Geoffrey Galt Harpham, "Symbolic Terror," *Critical Inquiry* 28, no. 2 (2002): 573.

3 Harpham, "Symbolic Terror," 574.

4 Harpham, "Symbolic Terror," 574.

5 Althusser, "The International of Decent Feelings," 25.
6 Harpham, "Symbolic Terror," 578.
7 Jacques Derrida, "Onto-theology of National Humanism (Prolegomena to a Hypothesis)," *Oxford Literary Review* 14, nos. 1–2 (1992): 3–23.
8 Althusser, "The International of Decent Feelings," 25.
9 Althusser, "The International of Decent Feelings," 27.
10 Noam Chomsky, "The Responsibility of Intellectuals," in *American Power and the New Mandarins* (New York: Pantheon, 1967), 329. I should note that the ideas Chomsky expresses, by way of Dwight Macdonald, in the essay's opening paragraphs have much the same resonance that they did thirty-five years ago though the climate for their reception is now not nearly as hospitable.
11 Chomsky, "The Responsibility of Intellectuals," 329.
12 Harpham, "Symbolic Terror," 579.
13 Althusser, "The International of Decent Feelings," 30; emphasis in original.
14 Harpham, "Symbolic Terror," 574.
15 Harpham, "Symbolic Terror," 574.
16 Gitlin is quoted in Alexander Cockburn, "Wild Justice," *New York Press*, January 30, 2002, 17: "To the Left-wing fundamentalist, the only interesting or important brutality is at least indirectly the United States' doing. . . . In the United Stated adherents of this kind of reflexive anti-Americanism are a minority (isolated, usually, on campuses and in coastal cities, in circles where reality checks are scarce)."
17 See Judith Butler, *The Psychic Life of Power* (Stanford, CA: Stanford University Press, 1995), 6–10.

Chapter 5: Rilya Wilson. Precious Doe. Buried Angel.

1 See Sylvia Wynter, "Unsettling the Coloniality of Being/Power/Truth/Freedom: Towards the Human, After Man, Its Overrepresentation—An Argument" in *CR: The New Centennial Review* 3, no. 3 (2003): 257–337.

Chapter 6: Black Op

1 I dedicate this essay to the memory of Lindon Barrett, a scholar of beautiful, severe, generous brilliance. His influence on me—and our friendship—overcame delay and survived estrangement. His work was driven by love.
2 Chuck Morse, "Capitalism, Marxism, and the Black Radical Tradition: An Interview with Cedric Robinson," in *Perspectives on Anarchist Theory* 3, no. 1 (spring 1999). Accessed July 10, 2007. http://www.hartford-hwp.com/archives /45a/568.html.

Chapter 7: The Touring Machine (Flesh Thought Inside Out)

1 Jerry Fodor, "Fire the Press Secretary," *London Review of Books*, April 28, 2011, 24.
2 Fodor, "Fire the Press Secretary," 25; Michel Foucault, "Technologies of the Self," in *Technologies of the Self: A Seminar with Michel Foucault*, ed. Luther H. Martin,

Huck Gutman, and Patrick H. Hutton (Amherst: University of Massachusetts Press, 1988), 31.

3 See Judith Butler, *Giving an Account of Oneself* (New York: Fordham University Press, 2005).

4 See Theodore A. Harris and Amiri Baraka, *Our Flesh of Flames* (Philadelphia: Anvil Arts Press, 2008).

5 Foucault, "Technologies of the Self," 18.

6 See Nahum Chandler, "Of Exorbitance: The Problem of the Negro as a Problem for Thought," *Criticism* 50, no. 3 (2008): 345–410.

7 Fodor, "Fire the Press Secretary," 24.

8 Robert Kurzban, *Why Everyone (Else) Is a Hypocrite: Evolution and the Modular Mind* (Princeton, NJ: Princeton University Press, 2011), 22.

9 Fodor, "Fire the Press Secretary," 24.

10 See David Kazanjian, *The Colonizing Trick: National Culture and Imperial Citizenship in Early America* (Minneapolis: University of Minnesota Press, 2003), 27. There, Kazanjian writes that "in the strictest sense the term refers to the process of igniting a liquid, of turning a liquid into flame. Here, I interpret such a process less as a breaking out of chaos than as a material transformation with powerful effects. 'Flashpoint' in this sense refers to the process by which someone or something emerges or bursts into action or being, not out of nothing but transformed from one form to another; and, it refers to the powerful effects of that emergence or transformation." In his concern with the conjunction of form and explosiveness, Kazanjian takes a theoretical path that can be said to parallel that of Catharine Malabou. In his concern with the irreducible sociality of the flash, Kazanjian can be said to diverge from or overrun Malabou, about whom more later.

11 Fodor, "Fire the Press Secretary," 25.

12 I'm thinking a very specific interpenetration, which is, I think, only disguised as an impenetrability. The first permutation/permeation emerges in part of an epigraph for Polly Greenberg, *The Devil Has Slippery Shoes: A Biased Biography of the Child Development Group of Mississippi* (London: Macmillan, 1969), xv: "'Course CDGM's good,' said a large lady from Lauderdale County. ''Cept the things about it that's bad. There's a lotta good folks come here to help us. 'Course, there's a lot just come to cause a fuss too. And the federal government's finally recognized us down here—'course sometimes that ain't so good, 'cause for every smile it gives us, it gives us a kick too. Well, at least it's got us colored peoples workin' for oursel's. 'Cept the ones that won't. One thing, though, it's great for the kids. On'y thing, it's kinda hard on 'em when they get to real school and it ain't like our school. God's helpin' us, ain't no doubt. It's just that the Devil keeps skippin' in and outa things so's we won't get spoilt. He really keeps you guessin'! Each thing, you gotta study it to see if it's God in the disguise of difficulty, or the Devil in the disguise of somebody good. This whole thing really keep us workin' our mind.'"

The second comes into relief in Noam Chomsky, "What We Know: On the Universals of Language and Rights," *Boston Review* 30, nos. 3–4 (2005): 25.

"A significant insight of the first cognitive revolution was that properties of the world that are informally called mental may involve unbounded capacities of a finite organ, the 'infinite use of finite means,' in Wilhelm von Humboldt's phrase. In a rather similar vein, Hume had recognized that our moral judgments are unbounded in scope, and must be founded on general principles that are part of our nature though they are beyond our 'original instincts.' That observation poses Huarte's problem in a different domain, where we might find part of the thin thread that links the search for cognitive and moral universals. By mid-20th century, it had become possible to face such problems in more substantive ways than before. By then, there was a clear understanding, from the study of recursive functions, of finite generative systems with unbounded scope—which could be readily adapted to the reframing and investigation of some of the traditional questions that had necessarily been left obscure— though only some, it is important to stress. Humboldt referred to the infinite use of language, quite a different matter from the unbounded scope of the finite means that characterizes language, where a finite set of elements yields a potentially infinite array of discrete expressions: discrete, because there are six-word sentences and seven-word sentences, but no 6.2 word sentences; infinite because there is no longest sentence (append 'I think that' to the start of any sentence). Another influential factor in the renewal of the cognitive revolution was the work of ethologists, then just coming to be more widely known, with their concern for 'the innate working hypotheses present in subhuman organisms' (Nikolaas Tinbergen) and the 'human a priori' (Konrad Lorenz), which should have much the same character. That framework too could be adapted to the study of human cognitive organs (for example, the language faculty) and their genetically determined nature, which constructs experience and guides the general path of development, as in other aspects of growth of organisms, including the human visual, circulatory, and digestive systems, among others."

13 Angela Mitropoulos, "Oikopolitics, and Storms," *Global South* 3, no. 1 (2009): 68.

14 Thomas Hobbes, *Leviathan*, ed. J. C. A. Gaskin (Oxford: Oxford University Press, 1998), 84.

15 Catherine Malabou, "Will Sovereignty Ever Be Deconstructed?" In *Plastic Materialities: Politics, Legality, and Metamorphosis in the Work of Catherine Malabou*, ed. Brenna Bhandar and Jonathan Goldberg-Hiller (Durham, NC: Duke University Press, 2015), 39.

16 Frantz Fanon, *Black Skin, White Masks*, trans. Richard Philcox (New York: Grove Press, 2008), 90–91.

17 Maurice Merleau-Ponty, *The Visible and the Invisible*, ed. Claude Lefort, trans. Alphonso Lingis (Evanston, IL: Northwestern University Press, 1968), 248–50.

18 Toni Morrison, *Beloved* (New York: Plume, 1988), 88.

19 Hortense J. Spillers, "Mama's Baby, Papa's Maybe: An American Grammar Book," *Diacritics* 17, no. 2 (1987): 67.

20 Spillers, "Mama's Baby," 68.

21 Cathine Malabou, "Will Sovereignty Ever Be Deconstructed?," unpublished manuscript, p. 7.

22 Jacques Derrida, "*Différance*," trans. Alan Bass, in *Margins of Philosophy* (Chicago: University of Chicago Press, 1985), 11.

23 Malabou, "Will Sovereignty Ever Be Deconstructed?," 40.

24 Malabou, "Will Sovereignty Ever Be Deconstructed?," 43.

Chapter 8: Seeing Things

1 Cedric J. Robinson, *Black Marxism: The Making of the Black Radical Tradition*, 2nd ed. (Chapel Hill: University of North Carolina Press, 2000).

2 Mário Pedrosa, "Antonio Manuel. On Antonio Manuel's Presentation at the Opening of the Salão Nacional de Arte Moderna, as a Work of Art," in *Primary Documents*, ed. Glória Ferreira and Paulo Herkenhoff, trans. Stephen Berg (New York: Museum of Modern Art, 2015), 326.

3 Karl Marx, "Private Property and Communism," in *Early Writings*, trans. Rodney Livingstone and Gregor Benton (New York: Vintage, 1975), 345–58.

4 Stuart Hall, Chas Critcher, Tony Jefferson, John Clarke, and Brian Roberts, *Policing the Crisis: Mugging, The State, and Law and Order* (London: Palgrave, 1978).

5 Michael Herzfeld, *Cultural Intimacy: Social Poetics in the Nation-State* (New York: Routledge, 2004), 3.

Chapter 9: Air Shaft, Rent Party

1 In addition to being dedicated, with the utmost respect, to Richard Iton's memory, this writing is also dedicated to, and emphatically under the influence of, Denise Ferreira da Silva.

2 "Eternal middle passage" is one of Ruth Wilson Gilmore's resonant phrases. See Gilmore, *Golden Gulag: Prison, Surplus, Crisis, and Opposition in Globalizing California* (Berkeley: University of California Press, 2007).

Chapter 10: Notes on Passage

"Die schärfsten Dialektiker sind die Flüchtlinge. Sie sind Flüchtlinge infolge von Veränderungen und sie studieren nicht als Veränderungen." Bertolt Brecht, "Dänemark oder Der Humor über Die Hegelische Dialektik," in *Flüchtlingsgespräche*. Translation quoted in Martin Jay, *Permanent Exiles: Essays on the Intellectual Migration from Germany to America* (New York: Columbia University Press, 1986), 28.

1 Immanuel Kant, "Idea for a Universal History with a Cosmopolitan Aim," trans. Allan W. Wood, in *Anthropology, History, and Education*, ed. Günter Zöller and Robert B. Louden (Cambridge: Cambridge University Press, 2007), 118, 112, 114.

2 See Jacques Derrida, "Onto-theology of National Humanism (Prolegomena to a Hypothesis)," *Oxford Literary Review* 14, nos. 1–2 (1992): 3–23; and Noam Chomsky, *The New Military Humanism: Lessons from Kosovo* (Monroe, ME. Common Courage Press, 2002).

3 Asexualization usually denotes sterilization and I mean to evoke that sense here since what's at stake is not only a regulation of sexual difference but also standardized control over sexual, and social, reproduction.

4 Édouard Glissant, "One World in Relation: Édouard Glissant in Conversation with Manthia Diawara," trans. Christopher Winks, *Nka Journal of Contemporary African Art* 28 (spring 2011): 5.

5 See Walter Rodney, *The Groundings with My Brothers* (London: Bogle-L'Ouverture, 1975); and Kamau Brathwaite, *Contradictory Omens: Cultural Diversity and Integration* (Mona, Jamaica: Savacou, 1974), 64.

6 See Nathaniel Mackey, *Atet A.D.* (San Francisco: City Lights Books, 2001), 118–19.

7 See G. W. F. Hegel, *Elements of the Philosophy of Right*, ed. Allen W. Wood, trans. H. B. Nisbet (Cambridge: Cambridge University Press, 1991), 275–380; and Hannah Arendt, *The Origins of Totalitarianism* (San Diego, CA: Harcourt Brace, 1973), 267–302.

8 See Hannah Arendt, *The Human Condition* (Chicago: University of Chicago Press, 1998); and Orlando Patterson, *Slavery and Social Death: A Comparative Study* (Cambridge, MA: Harvard University Press, 1985).

9 Space and time do not permit me to approach even a gesture toward the implications that emerge from reading certain passages of Arendt's that indicate some commerce between "the fact of natality, in which the faculty of action is ontologically rooted," the unobservable insurgency of *animal laborans*, and "the disappearance of the sensually given world, the transcendent world . . . and with it the possibility of transcending the material world in concept and thought." Unobservable things, in their fugitive uprising, their runaway digging, have been found to perform such vanishing in the age of quantum mechanics; on the other hand, "serious slave rebellions" are, for Arendt, striking in their absence in ancient and modern times, because when it comes to the social life of the enslaved, how they felt and feel (about) each other, if Patterson is to be believed, there is no data though even if there were it would have no purchase in the "realm of human affairs." Moreover, the ones described as alienated from their natality, when Patterson is read in light of Arendt's influence, are not only detached from heritage and patrimony but also from that capacity "for distinction and hence for action and speech" that "can bestow upon human affairs faith and hope." What remains to be seen and heard, in what is supposed to be the absence of rebellion, is the material that eludes man, that escapes (in) the experiment, remaining, as the incalculable, immeasurable miracle that ends, in order to begin, the world. It is the slave revolt, in all seriousness, that puts this interval into play. See Arendt, *The Human Condition* (215, 247, 285–89); and Patterson, *Slavery and Social Death* (11).

10 See Bernard Bailyn, *Voyagers to the West: A Passage in the Peopling of America on the Eve of the Revolution* (New York: Knopf, 1986).

11 See Peter Linebaugh, "All the Atlantic Mountains Shook," *Labour/La Travail* 10 (1982): 87–121; and Ronald A. T. Judy, *(Dis)Forming the American Canon: African-Arabic Slave Narratives and the Vernacular* (Minneapolis: University of Minnesota Press, 1993).

12 See Paul Gilroy, *The Black Atlantic: Modernity and Double Consciousness* (Cambridge, MA: Harvard University Press, 1993), and *Darker than Blue: On the Moral Economies of Black Atlantic Culture* (Cambridge, MA: Harvard University Press, 2010).

13 See Melinda Cooper and Angela Mitropoulos, "In Praise of Usura," *Mute*, May 27, 2009, www.metamute.org/editorial/articles/praise-usura.

14 See Frank B. Wilderson III, *Red, White and Black: Cinema and the Structure of US Antagonisms* (Durham, NC: Duke University Press, 2010); and Nathaniel Mackey, "On Antiphon Island," in *Splay Anthem* (New York: New Directions, 2006), 64–65.

15 See Nahum Dimitri Chandler, "The Figure of the X: An Elaboration of the Du Boisian Autobiographical Example," in *Displacement, Diaspora, and Geographies of Identity*, ed. Smadar Lavie and Ted Swedenburg (Durham, NC: Duke University Press, 1996), 235–72, and "The Figure of W. E. B. Du Bois as a Problem for Thought," *CR: The New Centennial Review* 6, no. 3 (2006): 29–55.

16 Lindon Barrett, *Blackness and Value: Seeing Double* (Cambridge: Cambridge University Press, 1998).

17 Bryan Wagner, *Disturbing the Peace: Black Culture and the Police Power after Slavery* (Durham, NC: Duke University Press, 2009), 1.

18 Art Ensemble of Chicago, *Certain Blacks*, Verve B00008S7JX, CD, 2005.

19 See Kamari Maxine Clarke, "New Spheres of Transnational Formations: Mobilizations of Humanitarian Diasporas," in "Language, Inequality, and Endangerment: African Americans and Native Americans," ed. Arthur K. Spears, special issue, *Transforming Anthropology* 18, no. 1 (2010): 48–79. The forum also includes responses to Clarke written by Jean Muteba Rahier and Paul Tiyambe Zeleza.

20 Clarke, "New Spheres," 51.

21 Michelle M. Wright, "Black in Time: Exploring New Ontologies, New Dimensions, New Epistemologies of the African Diaspora," in "Language, Inequality, and Endangerment: African Americans and Native Americans," ed. Arthur K. Spears, 70.

22 Clarke, "New Spheres," 49.

23 W. E. B. Du Bois, *The Souls of Black Folk* (New York: Modern Library, 2003), 15.

24 Kamari Clarke, "Response by Author," in "Language, Inequality, and Endangerment: African Americans and Native Americans," ed. Arthur K. Spears, 79.

25 For more on the concept of anarchrony see Tom Sheehan, "Anarchy and Anarchrony: Spatio-Temporality and Framing in Joyce, Proust and Rhys," unpublished manuscript, 2000.

26 See Melville J. Herskovitz, *The Myth of the Negro Past* (New York: Harper, 1941); and J. Lorand Matory, *Black Atlantic Religion: Tradition, Transnationalism, and Matriarchy in the Afro-Brazilian Candomblé* (Princeton, NJ: Princeton University Press, 2005).

27 See Cedric J. Robinson, *Black Marxism: The Making of the Black Radical Tradition* (Chapel Hill: University of North Carolina Press, 2000), 171; Laura Harris, "What Happened to the Motley Crew: C. L. R. James, Hélio Oiticica, and the Aesthetic Sociality of Blackness," *Social Text* 30, no. 3 (2012): 49–75; and Michel Foucault, *History of Madness*, trans. Jonathan Murphy and Jean Khalfa (London: Routledge, 2006), 11.

28 See Michelle M. Wright, *Becoming Black: Creating Identity in the African Diaspora* (Durham, NC: Duke University Press, 2004).

29 Clarke, "Response," 79.

30 Clarke, "Response," 79.

31 Clarke, "New Spheres," 58.

32 Here, I borrow and abuse a phrase of Ruth Wilson Gilmore's. See her *Golden Gulag: Prison, Surplus, Crisis, and Opposition in Globalizing California* (Berkeley: University of California Press, 2007), 245. Gilmore brilliantly analyzes how California is an innovator in the process by which the state is made to grow precisely by way of the promise of its eventual shrinkage and how the prison is the exemplary theater wherein this paradox is played out, with blacks forced to populate the stage, as the living enfleshment of the very state that incarcerates them and which is enlarged as a result of their confinement. This same black flesh, and this is no accident, is made to stand in for a similarly tangled ensemble of statist and antistatist desires precisely insofar as it is understood to exist, as it were, in a condition that is before the state.

33 *É Minha Cara/That's My Face*, directed by Thomas Allen Harris (2001; New York: Fox Lorber Home Video, 2004), DVD.

34 Frantz Fanon, *Black Skin, White Masks*, trans. Richard Philcox (New York: Grove, 2008), 90.

35 Wright, "Black in Time," 72.

36 Annette Henry, "'There's Salt-Water in Our Blood': The 'Middle Passage' Epistemology of Two Black Mothers regarding the Spiritual Education of Their Daughters," *International Journal of Qualitative Studies in Education* 19, no. 3 (2006): 340. See also, among Henry's prolific scholarly/creative writing, "Growing Up Black, Female and Working Class: A Teacher's Narrative," *Anthropology and Education Quarterly* 26, no. 3 (1995): 279–305; "African Canadian Women Teachers' Activism: Recreating Communities of Caring and Resistance," *Journal of Negro Education* 61, no. 3 (1992): 392–404; and "A Wha' Dem A Go On Wid? (Student Resistance in a Doctoral Seminar on Black Feminist Thought)," *Frontiers* 16, no. 1 (1996): 27.

37 Henry, "Salt-Water," 340. Quoted in Wright, "Black in Time," 72.

38 Wright, "Black in Time," 72.

39 Henry, "Salt-Water," 334, 332.

40 Louis Althusser, "Ideology and Ideological State Apparatuses (Notes towards an Investigation)," in *Lenin and Philosophy and Other Essays*, trans. Ben Brewster (New York: Monthly Review Press, 1971), 127–86.

41 See Michelle M. Wright, *Physics of Blackness: Beyond the Middle Passage Epistemology* (Minneapolis: University of Minnesota Press, 2015), 109–40.

42 See Kamau Brathwaite, *Roots* (Ann Arbor: University of Michigan Press, 1993).

43 See Augusto Boal, *Theatre of the Oppressed*, trans. Charles A. McBride (New York: Theatre Communications Group, 1993); and Paolo Freire, *Pedagogy of the Oppressed*, trans. Myra Bergman Ramos (New York: Continuum, 1970).

44 Clarke, "New Spheres," 49.

45 Clarke, "Response," 79.

46 See M. Jacqui Alexander, *Pedagogies of Crossing: Meditations on Feminism, Sexual Politics, Memory, and the Sacred* (Durham, NC: Duke University Press, 2006).

47 Lee Smolin, *The Trouble with Physics: The Rise of String Theory, The Fall of a Science, and What Comes Next* (Boston: Houghton Mifflin, 2006), 257.

48 For his formulation of *das vulgäre Zeitverständnis* [the vulgar understanding of time], see Martin Heidegger, *Sein und Zeit*, Sechzehnte Auflage [*Being and Time*, 16th ed.] (Tübingen, Germany: Max Niemeyer Verlag, 1986), 426; and Smolin, *The Trouble with Physics*, 38–53.

49 Darby English, *How to See a Work of Art in Total Darkness* (Cambridge, MA: MIT Press, 2007), 27–70.

50 Mackey, "On Antiphon Island," 64.

51 See Ed Roberson, *To See the Earth before the End of the World* (Middletown, CT: Wesleyan University Press, 2010). Having done so, ask if the Earth can survive the world.

52 See Denise Ferreira da Silva, "No-Bodies: Law, Raciality and Violence," *Griffith Law Review* 18, no. 2 (2009): 212–36.

53 See Elizabeth Alexander, "Today's News," in *The Venus Hottentot* (Charlottesville: University of Virginia Press, 1990), 51. Having done so, ask if blackness is (a) color. Having done so, ask if black(ness) is (another) country.

Chapter 11: Here, There, and Everywhere

1 Ariella Azoulay and Adi Ophir, *The One-State Condition: Occupation and Democracy in Israel/Palestine* (Stanford, CA: Stanford University Press, 2012). In this and other essays I have used the term *incorporative exclusion*, which is a slight variation, with what I hope are more than insignificant theoretical implications, on their notion of "inclusive exclusion."

2 Nicholas Payton, "Why Nicholas Payton Refuses to Boycott Israel." Accessed August 11, 2013, https://nicholaspayton.wordpress.com/2013/08/08why -nicholas-payton-refuses-to-boycott-israel/. Citation has since been deleted.

Chapter 12: Anassignment Letters

1 OK, rather than hope that nobody notices this grammatical mess I've gotten myself into, let's think of this as a kind of mathematical problem. It seems like the problem of how a many becomes a one, though black study is more and less than that. Strangely, this movement comes more sharply into relief if we consider its reversal. In a paragrammatical way, the shift from black study to black studies more closely parallels that from (anti-national, impersonal) difference to (national, personal) identity. It's a professional maneuver with which I have been

both happily and unhappily involved. Out of that ambivalence I've been trying to practice a bit of amateurism. And you can see, now, that this just folds right back into the intersection of our classes.

Chapter 13: The Animaternalizing Call

1 Avital Ronell, *The Telephone Book: Technology, Schizophrenia, Electric Speech* (Lincoln: University of Nebraska Press, 1990), 23–24.

Chapter 14: Erotics of Fugitivity

1 Nahum Dimitri Chandler, "Originary Displacement," *boundary 2* 27, no. 3 (2000): 249–86.
2 Nathaniel Mackey, *From a Broken Bottle Traces of Perfume Still Emanate: Bedouin Hornbook, Djbot Baghostus's Run, ATet A.D.* (vols. 1–3), (New York: New Directions, 2010).
3 Gayle Salamon, *Transgender and Rhetorics of Materiality* (New York: Columbia University Press, 2010).
4 Aldon Lynn Nielsen, "Face to Face with the Blues," Accessed July 11, 2017, https://www.academia.edu/472598/FACE_TO_FACE_WITH_THE_BLUES.
5 Sora Han, "Slavery as Contract: *Betty's Case* and the Question of Freedom," *Law and Literature* 27, no. 3 (2015): 395–96.
6 Han, "Slavery as Contract," 407–8.
7 Han, "Slavery as Contract," 398; emphasis in original.
8 Han, "Slavery as Contract," 400.
9 Friends of Freedom, *The Liberty Bell* (Boston: Prentiss, Sawyer, and Co., 1857), 312.
10 Robert M. Cover, *Justice Accused: Anti-Slavery and the Judicial Process* (New Haven, CT: Yale University Press, 1975), 2–7.
11 Adrian Heathfield, "Impress of Time," in Adrian Heathfield and Tehching Hsieh, *Out of Now: The Lifeworks of Tehching Hsieh* (Cambridge, MA: MIT Press, 2015), 11.
12 Peggy Phelan, *Unmarked: The Politics of Performance* (London: Routledge, 1993).
13 Huey Copeland, *Bound to Appear: Art, Slavery, and the Site of Blackness in Multicultural America* (Chicago: University of Chicago Press, 2013).
14 Han, "Slavery as Contract," 401.
15 Han, "Slavery as Contract," 401.
16 See Hortense Spillers, "Mama's Baby, Papa's Maybe: An American Grammar Book," *Diacritics* 17, no. 2 (1987): 78; quoted in Han, "Slavery as Contract," 402.
17 See M. NourbeSe Philip, *Zong!* (Middletown, CT: Wesleyan University Press, 2008).
18 Han, "Slavery as Contract," 403–4.
19 Orlando Patterson, *Slavery and Social Death: A Comparative Study* (Cambridge, MA: Harvard University Press, 1985).
20 Robert M. Cover, "The Bonds of Constitutional Interpretation: Of the Word, the Deed, and the Role," *Georgia Law Review* 20 (1986): 833.

21 Han, "Slavery as Contract," 404.

22 Han, "Slavery as Contract," 405.

23 Han, "Slavery as Contract," 406.

24 Han, "Slavery as Contract," 408.

25 Spillers, "Mama's Baby, Papa's Maybe," 74; quoted in Han, "Slavery as Contract," 409.

26 Han, "Slavery as Contract," 411.

27 See Oscar Zeta Acosta, *The Revolt of the Cockroach People* (New York: Vintage Books, 1989), 258.

28 Saidiya V. Hartman, *Scenes of Subjection: Terror, Slavery, and Self-Making in Nineteenth-Century America* (Oxford: Oxford University Press, 1997), 130.

29 Hartman, *Scenes of Subjection*, 116–17.

WORKS CITED

Acosta, Oscar Zeta. *The Revolt of the Cockroach People*. New York: Vintage Books, 1989.

Adorno, Theodor. *Aesthetic Theory*. Translated by Robert Hullot-Kentor. Minneapolis: University of Minnesota Press, 1997.

——. *Negative Dialectics*. Translated by E. B. Ashton. New York: Continuum, 1973.

Ahmad, Aijaz. *In Theory: Nations, Classes, Literatures*. London: Verso, 1992.

Alexander, Elizabeth. "Today's News." In *The Venus Hottentot*. Charlottesville: University of Virginia Press, 1990.

Alexander, Jacqui M. *Pedagogies of Crossing: Meditations on Feminism, Sexual Politics, Memory, and the Sacred*. Durham, NC: Duke University Press, 2006.

Althusser, Louis. "Ideology and Ideological State Apparatuses (Notes towards an Investigation)." In Althusser, *Lenin and Philosophy and Other Essays*. Translated by Ben Brewster, 127–86. New York: Monthly Review Press, 1971.

——. "The International of Decent Feelings." In *The Spectre of Hegel*. Translated by G. M. Goshgarian, 21–35. New York: Verso, 1997.

Althusser, Louis, and Etienne Balibar. *Reading Capital*. Translated by Ben Brewster. London: Verso, 1979.

Arendt, Hannah. *The Human Condition*. Chicago: University of Chicago Press, 1998.

——. *Lectures on Kant's Political Philosophy*. Edited by Ronald Beiner. Chicago: University of Chicago Press, 1982.

——. *The Origins of Totalitarianism*. San Diego, CA: Harcourt Brace, 1973.

Art Ensemble of Chicago. *Certain Blacks*. Verve B00008S7JX, CD. 2005.

Austin, J. L. *How to Do Things with Words*. Edited by J. O. Urmson and Marina Sbisá. 2nd ed. Cambridge, MA: Harvard University Press, 1975.

Azoulay, Ariella, and Adi Ophir. *The One-State Condition: Occupation and Democracy in Israel/Palestine*. Stanford, CA: Stanford University Press, 2012.

Bailyn, Bernard. *Voyagers to the West: A Passage in the Peopling of America on the Eve of the Revolution*. New York: Knopf, 1986.

Baker, Houston. *Blues, Ideology, and Afro-American Literature: A Vernacular Theory*. Chicago: University of Chicago Press, 1985.

Barrett, Lindon. *Blackness and Value: Seeing Double*. Cambridge: Cambridge University Press, 1998.

——. *Racial Blackness and the Discontinuity of Western Modernity*. Edited by Justin A. Joyce, Dwight A. McBride, and John Carlos Rowe. Urbana: University of Illinois Press, 2014.

Beckett, Samuel. *The Unnameable*. In *Three Novels by Samuel Beckett*. New York: Grove Press, 1965.

Bell, Daniel. *The End of Ideology: On the Exhaustion of Political Ideas in the Fifties*. Cambridge, MA: Harvard University Press, 1960.

Benjamin, Andrew. *Translation and the Nature of Philosophy: A New Theory of Words*. New York: Routledge, 1989.

Berlant, Lauren. "The Subject of True Feeling: Pain, Privacy and Politics." In *Cultural Studies and Political Theory*, edited by Jodi Dean, 42–62. Ithaca, NY: Cornell University Press, 2000.

Bernasconi, Robert, ed. "Who Invented the Concept of Race? Kant's Role in the Enlightenment Construction of Race." In *Race*, 11–36. London: Blackwell, 2001.

Bhabha, Homi. "Interrogating Identity: The Postcolonial Prerogative." In *Anatomy of Racism*, edited by David Theo Goldberg, 183–209. Minneapolis: University of Minnesota Press, 1990.

Boal, Augusto. *Theatre of the Oppressed*. Translated by Charles A. McBride. New York: Theatre Communications Group, 1993.

Brathwaite, Kamau. *Contradictory Omens: Cultural Diversity and Integration*. Mona, Jamaica: Savacou, 1974.

———. *Roots*. Ann Arbor: University of Michigan Press, 1993.

Brooks, Daphne. *Bodies in Dissent: Spectacular Performances of Race and Freedom, 1850–1910*. Durham, NC: Duke University Press, 2006.

Brooks, Peter. *The Melodramatic Imagination: Balzac, Henry James, Melodrama, and the Mode of Excess*. New Haven: Yale University Press, 1976.

Brown, Richard Maxwell. *No Duty to Retreat: Violence and Values in American History and Society*. Norman: University of Oklahoma Press, 1994.

Brown, Wendy. *States of Injury: Power and Freedom in Late Modernity*. Princeton, NJ: Princeton University Press, 1995.

Butler, Judith. "Merely Cultural." *Social Text* 52–53 (1997): 265–77.

———. *The Psychic Life of Power*. Stanford, CA: Stanford University Press, 1997.

Caretta, Vincent. "Possible Gustavus Vassa/Olaudah Equiano Attributions." In *The Faces of Anonymity: Anonymous and Pseudonymous Publications from the Sixteenth to the Twentieth Century*, edited by Robert J. Griffin, 103–40. New York: Palgrave Macmillan, 2003.

———. "Explanatory and Textual Notes," In Olaudah Equiano, *The Interesting Narrative and Other Writings*. New York: Penguin, 2003.

Chakrabarty, Dipesh. *Provincializing Europe: Postcolonial Thought and Historical Difference*. Princeton, NJ: Princeton University Press, 2000.

———. *Re-thinking Woking Class History: Bengal, 1890 to 1940*. Princeton: Princeton University Press, 1989.

Chandler, Nahum Dimitri. "Delimitations: The Positions of W. E. B. Du Bois in the History of Thought." Unpublished manuscript. 2002.

———. "The Figure of W. E. B. Du Bois as a Problem for Thought." *CR: The New Centennial Review* 6, no. 3 (2006): 29–55.

———. "The Figure of the X: An Elaboration of the Du Boisian Autobiographical Example." In *Displacement, Diaspora, and Geographies of Identity*, edited by Smadar Lavie and Ted Swedenburg, 235–72. Durham, NC: Duke University Press, 1996.

———. "Introduction: Toward a New History of the Centuries: On the Early Writings of W. E. B. Du Bois." In W. E. B. Du Bois, *The Problem of the Color Line at the Turn of the Twentieth Century: The Essential Early Essays*, edited by Nahum Dimitri Chandler, 1–32. New York: Fordham University Press, 2014.

———. "Of Exorbitance: The Problem of the Negro as a Problem for Thought." *Criticism* 50, no. 3 (2008): 345–410.

———. "Originary Displacement." *boundary 2* 27, no. 3 (2000): 249–86.

———. "The Problem of the Centuries: A Contemporary Elaboration of 'The Present Outlook for the Dark Races of Mankind' circa the 27th of December 1899." Unpublished manuscript. 2007.

———. *X: The Problem of the Negro as a Problem for Thought* (New York: Fordham University Press, 2013).

Chomsky, Noam. *Knowledge of Language: Its Nature, Origin and Use.* New York: Praeger, 1986.

———. *The New Military Humanism: Lessons from Kosovo.* Monroe, ME: Common Courage Press, 2002.

———. "The Responsibility of Intellectuals." In *American Power and the New Mandarins: Historical and Political Essays*, 323–66. New York: Pantheon, 1967.

———. "What We Know: On the Universals of Language and Rights." *Boston Review* 30, nos. 3–4, (2005): 23–27.

Clarke, Kamari Maxine. "New Spheres of Transnational Formations: Mobilizations of Humanitarian Diasporas." In "Language, Inequality, and Endangerment: African Americans and Native Americans," edited by Arthur K. Spears, special issue, *Transforming Anthropology* 18, no. 1 (2010): 48–65.

———. "Response by Author." In "Language, Inequality, and Endangerment: African Americans and Native Americans," edited by Arthur K. Spears. Special issue, *Transforming Anthropology* 18, no. 1 (2010): 79.

Cohen, Tom, Barbara Cohen, J. Hillis Miller, and Andrzej Warminski, eds. *Material Events: Paul de Man and the Afterlife of Theory.* Minneapolis: University of Minnesota Press, 2001.

Cooper, Melinda, and Angela Mitropoulos. "In Praise of Usura." *Mute.* May 27, 2009. www.metamute.org/editorial/articles/praise-usura.

Copeland, Huey. *Bound to Appear: Art, Slavery, and the Site of Blackness in Multicultural America.* Chicago: University of Chicago Press, 2013.

Cover, Robert M. "The Bonds of Constitutional Interpretation: Of the Word, the Deed, and the Role." *Georgia Law Review* 20 (summer 1986): 815–33.

———. *Justice Accused: Anti-Slavery and the Judicial Process.* New Haven: Yale University Press, 1975.

———. "The Supreme Court, 1982 Term—Foreword: *Nomos* and Narrative." *Harvard Law Review* 97, no. 1 (1983): 4–65.

Dayan, Joan. "Cruel and Unusual: The End of the Eighth Amendment." *Boston Review* 15, no. 3 (2004), bostonreview.net/dayan-cruel-and-unusual.

Dent, Gina. *Anchored to the Real: Black Literature in the Wake of Anthropology.* Durham, NC: Duke University Press. Forthcoming.

Deleuze, Gilles. *Kant's Critical Philosophy.* Translated by Hugh Tomlinson. New York: Columbia University Press, 1993.

Deleuze, Gilles, and Félix Guattari. *A Thousand Plateaus.* Minneapolis: University of Minnesota Press, 1987.

Derrida, Jacques. *Dissemination.* Translated by Barbara Johnson. Chicago: University of Chicago Press, 1981.

———. "Force of Law: The Mystical Foundation of Authority." In *Deconstruction and the Possibility of Justice,* edited by Drucilla Cornell, Michel Rosenfeld, and David Gray Carlson, 3–68. New York: Routledge, 1992.

———. "In Discussion with Christopher Norris." In *Deconstruction: Omnibus Volume,* edited by Andreas Papadakis, Catherine Cooke, and Andrew E. Benjamin, 71–78. New York: Rizzoli, 1989.

———. "The Law of Genre." In *On Narrative,* edited by W. J. T. Mitchell, 51–77. Translated by Avital Ronell. Chicago: University of Chicago Press, 1980.

———. *Margins of Philosophy.* Translated by Allan Bass. Chicago: University of Chicago Press, 1982.

———. "Onto-theology of National Humanism (Prolegomena to a Hypothesis)," *Oxford Literary Review* 14, nos. 1–2 (1992): 3–23.

———. "This Strange Institution Called Literature: An Interview with Jacques Derrida." In *Acts of Literature,* edited by Derek Attridge, 33–75. New York: Routledge, 1992.

———. *The Truth in Painting.* Translated by Geoff Bennington and Ian McLeod. Chicago: University of Chicago Press, 1987.

Diderot, Denis. "In Praise of Richardson." In *Selected Writings on Art and Literature,* translated by Geoffrey Bremner, 82–97. New York: Penguin, 1994.

Du Bois, W. E. B. *The Philadelphia Negro: A Social Study.* Revised ed. Philadelphia: University of Pennsylvania Press, 1996.

———. *The Problem of the Color-Line at the Turn of the Twentieth Century: The Essential Early Essays.* Edited by Nahum Dimitri Chandler. New York: Fordham University Press, 2015.

———. "Sociology Hesitant." *boundary 2* 27, no. 3 (2000): 37–44.

———. *The Souls of Black Folk.* In *Writings.* Edited by Nathan Huggins, 357–547. DVD New York: Library of America, 1986.

———. *The Souls of Black Folk.* New York: Modern Library, 2003.

Du Bois, W. E. B, and Moses Asch. *W. E. B. Du Bois: A Recorded Autobiography.* FH-5511 LP New York: Folkways Records, 1961.

É Minha Cara/That's My Face. DVD. Directed by Thomas Allen Harris. New York: Fox Lorber Home Video, 2004.

Edwards, Brent Hayes. *The Practice of Diaspora: Literature, Translation, and the Rise of Black Internationalism.* Cambridge, MA: Harvard University Press, 2003.

Ellison, Ralph. *Invisible Man.* 2nd ed. New York: Vintage International, 1995.

English, Darby. *How to See a Work of Art in Total Darkness*. Cambridge, MA: MIT
 Press, 2007.

Equiano, Olaudah. *The Interesting Narrative and Other Writings: Revised Edition*.
 Edited and with an introduction and explanatory and textual notes by Vincent
 Caretta. New York: Penguin, 2003.

——. *The Interesting Narrative of the Life of Olaudah Equiano or Gustavus Vassa,
 the African, Written by Himself*. Leeds, UK: James Nichols, 1814. Republished in
 The Classic Slave Narratives, edited by Henry Louis Gates Jr., 1–182. New York:
 Mentor, 1987.

Fanon, Frantz. *Black Skin, White Masks*. Translated by Charles Lam Markmann.
 London: Paladin, 1970.

——. *Black Skin, White Masks*. Translated by Richard Philcox. New York: Grove,
 2008.

——. *The Wretched of the Earth*. Translated by Constance Farrington. New York:
 Grove Press, 1966.

Ferreira da Silva, Denise. "No-Bodies: Law, Raciality and Violence." *Griffith Law
 Review* 18, no. 2 (2009): 212–36.

——. "On Difference without Separability." *32nd Bienal de São Paulo—Incerteza Viva*.
 Edited by Jochen Volz and Júlia Rebouças. São Paulo: Fundação Bienal de São
 Paulo, 2016.

——. *Toward a Global Idea of Race*. Minneapolis: University of Minnesota Press,
 2007.

Fodor, Jerry. "Fire the Press Secretary." *London Review of Books*, April 28, 2011, 24–25.

Ford, Richard. *Racial Culture: A Critique*. Princeton, NJ: Princeton University Press,
 2004.

Foucault, Michel. *History of Madness*. Translated by Jonathan Murphy and Jean
 Khalfa. London: Routledge, 2006.

——. *The History of Sexuality, Volume I: An Introduction*. Translated by Robert
 Hurley. New York: Vintage Books, 1978.

——. "Technologies of the Self." In *Technologies of the Self: A Seminar with Michel
 Foucault*, edited by Luther H. Gutman, Huck Gutman, and Patrick H. Hutton,
 16–49. Amherst: University Press of Massachusetts, 1988.

Freire, Paolo. *Pedagogy of the Oppressed*. Translated by Myra Bergman Ramos. New
 York: Continuum, 1970.

Friends of Freedom. *The Liberty Bell*. Boston: Prentiss, Sawyer, and Co., 1857.

Gaines, Kevin K. *Uplifting the Race: Black Leadership, Politics, and Culture in the
 Twentieth Century*. Chapel Hill: University of North Carolina Press, 1996.

Gates, Henry Louis, Jr., "The Master's Pieces: On Canon Formation and the
 Afro-American Tradition." In *The Bounds of Race: Perspectives on Hegemony
 and Resistance*, edited by Dominick LaCapra, 17–38. Ithaca, NY: Cornell
 University Press, 1991.

Gilmore, Ruth Wilson. *Golden Gulag: Prison, Surplus, Crisis, and Opposition in
 Globalizing California*. Berkeley: University of California Press, 2007.

Gilroy, Paul. *The Black Atlantic: Modernity and Double Consciousness*. Cambridge,
 MA: Harvard University Press, 1993.

――――. *Darker than Blue: On the Moral Economies of Black Atlantic Culture.* Cambridge, MA: Harvard University Press, 2010.

Glissant, Édouard. "One World in Relation: Édouard Glissant in Conversation with Manthia Diawara." Translated by Christopher Winks. *Nka Journal of Contemporary African Art* 28 (spring 2011): 4–19.

Gould, Stephen Jay. *The Mismeasure of Man.* Revised ed. New York: W. W. Norton, 1996.

Greenberg, Polly. *The Devil Has Slippery Shoes: A Biased Biography of the Child Development Group of Mississippi.* London: Macmillan, 1969.

Guyer, Paul. *Kant and the Claims of Taste.* 2nd ed. Cambridge: Cambridge University Press, 1997.

Hahn, Steven. *A Nation under Our Feet: Black Political Struggles in the Rural South from Slavery to the Great Migration.* Cambridge, MA: Harvard University Press, 2003.

Hall, Stuart, Chas Critcher, Tony Jefferson, John Clarke, and Brian Roberts, *Policing the Crisis: Mugging, the State, and Law and Order.* London: Palgrave, 1978.

Han, Sora. "Slavery as Contract: *Betty's Case* and the Question of Freedom." *Law and Literature* 27, no. 3 (2015): 395–416.

Harney, Stefano, and Fred Moten. *The Undercommons: Fugitive Planning and Black Study.* Wivenhoe, UK: Minor Compositions, 2013.

Harpham, Geoffrey Galt. "Symbolic Terror." *Critical Inquiry* 28, no. 2 (2002): 573–79.

Harris, Laura. "Whatever Happened to the Motley Crew? C. L. R. James, Hélio Oiticica, and the Aesthetic Sociality of Blackness." *Social Text* 30, no. 3 (2012): 49–75.

Harris, Theodore A., and Amiri Baraka. *Our Flesh of Flames.* Philadelphia: Anvil Arts Press, 2008.

Hartman, Saidiya V. *Scenes of Subjection: Terror, Slavery, and Self-Making in Nineteenth-Century America.* Oxford: Oxford University Press, 1997.

Heathfield, Adrian. "Impress of Time." In *Out of Now: The Lifeworks of Tehching Hsieh*, by Adrian Heathfield and Tehching Hsieh, 10–61. Cambridge, MA: MIT Press, 2009.

Hegel, G. W. F. *Elements of the Philosophy of Right.* Edited by Allen W. Wood. Translated by H. B. Nisbet. Cambridge: Cambridge University Press, 1991.

Heidegger, Martin. *Sein und Zeit.* Sechzehnte Auflage. [*Being and Time*] 16th ed. Tübingen, Germany: Max Niemeyer Verlag, 1986.

Henry, Annette. "'A Wha' Dem A Go On Wid? (Student Resistance in a Doctoral Seminar on Black Feminist Thought)." *Frontiers* 16, no. 1 (1996): 27–28.

――――. "African Canadian Women Teachers' Activism: Recreating Communities of Caring and Resistance." *Journal of Negro Education* 61, no. 3 (1992): 392–404.

――――. "Growing Up Black, Female and Working Class: A Teacher's Narrative." *Anthropology and Education Quarterly* 26, no. 3 (1995): 279–305.

――――. "'There's Salt-Water in Our Blood': The 'Middle Passage' Epistemology of Two Black Mothers regarding the Spiritual Education of Their Daughters." *International Journal of Qualitative Studies in Education* 19, no. 3 (2006): 329–45.

Herskovitz, Melville J. *The Myth of the Negro Past.* New York: Harper, 1941.

Herzfeld, Michael. *Cultural Intimacy: Social Poetics in the Nation-State*. New York: Routledge, 2004.

Hobbes, Thomas. *Leviathan*. Edited by J. C. A. Gaskin. Oxford: Oxford University Press, 1998.

Holmes, Oliver Wendell. "Letter to Harold Laski, May 12, 1921." In *Holmes-Laski Letters*, edited by Mark De Wolfe Howe. Abridged by Alger Hiss. New York: Atheneum, 1963.

Hunter, Tera W. "'The "Brotherly Love" for Which This City Is Proverbial Should Extend to All': The Everyday Lives of Working-Class Women in Philadelphia and Atlanta in the 1890s." In *W. E. B. Du Bois, Race, and the City: The Philadelphia Negro and Its Legacy*, edited by Michael B. Katz and Thomas J. Sugrue, 127–51. Philadelphia: University of Pennsylvania Press, 1998.

———. *To 'Joy My Freedom*. Cambridge, MA: Harvard University Press, 1997.

Hurston, Zora Neale. "Characteristics of Negro Expression." In *The Sanctified Church*. Berkeley, CA: Turtle Island, 1981.

James, C. L. R. *The Black Jacobins: Toussaint L'Ouverture and the San Domingo Revolution*. 2nd ed. New York: Vintage Books, 1989.

James, Henry. Preface to *The Portrait of a Lady*. Edited by Nicola Bradbury. Oxford: Oxford University Press, 1981.

Jameson, Fredric. *The Political Unconscious*. Ithaca, NY: Cornell University Press, 1981.

———. "Third World Literature in the Age of Multinational Capitalism." *Social Text* 15 (1986): 65–88.

Jay, Martin. *Permanent Exiles: Essays on the Intellectual Migration from Germany to America*. New York: Columbia University Press, 1986.

Johnson, Barbara. "Writing." In *Critical Terms for Literary Study*, edited by Frank Lentricchia and Thomas McLaughlin, 39–49. 2nd ed. Chicago: University of Chicago Press, 1995.

Jones, LeRoi (Amiri Baraka). *Black Music*. New York: William Morrow, 1967.

———. *Blues People: Negro Music in White America*. New York: William Morrow, 1963.

———. *Home: Social Essays*. New York: William Morrow, 1966.

Judy, Ronald A. T. *(Dis)Forming the American Canon: African-Arabic Slave Narrative and the Vernacular*. Minneapolis: University of Minnesota Press, 1993.

———. "Introduction: On W. E. B. Du Bois and Hyperbolic Thinking." *boundary 2* 27, no. 3 (2000): 1–35.

Kant, Immanuel. *Anthropologie in Pragmatischer Hinsicht*. Hamburg: Felix Meiner Verlag, 2000.

———. *Anthropology from a Pragmatic Point of View*. Translated by Victor Lyle Dowdell. Carbondale: Southern Illinois University Press, 1978.

———. "Anthropology from a Pragmatic Point of View." Translated by Robert B. Louden. In *Anthropology, History and Education*, 227–429. Cambridge: Cambridge University Press, 2007.

———. *Critique of Judgment*. Translated by Werner S. Pluhar. Indianapolis: Hackett, 1987.

———. *Critique of Pure Reason.* Translated and edited by Paul Guyer and Allen W. Wood. Cambridge: Cambridge University Press, 1998.

———. *Critique of the Power of Judgment.* Edited by Paul Guyer. Translated by Paul Guyer and Eric Matthews. Cambridge: Cambridge University Press, 2000.

———. "Idea for a Universal History with a Cosmopolitan Aim." In *Anthropology, History, and Education,* edited by Günter Zöller and Robert B. Louden, 107–20. Translated by Allan W. Wood. Cambridge: Cambridge University Press, 2007.

Kaprow, Allen. *Essays on the Blurring of Art and Life.* Edited by Jeff Kelly. Berkeley: University of California Press, 1993.

Kazanjian, David. *The Colonizing Trick: National Culture and Imperial Citizenship in Early America.* Minneapolis: University of Minnesota Press, 2003.

Kelley, Robin D. G. *Freedom Dreams: The Black Radical Imagination.* New York: Beacon, 2002.

Kirk, Roland. *I Talk with the Spirits.* CD 558 076-2. New York: Verve Records, 1964.

Kittler, Friedrich A. *Discourse Networks 1800–1900.* Translated by Michael Metteer and Chris Cullens. Stanford, CA: Stanford University Press, 1990.

Kramer, Fritz W. *The Red Fez: Art and Spirit Possession in Africa.* Translated by Malcom R. Green. London: Verso, 1993.

Kurzban, Robert. *Why Everyone (Else) Is a Hypocrite: Evolution and the Modular Mind.* Princeton, NJ: Princeton University Press, 2011.

Lewis, David Levering. *W. E. B. Du Bois: Biography of a Race, 1868–1919.* New York: Henry Holt, 1993.

Lindfors, Bernth, ed. *Conversations with Chinua Achebe.* Jackson: University Press of Mississippi, 1997.

Linebaugh, Peter. "All the Atlantic Mountains Shook." *Labour/Le Travail* 10 (1982): 87–121.

Lippit, Akira. *Electric Animal: Toward a Rhetoric of Wildlife.* Minneapolis: University of Minnesota Press, 2000.

Litwak, Leon. *Been in the Storm So Long.* New York: Vintage, 1979.

Llewelyn, John. *The HypoCritical Imagination: Between Kant and Levinas.* New York: Routledge, 2000.

Lorde, Audre. "The Master's Tools Will Never Dismantle the Master's House." In *Sister Outsider: Essays and Speeches,* 110–13. Freedom, CA: Crossing Press, 1984.

Lyotard, Jean-François. *Enthusiasm: The Kantian Critique of History.* Translated by George Van Den Abbeele. Stanford, CA: Stanford University Press, 2009.

———. *Lessons on the Analytic of the Sublime.* Translated by Elizabeth Rottenberg. Stanford, CA: Stanford University Press, 1994.

McKittrick, Katherine. *Demonic Grounds: Black Women and the Cartographies of Struggle.* Minneapolis: The University of Minnesota Press, 2006.

Mackey, Nathaniel. *Atet A.D.* San Francisco: City Lights Books, 2001.

———. *Bedouin Hornbook.* Lexington: University Press of Kentucky, 1986.

———. "Cante Moro." In *Sound States: Innovative Poetics and Acoustical Technologies,* edited by Adalaide Morris, 194–212. Chapel Hill: University of North Carolina Press, 1997.

———. *Discrepant Engagement: Dissonance, Cross-Culturality, and Experimental Writing.* Cambridge: Cambridge University Press, 1993.

——— *From a Broken Bottle Traces of Perfume Still Emanate: Bedouin Hornbook, Djbot Baghostus's Run, ATet A.D.* Volumes 1–3. New York: New Directions, 2010.

———. *Splay Anthem.* New York: New Directions, 2006.

Malabou, Catherine. "Will Sovereignty Ever Be Deconstructed?" unpublished manuscript, 2011.

———. "Will Sovereignty Ever Be Deconstructed?" In *Plastic Materialities: Politics, Legality, and Metamorphosis in the Work of Catherine Malabou,* edited by Brenna Bhandar and Jonathan Goldberg-Hiller, 35–46. Durham, NC: Duke University Press, 2015.

Marder, Michael. *The Event of the Thing: Derrida's Post-Deconstructive Realism.* Toronto: Toronto University Press, 2009.

Martin, Susan, and Alma Ruiz, eds. *The Experimental Exercise of Freedom.* Los Angeles: Museum of Contemporary Art, 1999.

Marx, Karl. *Grundrisse: Foundations of the Critique of Political Economy.* Translated by Martin Nicolaus. New York: Vintage, 1973.

———. "Private Property and Communism." In *Early Writings.* Translated by Rodney Livingstone and Gregor Benton, 345–58. New York: Vintage, 1975.

Matory, J. Lorand. *Black Atlantic Religion: Tradition, Transnationalism, and Matriarchy in the Afro-Brazilian Candomblé.* Princeton, NJ: Princeton University Press, 2005.

Mbembe, Achille. "Subject and Experience." Translated by Robert Bononno. In *Keywords/Experience,* edited by Nadia Tazi, 1–18. New York: Other Press, 2004.

Mellon, John, ed. *Bullwhip Days: The Slaves Remember.* New York: Avon Books, 1988.

Menand, Louis. *The Metaphysical Club: A Story of Ideas in America.* New York: Farrar, Straus and Giroux, 2001.

Menninghaus, Winfried. *In Praise of Nonsense: Kant and Bluebeard.* Translated by Henry Pickford. Stanford, CA: Stanford University Press, 1999.

Merleau-Ponty, Maurice. *The Visible and the Invisible.* Edited by Claude Lefort. Translated by Alphonso Lingis. Evanston, IL: Northwestern University Press, 1968.

Miller, Elaine P. *The Vegetative Soul: From Philosophy of Nature to Subjectivity in the Feminine.* Albany, NY: State University of New York Press, 2002.

Mingus, Charles. "Scenes in the City." *A Modern Jazz Symposium of Music and Poetry.* Bethlehem Records BCP 62016 LP, 1957.

Mitropoulos, Angela. "Oikopolitics, and Storms," *Global South* 3, no. 1 (2009): 66–82.

Morgan, Diane. *Kant Trouble: The Obscurities of the Enlightenment.* London: Routledge, 2002.

Morrison, Toni. *Beloved.* New York: Plume, 1988.

Morse, Chuck. "Capitalism, Marxism, and the Black Radical Tradition: An Interview with Cedric Robinson." *Perspectives on Anarchist Theory* 3, no. 1 (spring 1999). http://www.hartford-hwp.com/archives/45a/568.html.

Moten, Fred. *In the Break: The Aesthetics of the Black Radical Tradition.* Minneapolis: University of Minnesota Press, 2003.

———. *Black and Blur (consent not to be a single being)*. Durham, NC: Duke University Press, 2017.

Moynihan, Daniel P. *The Negro Family: The Case for National Action*. Washington, DC: U.S. Department of Labor, 1965.

Mullen, Harryette. "Runaway Tongue: Resistant Orality in *Uncle Tom's Cabin, Our Nig, Incidents in the Life of a Slave Girl,* and *Beloved*." In *The Culture of Sentiment: Race, Gender, and Sentimentality in Nineteenth-Century America*, edited by Shirley Samuels, 244–64. New York: Oxford University Press, 1992.

The Negro in Virginia. Compiled by Workers of the Writers' Program of the Works Project Administration in the State of Virginia. Winston-Salem, NC: John F. Blair, 1994.

Nielsen, Aldon Lynn. *Black Chant: Languages of African-American Postmodernism*. Cambridge: Cambridge University Press, 1997.

———. "Face to Face with the Blues." Accessed July 11, 2017, https://www.academia.edu /472598/FACE_TO_FACE_WITH_THE_BLUES.

Norton, Anne. "Hearts of Darkness: Africa and African Americans in the Writings of Hannah Arendt." In *Feminist Interpretations of Hannah Arendt*, edited by Bonnie Honig, 247–61. University Park: Penn State University Press, 1995.

Patterson, Orlando. *Slavery and Social Death: A Comparative Study*. Cambridge, MA: Harvard University Press, 1985.

Payton, Nicholas. "Why Nicholas Payton Refuses to Boycott Israel. Accessed August 11, 2013. https://nicholaspayton.wordpress.com/2013/08/08why-nicholas-payton -refuses-to-boycott-israel/. No longer available.

Pedrosa, Mário. *Primary Documents*. Edited by Glória Ferreira and Paulo Herkenhoff. Translated by Stephen Berg. New York: Museum of Modern Art, 2015.

Phelan, Peggy. *Unmarked: The Politics of Performance*. London: Routledge, 1993.

Philip, M. NourbeSe. *Zong!* Middletown, CT: Wesleyan University Press, 2008.

Phillips, Ulrich B. *American Negro Slavery*. Baton Rouge: Louisiana State University Press, 1966.

Piper, Adrian M. S. "Critical Hegemony and Aesthetic Acculturation." *Noûs* 19, no. 1 (1985): 29–40.

———. *Rationality and the Structure of the Self, Volume II: A Kantian Conception*. 2nd ed. Berlin: Adrian Piper Research Archive Foundation. Accessed June 10, 2010. www.adrianpiper.com/rss/index.shtml.

Prince, Mary. *History of Mary Prince, A West Indian Slave, Related by Herself, with a Supplement by the Editor*. London: F. Westley and A. H. Davis, 1831. Republished in *The Classic Slave Narratives*, edited by Henry Louis Gates Jr., 183–242. New York: Mentor, 1987.

Pritchard, N. H. *The Matrix: Poems 1960–1970*. Garden City, NY: Doubleday, 1970.

———. "Gyre's Galax." In *New Jazz Poets*, edited by Walter Lowenfels. New York: Smithsonian Folkways FW-09751-CCD, 2004.

Rahier, Jean Muteba. "'The Diversity of Diasporic Subjectivities: Different and Separate Ontologies?' A Response to Kamari Clarke's 'New Spheres of Transnational Formations: Mobilizations of Humanitarian Diasporas.'" In "Language, Inequality, and Endangerment: African Americans and

Native Americans," edited by Arthur K. Spears. Special issue, *Transforming Anthropology* 18, no. 1 (2010): 66–69.

Roberson, Ed. *To See the Earth before the End of the World*. Middletown, CT: Wesleyan University Press, 2010.

———. "On the Calligraphy of Black Chant." In *When Thy King Is a Boy*. Pittsburgh: University of Pittsburgh Press, 1970.

Robinson, Cedric J. *Black Marxism: The Making of the Black Radical Tradition*. 2nd ed. Chapel Hill: University of North Carolina Press, 2000.

———. *The Terms of Order: Political Science and the Myth of Leadership*. Albany: State University of New York Press, 1980.

Rodney, Walter. *The Groundings with My Brothers*. London: Bogle-L'Ouverture, 1975.

Ronell, Avital. *The Telephone Book: Technology, Schizophrenia, Electric Speech*. Lincoln: University of Nebraska Press, 1990.

Rorty, Richard. *Achieving Our Country: Leftist Thought in Twentieth-Century America*. Cambridge, MA: Harvard University Press, 1998.

———. "Postmodernist Bourgeois Liberalism." In Rorty, *Objectivity, Relativism, and Truth: Philosophical Papers, Volume 1*, 197–202. Cambridge: Cambridge University Press, 1991.

Salamon, Gayle. *Transgender and Rhetorics of Materiality*. New York: Columbia University Press, 2010.

Schwabsky, Barry. "Review of Fredric Jameson, *The Seeds of Time*." *The Nation* 260, no. 21 (1994): 762–64.

Sheehan, Thomas W. "Anarchy and Anarchrony: Spatio-Temporality and Framing in Joyce, Proust and Rhys." Unpublished manuscript. 2000.

Smolin, Lee. *The Trouble with Physics: The Rise of String Theory, the Fall of a Science, and What Comes Next*. Boston: Houghton Mifflin, 2006.

Soyinka, Wole. *Art, Dialogue, and Outrage: Essays on Literature and Culture*. London: Methuen, 1993.

Spears, Arthur K., ed. "Language, Inequality, and Endangerment: African Americans and Native Americans." Special issue, *Transforming Anthropology* 18, no. 1 (2010).

Spillers, Hortense J. *Black, White, and in Color: Essays on American Literature and Culture*. Chicago: University of Chicago Press, 2003.

———. "Mama's Baby, Papa's Maybe: An American Grammar Book." *Diacritics* 17, no. 2 (1987): 64–81.

Spivak, Gayatri Chakravorty. *A Critique of Postcolonial Reason*. Cambridge, MA: Harvard University Press, 1999.

———. "Righting Wrongs." *South Atlantic Quarterly* 103, nos. 2/3 (2004): 523–81.

Taylor, Cecil. *Dark to Themselves*. Enja Records 2084 LP, 1976.

Thometz, Kurt, ed. *Life Turns Man Up and Down: High Life, Useful Advice, and Mad English: African Market Literature*. New York: Pantheon Books, 2001.

Wagner, Bryan. *Disturbing the Peace: Black Culture and the Police Power after Slavery*. Durham, NC: Duke University Press, 2009.

Warnock, Mary. *Imagination*. Berkeley: University of California Press, 1976.

Weber, Max. *The Rational and Social Foundations of Music.* Translated and edited by Don Martindale, Johannes Riedel, and Gertrude Neuwirth. Carbondale: Southern Illinois University Press, 1958.

Weheliye, Alexander. *Habeas Viscus: Racializing Assemblages, Biopolitics, and Black Feminist Theories of the Human.* Durham, NC: Duke University Press, 2014.

Wiegman, Robyn. *American Anatomies: Theorizing Race and Gender.* Durham, NC: Duke University Press, 1995.

Wilderson, Frank B, III. *Red, White and Black: Cinema and the Structure of US Antagonisms.* Durham, NC: Duke University Press, 2010.

Williams, Linda. *Playing the Race Card: Melodramas of Black and White from Uncle Tom to O. J. Simpson.* Princeton, NJ: Princeton University Press, 2001.

Wilson, James Q., and Richard J. Herrnstein. *Crime and Human Nature: The Definitive Study of the Causes of Crime.* New York: Simon and Schuster, 1985.

Wonder, Stevie. "Too Shy to Say," *Fullfillingness' First Finale.* Tamla T6-332s1 LP, 1974.

Wright, Michelle M. *Becoming Black: Creating Identity in the African Diaspora.* Durham, NC: Duke University Press, 2004.

———. "Black in Time: Exploring New Ontologies, New Dimensions, New Epistemologies of the African Diaspora." In "Language, Inequality, and Endangerment: African Americans and Native Americans," edited by Arthur K. Spears. Special issue, *Transforming Anthropology* 18, no. 1 (2010): 70–73.

———. *Physics of Blackness: Beyond the Middle Passage Epistemology.* Minneapolis: University of Minnesota Press, 2015.

Wynter, Sylvia. "Unsettling the Coloniality of Being/Power/Truth/Freedom: Towards the Human, After Man, Its Overrepresentation—An Argument." In *CR: The New Centennial Review* 3, no. 3 (2003): 257–337.

Zeleza, Paul T. "Reconceptualizing African Diasporas: Notes from a Historian." In "Language, Inequality, and Endangerment: African Americans and Native Americans," edited by Arthur K. Spears. Special issue, *Transforming Anthropology* 18, no. 1 (2010): 74–78.

INDEX

Baraka, Amiri, xii, 85, 117–18, 120, 130–31, 187
Barrett, Lindon, 9–10, 287n1
Baucom, Ian, 165–67
BDS (Boycott, Divestment and Sanctions) movement, 213–26
beauty, 29–30, 242. *See also* aesthetics
Beckett, Samuel, 7
Been in the Storm So Long (Litwack), 45–50
Beethoven, 283n28
Being and Time (Heidegger), 239
Bell, Daniel, 110
Beloved (Morrison), 153
Ben Ali's Diary, 51–52
Benjamin, Andrew, 39
Bernasconi, Robert, 2, 9–10
Bernstein, Charles, 166
Betty's Case (legal proceeding), 246–65
Bildung, 243
biology, 172, 174, 179, 181
biopolitics, ix, 172, 178, 180, 211, 214–15, 253
biopower, 173, 253
birth, 266
black art, 97, 223, 225, 265
Black Belt, the, 123–24
black biological inferiority, 127
black body, 10
black chant, 32
black communism, 138
black elitism, 121
black fantastic, the, 190
black feminism, 209
black instrumentalism, 113
black insurgency, 215
"Black in Time" (Wright), 198
Black Jacobins, The (James), 116–18
black Marxism, 138
Black Mountain College, 230
black nationalism, 196
blackness: abjection and, 276n85; as abolitionism, 100–102, 106, 110–11, 114; aesthetics of, 13–14, 97, 223, 225, 264; Africa and, 18, 21, 59; African

American studies and, 157; Agassiz and, 96; as an international force, 203; anti-anti-blackness and, 265; antiblackness and, 25, 73, 224, 226; antislavery and, 246; beauty and, 29; Bernasconi and, 9–10; *Bildung* and, 243; black radical tradition and, 20–21; black studies and, 156, 158–60; citizenship and, 79, 99, 101–4, 134, 136, 192, 197–98, 206, 208, 211, 219, 247, 254; the color line and, 33–35; and the conflict between the principle of freedom vs. principle of legal formalism, 249; consent and, 242–43; cosmopolitanism and, 191; criminality and, 282n18; as debt, 262–63; displacement and, 212; Du Bois and, 32–35; Edwards on, 281n7; epidermalization and, xii, 6, 9, 39, 184, 242; Equiano and, 59; exclusion from, 201; facticity of, 37; Fanon and, 6, 9, 11, 39, 184, 242, 279n9; fugitivity and, 8, 15, 32, 34, 109–10, 122–24, 131–32, 217, 220, 227–28, 251–64, 281n2; individuation and, 211–12, 265–66; invisibility and, 22–23; Kant and, 12, 16, 29, 269n1; kinship and, 77–78, 247, 260–61; maternity and, 238; nation-state and, 197; the nonexcluded middle and, 108; normativity and, x; no-thing-ness and, 244; origin of, 21–22, 27; performance and, 241–42, 245–48, 258–59, 261, 263, 266; physics and, 209; property and, 261; radicalism and, 3, 17, 20–21, 31, 36, 41–44, 47, 58, 61, 81, 100, 112, 114, 116–21, 125–26, 130, 134, 201, 221, 223–24, 284–85n36; refusal and, 194, 243; regulation of, 2, 6; and its relationship to black people, 18, 24, 241–43; Robinson on, 20; sensuality and, 13; slavery and, 18–19, 22; sovereignty and, 33; statelessness and, 26; stolen life and, 266; study of, ix–xii, 19, 38; theory of, ix, 8, 243; the transatlantic and, 78; and the transition from slavery to freedom, 125; Wagner on, 18–20; Williams and, 99–100, 103–5

black optimism, 158, 160

black ordinary, the, 115, 285n36

black performance, 112

black politics, 97, 112

black power, 98

black radicalism: Adorno and, 285n36; black aesthetic, the, 114; black Marxism and, 100; blackness and, 20–21; criminality and, 125–26; Du Bois and, 134; enlightenment and, 41, 44, 58; ensemble and, 47; essence of, 224; form and, 81; freedom and, 61; Kantian regulation and, 3; in music, 116–20; narrative and, 42–43; ownership and, 36; Palestine and, 221, 224; refusal of the state and, 201; Robinson and, 17, 120–21; romanticism of the, 31; song and, 120; and speech, 130; terror and, 41; world affairs and, 223

black rebellion, 129

Black Reconstruction (Du Bois), 138

black representational space, 210

black sexuality, 129–30

Blacks Law Dictionary, 258

black social life, 37–38, 124–25, 128, 201, 265

black struggle and relation to Palestinian struggle, 223

black studies, 34, 211; aim of, 155–60; BDS and, 215–16; Chandler and, 162; rules and, 234; statelessness and, 204; subjectivity and, 233

black vulnerability, 122

Blint, Rich, 152

Blues People (Baraka), 117–18

blur, 5, 13, 56–57, 78, 89, 152, 170, 233, 258

Boal, Augusto, 207

body: flesh and, 174, 176, 180; gender and, 77, 176, 178; race and, 174–76; soul and, 244. *See also* gender; race

bombing (military), 142, 149

"Bonds of Constitutional Interpretation, The," 7

bourgeoisie, 58

boycott, 213–26. *See also* BDS (Boycott, Divestment and Sanctions) movement

Boyd, Julian, 32

brain, the, 161, 163, 179–81

Brooks, Peter, 106–8

Brown, Nicole, 104

Butler, Judith, 151, 162

Butler, Octavia, xi

California, 293n32

Capital (Marx), 78, 80

capitalism, 22, 80, 85, 87–88, 181, 202. *See also* biopolitics

Caretta, Vincent, 53

Chakrabarty, Dipesh, 82–83, 85, 87

Chandler, Nahum Dimitri: anoriginal displacement, 243; black studies and, 162; Du Bois and, 11–12, 34, 36–39, 115–16, 199–200; originary displacement and, 20–21

change, 191, 227

children, 166, 216

Chomsky, Noam, 45, 93, 142–44, 146, 150

Christianity, 53

churches, 230, 243

cinema, 96

cities, 189

citizenship: Afro-American life and, 211; blackness and, 99; contractual relationships and, 247, 254; denial of, 136; education and, 206; immigrants and, 198; interpellation and, 208; rights of, 219; Simpson trial and, 101, 104; statelessness and, 192; state subjectivity and, 79

Civil War (U.S), 111

Clarke, Kamari Maxine, 198–203, 205, 207–9, 211–12

class, 100, 110–12, 121, 123–25, 132, 148, 150, 183

Clausewitz, Carl von, 37

clubs, 230, 243

Cochran, Johnny, 98

coercion, 228

invasion, xi. *See also* imperialism; settlement

Invisible Man (Ellison), 43

Iraq, 141

Irigaray, Luce, xii

Islam, 150

Israel: academic freedom and, 217, 220; boycott of, 213–26; criticism of, 213; right to exist and, 215, 218, 226; as a settler colony, 214; sovereignty and, 217; United States and, 213–15. *See also* BDS (Boycott, Divestment and Sanctions) movement; Palestine

Iton, Richard, 190, 290n1

Iyer, Vijay, 190

James, C. L. R., 116–17

James, Henry, 108

Jameson, Fredric, 272n62

jazz, 222, 225

Jews, 218, 276n85

journal, 231

journalism, 153

judges, xi

Judy, R. A., 50–52

juridical difference, 68–69

jurisgenerative principle, 6, 8, 94, 137, 184, 253, 255

jurisgenerativity of no-bodies, 251

justice, 45, 262

Kansas City, 152–53

Kant, Immanuel: blackness and, 16, 29–30, 269n1; cosmopolitanism and, 192; foresight and, 270n10; freedom and, 1; imagination and, 27–28, 60, 103; law and, 7; on poetry, 31; race and, 2–6, 9–10, 12, 29, 32, 242; teleological principle and, 13–14, 172–73

Kantorowicz, Ernst, 193

Kazanjian, David, 72–76, 78, 80–81, 83, 85–88, 164, 275n79

Kelley, Robin, 136

King, Rodney, 97–98, 104, 114

kings, 232–34

kinship, 77–78, 154, 247, 260–61

Kirk, Rahsaan Roland, 131

Kurzban, Robert, 161, 163

labor: abstract, 80, 85–86, 88; free, 125, 246; power, 82–83, 87; stolen, 122, 158. *See also* class; socialism

Ladd, Mike, 190

landlords, 122

language, 31, 65–69, 93, 118, 166, 210. *See also* discourse (music and)

law, xi, 7, 19–20, 23, 55, 68–69, 97, 111, 113, 138; blackness and, 243, 259; contract, 248, 252–54, 256–57, 259; origin of, 27; private law of slavery, 247, 253, 260, 262; resistance to, 16; and the sovereign, 173. *See also* contracts

lawfulness, 30

lawlessness, 15, 30

Law of Contracts (Parsons), 254

law of motion, 60–61

legal formalism, principle of, 249

Levinas, Emmanuel, 46, 242

Lewis, David Levering, 119–20

liberalism, 110, 112–13, 148

liberal political theory, 219

life, 253

"Lines to García Lorca" (Garcia Lorca), 130–31

Lippit, Akira, 130, 237

literary study, 237

Litwack, Leon, 45–46, 48–49, 58, 94–95

Lombroso, Cesare, 106

Lorde, Audre, 137

lordship, 70

Los Angeles Police Department, 105

Lose Your Mother (Hartman), 233

love, 189, 238, 252, 264; music and, 222

Lubiano, Wahneema, 52

lynching, 134

Mackey, Nathaniel, 32, 35, 55, 130–31

Madison, James, 73–75

Malabou, Catherine, 171–74, 177–79

Man, 42–43, 51–53, 66, 153